Linux
Programming

BY EXAMPLE

que®

201 West 103rd Street
Indianapolis, Indiana 46290

Kurt Wall

Linux Programming by Example

Copyright © 2000 by Que® Corporation

International Standard Book Number: 0-7897-2215-1

Library of Congress Catalog Card Number: 99-64403

Printed in the United States of America

First Printing: December, 1999

01   00   99   4   3   2   1

Trademarks

Warning and Disclaimer

Associate Publisher
Dean Miller

Executive Editor
Jeff Koch

Acquisitions Editor
Gretchen Ganser

Development Editor
Sean Dixon

Managing Editor
Lisa Wilson

Project Editor
Tonya Simpson

Copy Editor
Kezia Endsley

Indexer
Cheryl Landes

Proofreader
Benjamin Berg

Technical Editor
Cameron Laird

Team Coordinator
Cindy Teeters

Interior Design
Karen Ruggles

Cover Design
Duane Rader

Copy Writer
Eric Borgert

Production
Dan Harris
Heather Moseman

Contents at a Glance

Table of Contents

About the Author

Kurt Wall has been using UNIX since 1993 and has been hooked on Linux for nearly as long. He currently maintains the Informix on Linux FAQ and is president of the International Informix Users Group's Linux SIG. He is also vice president of the Salt Lake Linux Users Group.

In no particular order, he enjoys coffee, cats, coding, cooking, staying up late, and sleeping even later. He dislikes writing about himself in the third person.

Formerly employed by USWest, Kurt now writes and edits full time. He recently completed his first book, *Linux Programming Unleashed*.

Dedication

To Mom (Eleanor Claire Fleming Wall):

Having a great time, wish you were here.

Acknowledgments

Ashleigh Rae and Zane Thomas bravely and stoically resigned themselves to playing with their Nintendo and watching cartoons while I completed the book. They also helped me name some of the sample programs when my imagination became parched. Dad did not do anything in particular, but without his confidence, support, and cheerleading, I would not have had the brass to undertake writing a book. Mom, I miss you and wish you were here so I could share this with you. Somehow, though, I know you know. Rick, Amy, Morgan Leah, and young Master Isaac Benjamin are simply the best brother, sister-in-law, niece, and nephew anyone could have. Thanks to the El Paso gang for entertaining me via email and for letting me butt into their lives when I came up for air. Marty kept me working by asking how it was going. Nudge lived up to the Yiddish meaning of his name by keeping me company at 4:00 a.m., warming my lap, helping me type, and insisting on my attention at precisely the wrong time. Finally, the friends of Bill Wilson helped keep me sane enough to write; if any credit is to be given, it goes to God.

My technical editor, Cameron Laird, offered suggestions that improved the manuscript's overall quality, pointed out an alarming number of really stupid mistakes, kept me from sounding like a manual page, and generally saved me from looking like a complete moron. Thanks, Cameron.

The cast at Macmillan was terrific. Gretchen Ganser deserves credit that this book even exists—I *still* owe you lunch, Gretchen, and thanks for not panicking when the schedule slipped. Gretchen and Sean Dixon, my development editor, both exerted themselves to help me get back on schedule (thanks, y'all!). I do not *even* want to know how many rules they broke. Sean deserves lunch, too, if he ever comes to Salt Lake. Kezia Endsley did a fantastic job of copy editing and of reading my mind when I wrote byzantine prose. Sara Bosin, yet another editor, was pleasantly patient during the editing phase, especially when I mutilated her name. Did I get it right this time? Thanks to Sara, I know the difference between an em dash and an en dash. Tonya Simpson, Sara's replacement, deserves extra credit for her patience with me.

Thanks to all the net.citizens and the members of the Linux community who patiently and graciously answered my questions and offered suggestions. In particular, Thomas Dickey, current maintainer of the ncurses package, reviewed an early version of the ncurses chapters and corrected several boneheaded mistakes and lots of typos. Michael Olson at Sleepycat Software, makers of Berkeley DB, kindly reviewed the chapter on the database API—it is a much better chapter than it would have been otherwise. The linux-sound mailing list helped out with the chapter on the sound API. I especially appreciate Hannu Solavainen, the original author of this API, for his assistance.

Companies doing business in, with, and for the Linux community also provided support. Red Hat Software and Caldera Systems provided fully supported copies of their Linux Distributions, saving lots of download time and even more frustration. Holly Robinson at Metro Link Incorporated cheerfully gifted me with copies of its Motif and OpenGL products—Holly, we *will* cover this material in the next book. Chris Dibona, Assistant High Muckety-Muck at VA Research (or whatever they are calling themselves this week), lent me a fine system on which to develop the code used in the book—Chris didn't flinch or even blink when I explained I preferred to crash someone else's system than expose mine to the vagaries of rogue pointers. It is testimony to Linux's incredible stability and robustness that I never actually did that, although I sure got tired of examining core files—my keyboard's "g", "d", and "b" keys are now smooth and blank.

If I have forgotten someone, please accept my sincerest apologies and send email to kwall@xmission.com so that I can remedy the oversight. Despite all the assistance I have received, I take full responsibility for any remaining errors and blunders.

Linux Programming by Example

Welcome to *Linux Programming by Example*! It seems one can hardly turn on the television, listen to the radio, surf the World Wide Web, or read a newspaper or magazine without hearing or seeing some mention of the "free UNIX-like operating system, Linux, created by Linus Torvalds..." Although the rest of the world seems just to have discovered Linux, it has been well known on the Internet since 1991, when Linus first publicly released an early version of the kernel.

I first discovered Linux in early 1993, while trying to locate a version of UNIX that I could use at home to learn enough UNIX to enhance my prospects at work. I was stunned by its capabilities and was immediately bitten by the Linux bug. However, my computer lived a dual existence for two more years as I switched between Windows and Linux. Finally, becoming utterly disgusted with Windows in 1995, I wiped it off my system completely and began using and programming Linux full time. I have not looked back since. It has been fun, exciting, rewarding, and satisfying to see Linux mature.

About This Book

So, why does *Linux Programming by Example* exist? The answer, simply put, is to fill a clear need. Linux began life as a hacker's hobby. For its first three or four years, Linux's user base was technically sophisticated, programming savvy, and familiar with UNIX. Given this user base, there was no need for an introductory Linux programming book because the assumption, perhaps rightly, was that Joe or Jane Linux user already knew how to program in a UNIX-like environment.

As Linux has grown in popularity, its user community has changed dramatically. The number of new users unfamiliar with software development in a UNIX milieu wanting to program on and for Linux has swelled. Unfortunately, there has been a distinct lack of information targeted toward beginning Linux programmers. There are, of course, books that teach you how to use individual tools and that cover individual topics, but *Linux Programming by Example* collects all the relevant material into a single book. By the time you have finished reading this book, you will have a solid grasp of Linux programming fundamentals, including tools, such as the compiler, gcc, make, basic Linux/UNIX programming idioms like processes, signals, system calls, file handling, common programming interfaces like ncurses, interprocess communication, and network programming.

Who Should Read This Book?

This book assumes that you know how to use Linux and that you know how to program using the C language. You should be able to find your way around the filesystem, read manual pages, use a text editor, and execute commands. It will be helpful, although not required, if you have an Internet connection. As a C programmer, you must know how to write a program that compiles, understand basic pointer usage, and be familiar with C idioms. No advanced knowledge is necessary.

I wrote this book with two groups of people in mind. The first group is composed of people in the position I was in in 1993. I had used and programmed various DOSes and Windows, but when it came to compiling a program on Linux, I was lost. The plethora of tools overwhelmed me, as did the terminology and, to some degree, the whole UNIX philosophy—everything is a file, string lots of little tools together to make bigger programs, the command line is a joyous thing. So, if you know how to program using the C language, but have no idea about the tools and utilities available to you and are overwhelmed by the Spartan complexity of the Linux programming environment, this book is for you.

The next group of readers are Linux users who want to know how to write applications that fit seamlessly into the Linux environment. This group has figured out how to write and compile programs and can actually comprehend some of the manual pages, but has no idea what a process is, how to write a signal handler, or why they should even care. If this paragraph describes you, this book is also for you.

The topics covered should have an appeal beyond these two groups, though. Competent Linux users can extend their knowledge and gain insight into how Linux works. If you ever wondered, "How does that work?", this book should answer that question.

If, on the other hand, you want to hack the kernel, this is definitely *not* the right book because all the material here is application code that sits on top of the kernel and uses services that the kernel provides. Another topic not covered in this book is X Window programming. GUI programming is a complex subject and beyond the scope of this book, which is aimed primarily at the beginning programmer. X Window programming deserves its own book; even introductory material can easily run to a couple hundred pages.

Linux Programming by Example, Chapter by Chapter

The first part of the book introduces you to the Linux programming environment. Chapter 1, "Compiling Programs," teaches you how to use the GNU C compiler, gcc. You will explore its options and capabilities and learn some of the extensions to the C language that gcc supports. The next chapter looks at the make program, which automates the software-building process. The final chapter of this part of the book discusses the program you will build at the end of the book, a music CD database manager. The programming project will use many of the techniques and tools covered in the book.

THE CODE FOR THIS BOOK

To see the code for this book, go to www.mcp.com/info and type 0789722151 (this book's ISBN) to get to the Linux Programming by Example Web site.

Part II, "System Programming," devotes five chapters to low-level Linux programming. Processes are the first subject because they are the key to understanding how any Linux program works. You will learn what a process is, how to create, manipulate, and kill them, and how processes interact with file ownership and access to system resources. The next chapter (Chapter 5) explains what signals are, how to create your own custom signal handlers, and how to ignore signals.

System programming often involves interacting with and requesting services from the kernel. System calls provide the interface between your application code and the kernel, so this is covered in Chapter 6. Chapters 7 and 8 are devoted to Linux file handling. Everything (almost) in Linux is a file, so all but the simplest programs will need file services. The first of these chapters (Chapter 7) provides basic information on file permissions, including creating, opening, closing, and deleting files, and getting information about files.

Chapter 8 goes into advanced file-handling topics, such as interacting with the Linux filesystem, ext2, high-speed I/O using memory maps, and file locking. Finishing up this part is a chapter on writing *daemons*, which are programs that run non-interactively in the background and provide services on request or perform other tasks. Daemons have special requirements, and Chapter 9 shows you what they are and how to meet them.

The third part of the book, "Linux APIs," takes you through some of the key application programming interfaces (APIs) available on Linux. The database API is the first topic because most applications need to store data in some sort of ordered, easily retrievable fashion. The Berkeley DB database meets that need.

Chapters 11 and 12 focus on manipulating character mode screens using the ncurses API. Chapter 11 looks at basic ncurses usage: initialization, termination, output, and input. Chapter 12 looks at the advanced capabilities ncurses provides, such as using color, window management, interacting with mice, and creating and using forms and menus.

Chapter 13 covers the sound API integrated into the Linux kernel. Finally, Chapter 14, "Creating and Using Programming Libraries," closes this part of the book. All the APIs discussed are implemented via libraries, so knowing how to use them is essential. In addition, as you write more Linux programs, you will find yourself writing the same code over and over—the solution is to put this code into your own libraries.

Part IV of the book covers various means of interprocess communication available with Linux. Pipes are the subject of the first chapter in this section, followed by a chapter on shared memory and another on semaphores and message queues. Because Linux is a product of the Internet and has sophisticated networking capabilities, it should not surprise you that the last chapter of this section is devoted to the basics of network programming using TCP/IP.

The last part of the book, "Linux Programming Utilities," covers tools you will find useful as you gain experience programming Linux. Chapter 19 covers the source code control using the venerable Revision Control System. Your code will have bugs, so Chapter 20 teaches you how to use the gdb source code debugger and how to use a couple of memory debugging toolkits—Electric Fence and mpr.

When you finally complete that killer application, you will want to distribute it. Chapter 21 covers the two main methods for distributing software—tar and the Red Hat Package Manager, RPM.

The final chapter of the book is a complete, real-world program, a music CD database manager. Besides listing the complete source code for the project, this chapter explains how all the parts work together.

The programming project completes the book, and your introduction to Linux programming. If you are hungry for more, the first of the two appendixes provides a bibliography and pointers to additional Linux programming information. The second appendix points you toward additional "stuff"—languages, tools, companies, and certification programs. By the end of the book, you will have a solid foundation in Linux programming. Experience, the ultimate teacher by example, will further hone your skills.

What's Next?

Chapter 1, "Compiling Programs," starts your journey into Linux programming by showing you how to use the GNU C compiler, gcc. After you know how to use the compiler, you will meet make, which, in a way, automates the use of gcc. It works harder so you don't have to.

Part I

The Linux Programming Environment

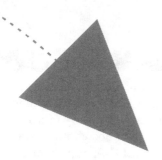

Compiling Programs

GNU cc (gcc) is the GNU project's compiler suite. It compiles programs written in C, C++, or Objective C. gcc also compiles FORTRAN (under the auspices of g77). This chapter focuses on the C compiler because C is Linux's *lingua franca*. The chapter also covers the differences between gcc and egcs version 1.1.2, the Experimental GNU Compiler Suite.

Topics covered in this chapter include

- Invoking gcc
- Options and arguments to control gcc's behavior
- Compiling multiple source files
- Using gcc's optmization features
- Using gcc's debugging features
- Handling compilation errors
- GNU extensions to the C language
- The new C compiler, egcs

Using GNU cc (gcc)

gcc gives the programmer extensive control over the compilation process. The compilation process includes up to four stages: *preprocessing*, *compilation*, *assembly*, and *linking*. You can stop the process after any of these stages to examine the compiler's output at that stage. gcc can also handle the various C dialects, such as ANSI C or traditional (Kernighan and Ritchie) C. You can control the amount and type of debugging information, if any, to embed in the resulting binary and, like most compilers, gcc can also perform code optimization.

gcc includes over 30 individual warnings and three "catch-all" warning levels. gcc is also a *cross-compiler*, so you can develop code on one processor architecture that will be run on another. Cross-compilation is important because Linux runs on so many different kinds of systems, such as Intel x86s, PowerPCs, Amigas, and Sun Sparcs. Each processor chip has a different physical architecture, so the way a binary should be constructed is different on each system. When used as a cross-compiler, gcc enables you to compile a program on, say, an Intel x86 system that is designed to run on a PowerPC.

Finally, gcc sports a long list of extensions to C. Most of these extensions enhance performance, assist the compiler's efforts at code optimization, or make your job as a programmer easier. The price is portability, however. I will mention some of the most common extensions because you will encounter them in the kernel header files, but I suggest you avoid them in your own code.

Invoking gcc

To use gcc, provide the name of a C source file and use its -o option to specify the name of the output file. gcc will preprocess, compile, assemble, and link the program, generating an executable, often called a *binary*. The simplest syntax is illustrated here:

```
gcc infile.c [-o outfile]
```

infile.c is a C source-code file and -o says to name the output file outfile. The [] indicate optional arguments throughout this book. If the name of the output file is not specified, gcc names the output file a.out by default.

Example

This example uses gcc to create the hello program from the source file hello.c. First, the source code:

EXAMPLE

```
/*
 * Listing 1.1
```

```
 * hello.c - Canonical "Hello, world!" program
 */
#include <stdio.h>

int main(void)
{
    puts( "Hello, Linux programming world!");
    return 0;

}
```

To compile and run this program, type

```
$ gcc hello.c -o hello
```

If all goes well, gcc does its job silently and returns to the shell prompt. gcc compiles and links the source file `hello.c`, creating a binary, which is specified using the `-o` argument, `hello`.

OUTPUT

The `ls` command shows that a new program, `hello`, exists. The last command executes the program, resulting in the following output:

```
$ ls
hello.c        hello*
$ ./hello
Hello, Linux programming world!
```

CAUTION

The command that executed the `hello` program specifically included the current directory, denoted with a `.`, because having the current directory in your path is a security risk. That is, instead of using a $PATH statement that resembles `/bin:/usr/bin:/usr/local/bin:.`, the statement should be `/bin:/usr/bin:/usr/local/bin` so that a cracker cannot put a dangerous command in your current directory that happens to match the name of the more benign command you really want to execute.

How does gcc know how to process files? It relies on file extensions to determine how to process a file correctly. The most common extensions and their interpretations are listed in Table 1.1.

*Table 1.1   How **gcc** Interprets Filename Extensions*

Extension	Type
.c	C language source code
.C, .cc	C++ language source code
.i	Preprocessed C source code

continues

Table 1.1   continued

Extension	Type
.ii	Preprocessed C++ source code
.S, .s	Assembly language source code
.o	Compiled object code
.a, .so	Compiled library code

Invoking gcc Step by Step

In the first example, a lot took place under the hood that you did not see. gcc first ran hello.c through the preprocessor, cpp, to expand any macros and insert the contents of #included files. Next, it compiled the pre-processed source code to object code. Finally, the linker, ld, created the hello binary. The entire compilation process is illustrated in Figure 1.1.

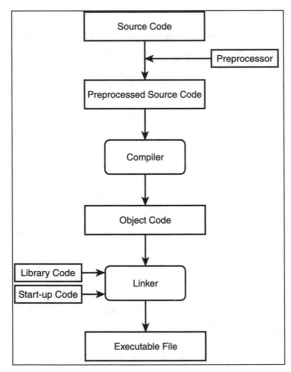

Figure 1.1: *Compiling a program consists of many steps.*

You can re-create these steps manually, stepping through the compilation process. To tell gcc to stop compilation after preprocessing, use gcc's -E option, as follows:

```
$ gcc -E infile.c -o outfile.cpp
```

The next step is to compile the preprocessed file to object code, using gcc's -c option. The correct syntax for this step is

```
$ gcc -x infile-type -c infile.cpp -o outfile.o
```

Linking the object file, finally, creates the binary image. The command for the link step should resemble the following:

```
$ gcc infile.o -o outfile
```

Example

Returning to the hello program from the previous example, step through the compilation process as the following example illustrates. First, pre-process hello.c:

```
$ gcc -E hello.c -o hello.cpp
```

If you examine hello.cpp with a text editor, you will see that the contents of stdio.h have indeed been inserted into the file, along with other prepro-cessing symbols. The following listing is an excerpt from hello.cpp:

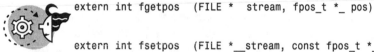

```
extern int fgetpos   (FILE *  stream, fpos_t *_ pos)   ;

extern int fsetpos   (FILE *_stream, const fpos_t *__pos)    ;
# 519 "/usr/include/stdio.h" 3
# 529 "/usr/include/stdio.h" 3

extern void clearerr   (FILE *__stream)    ;

extern int feof   (FILE *__stream)    ;

extern int ferror   (FILE *__stream)    ;

extern void clearerr_unlocked   (FILE *__stream) ;
extern int feof_unlocked   (FILE *__stream)    ;
extern int ferror_unlocked   (FILE *__stream)    ;

extern void perror   (__const char *__s)    ;

extern int sys_nerr;
extern __const char *__const sys_errlist[];
```

The next step is to compile hello.cpp to object code:

```
$ gcc -x cpp-output -c hello.cpp -o hello.o
```

You must use the -x option to tell gcc to begin compilation at a certain step, in this case, with preprocessed source code. Linking the object file, finally, creates a binary:

```
$ gcc hello.o -o hello
```

Hopefully, you can see that it is far simpler to use the "abbreviated" syntax, gcc hello.c -o hello. The step-by-step example demonstrated that you *can* stop and start compilation at any step, should the need arise.

One situation in which you want to step through compilation is when you are creating libraries. In this case, you only want to create object files, so the final link step is unnecessary. Another circumstance where you would want to walk through the compilation process is when an #included file introduces conflicts with your own code or perhaps with another #included file. Stepping through the process will make it clearer which file is introducing the conflict.

Using Multiple Source Code Files

Most C programs consist of multiple source files, so each source file must be compiled to object code before the final link step. This requirement is easily met. Just provide gcc with the name of each source code file it has to compile. It handles the rest. The gcc invocation would resemble:

```
$ gcc file1.c file2.c file3.c -o progname
```

gcc first creates file1.o, file2.o, and file3.o before linking them all together to create progname.

EXAMPLE

Example

Suppose you are working on newhello, which uses code from showit.c and msg.c:

```
showit.c
/*
 * showit.c _ Display driver
 */
#include <stdio.h>
#include "msg.h"

int main(void)
{
    char msg_hi[] = {"Hi there, programmer!"};
    char msg_bye[] = {"Goodbye, programmer!"};
```

```
        printf("%s\n", msg_hi);
        prmsg(msg_bye);
        return 0;
}
```

msg.h

```
/*
 * msg.h - Header for msg.c
 */

#ifndef MSG_H_
#define MSG_H_

void prmsg(char *msg);

#endif /* MSG_H_ */
```

msg.c

```
/*
 * msg.c - Define function from msg.h
 */
#include <stdio.h>
#include "msg.h"

void prmsg(char *msg)
{
    printf("%s\n", msg);
}
```

The command to compile these programs, and thus to create `newhello`, is

```
$ gcc msg.c showit.c -o newhello
```

Running this program, the output is

OUTPUT

```
$ ./newhello
Hi there, programmer!
Goodbye, programmer!
```

gcc goes through the same preprocess-compile-link steps as before, this time creating object files for each source file before creating the binary, newhello. Typing long commands like this *does* become tedious, however. In Chapter 2, "Controlling the Build Process—GNU make," you will see how to solve this problem. The next section introduces you to the multitude of gcc's command-line options.

EXAMPLE

Options and Arguments

The list of command-line options that gcc accepts runs to several pages, so Table 1.2 lists only the most common ones.

Table 1.2   **gcc** *Command-Line Options*

Option	Purpose
-o file	Name the output file file (not necessary when compiling object code). If the file is not specified, the default is a.out.
-c	Compile without linking.
-Dfoo=bar	Define a preprocessor macro foo with a value of bar on the command line.
-Idirname	Place the directory specified in dirname at the beginning of the list of directories gcc searches for include files.
-Ldirname	Place the directory specified in dirname at the beginning of the list of directories gcc searches for library files. By default, gcc links against shared libraries.
-static	Link against static libraries.
-lfoo	Link against the foo library.
-g	Include standard debugging information in the binary.
-ggdb	Include lots of debugging information in the binary that only the GNU debugger, gdb, can understand.
-O	Optimize the compiled code. This is equivalent to specifying -O1.
-On	Specify an optimization level n, 0<=n<=3.
-ansi	Places the compiler in ANSI/ISO C mode, disallowing GNU extensions that conflict with the standard.
-pedantic	Display all of the warnings the ANSI/ISO C standard requires.
-pedantic-errors	Display all of the errors the ANSI/ISO C standard requires.
-traditional	Enable support for the Kernighan and Ritchie C syntax (if you don't understand what this means, don't worry about it).
-w	Suppress all warning messages.
-Wall	Display all of the generally applicable warnings that gcc can provide. To see specific warnings, use -Wwarning.

Option	Purpose
-werror	Instead of generating warnings, gcc will convert warnings into errors, stopping compilation.
-MM	Output a make-compatible dependency list. Useful for creating a makefile in a complicated project.
-v	Show the commands used in each step of compilation.

You have already seen how -c and -o work. If you do not specify -o, though, for an input file named file.suffix, gcc's default behavior is to name the executable a.out, the object file file.o, and the assembly language file file.s. Preprocessor output goes to standard output.

LIBRARY AND INCLUDE FILES

If you have library or include files in non-standard locations, the -Ldirname and -Idirname options allow you to specify these locations and to ensure that they are searched before the standard locations. For example, if you store custom include files in /usr/local/myincludes, in order for gcc to find them, your gcc invocation would be something like

```
$ gcc infile.c -I/usr/local/myincludes
```

Similarly, suppose you are testing a new programming library, libnew.a, which is currently stored in /usr/local/mylibs, before installing it as a standard system library. Suppose also that the header files are stored in /usr/local/myincludes. Accordingly, to link against libnew.so and to help gcc find the header files, your gcc command line should resemble the following:

```
$ gcc myapp.c -I/usr/local/myinclues -L/usr/local/mylibs -lnew
```

The -l option tells the linker to pull in object code from the specified library. The example above linked against libnew.so.

TIP

A long-standing UNIX convention is that libraries are named lib{something}, and gcc, like most UNIX and Linux compilers, relies on this convention. If you do not use the -l option when linking against libraries or do not provide a pathname to the library against which to link, the link step will fail and gcc will emit a complaint about undefined references to "function_name."

By default, gcc uses shared libraries, so if you must link against static libraries, you have to use the -static option. This means that only static libraries will be used. The following example creates an executable linked against the static ncurses library:

```
$ gcc cursesapp.c -lncurses -static
```

✔ To learn about programming with ncurses, see "A Text-Mode User Interface API," p. 219.

When you link against static libraries, the resulting binary is much larger than when using shared libraries. Why use a static library, then? One common reason is to guarantee that users can run your program—in the case of shared libraries, the code your program needs to run is linked dynamically at runtime, rather than statically at compile-time. If the shared library your program requires is not installed on the user's system, she will get errors and not be able to run your program.

The Netscape browser is a perfect example of this problem. Netscape relies heavily on Motif, an expensive X programming toolkit. Most Linux users cannot afford to install Motif on their system because it costs too much money, so Netscape actually installs two versions of its browser on your system; one that is linked against shared libraries, netscape-dynMotif, and one that is statically linked, netscape-statMotif. The netscape executable itself is actually a shell script that determines whether you have the Motif shared library installed and launches one or the other of the binaries, as necessary.

EXAMPLE

Examples

1. This example creates a static library, libmsg.a. The necessary commands to do this are

```
$ gcc -c msg.c -o libmsg.o
$ ar rcs libmsg.a libmsg.o
```

Recall from earlier in the chapter that -c tells gcc to create an object file named, in this case, libmsg.o. The second line uses the ar command to create a static library named libmsg.a from the object module, libmsg.o. The next example uses this library.

✔ To learn more about the ar command, see "The ar Command," p. 299.

EXAMPLE

2. Now you have a library to link against. You have to tell gcc where to find the include file, using -I, where to find the library, using -L, and the name of the library, using -l, as illustrated here:

```
$ gcc showit.c -o newhello-lib   -I. -L. -lmsg
```

An earlier example created newhello by compiling showit.c and msg.c together. This time, we created newhello-lib by linking against the static library, libmsg.a. This example created a binary named newhello-lib (the name was chosen to distinguish it from the other example) by linking against libmsg.a (-lmsg) located in the current working directory (-L.). The . refers to the current directory. The output of this program is listed here:

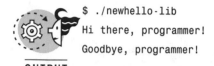

```
$ ./newhello-lib
Hi there, programmer!
Goodbye, programmer!
```

ERROR CHECKING AND WARNINGS

gcc boasts a whole class of error-checking, warning-generating, command-line options. These include -ansi, -pedantic, -pedantic-errors, and -Wall. To begin with, -pedantic tells gcc to issue all warnings demanded by strict ANSI/ISO standard C. Any program using forbidden extensions, such as those supported by gcc, will be rejected. –pedantic-errors behaves similarly, except that it emits errors rather than warnings. -ansi, turns off GNU extensions that do not comply with the standard. None of these options, however, guarantees that your code, even when it compiles without error using any or all of these options, is 100 percent ANSI/ISO-compliant.

The -Wall option instructs gcc to display all of the generally relevant warnings it can in relation to the code being compiled. -Wall emits warnings about code most programmers consider questionable and/or that is easy to modify to prevent the generated warning. One example of bad coding practice is to declare a variable but not otherwise to use it. Another example is declaring a variable without explicitly stating its type.

EXAMPLES

Consider the following example, which shows very bad programming form. It declares main as returning void, when in fact main returns int, and it uses the GNU extension long long int to declare a 64-bit integer.

```
pedant.c
/*
 * pedant.c - use -ansi, -pedantic or –pedantic-errors
 */
#include <stdio.h>

void main(void)
{
    long long int i =  01;
    puts("This is a non-conforming C program");
}
```

1. First, try to compile it using no conformance checking:

```
$ gcc pedant.c -o pedant
pedant.c: In function `main':
pedant.c:8: warning: return type of `main' is not `int'
```

2. Next, compile using the -ansi switch:

```
$ gcc -ansi pedant.c -o pedant
pedant.c: In function `main':
pedant.c:8: warning: return type of `main' is not `int'
```

The lesson here is that -ansi forces gcc to emit the diagnostic messages required by the standard. It does not ensure that your code is ANSI C-compliant. The program compiled despite main's incorrect declaration.

3. Now, use -pedantic:

```
$ gcc -pedantic pedant.c -o pedant
pedant.c: In function `main':
pedant.c:9: warning: ANSI C does not support `long long'
pedant.c:8: warning: return type of `main' is not `int'
```

Again, the code compiles, despite the emitted warnings.

4. Finally, use -pedantic-errors:

```
$ gcc -pedantic-errors pedant.c -o pedant
pedant.c: In function `main':
pedant.c:9: ANSI C does not support `long long'
pedant.c:8: return type of `main' is not `int'
```

The program fails to compile. gcc stops after displaying the required error diagnostics.

To reiterate, the -ansi, -pedantic, and -pedantic-errors compiler options do not ensure ANSI/ISO-compliant code. They merely help you along the road. It is instructive to point out the remark in the gcc's documentation on the use of -pedantic:

"This option is not intended to be useful; it exists only to satisfy pedants who would otherwise claim that GNU CC fails to support the ANSI standard. Some users try to use -pedantic to check programs for strict ANSI C conformance. They soon find that it does not do quite what they want: it finds some non-ANSI practices, but not all—only those for which ANSI C requires a diagnostic."

OPTIMIZATION OPTIONS

Code optimization is an attempt to improve performance. The tradeoff is longer compile times, increased memory usage during compilation, and, perhaps, larger code sizes.

Currently, gcc has three optimization levels. The bare -O option tells gcc to reduce both code size and execution time. It is equivalent to -O1. The types of optimization performed at this level depend on the target processor, but always include at least thread jumps and deferred stack pops. *Thread jump optimizations* attempt to reduce the number of jump operations. *Deferred stack pops* occur when the compiler allows arguments to accumulate on the stack as functions return and then pops them simultaneously, rather than popping the arguments piecemeal as each called function returns.

-O2 level optimizations include all level one optimizations plus additional tweaks that involve processor instruction scheduling. At this level, the compiler attempts to ensure that the processor has instructions to execute while waiting for the results of other instructions. The compiler also attempts to compensate for *data latency*, which is the delay caused by fetching data from cache or main memory. The implementation is highly processor-specific. -O3 options include all -O2 optimizations, loop unrolling, and other processor-specific features.

Depending on the amount of low-level knowledge you have about a given CPU family, you can use the -fflag option to request specific optimizations you want performed. Three of these flags bear consideration: -ffastmath, -finline-functions, and –funroll-loops. -ffastmath generates floating-point math optimizations that increase speed, but violate IEEE and/or ANSI standards. –finline-functions expands all "simple" functions in place, much like preprocessor macro replacements. The compiler decides what constitutes a simple function, however.

-funroll-loops instructs gcc to unroll all loops that have a fixed number of iterations, provided that the number of iterations can be determined at compile time. *Loop unrolling* means that each iteration of a loop will become an individual statement. So, a loop that has, for example, 100 iterations, becomes 100 sequential blocks of code, each executing the same statements. Figure 1.2 illustrates loop unrolling graphically.

Note that the figure simply illustrates the general principle of loop unrolling. The actual method that gcc uses may be dramatically different.

The optimizations that -finline-functions and -funroll-loops enable can greatly improve a program's execution speed because they avoid the overhead of function calls and variable lookups, but the cost is usually a large increase in the size of the executable or object file. You will have to experiment to see whether the increased speed is worth the increased file size. See the gcc info pages for more details on the -f processor flags.

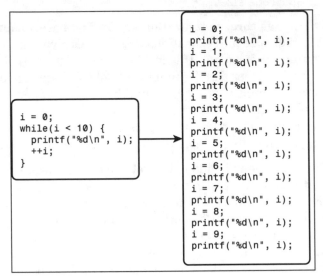

```
                          i = 0;
                          printf("%d\n", i);
                          i = 1;
                          printf("%d\n", i);
                          i = 2;
                          printf("%d\n", i);
                          i = 3;
                          printf("%d\n", i);
                          i = 4;
 i = 0;                   printf("%d\n", i);
 while(i < 10) {          i = 5;
   printf("%d\n", i);     printf("%d\n", i);
   ++i;                   i = 6;
 }                        printf("%d\n", i);
                          i = 7;
                          printf("%d\n", i);
                          i = 8;
                          printf("%d\n", i);
                          i = 9;
                          printf("%d\n", i);
```

Figure 1.2: Loop unrolling expands loops like the preprocessor does.

TIP

Generally, -O2 optimization is sufficient. Even on small programs, such as the one in the first "Example" section at the beginning of this chapter, you will see small reductions in code size and small increases in performance time.

EXAMPLE

Example

This example uses the maximum optimization level, O3, to compile Listings 1.2, 1.3, and 1.4. Compare the optimized program's size to the non-optimized program's size.

OUTPUT

```
$ gcc -O3 msg.c showit.c -o newhello
$ ls -l newhello
-rwxr-xr-x   1 kwall    users         12091 Jul 13 21:06 newhello*
$ gcc -O0 msg.c showit.c -o newhello
$ ls -l newhello
-rwxr-xr-x   1 kwall    users         12107 Jul 13 21:07 newhello*
```

The -O0 option turns off all optimization. Although the difference is small, only 16 bytes, it should be easy to understand that larger programs will see larger savings.

DEBUGGING OPTIONS

Bugs are as inevitable as death and taxes. To accommodate this sad reality, use gcc's -g and -ggdb options to insert debugging information into your compiled programs. These options facilitate debugging sessions.

The -g option can be qualified with 1, 2, or 3 to specify how much debugging information to include. The default level is 2 (-g2), which includes extensive symbol tables, line numbers, and information about local and external variables. Level 3 debugging information includes all of the level 2 information and all of the macro definitions present. Level 1 generates just enough information for creating backtraces and stack dumps. It does not generate debugging information for local variables or line numbers.

If you intend to use the GNU debugger, gdb (covered in Chapter 20, "A Debugging Toolkit"), using the -ggdb option creates extra information that eases the debugging chore under gdb. -ggdb accepts the same level specifications as -g, and they have the same effects on the debugging output. Using either of the two debug-enabling options will, however, dramatically increase the size of your binary.

EXAMPLE

This example shows you how to compile with debugging information and illustrates the impact debugging symbols can have on the size of a binary. Simply compiling and linking Listing 1.1 resulted in a binary of 4089 bytes on my system. The resulting sizes when I compiled it with the -g and -ggdb options may surprise you:

EXAMPLE

OUTPUT

```
$ gcc -g hello.c -o hello_g
$ ls -l hello_g
-rwxr--xr-x  1 kwall    users       6809 Jul 13 21:09 hello_g*
$ gcc -ggdb hello.c -o hello_ggdb
$ ls -l hello_ggdb
-rwxr-xr-x  1 kwall    users     354867 Jul 13 21:09 hello_ggdb*
```

As you can see, the -g option increased the binary's size by half, whereas the -ggdb option bloated the binary nearly 900 percent! Despite the size increase, you should provide binaries with standard debugging symbols (created using -g) in them in case someone encounters a problem and tries to debug your code for you.

TIP

As a general rule, debug first, optimize later. Do not, however, take "optimize later" to mean "ignore efficiency during the design process." Optimization, in this context, refers to the compiler magic discussed in this section. Good design and efficient algorithms have a far greater impact on overall performance than any compiler optimization magic ever will. Indeed, if you take the time up front to create a clean design and use fast algorithms, you may not need to optimize, although it never hurts to try.

GNU C Extensions

GNU's C implementation extends standard ANSI C in a variety of ways. If you don't mind writing blatantly non-standard code, some of these extensions can be very useful. For a complete discussion of the GNU project's extensions, the curious reader is directed to gcc's info pages (in particular, try the command `info gcc "C Extensions"`). The extensions covered in this section are the ones frequently seen in Linux's kernel headers and source code.

CAUTION

The problem with non-standard code is twofold. In the first place, if you are using GNU extensions, your code will only compile properly, if it compiles at all, with gcc. The other problem is that non-standard code does not adhere to ANSI/ISO standards. Many users use the strictest possible compilation switches with their compilers, so non-standard code will not compile. The wisest policy, if you wish to include non-ANSI features in your code, is to surround it with `#ifdefs` to enable conditional compilation. In the comp.lang.c newsgroup, you'll get flamed to a black crisp for using non-standard code.

To provide 64-bit storage units, for example, gcc offers the `long long int` type, used in Listing 1.5:

```
long long long_int_var;
```

NOTE

The `long long int` type is part of the new draft ISO C standard. It is still a *draft* standard, however, which few, if any, compilers support.

On the x86 platform, this definition results in a 64-bit memory location named `long_int_var`. Another gcc extension you will encounter in Linux header files is the use of inline functions. Provided it is short enough, an inline function expands in your code much as a macro does, thus eliminating the cost of a function call. Inline functions are better than macros, however, because the compiler type-checks them at compile-time. To use inline functions, you have to compile with at least -O optimization and precede the function definition with the inline keyword, as illustrated here:

```
inline int inc(int *a)
{
    (*a)++;
}
```

The attribute keyword tells gcc more about your code and helps the code optimizer work its magic. To use a function attribute, the general rule is to append __attribute__ ((attribute_name)) after the closing parenthesis of the function declaration.

For example, standard library functions, such as exit and abort, never return, so the compiler can generate slightly more efficient code if it knows that the function does not return. Of course, user-level programs may also define functions that do not return. gcc allows you to specify the noreturn attribute for such functions, which acts as a hint to the compiler to optimize the function.

Thus, suppose you have a function named die_on_error that never returns. Its declaration would look like:

```
void die_on_error(void) __attribute__ ((noreturn));
```

You would define it normally:

```
void die_on_error(void)
{
    /* your code here */
    exit(1);
}
```

You can also apply attributes to variables. The aligned attribute instructs the compiler to align the variable's memory location on a specified byte boundary. Conversely, the packed attribute tells gcc to use the minimum amount of space required for variables or structs. Used with structs, packed will remove any padding that gcc would ordinarily insert for alignment purposes.

One terrifically useful extension is case ranges. The syntax looks like this:

```
case LOWVAL ... HIVAL:
```

Note that the spaces before and after the ellipsis are required. Case ranges are used in switch statements to specify values that fall between LOWVAL and HIVAL, as the following code snippet illustrates:

```
switch(int_var) {
    case 0 ... 2:
        /* your code here */
        break;
    case 3 ... 5:
...
}
```

This fragment is equivalent to:

```
switch(int_var) {
    case 1:
    case 2:
        /* your code here */
        break;
    case 3:
    case 4:
    case 5:
...
}
```

Obviously, the case range is just a shorthand notation for the traditional switch statement syntax, but it is a darn convenient one.

EXAMPLE

Examples

1. This example illustrates using the inline keyword. The program loops 10 times, incrementing a variable in each iteration.

```
inline.c
/*
 * inline.c
 */
#include <stdio.h>

inline int inc(int *a)
{
```

```
        (*a)++;
}

int main(void)
{
    int i = 0;
    while(i < 10) {
        inc(&i);
        printf("%d ", i);
    }
    printf("\n");

    return 0;
}
```

In such a simple example, you are not likely to see significant increases or decreases in speed or code size, but this should illustrate how to use the inline keyword.

EXAMPLE

2. This example shows you how to use the attribute keyword and the noreturn attribute and also how to use case ranges.

noret.c

```
/*

 * noret.c
 */
#include <stdio.h>

void die_now(void) __attribute__ ((noreturn));

int main(void)
{
    int i = 0;

    while(1) {
        switch(i) {
        case 0 ... 5:
            printf("i = %d\n", i);
            break;
```

```
            default:
                die_now();
            }
            ++i;
        }
        return 0;
}


void die_now(void)
{
    printf("dying now\n");
    exit(1);
}
```

Be careful, when writing code that has an infinite loop like the while loop in this program, that an escape point exists, such as breaking out of the loop when a loop counter reaches a certain value. For our purposes, however, it perfectly illustrates how the case range extension works. The output of this program is

OUTPUT

```
$ ./noret
i = 0
i = 1
i = 2
i = 3
i = 4
i = 5
dying now
```

The case range extension behaves just as a regular case statement would. When i becomes 6, program flow reaches the default block, die_now executes, and the program terminates.

3. The final example illustrates the effect of using the packed attribute on a structure. The program merely prints the size of the structures and their constituent members.

EXAMPLE   packme.c

```
/*


 * packme.c - Using gcc's packed attributed
 */
```

```c
#include <stdio.h>

/* a "packed" structure */
struct P {
    short s[3];
    long l;
    char str[5];
} __attribute__ ((packed));

/* a normal unpacked structure */
struct UP {
    short s[3];
    long l;
    char str[5];
};

int main(void)
{
    struct P packed;
    struct UP unpacked;

    /* print the size of each member for comparison */
    fprintf(stdout, "sizeof char str[5] = %d bytes\n", sizeof(char) * 5);
    fprintf(stdout, "      sizeof long = %d bytes\n", sizeof(long));
    fprintf(stdout, " sizeof short s[3] = %d bytes\n", sizeof(short) * 3);

    /* how big are the two structures */
    fprintf(stdout, "    sizeof packed = %d bytes\n", sizeof packed);
    fprintf(stdout, "  sizeof unpacked = %d bytes\n", sizeof unpacked);

    return 0;
}
```

No special compilation command is necessary to use any of the GNU extensions to the C language. Compiled and executed, the output from this program is

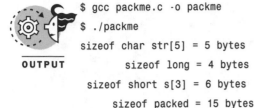

OUTPUT

```
$ gcc packme.c -o packme
$ ./packme
sizeof char str[5] = 5 bytes
        sizeof long = 4 bytes
 sizeof short s[3] = 6 bytes
     sizeof packed = 15 bytes
   sizeof unpacked = 20 bytes
```

The two elements were defined with identical members. The only difference was the addition of the packed attribute to struct P. As the output makes clear, the members of each struct require 15 bytes of storage. On an x86 architecture, the normal, unpacked structure, UP, gains five bytes, while the packed structure, P, is the sum of its members. Although a mere five bytes of saved memory may not seem like much, imagine you had an array of 1,000,000 of them (not unrealistic in some applications)—this amounts to almost five megabytes of saved RAM. Big difference!

NOTE

The padding in the normal structure was probably the result of aligning str and s on appropriate boundaries, adding three and two bytes, respectively, to the "actual" sizes. ANSI permits implementers of the C language to pad structures to the natural word lengths of the host architecture. So, while the packed attribute has some obvious benefits, it comes at the price of portability.

Using egcs

egcs is the Experimental(or Enhanced) GNU Compiler Suite. It originally started as an experimental step to speed up the development of gcc and to open up gcc's development environment. Other goals of the egcs (pronounced *eggs*, the c is silent) project were to add new languages, new optimizations, and new targets (host processor architectures) to gcc.

In April 1999, the GNU project formally appointed the egcs steering committee as official maintainer of gcc. gcc has since been renamed the GNU Compiler Collection. The point of this history lesson is to suggest that, at some point, egcs may well merge with gcc. In the meantime, however, egcs is a separate product. It is also the default C/C++ compiler on at least two distributions, so an understanding of its differences from and enhancements to gcc is important. For more information about egcs, visit the web site at http://egcs.cygnus.com/.

NOTE

It appears that the current release of egcs, 1.1.2, will be the last version of egcs *per se*. The next release, according to egcs's web site, will be version 2.95 of gcc.

---

egcs is completely backward-compatible with gcc, so everything this chapter said about gcc also applies to egcs. In fact, although doing so is not officially sanctioned by the kernel development team, you can compile the Linux 2.2.x kernel with egcs without incident and it should run very well. egcs represents significant improvement over the standard gcc compiler, 2.7.2.3. The next section covers some of these improvements.

Enhancements to gcc

Most of egcs' enhancements over gcc affect the operation of the compiler itself rather than its command-line interface, so they are far beyond the scope of this book. However, some changes in the command-line interface have been made, and are covered in this section.

Several new warnings have been added. -Wundef and -Wno-def generate warnings when an #if preprocessor directive attempts to evaluate an undefined identifier. -Wsign-compare causes egcs (and gcc) to warn when code compares signed and unsigned values. The -Wall flag has been extended to cause egcs to issue warnings when integers are implicitly declared. Similarly, the warning flag -Wimplicit-function-declarations catches implicit declaration of functions.

Debugging and optimization improvements have also been made. For example, in addition to the numeric arguments to the optimization switch, -O, you can now use -Os to select code size optimizations over code speed optimizations. Choosing between size or speed optimizations depends mostly on whether you need high performace or to conserve disk space. These days, with both RAM and disk space pretty inexpensive, it is easy to choose speed over size. A program's size, however, must be considered in terms of its disk footprint as well as the amount of memory it requires while executing. In situations where disk and RAM are at a premium, choose to reduce size rather than to increase speed because the fastest program in the world is useless if it will not fit on your disk or in memory.

The -fstack-check switch checks for stack overflow on systems that lack such a feature. To enhance debugging capabilities, new flags for *performance profiling* have been added. Performance profiling enables you to determine precisely how fast your code executes, which functions it calls most often, which variables it uses most often, and to identify unused sections of code (often called *dead code*) or variables. With this information, you can modify the source code to make your program more efficient. egcs also has built-in support for the Checker memory checking tool. Additional processor-specific flags are listed here:

- `-fprofile-arcs`—Enables egcs to count the number of times a function is executed.

- `-ftest-coverage`—Creates data files for the gcov code coverage analysis tool.

- `-fbranch-probabilities`—Improves egcs's prediction of code branches.

Finally, output from the `--help` options has been dramatically improved.

What's Next

In this chapter, you learned how to use the GNU C compiler, gcc, and, due to its similarity to gcc, how to use egcs. Most programs that you build, even single file programs, will require long compiler invocations. This flexibility can be hard on your fingers and tedious to type, so the next chapter will show you how to automate the software-building process using another great UNIX/Linux tool, make. With a basic understanding of these two tools, you will be ready to move on to the system programming topics that get you started programming Linux by example.

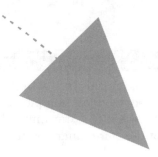

Controlling the Build Process
—GNU make

make is a tool used to control the process of building and rebuilding software. make automates what software is built, how it gets built, and when it gets built, freeing you to concentrate on writing code. It also saves a lot of typing, since it contains logic that invokes the C compiler with appropriate options and arguments.

In this chapter, you learn the following:

- How to invoke make
- make's command-line options and arguments
- Creating makefiles
- Writing make rules
- Using make variables
- Dealing with make errors

Why make?

For all but the simplest software projects, make is essential. In the first place, projects composed of multiple source files require long, complex compiler invocations. make simplifies this by storing these difficult command lines in a *makefile*, a text file that contains all of the commands required to build software projects.

make is convenient for both you and anyone else wanting to build your program. As you make changes to your program, whether you are adding new features or incorporating bug fixes, make allows you to rebuild it with a single, short command, to rebuild only a single component, such as a library file, or to customize the kind of build you want, depending on the circumstances. make is also convenient for other people who might build your program. Rather than creating documentation that explains in excruciating detail how to build it, you simply instruct them to type make. You will appreciate having to write less documentation, and they will appreciate the convenience of simple build instructions.

✔ For more information about distributing software, see "Software Distribution," page 443.

Finally, make speeds up the edit-compile-debug process. It minimizes rebuild times because it is smart enough to determine which files have changed, and thus only rebuilds files whose components have changed. The makefile also constitutes a database of dependency information for your projects, allowing you automatically to verify that all of the files necessary for building a program are available each time you start a build. As you gain experience with Linux programming, you will come to appreciate this feature of make.

Using make

This section explains how to use make. In particular, it explains how to create makefiles, how to invoke make, how to unravel its plethora of options, arguments, and switches, and how to handle the inevitable errors that occur along the way.

Creating Makefiles

So, how does make accomplish its magical feats? By using a makefile. A *makefile* is a text file database containing rules that tell make what to build and how to build it. A *rule* consists of the following:

- A *target*, the "thing" make ultimately tries to create
- A list of one or more *dependencies*, usually files, required to build the target
- A list of *commands* to execute in order to create the target from the specified dependencies

When invoked, GNU make looks for a file named GNUmakefile, makefile, or Makefile, in that order. For some reason, most Linux programmers use the last form, Makefile.

Makefile rules have the general form

```
target : dependency [dependency] [...]
        command
        [command]
        [...]
```

CAUTION

The first character in a command must be the tab character; eight spaces will not suffice. This often catches people unaware, and can be a problem if your preferred editor "helpfully" translates tabs to eight spaces. If you try to use spaces instead of a tab, make displays the message "Missing separator" and stops.

---

target is usually the binary or object file you want created. dependency is a list of one or more files required as input in order to create target. The commands are the steps, such as compiler invocations or shell commands, necessary to create target. Unless specified otherwise, make does all of its work in the current working directory.

"All well and good," you are probably thinking, "but how does make know when to rebuild a file?" The answer is stunningly simple: if a specified target does not exist in a place where make can find it, make (re)builds it. If the target does exist, make compares the timestamp on the target to the timestamp of the dependencies. If at least one of the dependencies is newer than the target, make rebuilds the target, assuming that the newer dependency implies some code change that must be incorporated into the target.

Example

This sample makefile will make the discussion more concrete. It is the makefile for building a text editor imaginatively named editor.

```
#
# Makefile.1
#

editor : editor.o screen.o keyboard.o
        gcc -o editor editor.o screen.o keyboard.o

editor.o : editor.c editor.h keyboard.h screen.h
        gcc -c editor.c

screen.o : screen.c screen.h
        gcc -c screen.c

keyboard.o : keyboard.c keyboard.h
        gcc -c keyboard.c

clean :
        rm editor *.o
```

To compile editor, you would simply type make in the directory containing the makefile. It's that simple.

This makefile has five rules. The first target, editor, is called the *default* target—this is the file that make ultimately tries to create. editor has three dependencies, editor.o, screen.o, and keyboard.o; these three files must exist in order to build editor. The next line is the command that make executes to create editor. As you recall from Chapter 1, "Compiling Programs," this compiler invocation builds an executable named editor from the three object modules, editor.o, screen.o, and keyboard.o. The next three rules tell make how to build the individual object modules.

Here is where make's value becomes evident: ordinarily, if you tried to build editor using the command from line 2, gcc would complain loudly and quit if the dependencies did not exist. make, on the other hand, after determining that editor requires these files, first verifies that they exist and, if they do not, executes the commands to create them. Then it returns to the first rule to create the editor executable. Of course, if the dependencies for the components, keyboard.c or screen.h, don't exist, make will also give up, because it lacks targets named, in this case, keyboard.c and screen.h.

Invoking make

Invoking make is as simple as typing make in the directory containing the makefile. Of course, like most GNU programs, make accepts a cornucopia of command-line options. The most common ones are listed in Table 2.1.

Table 2.1   Common **make** *Command-Line Options*

Option	Purpose
-f file	Use the makefile named file instead of one of the standard names (GNUmakefile, makefile, or Makefile).
-n	Display the commands make would execute without actually doing so. Useful for testing a makefile.
-Idirname	Add dirname to the list of directories make should search for included makefiles.
-s	Execute silently, not printing the the commands make executes.
-w	Print directory names when make changes directories.
-Wfile	Execute make as if file has been modified. Like -n, very useful for testing makefiles.
-r	Disable all of make's built-in rules.
-d	Print lots of debugging information.
-i	Ordinarily, make stops if a command returns a non-zero error code. This option disables this behavior.
-k	Keep executing even if one target fails to build. Normally, make terminates when a target fails to build.
-jN	Run N commands in parallel, where N is a small, non-zero integer.

make can generate a lot of output, so if you are not interested in looking at it, use the -s option to limit make's output. The -W and -n options allow you to say "what if file X changed?" The -i option exists because not all programs return a 0 on success. If you use such a command as part of a makefile rule, you will need to use -i in order for a build to continue.

The -k option is particularly useful when you are building a program for the first time. Because it tells make to continue even if one or more targets fail to build, the -k option enables you to see which targets build successfully and which do not, allowing you to focus your debugging efforts on the problem children.

If you have an especially long build, the -jN option instructs make to execute N commands simultaneously. While this may reduce the overall build time, it also creates a heavy load on the system. This is probably tolerable on a

stand-alone system or on an individual workstation, but it is absolutely
unacceptable on a production system that requires quick response times,
such as on a web server or database server.

Examples

These examples all use the following makefile, the makefile for most of the
programs from Chapter 1. The associated source code is also taken from
Chapter 1. Do not worry if you do not understand some of the features of
this makefile, because they are covered later in this chapter.

```
#
# Makefile
#
LDFLAGS :=

# Switch the comment characters on the next two lines if
# you want to optimize
CFLAGS := -g $(CPPFLAGS)
#CFLAGS := -O2 $(CPPFLAGS)

PROGS =      \
    hello \
    pedant \
    newhello \
    newhello-lib \
    noret \
    inline \
        packme

all: $(PROGS)

.c.o:
    $(CC) $(CFLAGS) -c $*.c

.SUFFIXES: .c .o

hello: hello.c

pedant: pedant.c
```

```
newhello: showit.c msg.c
    $(CC) $(CFLAGS) $^ -o $@

newhello-lib: showit.c libmsg.a
    $(CC) $(CFLAGS) $< -o $@ -I. -L. -lmsg

libmsg.a: msg.c
    $(CC) $(CFLAGS) -c $< -o libmsg.o
    $(AR) rcs libmsg.a libmsg.o

noret: noret.c

inline: inline.c
    $(CC) -O2 $< -o $@

packme: packme.c

.PHONY : clean zip

clean:
    $(RM) $(PROGS) *.o *.a *~ *.out

zip: clean
    zip 215101cd.zip *.c *.h Makefile
```

EXAMPLE

1. The first example illustrates how to simulate a build using the -W and -n options.

OUTPUT

```
$ make -Wmsg.c -Wshowit.c -n newhello-lib
cc -g   -c msg.c -o libmsg.o
ar rcs libmsg.a libmsg.o
cc -g   showit.c -o newhello-lib -I. -L. -lmsg
```

The -Wfile option tells make to act as if file has changed, whereas -n displays the commands that would be executed without actually executing them. As you can see from the output, make would first build the library file, libmsg.a, then compile showit.c and link it with the library to create newhello-lib. This technique is an excellent way to test makefile rules.

EXAMPLE

OUTPUT

2. This example compares the make's normal output with the result obtained when you use the -s option to suppress make's output.

```
$ make all
cc -g      hello.c    -o hello
cc -g      pedant.c    -o pedant
cc -g  showit.c msg.c -o newhello
cc -g  -c msg.c -o libmsg.o
ar rcs libmsg.a libmsg.o
pedant.c: In function 'main':
pedant.c:8: warning: return type of 'main' is not 'int'
cc -g      noret.c    -o noret
cc -02 inline.c -o inline
cc -g      packme.c    -o packme
cc -g  showit.c -o newhello-lib -I. -L. -lmsg

$ make -s all
pedant.c: In function 'main':
pedant.c:8: warning: return type of 'main' is not 'int'
```

As you can see, -s suppresses all of make's output. The warning about main's return value is diagnostic output from gcc, which make cannot, of course, suppress.

Creating Rules

This section goes into more detail about writing makefile rules. In particular, it discusses phony targets, makefile variables, environment variables, predefined variables, implicit rules, and pattern rules.

Phony Targets

In addition to the normal file targets, make allows you to specify *phony targets*. Phony targets are so named because they do not correspond to actual files. Phony targets, like normal targets, have rules that list commands make should execute. The final target of the makefile in the last example, clean, was a phony target. However, because clean did not have any dependencies, its commands were not automatically executed.

This behavior follows from the explanation of how make works: Upon encountering the clean target, make determines whether the dependencies exist and, because clean has no dependencies, make assumes the target is up to date. In order to build this target, you have to type make clean. In our case, clean removes the editor executable and its constituent object files. You might create such a target if you wanted to create a source-code *tarball*, an archive file created using the tar command, or wanted to start a build with a clean build tree.

✔ For a detailed discussion of the tar command, see "tar Usage," page 444.

If, however, a file named clean happened to exist, make would see it. Again, because it lacks dependencies, make would assume that it is up to date and would not execute the commands associated with the clean target. To deal with this situation, use the special make target, .PHONY. Any dependencies of the .PHONY target will be evaluated as usual, but make will disregard the presence of a file whose name matches one of .PHONY's dependencies and execute the corresponding commands anyway.

Examples

EXAMPLE

1. Refer to the previous makefile for this example. Without the .PHONY target, if a file named clean exists in the current directory, the clean target will not work correctly.

OUTPUT

```
$ touch clean
$ make clean
make: 'clean' is up to date.
```

As you can see, without the .PHONY target, make evaluated the clean target's dependencies, saw that it did not have any and that a file named clean already existed in the current directory, concluded that the target was up to date, and did not execute the rule's commands.

EXAMPLE

2. However, with the .PHONY special target, the clean target works perfectly, as illustrated:

OUTPUT

```
$ make clean
rm -f hello pedant newhello newhello noret inline packme *.o *.a *~
```

The .PHONY target clean forced make to ignore the presence of the file named clean. Under ordinary circumstances, it would be best not to have such unfortunately named files in a source tree. Since mistakes and coincidences will happen, however, .PHONY can be a lifesaver.

Variables

To simplify makefile editing and maintenance , make allows you to create and use variables. A *variable* is simply a name defined in a makefile that represents a string of text; this text is called the variable's *value*. make distinguishes between four kinds of variables: user-defined variables, environment variables, automatic variables, and predefined variables. Their usage is identical.

USER-DEFINED VARIABLES

Define variables using the general form:

```
VARNAME = value [...]
```

By convention, makefile variables are all uppercase, but this is not required. To obtain VARNAME's value, enclose it in parentheses and prefix it with a $:

```
$(VARNAME)
```

VARNAME expands to the text stored in value, the value on the right side of the assignment. Variables are usually defined at the top of a makefile.

Using makefile variables is primarily a convenience. If the value changes, you need to make only one change instead of many, simplifying makefile maintenance.

EXAMPLE

Example

This makefile shows how user-defined variables work. It uses the shell's echo command to demonstrate how variables expand.

```
PROGS = prog1 prog2 prog3 prog4


.PHONY : echoit


echoit :
    echo $(PROGS)
```

OUTPUT

```
$ make -s echoit
prog1 prog2 prog3 prog4
```

As you can see, PROGS expanded into its value when passed to the echo command. This example also illustrates that the commands in a rule can be any valid shell command or system utility or program, not just compiler invocations. It is necessary to use the -s option because make echoes the commands it executes as it executes them. In the absence of -s, the output would have been:

```
$ make echoit
echo prog1 prog2 prog3 prog4
prog1 prog2 prog3 prog4
```

OUTPUT

RECURSIVELY EXPANDED VERSUS SIMPLY EXPANDED VARIABLES

make actually uses two kinds of variables, recursively expanded and simply expanded. *Recursively expanded* variables are expanded verbatim as they are referenced, that is, if the expansion contains another variable reference, it is also expanded. The expansion continues until no further variables exist to expand, hence the name, recursively expanded. For example, consider the variables TOPDIR and SRCDIR defined as follows:

```
TOPDIR = /home/kwall/myproject
SRCDIR = $(TOPDIR)/src
```

Thus, SRCDIR will have the value /home/kwall/myproject/src. This works as expected and desired. However, you cannot append text to the end of a previously defined variable. Consider the next variable definition:

```
CC = gcc
CC = $(CC) -g
```

Clearly, what you ultimately want is CC = gcc -g. That is not what you will get, however. $(CC) is recursively expanded when it is referenced, so you wind up with an infinite loop: $(CC) will keep expanding to $(CC), and you never pick up the -o option. Fortunately, make detects this and reports an error:

```
*** Recursive variable 'CC' references itself (eventually). Stop.
```

Figure 2.1 illustrates the problem with recursive variable expansion.

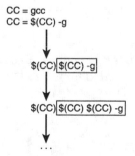

Figure 2.1: *The pitfalls of recursively expanded* make *variables.*

As you can see in the figure, recursive expansion when you try to append something to a previously defined variable starts an infinite loop. The boxed text represents the result of the previous expansion, while the recursive element is represented by prepending $(CC) to the front of the previous expansion. Clearly, the CC variable will never resolve.

To avoid this difficulty, make also uses simply expanded variables. Rather than being expanded when they are referenced, *simply expanded* variables are scanned once when they are defined; all embedded variable references are immediately resolved. The definition syntax is slightly different:

```
CC := gcc
CC += -g
```

The first definition uses := to set CC equal to gcc and the second definition uses += to append -g to the first definition, so that CC's final value is gcc -g (+= works in make the same way it does in C). Figure 2.2 illustrates graphically how simply expanded variables work. If you run into trouble when using make variables or get the "VARNAME references itself" error message, it's time to use the simply expanded variables. Some programmers use only simply expanded variables to avoid unanticipated problems. Since this is Linux, you are free to choose for yourself!

Figure 2.2: *Simply expanded variables resolve completely when first scanned.*

Figure 2.2 shows that each time a variable is referenced, it is expanded completely. The variable assignments on the left side have the values show on the right side, and the values contain no variable references.

Examples

1. This makefile uses recursively expanded variables. Because it repeatedly references the CC variable, the make will fail. The file hello.c (in the source code directory for this chapter on the CD-ROM) is taken from Chapter 1.

EXAMPLE

```
CC = gcc
CC = $(CC) -g


hello: hello.c
    $(CC) hello.c -o hello
```

```
$ make hello
Makefile:5: *** Recursive variable 'CC' references itself (eventually). Stop.
```

OUTPUT As you would expect, make detected the recursive use of CC and stopped.

2. This makefile uses simply expanded variables in place of the recursively expanded variables in the first example.

```
CC := gcc
CC += -g


hello: hello.c
    $(CC) hello.c -o hello
```

```
$ make hello
gcc -c hello.c -o hello
```

This time, the program compiled normally.

ENVIRONMENT VARIABLES

Environment variables are make's copies of all the shell's environment variables. When it starts, make reads every variable defined in its environment and creates variables with the same name and value. However, similarly named variables in the makefile override the environment variables, so beware.

Example

This makefile uses the $HOME variable it inherits from the shell as part of a rule for making the foo target.

```
foo : $(HOME)/foo.c
    gcc $(HOME)/foo.c -o $(HOME)/foo
```

```
$ make all
make: *** No rule to make target '/home/kwall/foo.c', needed by 'foo'.  Stop.
```

The error message displayed is somewhat misleading. When make failed to find /home/kwall/foo.c, listed as a dependency of the foo target, it assumed that it needed to somehow build foo.c first. However, it failed to find a rule for doing so, so it complained and exited. The point, though, was to demonstrate that make inherited the $HOME variable from shell environment (/home/kwall in this case).

AUTOMATIC VARIABLES

Automatic variables are variables whose values are evaluated each time a rule is executed, based on the target and the dependencies of that rule. Automatic rules are used to create pattern rules. Pattern rules are generic instructions, such as a rule that says how to compile an arbitrary .c file to its corresponding .o file. Automatic variables are pretty cryptic looking. Table 2.2 contains a partial list of automatic variables.

✔ To learn about pattern rules in greater detail, see "Pattern Rules," p. 49.

Table 2.2   Automatic Variables

Variable	Description
$@	Represents the target filename in a rule
$*	Represents the basename (or stem) of a filename
$<	Represents the filename of a rule's first dependency
$^	Expands to a space-delimited list of all of a rule's dependencies
$?	Expands to a space-delimited list of all of a rule's dependencies that are newer than the target
$(@D)	If the named target is in a subdirectory, this represents the directory part of the target's pathname
$(@F)	If the named target is in a subdirectory, this represents the file-name part of a target's pathname

EXAMPLE

Example

The makefile excerpt that follows (from the makefile for Chapter 4, "Processes") uses the $*, $<, and $@ automatic variables.

```
CFLAGS := -g
CC := gcc
.c.o:
        $(CC) $(CFLAGS) -c $*.c


prpids: prpids.c
        $(CC) $(CFLAGS) $< -o $@


ids: ids.c
        $(CC) $(CFLAGS) $< -o $@
```

OUTPUT

```
$ make prpids ids
gcc -g prpids.c -o prids
gcc -g ids.c -o ids
```

The first target is an implicit rule. (Implicit rules are explained in detail later in this chapter.). It says that for each filename ending in .c, create an object file ending in .o using the command $(CC) $(CFLAGS) -c. $*.c matches any filename in the current directory ending in .c, in this case, prpids.c and ids.c.

As the echoed commands in the output showed, make replaced $< with the first dependency for each rule, prpids.c and ids.c. Similarly, the automatic variable $@ in the commands for building prpids and ids is replaced by the target names for these rules, prpids and ids, respectively.

PREDEFINED VARIABLES

In addition to the automatic variables listed in Table 2.2, GNU make predefines a number of other variables that are used either as names of programs or to pass flags and arguments to these programs. Table 2.3 lists make's most commonly used predefined variables. You have already seen some of these in this chapter's example makefiles.

Table 2.3   Predefined Variables for Program Names and Flags

Variable	Description	Default Value
AR	Filename of the archive-maintenance program	ar
AS	Filename of the assembler	as
CC	Filename of the C compiler	cc
CPP	Filename of the C Preprocessor	cpp
RM	Program to remove files	rm -f
ARFLAGS	Flags for the archive-maintenance program	rv
ASFLAGS	Flags for the assembler	No default
CFLAGS	Flags for the C compiler	No default
CPPFLAGS	Flags for the C preprocessor	No default
LDFLAGS	Flags for the linker	No default

The last makefile example used several of these predefined variables. You can redefine these variables in your makefile, although in most cases their default values are reasonable. Redefine them when the default behavior does not meet your needs or when you know that a program on a given system does not have the same calling syntax.

Example

The makefile in this example rewrites the one from the previous example to use only automatic and predefined variables wherever possible, and does not redefine the default values of the predefined variables that make provides.

```
prpids: prpids.c
        $(CC) $(CFLAGS) $< -o $@ $(LDFLAGS)

ids: ids.c
        $(CC) $(CFLAGS) $< -o $@ $(LDFLAGS)
```

The output this makefile generates is slightly different from the last example:

OUTPUT

```
$ make
cc  prpids.c -o prpids
cc  ids.c -o ids
```

The output shows that make used the default value of CC, cc, rather than gcc. On most Linux systems, however, cc is a symbolic link to gcc (or egcs), so the compile worked correctly.

Implicit Rules

So far, the makefiles in the chapter have used *explicit rules*, rules that you write yourself. make comes with a comprehensive set of *implicit*, or predefined, rules, too. Many of these are special-purpose and of limited usage, so the chapter covers only a few of the most commonly used implicit rules. Implicit rules simplify makefile maintenance.

Suppose you have these two makefile rules:

```
prog : prog1o


prog.o : prog.c
```

The two rules list dependencies but no rules for building their targets. Rather than failing, however, make will attempt to find and use implicit rules to build the targets (you can verify that make searches for implicit rules by watching the debugging output generated when you use the -d option).

EXAMPLE

Example

The very spare-looking makefile that follows will create prpids using two of make's implicit rules. The first defines how to create an object file from a C source code file. The second defines how to create a binary from an object file.

```
prpids : prpids.o


prpids.o : prpids.c
```

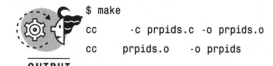

```
$ make
cc      -c prpids.c -o prpids.o
cc      prpids.o    -o prpids
```

make invokes two implicit rules to build prpids. The first rule says, in essence, that for each object file somefile.o, look for a corresponding source file somefile.c and build the object file with the command cc -c somefile.c -o somefile.o. So, make looked for a C source file named prpids.c and compiled it to the object file prpids.o. To build the default target, prpids, make used another implicit rule that says for each object file somefile.o, link the final executable using the command cc somefile.o -o somefile.

Pattern Rules

Pattern rules provide a way for you to define your own implicit rules. Pattern rules look like normal rules, except that the target contains exactly one character (%) that matches any non-empty string. The dependencies of such a rule also use % in order to match the target. So, for example, the rule

```
%.o : %.c
```

tells make to build any object file somename.o from a corresponding source file named somename.c. This pattern rule also happens to be one of make's predefined pattern rules but, as with predefined variables, you can redefine them to suit your own needs.

```
%.o : %.c
        $(CC) -c $(CFLAGS) $(CPPFLAGS) $< -o $@
```

Example

The makefile that follows is a version of the last one, except that it uses a pattern rule to create a custom, user-defined implicit rule for compiling and linking C source code, and uses a predefined implicit rule for linking the object file to create the binary.

```
CFLAGS := -g -O3 -c
CC := gcc

#
# Redefine the default pattern rule
# %.o : %.c
#
```

```
%.o : %.c
    $(CC) $(CFLAGS) $< -o $@


#
# This is a totally gratuitous comment
#
prpids : prpids.o


prpids.o : prpids.c

$ make
gcc -g -O3 -c prpids.c -o prpids.o
gcc    prpids.o    -o prpids
```

OUTPUT

The user-defined pattern rule did several things:

- Changed CC to gcc

- Added gcc's debugging switch, -g, and the optimization switch -O3, to CFLAGS

- Used the automatic variables $< and $@ to substitute the names of the first dependency and the target each time the rule is applied

As you can see from make's output, the custom rule was applied as specified in the makefile, creating a highly optimized binary with debugging information embedded in it.

Comments

You can insert comments in a makefile by preceding the comment with the hash sign (#). When make encounters a comment, it ignores the hash symbol and the rest of the line following it. Comments can be placed anywhere in a makefile. Special consideration must be given to comments that appear in commands, because most shells treat # as a *metacharacter* (usually as a comment delimiter). As far as make is concerned, a line that contains only a comment is, for all practical purposes, blank. The previous example illustrated the use of comments. make totally ignored the four lines that consisted only of the comment delimiter and the two lines containing useless text.

Useful Makefile Targets

In addition to the clean target illustrated earlier in this chapter, several other targets typically inhabit makefiles. A target named install moves the final binary, any supporting libraries or shell scripts, and documentation to their final homes in the filesystem and sets file permissions and ownership appropriately.

An `install` target typically also compiles the program and may also run a simple test to verify that the program compiled correctly. An `uninstall` target deletes the files installed by an `install` target.

A `dist` target is a convenient way to prepare a distribution package. At the very least, the `dist` target removes old binary and object files from the build directory and creates an archive file, such as a gzipped (compressed) tarball, ready for uploading to World Wide Web pages and FTP sites.

NOTE

The gzip program is a general purpose file compressor and uncompressor that is compatible with the classic UNIX `compress` utility. It is one of the GNU projects most popular programs and is available for almost every operating system available.

Example

The following makefile illustrates how to create `install`, `dist`, and `uninstall` targets, using the terribly overworked `hello.c` program.

EXAMPLE

```
hello : hello.c

install : hello
    install $< $(HOME)

.PHONY : dist uninstall

dist :
    $(RM) hello *.o core
    tar czvf hello.tar.gz hello.c Makefile

uninstall :
    $(RM) $(HOME)/hello
```

OUTPUT

```
$ make install
cc      hello.c    -o hello
install hello /home/kwall
$ make dist
rm -f hello *.o core
tar czvf hello.tar.gz hello.c Makefile
hello.c
```

```
Makefile
$ make uninstall
rm -f /home/kwall/hello
```

make install first compiles hello and installs it in the designated directory. This illustrates one of the bonuses of using make variables: $HOME evaluates to the correct value on whatever system make runs, thus it does not have to be hard coded into the makefile. make dist cleans up the detritus from the build, such as object modules and other temporary files, and creates what amounts to a source code distribution ready for uploading to the Internet. The uninstall target, finally, silently deletes the freshly installed program.

Handling Errors

When you run into trouble using make, the -d option tells make to print lots of extra debugging information in addition to the commands it is executing. The output can be overwhelming because the debugging dump will display what make does internally and why. The debug option's output includes the following information:

- Which files make evaluates for rebuilding

- Which files are being compared and what the comparison results are

- Which files actually need to be remade

- Which implicit rules make thinks it will use

- Which implicit rules make decides to use, and the commands it actually executes

The list that follows contains the most common error messages you will encounter while using make and suggests how to resolve them. For complete documentation, refer to the make manual or, better yet, make's info pages (use the command info "GNU make").

- No rule to make target 'target'. Stop—make could not find an appropriate rule in the makefile to build the named target and no default rules apply. The solution is to locate the target causing the problem and add a rule to create it or to fix the existing rule.

- 'target' is up to date—The dependencies for the named target have not changed (are older than the target).This is not really an error message, but, if you want to force the target to be remade, simply use the touch utility to change the timestamp on the file. This will cause make to rebuild the target in question.

- `Target 'target' not remade because of errors`—An error occurred while building the named target. This message only appears when using make's `-k` option, which forces make to continue even if errors occur (see Table 2.1, page 37). There are many possible solutions when you get this error message. The first step would be to try to make just the target in question and, based on the errors generated, determine the next appropriate step.

✔ make's `-k` option is covered in more detail in Table 2.1, "Common make Command-Line Options," page 37.

- `progname: Command not found`—make could not find progname. This usually occurs because progname has been misspelled or is not in the $PATH environment variable. Either use the command's complete file-name or add the path to progname to the makefile's PATH variable.

- `Illegal option - option`—The invocation of make included an option that it does not recognize. Don't use the offending option or check the syntax.

What's Next?

This chapter introduced you to the make command, explaining why it is useful and how to use it. You now have enough of a foundation to start writing and building simple programs in the Linux development environment. After previewing the program you will build after completing the book (Chapter 3, "About the Project"), Part II gets you started with *real* programming by teaching you how to program Linux at the system level. You will begin with the Linux process model, covered in Chapter 4, "Processes."

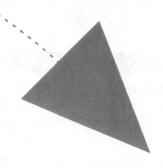

About the Project

At the end of the book is the complete source code for a working, fully functional music CD database program. It was designed to tie together many of the techniques you learn in the book so you can see how many of these topics, such as file handling, character-mode screen painting, and the database API, fit together and work as a cohesive whole.

One of the shortcomings of many beginner-level programming books is that, although they do a terrific job of showing you all sorts of techniques, tools, tips, and tricks, they do not demonstrate how all the material fits together. This is not the fault of the writer, but of the material, which necessarily has to cover a lot of territory. It also reflects the format of the genre, which assumes, rightly, that you want to learn how to do X, Y, and Z, but which usually ignores, due to the economics of book publishing, the necessity of connecting all the material together. My hope is that this programming project remedies this potential defect.

The Music CD Database Program

The project you will complete is a music CD database program. Actually, it is already complete. You will step through its design and creation module by module, often block by block, to gain insight into how the material you learn in this book fits together.

I sought to make the program as modular as possible, thus separating the user interface from the database manager and isolating nonportable code into as few modules as possible. In addition, library code, such as that from the ncurses and database libraries, is wrapped by application code, so that the implementation can change while the interface stays the same.

The project is a highly personal project, at least from my perspective. There are already many such programs out there, some far richer in features and *eye candy*, or visual appeal, than this one. But none of them do what I want them to do the way I want them to do it. That is, this program scratches an itch, which is one of the motivations behind the whole open source endeavor, as Eric Raymond argues in his excellent paper, *The Cathedral and the Bazaar*. See `http://www.tuxedo.org/~esr/writings/cathedral-bazaar/cathedral-bazaar.html` for the complete text of this seminal work.

Components and Subsystems

At the simplest level, the project consists of a command-line program, `mcdcli.c`, suitable for use in shell scripts, an interactive GUI client, `mcdui.c`, and three helper modules, `mcdscr.c`, `mcddb.c`, and `mcdutil.c`. The relationships between each of these modules are illustrated in Figure 3.1.

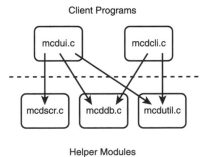

Figure 3.1: *The relationships between the programs and the helper code.*

As you can see in Figure 3.1, the client programs rely on the routines, or *services*, that `mcdscr.c`, `mcddb.c`, and `mcdutil.c` provide.

mcdcli.c parses command-line options and their associated arguments to add, delete, fetch, and search for records in the CD database. Its entire design is centered around being a command-line utility suitable for use in shell scripts. It is noninteractive and returns appropriate error codes that can be used in a shell script. mcdcli.c calls routines defined in mcddb.c to do the work of accessing and moving around in the database.

In addition to using the database manager mcddb.c and the utility functions in mcdutil.c, mcdui.c also calls functions in mcdscr.c. mcdscr.c encapsulates functionality provided by the ncurses screen-handling library, giving mcdui.c the capability to paint the screen, interpret keystrokes, and display data from the database.

The helper modules, in turn, rely heavily on system calls and other supporting libraries. mcddb.c *abstracts*, or encapsulates, all the database functionality that mcdcli.c requires. The database module consists of high-level function wrappers that interact with the database. However, mcdcli.c, aside from using a few database-specific declarations, need know nothing about the underlying database interface in order to use the database's API. By implementing the nitty-gritty database functionality in a separate module, the actual implementation can change without needing to change the application code. This kind of modularity is essential to writing easily maintained programs.

The screen-handling code in mcdscr.c performs a similar function for the GUI client, mcdui.c. It insulates the application code from the details of the underlying screen-handling library—ncurses—which allows the implementation of screen manipulation to change without affecting the application. mcdscr.c also allows mcdui.c to focus on transferring data from the database to the screen, which is its purpose, rather than concerning itself with redrawing the screen or displaying a dialog box.

What's Next?

This chapter gave you a brief introduction to the programming project that you will encounter at the end of the book.

✔ The complete source code for the programming project, along with explanatory text, is found in "Programming Project: A Music CD Database," page 461.

Between now and then, though, you have a lot of ground to cover. Part II, "System Programming," begins with a discussion of Linux processes, followed by a chapter on signals and signal handling. Few applications can accomplish much without being able to manipulate processes and handle signals, so this material is a good base on which to build your knowledge of Linux programming.

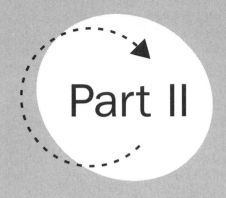

Part II

System Programming

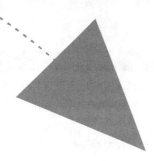

4

Processes

Understanding the Linux process model is central to understanding most of Linux's low-level behavior. The notion of the process underlies most file access rights, signals, and job control. This chapter covers the following subjects:

- What is a process?
- Process information
- Process identifiers
- Creating processes
- Killing processes
- Manipulating processes

What Is a Process?

A *process* is an instance of an executing program and also the operating system's basic scheduling unit. A process is considered a running program and consists of the following elements:

- The program's current *context*, which is the program's current execution status
- The program's current working directory
- The files and directories to which the program has access
- The program's *credentials* or access rights, such as its file mode and ownership
- The memory and other system resources allocated to the process

Processes are also Linux's basic scheduling unit. The kernel uses processes to control access to the CPU and other system resources. Linux processes determine which programs run on the CPU, for how long, and with what characteristics. The kernel's scheduler allocates CPU execution time, called *time slices*, among all processes, preempting each process in turn when its time slice expires.

The time slices are small enough that, on a single processor system, several processes appear to be running simultaneously. Each process also contains enough information about itself that the kernel can switch it in and out of execution as necessary.

Process Attributes

Processes have attributes or characteristics that identify them and define their behavior. The kernel also maintains a great deal of information about each process internally and provides an *interface* or group of function calls to obtain this information. The following sections discuss what this information is and the interfaces for obtaining and manipulating it.

Process Identifiers

The basic attributes of a process are its process ID, *PID*, and its parent process ID, *PPID*. Both the PID and the PPID are positive, non-zero integers. A PID uniquely identifies a process. A process that creates a new process is said to have created a *child process*. Conversely, the process that created a child process is called the *parent process*.

All processes ultimately trace their lineage to the process with PID 1, which is the init process. init is the first process to start after the kernel boots. init brings up the system, starts daemons, and runs other programs as necessary. Although the internals of the boot process are beyond the scope of this book, it is important to point out that init is the father of all processes.

The functions that allow a process to obtain its PID and PPID are getpid and getppid. Declared in the system header file <unistd.h>, their proto-types are

```
pid_t getpid(void);
pid_t getppid(void);
```

getpid returns the PID of its caller (the calling process), and getppid returns the PPID of its caller, which would be the PID of its parent.

Why would a process need to know its PID or the PID of its parent? One common use of a PID is to create unique filenames or directories. After a call to getpid, for example, the process could then use the PID to create a temporary file. Another typical task is to write the PID to a log file as part of a log message, making it clear which process recorded the log message. A process can use its PPID to send a signal or other message to its parent process.

EXAMPLE

Example

This short program prints its PID and PPID:

```c
/*
 * prpids.c - Print PID and PPID
 */
#include <stdio.h>
#include <unistd.h>
#include <stdlib.h>

int main(void)
{
    printf("PID = %d\n", getpid());
    printf("PPID = %d\n", getppid());
    exit(EXIT_SUCCESS);
}
```

The output from this program, on the author's system, was

OUTPUT

```
$ ./prids
PID = 15249
PPID = 15214
```

Of course, the displayed values will be different on your system.

NOTE

<unistd.h> declares many functions that are part of the POSIX standard. Briefly, POSIX, which stands for the Portable Operating System Interface, is a family of standards that defines the services and capabilities an operating system must provide if it is to be considered "POSIX compliant." However, POSIX defines only the standard interface, not an implementation. Many non-UNIX operating systems, such as Microsoft's Windows NT, claim POSIX compliance.

POSIX compliance is important because, at least in theory, it makes applications written to run on one type of system easy to port to another system. By using the standard POSIX interface to obtain a user's ID, for example, the program would not have to be rewritten to run on another system. Instead, the program would simply be recompiled on the other system. Finally, because POSIX is a generally accepted standard, many companies require software they purchase to be POSIX compliant.

Real and Effective IDs

In addition to their PIDs and PPIDs, each process has several other identifying attributes, which are listed in Table 4.1 along with their C language type and the functions that return them. To use the functions listed in Table 4.1's third column, you must include both <sys/types.h> and <unistd.h> in your code.

Table 4.1:   Process Attributes

Attribute	Type	Function
Process ID	pid_t	getpid(void);
Parent Process ID	pid_t	getppid(void);
Real User ID	uid_t	getuid(void);
Effective User ID	uid_t	geteuid(void);
Real Group ID	gid_t	getgid(void);
Effective Group ID	gid_t	getegid(void);

Each process has three user IDs (UIDs) and three group IDs (GIDs). They are used primarily for security purposes, such as assigning file access permissions and limiting who can run certain programs. The real user ID and real group ID are who you really are. They are read from /etc/passwd when you log in. They are the numeric representations of your login name and your primary group membership.

For example, on my system, my UID is 500, which corresponds to kwall, my login name. My GID is 100, which corresponds to the group named users. The getuid and geteuid functions return the real UID and effective UID, respectively, of the process from which they were called. Similarly, the getgid and getegid functions return the calling process's real and effective

GIDs. The effective user and group IDs are used primarily for security purposes but, under most circumstances, match the real user and group IDs. The difference between real and effective IDs matters primarily with programs that are setuid or setgid, a topic discussed in the next section.

Examples

EXAMPLE

1. Using the functions listed in Table 4.1, this program displays the process's real and effective UIDs and GIDs.

```
/*
 * ids.c - Print UIDs and GIDs
 */
#include <stdio.h>
#include <unistd.h>
#include <stdlib.h>

int main(void)
{
    printf("Real user ID: %d\n", getuid());
    printf("Effective user ID: %d\n", geteuid());
    printf("Real group ID: %d\n", getgid());
    printf("Effective group ID: %d\n", getegid());
    exit(EXIT_SUCCESS);
}
```

The output from running this program, on the author's system, is

OUTPUT

```
$ ./ids
Real user ID: 500
Effective user ID: 500
Real group ID: 100
Effective group ID: 100
```

EXAMPLE

2. As noted previously, under normal circumstances, the real and effective UIDs and GIDs match, and the previous output illustrated this. To confirm that this in fact the case, use su to become another user and execute the program. The UIDs and GIDs will still match, as the following example shows:

OUTPUT

```
$ su dummy
Password:
$ id
uid=502(dummy) gid=100(users) groups=100(users)
```

```
$ ./ids
Real user ID: 502
Effective user ID: 502
Real group ID: 100
Effective group ID: 100
```

The id command prints the real and effective UIDs and GIDs of the user that executes it (see man id for more information). When the user dummy executes ids, the output matches that of the system's id command. More importantly, despite the user and group ownership on ids, the effective and real UID and GID are those of the user executing it.

The third set of IDs are the saved UID and the saved GID. They are called *saved* IDs because they are saved by the exec function, covered in the section "Manipulating Processes," when it executes programs. Ordinarily, programmers need only concern themselves with the real and effective IDs.

setuid and setgid Programs

As stated earlier, one situation in which a process's real and effective IDs differ occurs when the program it is executing is setuid or setgid. setuid and setgid programs are so named because the effective UID or GID is set to the file's UID or GID rather than to the owner or group ID of the user executing the program. The purpose of setuid and setgid programs is to give the user executing the program special permissions.

For example, consider the passwd program, used to change passwords. Most Linux systems store passwords in /etc/passwd. This file is readable by all users but writable only by the root user. You can see this very clearly when you run ls -l /etc/passwd, as follows:

```
$ ls -l /etc/passwd
-rw-r--r--   1 root      bin    703  Aug 10 16:44  /etc/passwd
```

As a result, the passwd program must be owned by the root user. However, because passwd can be executed by any user, it would not normally be capable of updating the /etc/passwd file. The solution to this dilemma is that passwd is a setuid root program; that is, when it executes, its effective UID is set to the root UID, allowing it to update /etc/passwd.

NOTE

Actually, most modern Linux systems use shadow passwords, so the actual password is stored in /etc/shadow, which is readable and writable only by the root users. The password field in /etc/password is the letter x.

A setuid program has an s instead of an x in the owner's execute bit, as the next listing shows:

```
$ ls -l /usr/bin/passwd

-rwsr-xr-x    1 root      bin      703 Aug 10 16:44  /etc/passwd
```

Similarly, a setgid program has an s in its group execute bit. To make a program setuid, execute the following command:

```
$ chmod u+s mybinary
```

The next command makes a program setgid:

```
$ chmod g+s mybinary
```

CAUTION

Programs that are setuid or setgid root are security risks because, although executable by merely mortal users, they run with superuser privileges and so have complete access to the system. They can break anything. Exercise extreme caution when executing or creating a setuid root program.

User Information

Although machines work well with numbers, humans work much better with names. Fortunately, there are two ways to turn UIDs into human-readable names. The getlogin function returns the login name of the user executing a process. When you have the login name, you can pass it to the getpwnam function, which returns the complete entry in /etc/passwd corresponding to that login name. The other method is to pass a process's UID to the getpwuid function, which also returns the appropriate entry from /etc/passwd.

getlogin, declared in <unistd.h>, is prototyped as follows:

```
char *getlogin(void);
```

It returns a pointer to a string containing the login name of the user running the process or NULL if this information is not available. getpwnam is declared in <pwd.h>. Its prototype is

```
struct passwd *getpwnam(const char *name);
```

name must be a pointer to a string containing the login name of interest. getpwnam returns a pointer to a passwd structure. The pointer to the returned passwd structure points to statically allocated memory that will be overwritten by the next call to getpwnam, so if you will need this information later, save the structure information before calling getpwnam again.

Example

This example illustrates getlogin's and getpwname's behavior:

EXAMPLE

```
/*
 * getname.c - Get login names
 */
```

```c
#include <stdio.h>
#include <stdlib.h>
#include <sys/types.h>
#include <unistd.h>
#include <pwd.h>

int main(void)
{
    char *login;
    struct passwd *pentry;

    /* Get the login name */
    if((login = getlogin()) == NULL) { /* oops */
        perror("getlogin");
        exit(EXIT_FAILURE);
    }
    printf("getlogin returned %s\n", login);

    /* get the password entry for login */
    if((pentry = getpwnam(login)) == NULL) {
        perror("getpwnam");
        exit(EXIT_FAILURE);
    }
    /* display the full name */
    printf("gecos: %s\n", pentry->pw_gecos);

    exit(EXIT_SUCCESS);
}
```

```
$ ./getname
getlogin returned kwall
gecos: Kurt Wall
```

OUTPUT

The if statements guard against the possibility of getlogin or getpwnam returning NULL. If either function returns NULL, perror will print an error message and the program exits. First, the program uses getlogin to retrieve and display the login name running the program. Then, it uses that name to retrieve the password entry and displays the user's full name (stored in the GECOS field of /etc/passwd—see man 5 passwd for more information).

Additional Process Information

More information than just process, user, and group IDs is available about processes, such as their resource usage and execution times. Note that I wrote execution *times*, not *time*. This is because the Linux kernel maintains three separate time values for processes, as follows:

- *Wall clock time* is elapsed time.
- *User CPU time* is the amount of time the processor spends executing user mode (non-kernel mode) code.
- *System CPU time* is the amount of time spent executing kernel code.

✔ The difference between user mode and kernel mode is discussed in "What Is A System Call?" page 120.

You can obtain this information by calling times or getrusage. A process's resource usage, however, can be obtained only from the getrusage call. These resources are all concerned with memory-access statistics. This section discusses obtaining timing information first, and then covers resource usage.

TIP

Which call, times or getrusage, should you use to obtain timing information? Well, Linux has inherited functionality from both BSD and SVR4 UNIX, and they both have both functions. POSIX, a standard Linux attempts to follow, only mandates times. However, getrusage gives programmers a more complete picture of a process's resource usage, at least in theory. It is theoretical because Linux (as of version 2.2.10) implements only five of the sixteen resources defined in the rusage structure. Finally, the timing information times returns is more finely grained than that returned by getrusage. So, if you only need timing information or want to adhere to the POSIX standard, use times. If you do not care about POSIX compliance or if you need the additional information provided by getrusage, use it instead.

PROCESS TIMING

The times function is prototyped in <sys/times.h> as follows:

```
clock_t times(struct tms *buf);
```

times returns the number of clock ticks that have elapsed since the system was brought up, also known as wall clock time. buf is a pointer to a tms structure that stores the current process times.

Example

This program uses the system function to execute an external command, and then uses the times call to print the resulting timing information.

EXAMPLE

```
/*
 * resusg1.c - Get process times and resource usage
 */
```

```c
#include <stdio.h>
#include <stdlib.h>
#include <sys/times.h>
#include <time.h>
#include <unistd.h>

void doit(char *, clock_t);

int main(void)
{
    clock_t start, end;
    struct tms t_start, t_end;

    start = times(&t_start);
    /* redirect output to prevent screen clutter */
    system("grep the /usr/doc/*/* > /dev/null 2> /dev/null");
    end = times(&t_end);

doit("elapsed", end - start);

    s("parent times");
    doit("\tuser CPU", t_end.tms_utime);
    doit("\tsys  CPU", t_end.tms_stime);

    fputs("child times");
    doit("\tuser CPU", t_end.tms_cutime);
    doit("\tsys  CPU", t_end.tms_cstime);

    exit(EXIT_SUCCESS);
}

void doit(char *str, clock_t time)
{
    /* get clock ticks/second */
    long tps = sysconf(_SC_CLK_TCK);

    printf("%s: %6.2f secs\n", str, (float)time/tps);
}
```

On one system, a sample run created the following output:

```
$ ./resusg1
elapsed time: 19.91 secs
Parent times
    user CPU time:    0.00 secs
    sys  CPU time:    0.00 secs
Child times
    user CPU time:    2.34 secs
    sys  CPU time:    1.10 secs
```

The first thing to note is that no time appeared to accumulate in the parent process. Although this is covered in much more detail in the section "Creating Processes" later in this chapter, what happened was that when the program called the system function, it spawned a child process and it was the child, not the parent, that did all the work and accumulated the CPU time.

The second noteworthy observation is that the process's elapsed time, 19.91 seconds, does not equal the sum of the user and system CPU times, 3.44 seconds. The reason for this apparent discrepancy is that the grep operation that the child process executed was much more I/O intensive than it was CPU intensive. It had to scan 2331 header files, more than 10 megabytes of text, on the system in question. The missing 16 seconds were all devoted to reading the hard disk. Of course, the timing will be different on your system.

times' return value is in relative, not absolute, time (the number of clock ticks since the system was brought up), so to make it useful you have to take two measurements and use their difference. This results in the elapsed, or wall clock time. resusg1 accomplishes this by storing the starting and ending number of clock ticks in start and end, respectively. The other process timing values are taken from the tms structure defined in the header <sys/times.h>. The tms structure stores the current CPU time used by a process and its children. It is defined as

```
struct tms {
    clock_t tms_utime;      /* User CPU time */
    clock_t tms_stime;      /* System CPU time */
    clock_t tms_cutime;     /* User CPU time of children */
    clock_t tms_cstime;     /* System CPU time of children */
};
```

Again, these values are clock ticks, not the number of seconds. To convert clock ticks to seconds, use the sysconf function, which converts its

arguments into values that define system limits or options at runtime.
_SC_CLK_TCK is a macro that defines how many clock ticks there are per second; sysconf returns that value as a type long, and the program uses it to calculate how many seconds it took the process to run. The real workhorse of this program is the doit function. It takes a pointer to a string and a clock_t value, and then calculates and prints the actual timing information for each part of the process.

RESOURCE USAGE

A process's resource usage involves more than just CPU time. You also have to consider the process's memory footprint, how the memory is structured, the types of memory accesses the process makes, the amount and type of I/O it performs, and the quantity and type of network activity, if any, it generates. The kernel tracks all this information, and more, for each process. At least, it has the capability to do so. The structure in which this information is obtained is an rusage structure, defined in the <sys/resource.h> header file. This structure is defined as follows:

```
struct rusage {
    struct timeval ru_utime;    /* user time used */
    struct timeval ru_sutime;   /* system time used */
    long ru_maxrss;              /* maximum resident set size */
    long ru_maxixrss;            /* shared memory size */
    long ru_maxidrss;            /* unshared data size */
    long ru_maxisrss;            /* unshared stack size */
    long ru_minflt;              /* page reclaims */
    long ru_majflt;              /* page faults */
    long ru_nswap;               /* swaps */
    long ru_inblock;             /* block input operations */
    long ru_oublock;             /* block output operations */
    long ru_msgsnd;              /* messages sent */
    long ru_msgrcv;              /* messages received */
    long ru_nsignals;            /* signals received */
    long ru_nvcsw;               /* voluntary context switches */
    long ru_nivcsw;              /* involuntary context switches */
};
```

Linux, unfortunately, only keeps track of the resources listed in Table 4.2.

Table 4.2: *Tracked System Resources*

Resource	Description
ru_utime	Time spent executing user mode (non-kernel) code
ru_stime	Time spent executing kernel code (requests from user code for system services)
ru_minflt	The number of minor faults (memory accesses that do not result in disk accesses)
ru_majflt	The number of major faults (memory accesses that result in disk accesses)
ru_nswap	The number of memory pages read from disk due to major faults

As Table 4.2 indicates, there are two types of memory faults: minor faults and major faults. *Minor faults* occur when the CPU must access main memory (RAM). This kind of fault occurs because code or data the CPU needs is not in its registers or cache. *Major faults* occur when a process must read data from disk because the needed code or data is not in RAM. The ru_nswap member stores the number of memory pages that must be read from disk as a result of major faults.

To get this information, use the getrusage call, declared in <sys/resources.h>. The ru_utime and ru_stime members store the user and system CPU time the process accumulates. The only new information that getrusage gives you is the number of memory faults and fault-related disk accesses. Unlike the times function, getrusage must be called twice if you want to obtain information for both parent and child. getrusage is prototyped as follows:

```
int getrusage(int who, struct rusage *usage);
```

usage is a pointer to an rusage structure the function fills. The who parameter determines which resource usages are returned, the calling process's or its children's. who must be either RUSAGE_SELF or RUSAGE_CHILDREN. getrusage returns 0 if it succeeds, or −1 if an error occurs.

EXAMPLE

This program rewrites the previous example to use getrusage instead of times:

EXAMPLE

```
/*
 * resusg2.c - Get process times and resource usage
 */
#include <stdio.h>
#include <stdlib.h>
#include <sys/times.h>
```

```c
#include <sys/resource.h>
#include <time.h>
#include <unistd.h>

void err_quit(char *);
void doit(char *, long);

int main(void)
{
    struct rusage usage;

    /* redirect output to prevent screen clutter */
    system("grep the /usr/doc/*/* > /dev/null 2> /dev/null");

    /* get the resource structure for the parent */
    if((getrusage(RUSAGE_SELF, &usage)) == -1)
        err_quit("getrusage");

    puts("Parent times");
    doit("\tuser CPU", usage.ru_utime.tv_sec);
    doit("\tsys  CPU", usage.ru_stime.tv_sec);

    fputs("Parent memory stats");
    doit("\tminor faults", usage.ru_minflt);
    doit("\tmajor faults", usage.ru_majflt);
    doit("\tpage   swaps", usage.ru_nswap);

    /* get the resource structure for the child */
    if((getrusage(RUSAGE_CHILDREN, &usage)) == -1)
        err_quit("getrusage");

    puts("Child Times");
    doit("\tuser CPU", usage.ru_utime.tv_sec);
    doit("\tsys  CPU", usage.ru_utime.tv_sec);

    puts("Child memory stats");
    doit("\tminor faults", usage.ru_minflt);
    doit("\tmajor faults", usage.ru_majflt);
```

```
        doit("\tpage    swaps", usage.ru_nswap);

        exit(EXIT_SUCCESS);
}


void doit(char *str, long resval)
{
        printf("%s: %ld\n", str, resval);
}


void err_quit(char *str)
{
        perror(str);
        exit(EXIT_FAILURE);
}
```

This program executes the same grep command as the previous one.
However, in addition to the timing information, it also displays the memory
usage of both the parent and child processes. A sample run produced the
following output:

OUTPUT

```
$ ./resusg2
Parent times
        user CPU: 0
        sys  CPU: 0
Parent memory stats
        minor faults: 18
        major faults: 66
        page    swaps: 0
Child Times
        user CPU: 2
        sys  CPU: 2
Child memory stats
        minor faults: 2585
        major faults: 21412
        page    swaps: 0
```

As the output from the sample run makes clear, the timing information
getrusage produces is not as precise as that produced by times. On the
other hand, you get a very clear picture of a process's memory usage with

getrusage. In fact, the number of major faults in the sample run confirms the earlier discussion about the amount of disk I/O the program requires. The process read from the disk 21,412 times because the necessary data was not in memory. No page swaps occurred, however.

Sessions and Process Groups

There are situations in which the simple parent/child model insufficiently describes the relationships between processes. Consider, for example, an open xterm window. Suppose you execute three commands individually in the xterm: ls, cat, and vi. Is the xterm or the shell running in the xterm the parent? Obviously, all three commands are related to each other, but not as parent and child. Instead, they are all part of the same session.

Another example is the set of commands executed in a pipeline, such as ls -l ¦ sort ¦ more. Again, these commands are related to each other not as parent and child but as members of the same process group. Figure 4.1 illustrates the relationships between processes, sessions, and process groups.

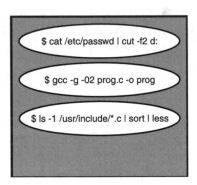

Figure 4.1: *Processes, sessions, and process groups.*

PROCESS GROUPS

A *process group* is a set of related processes, usually a sequence of commands in a pipeline. All the processes in a process group have the same process group ID, or PGID. The purpose of a process group is to facilitate job control. Suppose, for example, you run the command pipeline ls -l /usr/include ¦ sort ¦ wc -l. If, while it is still executing, you kill it (using Ctrl+C), the shell must be able to terminate all the processes. It does so by killing the process group rather than each individual process.

SESSIONS

A *session* consists of one or more process groups. A *session leader* is the process that created the session. Each session has a unique identifier, called the *session ID*, which is merely the PID of the session leader. Sessions serve the same purpose for process groups as process groups serve for individual processes.

Say that you execute the same pipeline command mentioned earlier (that is, ls -l /usr/include ¦ sort ¦ wc -l &) in the background and execute other commands in the foreground. Now, if you are running these commands in an X Window terminal and shut down the terminal window while all these processes are running, the kernel sends a signal to the controlling process (the session leader), which in turn kills each process group as described in the previous paragraph.

Manipulating process groups and sessions is an advanced topic and is beyond the scope of this book. It is important, however, to understand the concepts and terminology because they have important implications for signals, which are covered in Chapter 5, "Signals."

Manipulating Processes

This section discusses creating new processes, killing existing processes, and waiting on and monitoring processes. The system, fork, and exec calls create new processes. The kill function can be used to kill other processes, and a process can call either exit and abort in order to kill itself. Good resource management requires that parent processes wait for their children to terminate. The various wait functions handle this requirement.

Creating Processes

Programmers frequently need to create new processes from within their programs. For example, suppose you create a program that manages a database of CD-ROM titles. Rather than having to create your own sorting routine, you would like to use the sort program to do the work. Linux provides three ways to accomplish this. The system call, provided by the standard C library, is one method. The fork and exec calls, however, are the "Linux way." This section looks at all three calls.

USING system

The system function executes a shell command passed to it. Its prototype, declared in <stdlib.h>, is

```
int system(const char *string);
```

system executes the shell command string by passing it to /bin/sh, returning after the command completes. Previous examples have demonstrated its use already. If, for some reason, system fails to invoke /bin/sh, it returns 127. If another error occurs, system returns –1. The normal return value of system is the exit code of the command passed in string. If string is NULL, system returns 0 if /bin/sh is available or non-zero if it is not.

USING fork

The fork call creates a new process. The new or child process will be a copy of the calling or parent process. Declared in <unistd.h>, fork's syntax is

```
pid_t fork(void);
```

If it succeeds, fork returns the PID of the child process to the parent process, and it returns 0 to the child process. This means that even though you call fork only once, it returns twice.

The new process fork creates is an exact copy of the parent process, except for the PID and PPID. fork makes a complete copy of the parent process, including the real and effective UIDs and GIDs, the process group and session IDs, the environment, resource limits, open files, and shared memory segments.

The differences between the parent and child are few. The child does not inherit alarms set in the parent (using the alarm call), file locks the parent created, or pending signals. The key concept to understand is that fork creates a new process that is an exact duplicate of the parent.

EXAMPLE

EXAMPLE

Here is a simple example of using fork:

```c
/*
 * child.c - Simple fork usage
 */
#include <unistd.h>
#include <stdio.h>
#include <stdlib.h>

int main(void)
{
    pid_t child;

    if((child = fork()) == -1) {
        perror("fork");
        exit(EXIT_FAILURE);
    } else if(child == 0) {
        puts("in child");
        printf("\tchild pid = %d\n", getpid());
        printf("\tchild ppid = %d\n", getppid());
        exit(EXIT_SUCCESS);
    } else {
```

```
        fputs("in parent");
        printf("\tparent pid = %d\n", getpid());
        printf("\tparent ppid = %d\n", getppid());
    }
    exit(EXIT_SUCCESS);
}
```

The output of this program should resemble the following:

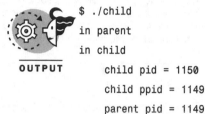

```
$ ./child
in parent
in child
        child pid = 1150
        child ppid = 1149
        parent pid = 1149
        parent ppid = 706
```

As you can see from the output, the child's PPID (the parent process ID) is the same as the parent's PID, 1149. The output also illustrates a critical point regarding fork's usage: You cannot predict whether a parent will execute before or after its child. This can be seen in the strange appearance of the output. The first line of output comes from the parent, the second through fourth lines from the child, and the fifth and sixth from the parent again. It has executed out of order; that is, *asynchronously*.

The asynchronous nature of fork's behavior means that you should not execute code in the child that depends on the execution of code in the parent, or vice versa. Doing so creates a potential *race condition*, which occurs when multiple processes want to use a shared resource but doing so depends on the order in which the processes execute. Race conditions can be hard to catch because the code that creates them works "most of the time." The potential impact of a race condition is hard to predict, but their symptoms might include unpredictable program behavior, an apparent system hang, slow system response on an otherwise lightly loaded system, or outright system crashes.

A fork call may fail because there are too many processes already running on the system or because the UID attempting to fork has exceeded the number of processes it is permitted to execute. If it fails, fork returns −1 to the parent process and does not create a child. The sample program guards against this possibility by checking fork's return value. The check also enables the program to determine whether it is in the child or the parent process.

N O T E

The process of forking involves copying the entire memory image of the parent to the child. This is an inherently slow process, so UNIX's designers created the vfork call. vfork also creates a new process, but it does not make a copy of the parent. Instead, until exec or exit is called, the new process runs in the parent's address space—if it accesses any of the parent's memory, that portion of memory is copied to the child process. This feature is called *copy-on-write*.

The rationale behind vfork is to speed up the creation of new processes. In addition, vfork has the additional feature of guaranteeing that the child executes before the parent, thus eliminating the threat of a race condition. Under Linux, however, vfork is merely a wrapper around fork because Linux has always used the copy-on-write mechanism. Linux's fork, therefore, is as fast as UNIX's vfork, but Linux's vfork, because it is an alias of fork, cannot guarantee that the child process will execute before the parent.

Using exec

The exec function is actually a family of six functions, each with slightly different calling conventions and uses. Despite the multiple functions, they are conventionally referred to as "the exec function." Like fork, exec is declared in <unistd.h>. The prototypes are

```
int execl(const char *path, const char *arg, ...);

int execlp(const char *file, const char *arg, ...);

int execle(const char *path, const char *arg, char *const envp[]);

int execv(const char *path, char *const argv[]);

int execve(const char *path, char *const argv[], char *const envp[]);

int execvp(const char *file, char *const argv[]);
```

exec completely replaces the calling process's image with that of the program being execed. While fork creates a new process, and so generates a new PID, exec initiates a new program, replacing the original process. Therefore, the PID of an execed process doesn't change.

execve takes three arguments: path, argv, and envp. path is the full path to the binary executable or script you want to execute. argv is the complete list of arguments you want to pass to the program, including argv[0], which is traditionally the name of the program to execute. envp is a pointer to a specialized environment, if any, for the execed program (it was NULL in the sample program).

EXAMPLE

In this example, execve is used to execute an ls command in the current directory.

EXAMPLE

```
/*
 * execs.c - Illustrate execve
 */
```

```
#include <unistd.h>
#include <stdlib.h>
#include <stdio.h>

int main(void)
{
    char *args[] = {"/bin/ls", NULL};

    if(execve("/bin/ls", args, NULL) == -1) {
        perror("execve");
        exit(EXIT_FAILURE);
    }

    puts("shouldn't get here");
    exit(EXIT_SUCCESS);
}
```

A test run of this program generated the following output:

OUTPUT

```
$ ./execve
Makefile   execve     getname.c  prprids.c   resusg2.c
child.c    execve.c   ids.c      resusg1.c
```

As you can see from the output, the fprintf statement did not execute. Why? If an exec succeeds, it does not return to the caller. This makes sense because, as stated previously, exec completely replaces the caller with the new program, so no trace of it remains. That is, there is no longer a caller to which to return! If exec fails, however, it returns –1 and sets the global variable errno. errno can be turned into a meaningful error message with strerror, part of the standard I/O library (see man errno for details about using this variable).

exec IN DETAIL

Because of the confusing similarity between the six functions in the exec family, a complete discussion of their syntax, behavior, similarities, and differences follows.

Four of the functions—execl, execv, execle, and execve—take pathnames as their first argument. execlp and execvp take filenames and, if the filename does not contain a slash, they will mimic the behavior of the shell and search $PATH to locate the binary to execute.

The three functions that contain an l expect a comma-separated list of arguments, terminated by a NULL pointer, that will be passed to the program being execed. The functions containing a v, however, take a vector, that is, an array of pointers to null-terminated strings. The array must be terminated with a NULL pointer. For example, suppose you want to exec the command /bin/cat /etc/passwd /etc/group. Using one of the l functions, you simply pass each of these values as an argument, terminating the list with NULL, as illustrated here:

```
execl("/bin/cat", "/bin/cat", "/etc/passwd", "/etc/group", NULL);
```

If you prefer to use one of the v functions, however, you first have to build the argv array, and then pass that array to the exec function. Your code would look something like the following:

```
char *argv[] = {"/bin/cat", "/etc/passwd", "/etc/group", NULL};
execv("/bin/cat", argv);
```

Finally, the two functions ending in e—execve and execle—allow you to create a specialized environment for the program being execed. This environment is stored in envp, which is also a pointer to a null-terminated array of null-terminated strings. Each string takes the form of a *name=value* pair, where *name* is the name of an environment variable and *value* is its value. For example,

```
char *envp[] = "PATH=/bin:/usr/bin", "USER=joeblow", NULL};
```

In this example, PATH and USER are the names, and /bin:/usr/bin and joeblow are the values.

The other four functions receive their environment implicitly through a global variable named environ that points to an array of strings containing the calling process's environment. To manipulate the environment these functions inherit, use the putenv and getenv functions. Declared in <stdlib.h>, they are prototyped as

```
int putenv(const char *string)
char *getenv(const char *name);
```

getenv looks for an environment variable named name and returns a pointer to its value, or returns NULL if there is no match. putenv adds or changes the *name=value* pair specified in string. If it succeeds, it returns zero. If it fails, it returns −1. Code using getenv and putenv would resemble the following snippet.

EXAMPLE

Example

The following program illustrates getenv's behavior:

```c
/*
 * testenv.c - Tests environment for an environment var
 */
#include <unistd.h>
#include <stdlib.h>
#include <stdio.h>

int main(void)
{
    char envval[] = {"MYPATH=/user/local/someapp/bin"};

    if(putenv(envval))
        puts("putenv failed");
    else
        puts("putenv succeeded");

    if(getenv("MYPATH"))
        printf("MYPATH=%s\n", getenv("MYPATH"));
    else
        puts("MYPATH unassigned");

    if(getenv("YOURPATH"))
        printf("YOURPATH=%s\n", getenv("YOURPATH"));
    else
        puts("YOURPATH unassigned");

    exit(EXIT_SUCCESS);
}
```

Running the program produces the following output:

OUTPUT

```
$ ./testenv
putenv succeeded
MYPATH=/usr/local/someapp/bin
YOURPATH unassigned.
```

Waiting on Processes

After you fork or exec a new process, the parent process should wait for it to terminate in order to collect its exit status and prevent the creation of zombies. As with exec, you have a variety of functions to use. To prevent utter confusion, however, this section focuses only on the wait and waitpid functions.

What is a zombie? A *zombie process* is a child process that terminates before the parent has a chance to collect its exit status with wait or waitpid. A parent *collects* a child process's exit status by using one of the wait functions to retrieve the exit status from the kernel's process table. A process is called a zombie because it is dead but still present in the process table. The child has exited and memory and other resources allocated to it have been freed, but it still occupies a slot in the kernel's process table. The kernel maintains the child's exit status until the parent harvests it.

One or two zombies are not a problem, but if a program forks and execs constantly and fails to collect exit statuses, the process table eventually fills up, which hampers performance and makes a system reboot necessary—not a desirable situation in a mission-critical production environment!

An *orphan* process, on the other hand, is a child process whose parent terminates before calling wait or waitpid. In this case, the init process becomes the child's parent and collects the exit status, thereby preventing zombies.

To collect a child's exit status, use the wait or waitpid calls. You must include the header files <sys/types.h> and <sys/wait.h>. They are prototyped as follows:

```
pid_t wait(int *status);

pid_t waitpid(pid_t pid, int *status, int options);
```

The status parameter stores the child process's exit status. pid is the PID of the process for which you want to wait. It can take one of the four values, listed in Table 4.3.

Table 4.3:   Possible Values of **pid**

Value	Description
< -1	Wait for any child process whose PGID equals the absolute value of PID
-1	Wait for any child process
0	Wait for any child process whose PGID equals that of the calling process
> 0	Wait for the child whose PID equals pid

options specifies how the wait call should behave. It can be WNOHANG, which causes waitpid to return immediately if no child has exited, WUNTRACED, which means it should return for children whose status has not been reported, or you can logically OR them to get both behaviors (that is, pass WNOHANG ¦¦ WUNTRACED for the options argument).

EXAMPLE

Example

waiter.c illustrates using waitpid.

```
/*
 * waiter.c - Simple wait usage
 */
#include <unistd.h>
#include <sys/types.h>
#include <sys/wait.h>
#include <stdio.h>
#include <stdlib.h>

int main(void)
{
    pid_t child;
    int status;

    if((child = fork()) == -1) {
        perror("fork");
        exit(EXIT_FAILURE);
    } else if(child == 0) {
        puts("in child");
        printf("\tchild pid = %d\n", getpid());
        printf(stdout, "\tchild ppid = %d\n", getppid());
        exit(EXIT_SUCCESS);
    } else {
waitpid(child, &status, 0);
        puts("in parent");
        printf("\tparent pid = %d\n", getpid());
        printf("\tparent ppid = %d\n", getppid());
        printf("\tchild exited with %d\n", status);
    }
    exit(EXIT_SUCCESS);
}
```

A sample run produced the following output:

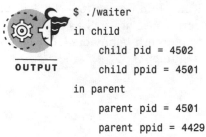

```
$ ./waiter
in child
     child pid = 4502
     child ppid = 4501
in parent
     parent pid = 4501
     parent ppid = 4429
     child exited with 0
```

This program is similar to the previous child.c, except that it adds a waitpid statement. It specifically waits for the child process specified by child to return and also displays the child's exit status. Notice that output from the parent and child processes is not mixed together like it was in child.c. The parent process's execution stops until the child exits. waitpid (and wait) returns the PID of the child that exited, 0 if WNOHANG was specified in options, or –1 if an error occurs.

Killing Processes

A process can terminate for one of five reasons:

- Its main function calls return

- It calls exit

- It calls _exit

- It calls abort

- It is terminated by a signal

The first three reasons are normal terminations, the last two are abnormal terminations. Regardless of why a process terminates, though, the same kernel code eventually executes, closing open files, releasing memory resources, and performing any other required cleanup. Because this book assumes C programming competency, hopefully the return function needs no explanation.

THE exit FUNCTIONS

You have seen the exit function, which is part of C's standard library, used in programs throughout this chapter. Rather than provide another example, its prototype is listed, as declared in <stdlib.h>:

```
int exit(int status);
```

exit causes normal program termination and returns status to the parent process. Functions registered with atexit are executed.

The _exit function is declared in <unistd.h>. It terminates the calling process immediately; functions that have been registered with atexit do not execute.

USING abort

Use the abort function if you need to terminate a program abnormally. Under Linux, abort has the additional side effect of causing a program to dump core, which most debuggers use to analyze the state of a program when it crashed. Although any open files are closed, abort is a harsh call and should be called only as a last resort, such as when you encounter an error that you cannot deal with programmatically, like a severe memory shortage. abort is also a standard library function (declared in <stdlib.h>). Its prototype is

```
void abort(void);
```

EXAMPLE

The following program shows how the abort function behaves:

```
/*
 * abort.c - Demonstrate the abort system call
 */
#include <stdlib.h>
#include <stdio.h>

int main(void)
{
    abort();

    /* Shouldn't get here */
    exit(EXIT_SUCCESS);
}
```

OUTPUT

```
$ ./abort
Aborted
$ ulimit -c unlimited
$ ./abort
Aborted (core dumped)
```

Note that your system might not generate a core file. If it does not, use the shell's ulimit command as shown in the output. The core file is useful when debugging a program.

✔ For more information on debugging with a core file, see "Starting gdb," page 426.

USING THE kill FUNCTION

The previous two sections focused on how a process can kill itself. How, though, can one process terminate another? Using the kill function, which is prototyped as follows:

```
int kill(pid_t pid, int sig);
```

To use it, you must include both <sys/types.h> and <signal.h> in your program. The pid parameter specifies the process you want to kill and sig is the signal you want to send. Because this section covers killing a process, the only signal you need to worry about right now is SIGKILL. Chapter 5 extends the discussion of signals. For now, just take this on faith.

EXAMPLE

EXAMPLE

This program shows how to kill a process:

```
/*
 * killer.c - Killing other processes
 */
#include <sys/types.h>
#include <sys/wait.h>
#include <signal.h>
#include <stdlib.h>
#include <stdio.h>

int main(void)
{
    pid_t child;
    int status, retval;

    if((child = fork()) < 0) {
        perror("fork");
        exit(EXIT_FAILURE);
    }
    if(child == 0) {
        /* sleep long enough to be killed */
        sleep(1000);
        exit(EXIT_SUCCESS);
    } else {
        /* use WNOHANG so wait will return */
```

```
            if((waitpid(child, &status, WNOHANG)) == 0) {
                retval = kill(child, SIGKILL);
                if(retval) {
                    /* kill failed, so wait on child to exit */
                    puts("kill failed\n");
                    perror("kill");
                    waitpid(child, &status, 0);
                } else
                    printf("%d killed\n", child);
            }
        }
        exit(EXIT_SUCCESS);
}
```

The output from this program should resemble the following:

```
$ ./killer
4511 killed
```

OUTPUT

After making sure that the fork succeeded, the child process will sleep for 1000 seconds and then exit. The parent process, meanwhile, calls waitpid on the child but uses the WNOHANG option so that the call returns immediately. Then it kills the process. If kill fails, it returns –1, otherwise it returns 0. If the kill fails, the parent calls waitpid a second time, ensuring that execution stops until the child exits. Otherwise, the parent displays a success message and exits. kill is usually used to terminate a process or process group, but it can also be used to send any signal to a process or process group. Chapter 5 covers signals in detail.

When to Manipulate Processes

What situations require the use of process manipulation discussed in this chapter? One has already been mentioned: when you want to or need to use the capabilities of an external program in your own code. Suppose you are creating (yet another) file manager. Although it might be ideal to write your own implementation of the ls command, it would be much faster in terms of development time to use the existing ls command and focus your programming efforts on using the ls command's output in your program.

If you create new processes using fork or exec, it is vital that you harvest their exit codes using one of the wait functions to maintain a smoothly functioning system. Similarly, you should always make sure your programs call return or exit so that other programs are able to harvest their exit codes. The point is that responsible process management necessitates using some of the techniques discussed in this chapter.

Finally, as you develop programs, either for your own use or for others, you will inevitably encounter problems. One of the best tools for solving code problems is the core file, the image of a running program that is written to disk. Thus, if you can isolate a problem to a specific section of your program, the judicious use of abort will generate a core file that you can use while debugging (debugging is covered in Chapter 20, "A Debugging Toolkit"). No doubt, as you become an accomplished Linux programmer, you will encounter many situations in which process management using the techniques discussed in this chapter will prove essential.

What's Next?

This chapter has taken a long look at Linux processes. The next chapter covers a complementary subject, signals, and deepens your understanding of processes and of Linux system programming in general.

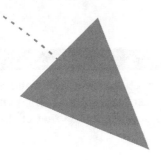

Signals

Signals are the simplest form of interprocess communication available in Linux. Processes use them to communicate with each other, and the kernel uses them to communicate with processes. Signals are also the key facilitator of *job control,* which is the ability to run jobs in the background or temporarily to stop them. If you are writing a non-trivial application program, you will use signals. Subjects this chapter covers include

- What is a signal?
- Signal terminology
- Early signal APIs and their problems
- The POSIX and Linux signal API
- Sending and receiving signals
- Manipulating signal sets

Signal Concepts

When discussing signals, several terms and concepts come up continuously. This section defines these terms and explains these concepts. At this point, a basic grasp of the terminology and concepts is sufficient; the rest of the chapter will explain them in more detail.

What Is a Signal?

A *signal* is the software analog to a hardware interrupt, an event that occurs at almost any time while a process is executing. This unpredictability means that signals are *asynchronous*. Not only can a signal occur at any time, the process receiving the signal has no control over when the signal is sent. Every signal has a name, beginning with SIG, such as SIGTERM or SIGHUP. These names correspond to positive integer constants, called the *signal number*, defined in the system header file <signal.h>.

Signals occur in many situations. A hardware exception, such as an illegal memory reference, generates a signal. A software exception, for example attempting to write to a pipe when it has no readers ("SIGPIPE), also generates a signal. The kill function discussed in Chapter 4, "Processes," sends a signal to the killed process, as does the kill command. Finally, terminal-generated actions, such as typing Ctrl+Z to suspend the foreground process, generate signals.

✔ For a complete discussion of writing to pipes, see "Reading and Writing Pipes," page 323.

When a process receives a signal, it can do one of three things with it:

- It can ignore the signal.
- It can trap or *catch* the signal, which causes a special piece of code, called the *signal handler,* to execute. This is called *handling the signal*.
- It can allow the signal's default action to occur.

This chapter looks at each of these options in detail.

Signal Terminology

A signal is *generated* for a process when the event that causes that signal occurs, such as a hardware exception. Conversely, a signal is said to be *delivered* when the process to which it was sent takes action on it. Between a signal's generation and delivery, it is considered to be *pending*. The delivery of a signal can be *blocked*, or delayed. It will be delayed until it is *unblocked* or until the receiving process changes the signal's disposition to ignore. A signal's *disposition* is how the process responds to that signal. A process can ignore a signal, allow its default action to take place, or *handle* it, which means to execute custom code in response to that signal. A blocked signal is also considered pending.

A *signal set* is a C data type, sigset_t, defined in <signal.h>, that is capable of representing multiple signals. Finally, a process's *signal mask* is the signal set that a process is currently blocking from delivery.

Over and over in this book, you will read that Linux, while designed to be POSIX compliant, has liberally adopted features from the two main branches of its UNIX forebears, AT&T and BSD UNIX. This inheritance shows in signals. As it happens, AT&T and BSD UNIX have also adopted a POSIX compliant signal API, so the differences between them do not matter terribly (so long as everyone writes to the POSIX API!). After a quick review of the development of the signal API, the next section shows you how to send, catch, and manipulate signals.

Signal History

Signals have been a part of UNIX almost from the beginning, but it took UNIX's designers a couple of attempts to get it right. Without going into all of the gory details, three main problems emerged with early signal implementations. The first problem was that signal handlers had to be re-installed each time they were triggered, resulting in a possible (or likely) *race condition*. If a second signal was delivered while the first was being handled and before the signal handler could be re-installed, the second signal would either be lost or the original, unhandled behavior of the signal would occur.

The second problem with early signal implementations was that they did not provide an easy way to pause a process until a signal arrived. As a result, a signal might be delivered to a process and it would not realize it. Finally, system calls were not restarted automatically if interrupted by a signal. The result was an enormous burden for programmers. After each system call, they had to check the errno variable and reissue the system call if errno was EINTR. Signal implementations that suffer these shortcomings are classified as *unreliable signals*.

The POSIX signal API that this chapter covers is considered a *reliable signal* API because it remedies these shortcomings. Under POSIX, signal handlers remain installed, avoiding the race condition and its consequences. Certain system calls restart automatically, relieving the programming burden, and POSIX also provides a reliable means to pause a process until a signal is delivered, eliminating the problem of missed signals.

Available Signals

Table 5.1 lists all the signals Linux supports.

Table 5.1:   *Linux Signals*

Signal	Description	Default Action
SIGABRT	Generated by the abort system call (POSIX)	Process terminates and dumps core
SIGALRM	A timer signal generated by the alarm system call (POSIX)	Process terminates
SIGBUS	Process attempted to use mis- or unaligned memory (4.2 BSD)	Process terminates and dumps core
SIGCHLD	A child has stopped or terminated (POSIX)	Ignore
SIGCONT	Process continues if it is stopped (POSIX)	Continue (ignore if process is not stopped)
SIGEMT	Bus (hardware) error	Process terminates and dumps core
SIGFPE	Floating-point exception (POSIX)	Process terminates and dumps core
SIGHUP	Process received a hang-up on its controlling terminal or its controlling process died	Process terminates
SIGILL	Illegal instruction (POSIX)	Process terminates and dumps core
SIGINFO	The same as SIGPWR	Ignore
SIGINT	User generated a keyboard interrupt (POSIX)	Process terminates
SIGIO	Asynchronous I/O received (4.2 BSD)	Ignore
SIGIOT	I/O trap. Same as SIGABRT (4.2 BSD)	Process terminates and dumps core
SIGKILL	Kill (POSIX)	Process terminates, cannot catch or ignore
SIGLOST	Process lost a file lock	Process terminates
SIGPIPE	Process attempted to write to a pipe with no readers (POSIX)	Process terminates
SIGPOLL	Pollable event occurred (System V)	Process terminates
SIGPROF	Profiling alarm clock set on a segment of code expired (4.2 BSD)	Process terminates

Signal	Description	Default Action
SIGPWR	System detected a power failure (System V)	Ignore
SIGQUIT	User generated a keyboard quit (POSIX)	Process terminates and dumps core
SIGSEGV	Process attempted to reference inaccessible memory (POSIX)	Process terminates and dumps core
SIGSTKFLT	Process generated a stack fault ("blew the stack")	Process terminates
SIGSTOP	Stop signal (POSIX)	Stop, cannot catch or ignore
SIGSYS	Bad argument to routine	Process terminates and dumps core
SIGTERM	Process received a termination signal (POSIX)	Process terminates
SIGTRAP	Process hit a trace or breakpoint trap (usually during debugging) (POSIX)	Process terminates and dumps core
SIGTSTP	User generated a stop from the keyboard (POSIX)	Stop
SIGTTIN	Process attempted to read from stdin while running in the background (POSIX)	Stop
SIGTTOU	Process attempted to write Stop to stdout while running in the background (POSIX)	
SIGUNUSED	Unused signal	Process terminates
SIGURG	Urgent condition on socket (4.2 BSD)	Ignore
SIGUSR1	User-defined signal 1 (POSIX)	Process terminates
SIGUSR2	User-defined signal 2 (POSIX)	Process terminates
SIGVTALRM	Interval alarm clock expired (4.2 BSD)	Process terminates
SIGWINCH	The size of a terminal window changed (4.3 BSD, Sun)	Ignore
SIGXCPU	Process exceeded the amount of CPU time it can use (4.2 BSD)	Process terminates and dumps core

continues

Table 5.1: *continued*

Signal	Description	Default Action
SIGXFSZ	Process tried to access or manipulate a file larger than the syste file size limit (4.2 BSD)	Process terminates and dumps core

As you can see from Table 5.1, the signals Linux recognizes are a hodge-podge of signals derived from BSD, System V or AT&T, and, of course, POSIX. Several signals listed, however, including SIGEMT, SIGCLD, SIGINFO, and SIGLOST, are not implemented (which is why they are nevertheless documented in the signal(7) manual page is a mystery!). The next few paragraphs discuss most of these signals in greater detail.

SIGABRT is generated by the abort function discussed in Chapter 4. SIGALRM and SIGVTALRM are generated when timers set using the alarm and setitimer calls, respectively, expire. The alarm call is discussed later in this chapter in the section, "Setting an Alarm." SIGBUS does not actually occur on Linux systems—when a process attempts to use misaligned memory, the kernel fixes the alignment problem and continues rather than generate SIGBUS. SIGCHLD is sent to a parent process when a child terminates or stops, allowing the parent to call one of the wait functions to reap the exit status.

✔ The wait functions are discussed in detail in "Waiting on Processes," page 84.

SIGHUP occurs when a session leader terminates or when a controlling terminal is closed. SIGFPE is sent for any arithmetic exception, such as overflows, underflows, or division by zero. SIGILL is another hardware exception, the execution of an illegal instruction. SIGINT causes all processes in the foreground process group to terminate because the user typed a keyboard interrupt, usually Ctrl+C.

SIGQUIT, similarly, is generated when the quit character, usually Ctrl+\, is signaled from the keyboard. Another keyboard signal, Ctrl+Z, generates SIGTSTP. SIGKILL and SIGTERM are generated by the kill function. Note that SIGKILL cannot be caught or ignored—this arrangement allows the superuser an unambiguous method to kill a misbehaving process.

SIGSTOP stops a process and, like SIGKILL, cannot be caught or ignored. However, unlike SIGKILL, SIGSTOP merely stops a running process. It can be restarted by sending it SIGCONT. Alas, there is no SIGRESURRECT for killed processes. SIGTTIN and SIGTTOU occur when a background process attempts to read input from or write output to its controlling terminal. When a terminal window changes size, all foreground processes receive the SIGWINCH signal. The SIGUSR1 and SIGUSR2 signals are reserved for process-defined purposes. SIGXCPU and SIGXFS, finally, are generated when a process exceeds its CPU time or file size limit, respectively.

Sending Signals

Programmatically, there are two ways to send a signal to a running process: using the kill command (kill(1)) and using the kill(2) function. The kill command is actually a user interface to the kill function.

✔ For a detailed discussion of the kill function, see "Killing Processes," page 86.

Using the kill Command

To use the kill command in your programs, you must call one of system, fork, or exec. As you learned in the last chapter, the first two calls spawn a new process to execute kill, whereas exec replaces the calling process before running kill. The result, however, is the same, the target process is terminated.

EXAMPLE

Example

This example first spawns a new process that does nothing but sleep. Then an exec call kills the child process before the program terminates.

```c
/*
 * pkill.c - Send a signal using kill(1)
 */
#include <sys/types.h>
#include <wait.h>
#include <unistd.h>
#include <stdio.h>
#include <stdlib.h>

int main(void)
{
    pid_t child;
    char *str;

    if((child = fork()) < 0) {
        perror("fork");
        exit(EXIT_FAILURE);
    } else if(child == 0) { /* in the child process */
        sleep(30);
    } else {
```

```
                /* in the parent, so kill the child */
                sprintf(str, "%d", child);
                printf("killing %s\n", str);
                if((execl("/bin/kill", "/bin/kill", str, NULL)) < 0) {
                    /* the exec failed, so wait and reap the status */
                    perror("execl");
                    waitpid(child, NULL, 0);
                    exit(EXIT_FAILURE);
                }
            }
        }
        exit(EXIT_FAILURE); /* shouldn't get here */
}
```

After making sure `fork` succeeded, the child process sleeps for 30 seconds, more than enough time for the parent to kill it. If, for some reason, the `exec` call fails, it is important to wait for the child to exit so you can reap its exit status. Recall from the last chapter that the `exec` functions never return to the caller unless an error occurs. The program also uses the `sprintf` function to turn the numeric PID (`child`) into a null-terminated string that can safely be passed to the `execl` function. Running the program, the output simply indicates that the parent is killing its child:

```
$ ./pkill
killing 759
```

OUTPUT

Of course, the actual PID will be different on your system.

Using the `kill` Function

Using the `kill` function is simpler than execing the `kill` command because you do not have to take extra steps to prepare an `exec` string. All you need is the PID and the signal you want to use. The rationale behind using `execl` in the example was simply to illustrate `/bin/kill`'s usage in a running program.

You might have noticed that no signal has the value 0. This is the *null signal* and it serves a special purpose. If you pass `kill` the null signal, it does not send a signal at all, but it does perform its normal error checking. This can be useful if you want to determine whether a given process is still running by looking for its PID. Keep in mind, however, that PIDs roll over periodically, so, on a busy machine, this is not a reliable method to test for the existence of a certain process.

Example

The next example uses the `kill` function to send two signals to a sleeping child process, one that will be ignored, and one that will kill the process.

```c
/*
 * fkill.c - Send a signal using kill(2)
 */
#include <sys/types.h>
#include <wait.h>
#include <unistd.h>
#include <signal.h>
#include <stdio.h>
#include <stdlib.h>

int main(void)
{
    pid_t child;
    int errret;

    if((child = fork()) < 0) {
        perror("fork");
        exit(EXIT_FAILURE);
    } else if(child == 0) { /* in the child process */
        sleep(30);
    } else { /* in the parent */
        /* send a signal that gets ignored */
        printf("sending SIGCHLD to %d\n", child);
        errret = kill(child, SIGCHLD);
        if(errret < 0)
            perror("kill:SIGCHLD");
        else
            printf("%d still alive\n", child);

        /* now murder the child */
        printf("killing %d\n", child);
        if((kill(child, SIGTERM)) < 0)
            perror("kill:SIGTERM");
        /* have to wait to reap the status */
        waitpid(child, NULL, 0 );
```

```
    }
  exit(EXIT_SUCCESS);
}
```

Here is the output from a couple of runs of this program:

OUTPUT

```
$ ./fkill
sending SIGCHLD to 871
871 is still alive
killing 871
$ ./fkill
sending SIGCHLD to 879
879 is still alive
killing 879
```

The first thing to notice is that, as strange as it may seem, kill can be used to send signals other than one to kill a process (SIGKILL, SIGTERM, SIGQUIT). Next, the child process did, in fact, ignore SIGCHLD. Finally, since my system is relatively inactive, I could use the null signal to confirm that the signaled process was still alive. Finally, SIGTERM terminated the child.

The waitpid call, again, is a safety measure in case kill fails. As noted in the last chapter, there is no way to know in advance whether the child terminates before or after the parent. If the parent exits first, the child becomes an orphan adopted by init, and init will reap the child's exit status. If the child dies first, however, the parent must reap its exit status to prevent it becoming a zombie process needlessly occupying a slot in the kernel's process table.

Catching Signals

Catching and handling signals are the flip side of sending signals. Each process can decide how to respond to all signals except SIGSTOP and SIGKILL, which, as you saw in Table 5.1, cannot be caught or ignored. The simplest way to catch signals involves not actually catching them but simply waiting for them to be sent. The alarm function sets a timer that sends the SIGALRM signal when the timer expires. The pause function behaves similarly, except that it suspends a process until the process receives *any* signal.

Setting an Alarm

The alarm function, prototyped in <unistd.h>, sets a timer in the calling process. When the timer expires, it sends SIGALRM to the caller and, unless the caller catches the signal, the default action for SIGALRM is to terminate the process. alarm's prototype is

```
unsigned int alarm(unsigned int seconds);
```

seconds is the number of clock seconds after which the timer expires. The return value is 0 if no other alarm was set, or the number of seconds remaining in a previously scheduled alarm, if any. A process can have only one alarm. Setting seconds to 0 cancels any previously set alarm.

Examples

EXAMPLE

1. This program sets a five-second alarm, after which it terminates.

```c
/*
 * mysleep.c - Naive implementation of sleep(1)
 */
#include <unistd.h>
#include <stdio.h>
#include <stdlib.h>

int main(void)
{
    /* Set the alarm */
    if((alarm(5)) > 0)
        puts("an alarm was already set");
    /* Sleep long enough for the alarm to expire */
    sleep(30);

    /* shouldn't get here */
    puts("how did we get here?");
    exit(EXIT_FAILURE);
}
```

```
$ ./mysleep
Alarm clock
```

OUTPUT

This program sets a five-second alarm, notes if another alarm was already set, and then goes to sleep for 30 seconds to give the alarm ample time to expire. On busy systems, additional time can elapse between the generation of SIGALRM and its delivery (hopefully not 25 seconds, though!). When the SIGALRM signal arrives, mysleep terminates. The kernel generated the "Alarm clock" message, not mysleep.

EXAMPLE

2. This example sets two alarms, calling alarm a third time to cancel the second alarm.

```
/*
 * 2alarm.c - Cancelling alarms
 */
#include <sys/types.h>
#include <unistd.h>
#include <stdio.h>
#include <stdlib.h>

int main(void)
{
    long int errret;

    /* Set the alarm */
    if((alarm(15)) > 0)
        puts("an alarm was already set");

    /* Set a new one */
    sleep(3);
    errret = alarm(5);
    if(errret > 0)
        printf("%ld seconds left in first alarm\n", errret);

    /* Cancel the second alarm */
    sleep(2);
    printf("%d seconds left on second alarm\n", alarm(0));

    exit(EXIT_FAILURE);
}
```

```
$ ./2alarm
12 seconds left in first alarm
3 seconds left in second alarm
```

OUTPUT

Because the program canceled the second alarm before it had a chance to expire, by passing 0 as alarm's seconds argument, the program did not display the "Alarm clock" message. Again, on a heavily loaded system, alarms may be delivered later than anticipated. One reason you might want to use alarms is to set a ceiling on potentially long operations, such as sorting a very large file or waiting for a user response to a prompt. Most programs that set alarms also catch them, rather than allowing them to terminate the process.

Using the pause Function

The pause function suspends the calling process until *any* signal arrives. The caller must be equipped to handle the delivered signal, or the signal's default disposition will occur. pause is also prototyped in <unistd.h>:

```
int pause(void);
```

pause returns to the calling process only if the process catches a signal. If the delivered signal invokes a handler, it will execute before pause returns. pause always returns -1 and sets errno to EINTR.

EXAMPLE

Example

This simple program just waits for a signal to be delivered, and then exits.

```
/*
 * pause.c - Pause then exit
 */
#include <unistd.h>
#include <stdlib.h>

int main(void)
{
    pause();
    exit(EXIT_SUCCESS);
}
```

OUTPUT

```
$ ./pause
[Ctrl+z]
[1]+  Stopped                 ./pause
fg
./pause
[Ctrl+\]
Quit (core dumpsed)
$ ./pause
User defined signal 1
```

In the first run, pause just goes into an eternal holding pattern. First, Ctrl+Z (entered from the keyboard), suspends the program; the fg command brings it to the foreground again, at which point Ctrl+\ (SIGQUIT) kills it and causes it to dump core. If you had not killed it, it would have continued in pause until it received another signal or until the system was restarted.

During the second run, the program ran in one window. In a second window, the PID was obtained using ps, and then kill -USR1 <PID> was issued. Because a signal handler was not established for the SIGUSR1 signal, its default action—termination—occurred.

Defining a Signal Handler

In some cases, a signal's default action is the desired behavior. In others, probably most, you want to alter that behavior, or perform additional tasks. In these cases, you have to define and install a custom signal handler to override the default action.

Consider the case of a parent process that spawns several children. When the children terminate, the parent receives the SIGCHLD signal. To keep track of its children and monitor their exit status, the parent can either call wait immediately after spawning each child, or, more efficiently, establish a signal handler that calls wait (or waitpid) each time it receives SIGCHLD.

POSIX defines a set of functions for creating and manipulating signals. The general procedure is to create a signal set, set the signals you want to catch, register a signal handler with the kernel, and wait to catch the signal.

THE SIGNAL HANDLING API

To create, set, and query a signal set, use the following five functions, all defined in <signal.h>:

- int sigemptyset(sigset_t *set);

- int sigfillset(sigset_t *set);

- int sigaddset(sigset_t *set, int signum);

- int sigdelset(sigset_t *set, int signum);

- int sigismember(const sigset_t *set, int signum);

set is a signal set of type sigset_t, as explained at the beginning of the chapter. sigemptyset initializes signal set set so that all signals are excluded from the set. sigfillset, conversely, initializes set so that all signals are included. sigaddset adds the signal signum to set. sigdelset removes signum from set.

These four functions return 0 on success or -1 if an error occurs. sigismember, finally, tests whether signum is in set, returning 1 (true) if it is or 0 (false) if it is not.

CREATE A SIGNAL SET

To create a signal set, then, use sigemptyset or sigfillset to initialize a signal set. If you create an empty signal set, you will need to use sigaddset to add signals in which you are interested. If you create a full signal set, use sigdelset to remove signals from the signal mask.

EXAMPLE

Examples

1. This program adds a signal to an empty signal set, and then uses sigismember to confirm that the signal is in the set.

```c
/*
 * mkset.c - Create a signal set
 */
#include <signal.h>
#include <stdlib.h>
#include <stdio.h>

void err_quit(char *);

int main(void)
{
    sigset_t newset;

    /* Create the set */
    if((sigemptyset(&newset)) < 0)
        err_quit("sigemptyset");
    /* Add SIGCHLD to the set */
    if((sigaddset(&newset, SIGCHLD)) < 0)
        err_quit("sigaddset");

    /* Check the signal mask */
    if(sigismember(&newset, SIGCHLD))
        puts("SIGCHLD is in signal mask");
    else
        puts("SIGCHLD not in signal mask");
    /* SIGTERM shouldn't be there */
    if(sigismember(&newset, SIGTERM))
        puts("SIGTERM in signal mask");
    else
        puts("SIGTERM not in signal mask");
```

```
        exit(EXIT_SUCCESS);
    }


    void err_quit(char *msg)
    {
        perror(msg);
        exit(EXIT_FAILURE);
    }
```

OUTPUT

```
$ ./mkset
SIGCHLD is in signal mask
SIGTERM not in signal mask
```

mkset first creates an empty signal set, passing the address of a sigset_t structure to sigemptyset. Next it adds SIGCHLD to the process's signal mask. Finally, using sigismember, it confirms that SIGCHLD *is* part of the set and that SIGTERM *is not* part of the mask.

2. This example illustrates the process of removing a signal from a process's signal mask.

EXAMPLE

```
/*
 * rmset.c - Remove signals from a set
 */
#include <signal.h>
#include <stdlib.h>
#include <stdio.h>


void err_quit(char *);


int main(void)
{
    sigset_t newset;

    /* Create the set */
    if((sigfillset(&newset)) < 0)
        err_quit("sigfillset");
    /* Remove SIGALRM from the set */
    if((sigdelset(&newset, SIGALRM)) < 0)
        err_quit("sigaddset");
```

```
    /* SIGALRM should be gone */
    if(sigismember(&newset, SIGALRM))
        puts("SIGALRM is in signal mask");
    else
        puts("SIGALRM not in signal mask");
        /* SIGTERM should still be there */
    if(sigismember(&newset, SIGTERM))
        puts("SIGTERM in signal mask");
    else
        puts("SIGTERM not in signal mask");


    exit(EXIT_SUCCESS);
}


void err_quit(char *msg)
{
    perror(msg);
    exit(EXIT_FAILURE);
}
```

```
$ ./rmset
SIGALRM not in signal mask
SIGTERM in signal mask
```

OUTPUT

rmset behaves the opposite of the last example by creating a full signal set, one that contains all signals. It then removes SIGALRM. Again, the sigismember calls confirm that the removed signal is removed and that other signals are not.

REGISTERING THE HANDLER

Simply creating a signal set and adding or deleting signals, however, does not create a signal handler or enable you to catch or block signals. There are more steps to take. First, you have to use sigprocmask to set or modify (or both) the current signal mask—if a signal mask has not yet been set, all signals will have their default disposition. Once you set a signal mask, you need to register a signal handler for the signal or signals you want to catch, using sigaction.

As you might expect by now, sigaction and sigprocmask are prototyped in <signal.h>. Their prototypes are as follows:

```
int sigprocmask(int how, const sigset_t *set, sigset_t *oldset);
```

`sigprocmask` sets or examines the current signal mask, depending on the value of how, which can be one of the following:

- `SIG_BLOCK`—set contains additional signals to block

- `SIG_UNBLOCK`—set contains signals to unblock

- `SIG_SETMASK`—set contains the new signal mask

If how is NULL, it is ignored. If set is NULL, the current mask is stored in oldset; if oldset is NULL, it is ignored. `sigprocmask` returns 0 on success and -1 on error.

```
int sigaction(int signum, const struct sigaction *act,
	struct sigaction *oldact);
```

`sigaction` sets the signal handler for the signal specified in signum. The structure struct sigaction describes a signal's disposition. Its complete definition, from (you guessed it) <signal.h>, is

```
struct sigaction {
    void (*sa_handler)(int);
    sigset_t sa_mask;
    int sa_flags;
    void (*sa_restorer)(void);
};
```

`sa_handler` is a pointer to a function that specifies the handler, or function, to invoke when the signal in signum is generated. The function must be defined to return type void and accept an int argument. Alternatively, the sa_handler argument may also be SIG_DFL, causing signum's default action to occur, or SIG_IGN, which will cause this signal to be ignored.

While a signal handler is executing, the signal that triggered it is blocked. sa_mask defines the signal mask of a set of additional signals that should be blocked during execution of the handler. sa_flags is a mask that modifies sa_handler's behavior. It can be one or more of the following:

- `SA_NOCLDSTOP`—The process will ignore any SIGSTOP, SIGTSTP, SIGTTIN, and SIGTTOU signals generated by child processes.

- `SA_ONESHOT` or `SA_RESETHAND`—The registered custom signal handler will execute only once. After it executes, the signal's default action will be restored.

- `SA_RESTART`—Enables restartable system calls.

- `SA_NOMASK` or `SA_NODEFER`—Do not prevent the signal from being received within its own handler.

Ignore the sa_restorer element; it is obsolete and should not be used.

To summarize, sigprocmask manipulates the set of signals you want to block and queries the current signal mask. The function sigaction registers a signal handler for one or more signals with the kernel and sets the exact behavior of the handler.

EXAMPLE

Examples

1. The first example simply blocks SIGALRM and SIGTERM without installing a handler to take special action.

```
/*
 * mkset.c - Create a signal set
 */
#include <signal.h>
#include <stdlib.h>
#include <stdio.h>

void err_quit(char *);

int main(void)
{
    sigset_t newset;

    /* Create the set */
    if((sigemptyset(&newset)) < 0)
        err_quit("sigemptyset");
    /* Adding SIGTERM and SIGALRM */
    if((sigaddset(&newset, SIGTERM)) < 0)
        err_quit("sigaddset:SIGTERM");
    if((sigaddset(&newset, SIGALRM)) < 0)
        err_quit("sigaddset:SIGALRM");

    /* Block the signals without handling them */
    if((sigprocmask(SIG_BLOCK, &newset, NULL)) < 0)
        err_quit("sigprocmask");

    /* Wait for a signal */
    pause();

    exit(EXIT_SUCCESS);
```

```
    }

    void err_quit(char *msg)
    {
        perror(msg);
         exit(EXIT_FAILURE);
    }
```

A test of this program produced the following output. The program ran in one window and was sent signals using the `kill` command from another window (commands sent from the second are shown in brackets).

OUTPUT
```
$ ./block
[$ kill -TERM $(pidof ./block)]
[$ kill -ALRM $(pidof ./block)]
[$ kill -QUIT $(pidof ./block)]
Quit (core dumped)
```

As you can see from the output, sending the process SIGTERM and SIGALRM had no effect, although both signals' default action is to terminate the process. The command `pidof ./block` returns the PID associated with `./block`, whereas the `$(...)` construct substitutes the results of the command and passes it to the `kill` command. When the process receives SIGQUIT, it quits, as the output shows. Note that because the program blocks SIGTERM and SIGALRM, pause never returns because the process does not receive the signal.

2. This program establishes a handler for SIGUSR1. SIGUSR1's default action is to terminate the process. The custom handler just says it was called.

EXAMPLE
```
/*
 * blkusr.c - Custom handler for SIGUSR1
 */
#include <unistd.h>
#include <signal.h>
#include <stdio.h>
#include <stdlib.h>

void err_quit(char *); /* err function */
void hndl_usr1(int);   /* signal handler */

int main(void)
{
```

```
        struct sigaction action;

        /* Set up the handler */
        action.sa_handler = hndl_usr1;
        sigemptyset(&action.sa_mask);
        action.sa_flags = SA_NOCLDSTOP;

        /* Register the handler */
        if((sigaction(SIGUSR1, &action, NULL)) < 0)
            err_quit("sigaction");
        /* Enough time to send a signal */
        sleep(60);

        exit(EXIT_SUCCESS);
}


void err_quit(char *msg)
{
    perror(msg);
    exit(EXIT_FAILURE);
}
void hndl_usr1(int signum)
{
    if(signum == SIGUSR1)
        puts("caught USR1");
    else
        printf("caught %d\n", signum);
}
```

hndl_usr1 is a simple signal handler, doing nothing more than reporting the fact that it caught SIGUSR1. Since the sa_mask member of action, the sigaction structure, should contain additional signals to block while the signal handler is running, you simply initialize it to an empty set by passing it directly to sigemptyset. With the handler set up, sigaction registers the handler for SIGUSR1. Since you are not interested in the old disposition of the handler, you pass NULL as the value for oset. Finally, the program sleeps for 60 seconds to give you enough time to send it a signal. Run this program in one window, then send it SIGUSR1 from another window, as illustrated:

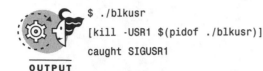

```
$ ./blkusr
[kill -USR1 $(pidof ./blkusr)]
caught SIGUSR1
```

The output shows that the handler registered successfully. After it executes, the program exits.

TIP

SIGUSR1 and SIGUSR2 have been specifically reserved as programmer-defined signals. You should use them to enable special behavior, such as re-reading a configuration file, rather than using a signal handler to redefine one of the standard signals, whose semantics are already well-defined.

Detecting Pending Signals

sigpending allows a process to detect *pending signals* (signals that were raised while they were blocked) and then decide whether to ignore them or to let them be delivered. Why find out what signals are pending? Suppose you want to write to a file, and the write operation must not be interrupted in order to maintain the file's integrity. During the write, then, you want to block SIGTERM and SIGQUIT, but ordinarily you want either to handle them or allow their default action. So, before you start the write operation, you block SIGTERM and SIGQUIT. Once the write completes successfully, you check for pending signals and, if SIGTERM or SIGQUIT are pending, you unblock them. Or, you can simply unblock them without bothering to check whether they are pending. Whether to check for pending signals is up to you. If you want to execute a special block of code if a certain signal is pending, check for it. Otherwise, just unblock it.

Like the other signal functions, sigpending is prototyped in <signal.h>. sigpending's prototype is

```
int sigpending(sigset_t *set);
```

The set of pending signals is returned in set. The call itself returns 0 on success and -1 on error. Use sigismember to determine whether the signals in which you are interested are pending, that is, whether they are in set.

Example

For the purposes of demonstration, this program blocks SIGTERM, determines whether it is pending, then ignores it and terminates normally.

```
/*
 * pending.c - Fun with sigpending
 */
#include <sys/types.h>
```

```
#include <unistd.h>
#include <signal.h>
#include <stdio.h>
#include <stdlib.h>

int main(void)
{
    sigset_t set, pendset;
    struct sigaction action;

    sigemptyset(&set);

    /* Add the interesting signal */
    sigaddset(&set, SIGTERM);
    /* Block the signal */
    sigprocmask(SIG_BLOCK, &set, NULL);

    /* Send SIGTERM to myself */
    kill(getpid(), SIGTERM);

    /* Get pending signals */
    sigpending(&pendset);
    /* If SIGTERM pending, ignore it */
    if(sigismember(&pendset, SIGTERM)) {
        sigemptyset(&action.sa_mask);
        action.sa_handler = SIG_IGN; /* Ignore SIGTERM */
        sigaction(SIGTERM, &action, NULL);
    }

    /* Unblock SIGTERM */
    sigprocmask(SIG_UNBLOCK, &set, NULL);

    exit(EXIT_SUCCESS);
}
```

For brevity's sake, error checking has been omitted. The code is straightforward. It creates a signal mask that blocks SIGTERM, and then uses kill to send SIGTERM to itself. Because it is blocked, the signal is not delivered. You use sigpending and sigismember to determine whether SIGTERM is pending and, if so, to set its disposition to SIG_IGN. When you unblock, SIGTERM is not delivered, and the program terminates normally.

What's Next?

With a basic understanding of process management and signal processing, you are ready to move on to more advanced topics, such as elementary file I/O and more sophisticated file handling such as multiplexing and file locking. *I/O multiplexing,* which is the process of reading from and writing to multiple input and output sources simultaneously, requires a good understanding of signals. *Daemons*, background processes running without user intervention, depend on both the ability to fork and monitor multiple processes and to catch interesting signals from child processes and act accordingly. First, however, the next chapter explains *system calls*, the programmatic interface between application programs and services provided by the kernel.

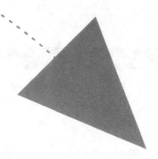

System Calls

In this chapter, you meet *system calls*, the interface between your program and the kernel. In particular, you learn

- What is a system call?
- Why and when to use system calls
- Common system calls
- Errors system calls generate
- Handling errors

Understanding System Calls

In this section, you learn what system calls are, what they are used for, and why you would use them.

What Is a System Call?

Obviously, a running Linux system is made up of many hundreds of pieces of code, such as utility and application programs, libraries, device drivers, filesystems, compilers, GUI interfaces, window managers, and, of course, the kernel itself. However, all of this code executes in one of two modes, user mode or kernel mode.

Unless you become a kernel hacker or write device drivers, all of the code you write will run in *user mode*. Programs running in user mode take advantage of both software and processor features to protect themselves from other misbehaving applications—generally, the memory and resources allocated to application A cannot be accessed by application B. At the same time, user mode programs are strictly prohibited from damaging the system itself.

Kernel mode code, while protected from the ravages of poorly written user mode programs, has complete access to the entire system. It can use, or break, anything. Examples of kernel mode code include device drivers, filesystems, and, naturally, the kernel itself. Consider a device driver, for example. In order to function properly, it needs complete access to the physical device it controls, such as a disk drive, as well as to the code and data associated with that device. At the same time however, the device has to be protected from psychopathic programs that might potentially corrupt this code and data, or might even damage the physical device somehow. Thus, device drivers must run in kernel mode.

Simply stated, the Linux kernel's job is to provide a variety of services to application programs while maintaining the integrity of the system. Put another way, user mode code (applications) requests various services from kernel mode code (memory managers, device drivers, and so forth). System calls are the method by which user code requests these services from the protected code running in kernel mode.

By design, system calls look like standard C functions. Because of the barrier erected between kernel and user mode, the interface that allows user code to cross this barrier is pretty ugly. Functions in the standard C library hide this ugly, awkward interface. User code calls the library functions, which are wrappers around the actual system call.

System Call Limitations

The real system calls are optimized for speed and, in order to maintain the integrity of kernel mode code, have three significant restrictions:

- Each argument passed from user to kernel mode is the same length, usually the native word size of the host processor architecture.

- System calls always return signed integers.

- To minimize the size of the kernel and to keep it fast, all data passed to kernel mode is passed by reference. This is particularly important when dealing with potentially large data structures.

In reality, the first two limitations have little meaningful effect on the programs you write. The third restriction simply means that you have to use pointers to structures, rather than structures themselves, when invoking system calls.

Why Use System Calls?

As the previous section suggested, the main reason to use system calls is to request a service from the kernel that user code cannot provide itself. What sort of system services are available? As of kernel version, 2.2.5, there were 190 system calls enumerated in the file /usr/include/asm/unistd.h, which contains all of the system calls and defines the relevant function calls and macros for using them. The list of available services includes the following:

- Process management, such as fork, exec, setgid, getuid, and so on

- The complete signal handling interface, such as sigaction, sigsuspend, sigprocmask, and sigreturn

- Filesystem services, such as mkdir, chdir, fstat, read, write, open, and close

- Memory management such as mmap, munmap, sbrk, mlock, and munlock

- Network services, including sethostname and setdomainname

- Process scheduling, which merely mortal programmers should never need to use

One reason you might want to use system calls is to implement your own memory management scheme for your application. As you know, the standard C library provides malloc for requesting memory from the operating system. What you may not realize, however, is that you can create your own malloc using the brk and sbrk system calls (brk and sbrk manipulate a program's data space). This would perhaps remedy some of the standard library `malloc`'s shortcomings, such as memory fragmentation or the lack of automatic freeing of unused memory (garbage collection). You will also use system calls without realizing it. Almost every system call has a function of the same name in the standard C library. Moreover, many functions in the standard library invoke system calls. `printf`, for example, uses the `write` system call. You can also call `write` directly.

> ✔ To find detailed coverage of the `write` system call, see "Reading and Writing Files," page 141.

Using System Calls

Using system calls is as simple as calling a function. From the point of view of application programmers, the distinction between system calls and regular library functions is inconsequential. The interface is the same. To use them, all you need to do is include the header file `<unistd.h>` in your code.

Of course, you will need to understand what system calls do. Their behavior, parameters, and return values are documented in the section 2 manual pages. Because system calls have similarly named library functions, which are documented in the section 3 manual pages, it is generally wise to look at both sections to obtain a complete understanding of how they behave.

Common System Calls

With over 190 system calls, it is beyond the scope of this book to discuss each one. Nevertheless, you learn many of them in other chapters. This section introduces the most common system calls, referring you to the appropriate chapters in which each group of calls is discussed.

PROCESS MANAGEMENT

Process management is covered in Chapter 4, "Processes." This group of system calls handles the creation and manipulation of programs. The `fork`, `vfork`, and `execve` calls create new processes. Similarly, `kill` and `exit` terminate processes. Processes have a unique PID, owner, creator and other identifiers that can be obtained with the system calls listed here:

- `getpid`   Returns the calling process's process ID
- `getuid`   Returns the user ID of the user that created the process
- `getgid`   Returns the group ID of the user that created the process
- `getppid`   Returns the calling process's parent process ID
- `geteuid`   Returns the calling proccess's effective user ID
- `getegid`   Returns the calling process's effective group ID

The wait and waitpid system calls enable the parent process to wait for its child processes to exit and collect their exit status. A process can discover how many system resources it can consume, as well as other limits to which it is subject, using the ulimit and getrlimit system calls.

FILE I/O

Many of Linux's system calls involve file input and output. Chapter 7, "Basic Linux File Handling," and Chapter 8, "Advanced Linux File Handling," cover many of these routines in detail. The calls to create, open, and close files, for example, are creat, open, and close, respectively. Similarly, to read and write files, use the read and write functions.

The unlink system call deletes a file. The symlink call creates a symbolic link to a file. The system call that to set and change file permissions is chmod, while chown changes ownership, like its identically named user command. Multiplexed input and output is enabled through the select and poll calls. If you want to shorten a file without reading or writing, truncate is the call you want to use. To obtain information about a file, such as its size, creation date, and so forth, the stat, lstat, and ustat calls obtain file status data. File locking, finally, controlling simultaneous access to a file or its contents, is accomplished through the flock or fcntl calls.

MEMORY MANAGEMENT

Memory management extends beyond the standard C library's malloc and calloc routines. In fact, malloc and related memory allocation routines are implemented via the brk and sbrk calls. In addition to these two functions, a whole family of system calls exist to provide a form of high-speed file I/O, memory mapped files. The names of these functions are mmap, munmap, mlock, munlock, mlockall, munlockall, msync, mremap, and mprotect.

✔ To learn about memory-mapped files, see "Memory Mapping Files," page 174.

SIGNAL HANDLING

The signal handling system, discussed in Chapter 5, "Signals," is entirely implemented as kernel level system calls and consists of the following functions:

- sigaction   Changes the action a process takes when it receives a given signal

- sigsuspend   Temporarily replaces a process's signal mask with a new one, then pauses the process until a signal is received

- sigpending   Returns a signal mask containing all of the signals that are blocked want waiting to be delivered to the calling process

- sigprocmask   Sets or modifies the list of signals that a process wants to block

System Call Return Codes

System calls almost always return 0 when they succeed and return a negative number (almost always -1) when an error occurred, so there are (at least) two ways to check the return value.

Examples

EXAMPLE

1. This code snippet compares a system call return code to 0.

```
if(open("/usr/src/linux/Makefile", O_RDONLY)) {
    /* an error occurred, handle it here */
} else {
    /* open the file successfully */
}
```

This example uses the fact that successful system calls return 0. The if condition will test true if the open call fails, so the appropriate error handling code will execute.

EXAMPLE

2. This snippet specifically evaluates whether the system call returns a negative value and acts appropriately.

```
if(open("/usr/src/linux/Makefile", O_RDONLY) < 0) {
    /* an error occurred, handle it here */
} else {
    /* opened the file successfully */
}
```

The second example explicitly tests for a negative return value from open. Other than the different if conditions, the two examples behave precisely the same way. The first one is a common C idiom, so you will encounter it a great deal. I prefer the second example because it is easier for novices to understand, but the choice is yours (this is Linux, after all).

Table of System Call Error Codes

Table 6.1 contains an annotated list of the errors that system calls generally return. Because you are still learning to program in the Linux environment, you probably will not understand a lot of these errors. Read through the list to get a general idea, and then, as you read the rest of this book and work through the example programs, review the list.

The manual page for each system call documents all of the error codes it generates. In addition, all of the error codes defined by POSIX, the standard Linux most closely follows, are documented in the section 3 manual page errno (type man 3 errno).

Table 6.1: *System Call Error Codes*

Error	Description
EPERM	The process lacks sufficient permissions to perform the operation it is attempting to perform.
ENOENT	The process is attempting to access a file or directory that does not exist.
ESRCH	No such process exists.
EINTR	A system call was interrupted.
EIO	Some sort of (usually hardware-related) I/O error occurred.
ENXIO	The I/O device or address does not exist.
E2BIG	The argument list passed to an exec call was too long.
ENOEXEC	The format of a binary that a process attempted to execute was incorrect (such as trying to run a SPARC binary on an x86 processor).
EBADF	An invalid file number was passed to a function that opens/close/reads/writes a file.
ECHILD	The process had no child process on which to wait.
EAGAIN	A process attempted to perform non-blocking I/O when no input was available.
ENOMEM	Insufficient memory is available for the requested operation.
EACCESS	Access to a file or other resource *would be* denied.
EFAULT	A bad pointer (one that points to inaccessible memory) was passed to a system call.
ENOTBLK	A process attempted to mount a device that is not a block device.
EBUSY	A process attempted to mount a device that is already mounted or attempted to unmount a filesystem currently in use.
EEXIST	Returned when you try to create a file that already exists.
EXDEV	Returned by the link call if the source and destination files are not on the same filesystem.
ENODEV	A process attempted to use a filesystem type that the kernel does not support.
ENOTDIR	A directory component in a pathname is not, in fact, a directory.
EISDIR	The filename component of a pathname is a directory, not a filename.
EINVAL	A process passed an invalid argument to a system call.

continues

Table 6.1: *continued*

Error	Description
ENFILE	The system has reached the maximum number of open files it supports.
EMFILE	The calling process cannot open any more files because it has already opened the maximum number allowed.
ENOTTY	A process attempted to do terminal style I/O on a device or file that is not a terminal. This error is the famous "not a typewriter" message.
ETXTBSY	A process attempted to open a binary or library file that is currently in use.
EFBIG	The calling process attempted to write a file longer than the system maximum or the process's resource limits permit.
ENOSPC	A filesystem or device is full.
ESPIPE	A process attempted to lseek on a non-seekable file.
EROFS	A process attempted to write on a read-only filesystem.
EMLINK	The file being linked has reached the maximum number of links allowed.
EPIPE	The read end of a pipe is closed and SIGPIPE is being ignored or trapped.
EDOM	Set by math functions when an argument exceeds the function's domain.
ERANGE	Set by math functions when the result of the function can't be represented by the function's return type.
ENAMETOOLONG	A path or filename is too long.
ENOSYS	The system call invoked has not been implemented.
ENOTEMPTY	A directory on which rmdir was called is not empty.
ELOOP	A path involves too long a chain of symbolic links.

Handling Errors

You have two ways to test for and handle errors when using system calls. One is to test for the return values discussed in the previous section and write code to handle them. The second is to use the global variable errno that is declared in <errno.h>. All system calls, and many library functions, set errno when an error occurs. There are two ways to use this variable. The first relies on the perror function call, which is declared in <stdio.h> and prototyped as follows:

```
void perror(const char *s);
```

perror displays the string s, followed by :, a space, and the error message associated with errno.

Examples

EXAMPLE

1. Using perror is the most common way to display an error code.

```
/*
 * oops.c
 */
#include <stdio.h>
#include <stdlib.h>
#include <errno.h>

int main(void)
{
    FILE *pfile;

    if((pfile = fopen("foobar", "r")) == NULL) {
        perror("fopen");
        exit(EXIT_FAILURE);
    } else {
        fprintf(stdout, "how did that happen!\n");
        fclose(pfile);
    }

    exit(EXIT_SUCCESS);
}
```

The program attempts to open a (hopefully) non-existent file, foobar. If it fails, it calls perror and exits. If it somehow succeeds, the program closes the file and exits. The output from this program follows:

OUTPUT

```
$ ./oops
fopen: No such file or directory
```

As you can see, the string passed to perror, fopen, is printed, followed by the error message associated with errno. perror makes it very simple to implement basic but informative error handling in your programs. Most of the programs you will see in this book use perror.

EXAMPLE

2. The second way to use errno is via the strerror call, which is prototyped in <string.h> as follows:

```
char *strerror(int errnum);
```

strerror returns a string describing the error code errnum. The string returned may only be used until the next call to strerror. You can use strerror to implement your own perror function, as illustrated here:

```
/*
 * mperror.c
 */
#include <stdio.h>
#include <stdlib.h>
#include <string.h>
#include <errno.h>

void mperror(const char *msg, int errnum);

int main(void)
{
    FILE *pfile;

    if((pfile = fopen("foobar", "r")) == NULL) {
        mperror("fopen", errno);
        exit(EXIT_FAILURE);
    } else {
        fprintf(stdout, "how did that happen!\n");
        fclose(pfile);
    }

    exit(EXIT_SUCCESS);
}

void mperror(const char *msg, int errnum)
{
    fprintf(stderr, "%s: %s\n", msg, strerror(errnum));
}
```

This program defines a function, mperror, to emulate perror's behavior. It uses the global errno variable as the argument to strerror. The output from this program is identical to the output from the last example.

What's Next?

In this chapter, you learned about system calls, the interface between user and kernel mode code. As you become more proficient programming with Linux, you will find more and more situations in which it is advantageous or convenient to use services provided by the kernel rather than rolling your own. In the next two chapters—Chapter 7, "Basic Linux File Handling," and Chapter 8, "Advanced Linux File Handling"—you will see excellent examples of the sorts of services the kernel provides and why you might find them preferable to reinventing the wheel with your own code.

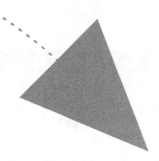

Basic Linux File Handling

In Linux, almost everything is a file, at least abstractly. This fact is one of Linux's most ingenious design features because it makes possible a uniform programming interface to a bewildering and wildly varying array of resources, such as memory, disk space, devices, interprocess communication channels, network communication channels, and even running processes! This chapter covers the fundamental featuers of Linux's file-handling interface, including the following:

- Basic concepts of Linux file handling

- File permissions

- File types

- Opening and closing files

- Reading and writing files

- Obtaining and changing file information

Characteristics and Concepts

Before you can start using the file-handling interfaces, you need to understand the concepts and core features underneath the idea of a file. This section discusses these ideas and notions in some detail before proceeding to real programming.

As stated, most Linux resources can be accessed as files. As a result, there are many different kinds of files. A partial list of the kinds of files present on a Linux system includes the following:

- Regular files
- Unnamed and named pipes
- Directories
- Devices
- Symbolic links
- Sockets

Regular files are called disk files and are defined as data storage units that allow random access. They are *byte-oriented*, meaning that the basic unit used to read from and write to them is a single byte, which also corresponds to a single character. Of course, you can and usually will read or write multiple bytes, but the fundamental unit is still a single character or byte.

A *pipe* (discussed at greater length in Chapter 15, "Pipes and FIFOs") is just what the name implies—a data channel that receives data in one end and transmits it on the other. One end is written and the other is read. There are two types of pipes: named and unnamed. *Unnamed pipes* are so called because they never appear on a system's hard drive with a name, such as /home/kwall/somefile. Instead, unnamed pipes are created and destroyed in memory (strictly speaking, in the kernel) on an as-needed basis. Moreover, as you will see in the section "The File-Handling Interface" later in this chapter, unnamed pipes are referred to only by numbers, never by a filename. Nevertheless, you use the same interface to read and write to unnamed pipes as you use to read and write regular disk-based files.

Unnamed pipes are usually created as the result of a shell command line like the one shown here:

EXAMPLE

```
$ cat /etc/passwd ¦ cut -f1 -d: ¦ head -5
```

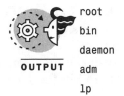

```
root
bin
daemon
adm
lp
```

The sample shell command creates two unnamed pipes, as indicated by the arrows in Figure 7.1.

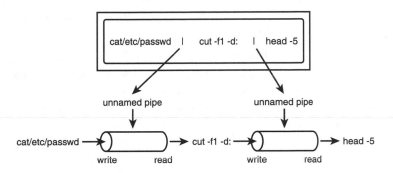

Figure 7.1: *Creating unnamed pipes with shell commands.*

As you can see in Figure 7.1, the kernel creates an unnamed pipe to receive the output of the cat command, which ordinarily writes its output to standard output (the screen). The cut command receives its input from the read end of the first pipe, performs its own transformation on the data, and then sends the output to the second unnamed pipe. In the meantime, after cut receives all of cat's output, the kernel destroys the first pipe because it is no longer needed. The head commmand, finally, displays the first five lines of input read from the pipe. After head receives all the data from the second unnamed pipe, the kernel destroys the second pipe, too. At no time, however, did either of the pipes have a name or exist on disk.

Named pipes, by contrast, do have filenames. They are most often used when two processes need to share data but do not share file descriptors (see "The File-Handling Interface" later in this chapter, for details).

Directories, also known as *directory files*, are simply files that contain a list of files stored in the directory.

Device files, also called *special files*, are files that provide an interface to most physical devices. They can either be character special or block special files. *Character special files* are written to and read from one byte (or character) at a time. Examples of character devices include modems, teminals, printers, sound cards, and mice. *Block special files*, on the other hand, must be read to and written from in multiples of some block size (a *block* is a chunk of data of some arbitrary size, for example, 512 bytes or 1 kilobyte). Block devices include CD-ROM drives, RAM drives, and disk drives. Generally speaking, character devices are used to transfer data, whereas block devices are used to store data. Device files are stored in the /dev directory.

Symbolic links are files that contain a path to another file. Functionally, they behave much like command aliases. Most file-handling calls deal with the real file to which a link points, rather than the link itself (this is called *following the link*). *Sockets*, finally, act much like pipes but allow processes on separate machines to communicate.

Regardless of the file type, however, the Linux file abstraction—that is, its habit of treating almost everything as a file—allows you to use the same interface to open, close, read, and write. That is, the file abstractions gives you a consistent, uniform interface for interacting with the entire spectrum of available devices and file types, freeing you from having to remember the different methods for writing to block devices, symbolic links, or directories.

The File Mode

A file's *mode* is a 16-bit octal number that expresses a file's type and its access permissions. Access permissions and their modifiers, if any, fill the lower 12 bits of the mode. The four high-order bits express the file's type. Figure 7.2 illustrates the file mode and its constituent elements.

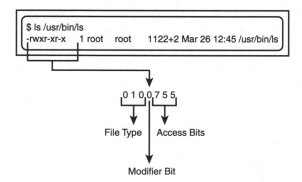

Figure 7.2: *The elements of the file mode.*

THE ACCESS BITS

The first three low-order bits express a file's access permissions. As you look at Figure 7.2 and read the octal mode from right to left, the bits specify access for other, group, and the owner. A value of 1 corresponds to execute privileges; a value of 2 corresponds to read privileges; and a value of 4 corresponds to write privileges. The file in Figure 7.2 is readable and executable for the group and other, and readable/writeable/executable for the owner, root.

THE MODIFIER BIT

The fourth bit in the file mode is the file mode *modifier*; it indicates whether the file is setuid, setgid, or sticky. As discussed in Chapter 4, "Processes," when a process executes a setuid or setgid file, its effective UID or GID is set to the file's owner or group, respectively. When a file's *sticky* bit is set (indicated by an uppercase S in the fourth bit), it forces the kernel to try to keep the file in memory as long as possible (hence the name, sticky), even if it is not being executed, because this reduces execution time. The modifier bit of the file in Figure 7.2 is not set, so the file is neither setuid, setgid, nor sticky.

NOTE

A file's modifier and permission bits are *bitmasks*, or integers that are manipulated and evaluated at the bit level using C's bit manipulation functions, such as << (left-shift) and ~ (bitwise complement). Fortunately, Linux provides a set of macros and symbolic constants (see Table 7.1) that make it easy to decode a file's mode.

Table 7.1: *File Access and Modifier Bitmask Macros*

Name	Mask	Description	POSIX
S_ISUID	0004000	Set UID bit	Yes
S_ISGID	0002000	Set GID bit	Yes
S_ISVTX	0001000	Sticky bit	No
S_IRWXU	00700	User (owner) has read/write/execute permission	Yes
S_IRUSR	00400	User has read permission	Yes
S_IWUSR	00200	User has write permission	Yes
S_IXUSR	00100	User has execute permission	Yes
S_IRWXG	00070	Group has read/write/execute permission	Yes
S_IRGRP	00040	Group has read permission	Yes
S_IWGRP	00020	Group has write permission	Yes
S_IXGRP	00010	Group has execute permission	Yes
S_IRWXO	00007	Others have read/write/execute permission	Yes

continues

Table 7.1: continued

Name	Mask	Description	POSIX
S_IROTH	00004	Others have read permission	Yes
S_IWOTH	00002	Others have write permission	Yes
S_IXOTH	00001	Others have execute permission	Yes

THE FILE TYPE

The *file type* is a simple numeric value that represents what kind of file it is. The following are Linux's file types:

- Socket
- Symbolic link
- FIFO
- Regular file
- Directory
- Block device
- Character device

Table 7.2 lists the symbolic constants you can use to determine the type of a file.

Table 7.2: File Type Constants

Name	Mask	Description	POSIX
S_IFMT	00170000	Bitmask for all file type fields	No
S_IFSOCK	0140000	File is a socket	No
S_IFLNK	0120000	File is a symbolic link	No
S_IFREG	0100000	File is a regular file	No
S_IFBLK	0060000	File is a block device	No
S_IFDIR	0040000	File is a directory	No
S_IFCHR	0020000	File is a character device	No
S_IFIFO	0010000	File is a FIFO	No

A later section of this chapter, "Getting File Information," illustrates how to use the symbolic constants to deduce a file's type.

The material in this section likely seems overwhelming. Relax! Although it is the foundation for the rest of the chapter, all you really need to comprehend at this point is that Linux has many different file types and that you can use the constants listed in Table 7.2 to determine a file's type. After you have read the rest of this chapter and worked through the sample programs, review Tables 7.1 and 7.2.

TIP

For information about manipulating the file mode from a user's perspetive rather than from a programmer's perspective, see *Sams Teach Yourself Linux in 24 Hours* (Bill Ball), *Linux Unleashed* (Tim Parker), or *Special Edition Using Linux* (Jack Tackett and Steven Burnett).

THE umask

You will discover in the next section, "The File-Handling Interface," that you can create new files and directories and can set the permissions on them as you do so. However, at both the system and the user level, the permissions you request will be modified by the process's *umask*, which contains a bitmask of the permission bits to turn off for newly created files and directories. The umask affects only a file's permission bits; you cannot change the modifier and file type via the umask.

You can change a process's umask, but only to make it more restrictive, not less restrictive. The call that enables this is the umask call, prototyped in <sys/stat.h> as follows:

```
mode_t umask(mode_t newmask);
```

This function sets the process's new umask to newmask, returning the old umask regardless of whether the call successfully changes the umask.

EXAMPLE

Example

The sample program calls umask to set a more restrictive umask.

```
/*
 * newmask.c - Reset the umask
 */
#include <sys/stat.h>
#include <sys/types.h>
#include <stdio.h>
#include <stdlib.h>

int main(void)
{
    mode_t newmask = 0666, oldmask;

    oldmask = umask(newmask);
    printf("old umask is %#o\n", oldmask);
    printf("new umask is %#o\n", newmask);
```

```
        system("touch foo");

        exit(EXIT_SUCCESS);
}
```

$ ./newmask

OUTPUT

```
old umask is 022
new umask is 0666
$ ls -l foo
---------- 1 kwall     users          0 Jul 24 10:03 foo
```

As the output from the program shows: the new umask is set to 0666. The touch utility ordinarily creates a file with a mode of 666. However, a umask of 0666 requests that all new files created have no permission bits set. As a result, foo is created with no permission bits set, which is precisely what ls reported.

The File-Handling Interface

Most file-handling options come in two forms: one that works with filenames and one that works with file descriptors. *File descriptors* are small, positive integers that act as indices into an array of open files that the kernel maintains for each process. For example, the stat and fstat functions return information about a file. They are prototyped as follows in <unistd.h>:

```
int stat(const char *filename, struct stat *buf);
int fstat(int filedes, struct stat *buf);
```

As you can see, stat expects a filename to be passed in filename, whereas fstat expects a file descriptor to be passed in filedes.

Each process is always given three open files: standard input, standard output, and standard error. These correspond to file descriptors 0, 1, and 2, respectively. However, three macros, defined in <unistd.h>, should be used instead: STDIN_FILENO, STDOUT_FILENO, and STDERR_FILENO. You are advised to use these macros rather than hard-coding 0, 1, or 2 because your program can get compiled on a system on which standard input, standard output, and standard error do not correspond to the integers 0, 1, and 2.

> **NOTE**
>
> The discussion of file-handling routines covered in the rest of this chapter does not include standard library routines such as fopen, fclose, and so on, because your knowledge of these is assumed. If you need a quick refresher, see *The C Programming Language, Second Edition*, by Brian Kernighan and Dennis Ritchie, Greg Perry's *C by Example*, or *Sams Teach Yourself C in 21 Days, Fifth Edition*, by Peter Aitken and Brad Jones.

Opening and Closing Files

There are two ways to open files, open and creat. They are prototyped in <unistd.h>, but you also must include the <fcntl.h> header file.

THE open SYSTEM CALL

```
int open(const char *pathname, int flags);

int open(const char *pathname, int flags, mode_t mode);
```

open attempts to open the file referred to in pathname, with the access specified in flags. The mode parameter contains the file mode if the file is being created. You must set flags to O_RDONLY, O_WRONLY, or O_RDWR, which specify read only, write only, or read/write access, respectively. Additionally, you may set zero or more of the values listed in Table 7.3. (You must bitwise OR the values together if you use more than one.) Use the first form of open if the default file mode suits your purposes. Use the second form of open if you want to set a specific file mode, as modified by the process's umask. Both forms of open return a file descriptor when they succeed. On failure, they return −1 and set errno.

Table 7.3:   Access Flags for **open** *and* **creat**

Flag	Description
O_CREAT	Creates the file if it does not already exist
O_EXCL	Used only with O_CREAT, open fails if the file already exists
O_NOCTTY	If the file is a terminal device, it will not become the process's controlling terminal
O_TRUNC	Sets the file's size to 0
O_APPEND	Writes occur at the end of the file
O_NONBLOCK	Opens the file in non-blocking mode, so that a read will return zero bytes rather than block
O_SYNC	All writes to the file are written to the disk before the call returns

THE creat SYSTEM CALL

creat also opens a file, creating it if it does not exist. It is prototyped as

```
int creat(const char *pathname, mode_t mode);
```

It is equivalent to the following:

```
open(pathname, O_CREAT | O_TRUNC | O_WRONLY, mode);
```

Programs in this book do not use `creat` for two reasons. First, it is misspelled. Second, the open call is more general and, provided you use the `O_CREAT` flag, achieves the same result. `creat` returns a file descriptor if it succeeds or, it if fails, sets `errno` and returns −1.

THE close SYSTEM CALL

To close a file, use the `close` call, prototyped in `<unistd.h>` as follows:

```
int close(int fd);
```

`close` closes the file associated with `fd` and returns 0 on success or −1 on error.

EXAMPLE

Example

The following program simply opens and closes a file named `hello`:

```c
/*
 * fopn.c - Opening/closing files
 */
#include <fcntl.h>
#include <unistd.h>
#include <stdlib.h>
#include <stdio.h>

int main(void)
{
    int fd;
    char path[] = "hello";

    if(fd = open(path, O_CREAT | O_TRUNC | O_WRONLY, 0644) < 0) {
        perror("open");
        exit(EXIT_FAILURE);
    } else
        printf("opened %s\n", path);
    if(close(fd) < 0) {
        perror("close");
        exit(EXIT_FAILURE);
    } else
        printf("closed %s\n", path);
```

```
    exit(EXIT_SUCCESS);
}
```

The open statement attempts to open the file, hello, in read-only mode. O_CREAT will cause the file to be created if it does not exist but, if it does, O_TRUNC sets the file's length to zero, as if it was newly created. When the file is open, fopn promptly closes it.

In particular, note that the source code checks close's return value. Although it is common not to do so, it is also a serious programming error for two reasons. First, on a networked filesystem, such as NFS, the close call may fail due to network latency. Second, many systems are configured with *write-behind caching*, meaning that a write call will return successfully, but the operating system will wait to perform the actual disk write until a more convenient time. As the close(2) manual page states:

> "The error status may be reported at a later write operation, but is is quaranteed to be reported on closing the file. Not checking the return value when closing the file may lead to silent loss of data."

Reading and Writing Files

Likely, you will want to read from, write to, and move around files. To read and write files, the following two functions are provided in <unistd.h>:

```
ssize_t read(int fd, void *buf, size_t count);
ssize_t write(int fd, const void *buf, size_t count);
```

read attempts to read up to count bytes from the file opened on the file descriptor fd, and stores the read data into the buffer specified by buf. It returns the number of bytes read on success (0 indicates an end-of-file condition), which may be less than the bytes requested, or −1 if an error occurs. errno will be set if an error occurs. After a successful read, the file pointer will be advanced by the number of bytes read, not necessarily by count.

Similarly, write writes up to count bytes to the file descriptor fd from the buffer pointed to by buf. A successful write returns the number of bytes written (0 meaning that nothing was written). On error, write returns −1 and sets errno.

Example

EXAMPLE

The following program reads in its own source code, and then writes it out to /dev/null and to a file named /tmp/foo.bar:

```
/*
 * fread.c - The read and write system calls
```

```c
    */
#include <fcntl.h>
#include <unistd.h>
#include <stdlib.h>
#include <stdio.h>

int main(void)
{
    int fdsrc, fdnull, fdtmp, numbytes;
    char fname[] = "fread.c";
    char buf[10];

    /* open the source file, /dev/null, and /tmp/foo.bar */
    if((fdsrc = open(fname, O_RDONLY)) < 0) {
        perror("open fdsrc");
        exit(EXIT_FAILURE);
    }
    if((fdnull = open("/dev/null", O_WRONLY)) < 0) {
        perror("open fdnull");
        close(fdsrc); /* close this since we've opened it
                    */           exit(EXIT_FAILURE);
    }    if((fdtmp = open("/tmp/foo.bar",
                    O_CREAT | O_TRUNC | O_WRONLY,
                    0644)) < 0) {
        perror("open fdtmp");
        close(fdsrc); /* have to close both of these now */
        close(fdnull);
        exit(EXIT_FAILURE);
    }

    /* read up to 10 bytes, write up to 10 bytes */
    while((numbytes = read(fdsrc, buf, 10)) != 0) {
        if(write(fdnull, buf, 10) < 0) /* the null device */
            perror("write /dev/null");
        if(write(fdtmp, buf, numbytes) < 0) /* a temporary file in /tmp */
            perror("write /tmp/foo.bar");
    }
```

```
/* close our files and exit */
close(fdsrc);
close(fdnull);
close(fdtmp);

exit(EXIT_SUCCESS);
}
```

The program opens three files, one to read and two to write. The file /tmp/foo.bar is relatively uninteresting, but note that the program opens a device file, /dev/null, as if it were a regular file. So, you should be able to see that you can treat most devices as files. Standard file-handling semantics that apply to regular files apply to devices and other special files as well. Another feature of the program is that when writing the disk file /tmp/ foo.bar, it writes only up to numbytes characters, which prevents blank bytes from being written to the end of the file. The last read before reaching end-of-file probably will not read the full 10 bytes, but the write will write as many bytes as it is told to. By writing only numbytes, the program does not append extra characters to the end of the file.

Positioning the File Pointer

If you want to read and write from random locations in a file, you must be able both to determine the file pointer's current position and to position the pointer. The lseek call is the tool for this purpose. Its prototype in <unistd.h> is as follows:

```
int lseek(int fd, off_t offset, int whence);
```

lseek positions the file pointer to position offset in the file opened on file descriptor fd based on the value of whence. whence can be one of the following three constants:

- SEEK_SET sets the pointer offset bytes into the file.
- SEEK_CUR sets the pointer's location to offset bytes into the file relative to the pointer's current location. offset can be negative.
- SEEK_END sets the location offset bytes from the end of the file.

lseek returns the new pointer location on success, or a value of off_t -1 on error, and sets errno appropriately.

Example

This example reads 10 bytes from its input file after positioning the cursor at various locations in the file.

EXAMPLE

```c
/*
 * seek.c - Using lseek
 */
#include <stdio.h>
#include <stdlib.h>
#include <fcntl.h>
#include <unistd.h>

int main(void)
{
    char ftmp[] = "tmpXXXXXX";
    char buf[10];
    int i, infd, outfd;

    /* open the input file */
    if((infd = open("devices.txt", O_RDONLY)) < 0) {
        perror("open devices.txt");
        exit(EXIT_FAILURE);
    }
    /* create a temporary file for output */
    if((outfd = mkstemp(ftmp)) < 0) {
        perror("mkstemp");
        exit(EXIT_FAILURE);
    }
    fprintf(stdout, "output file is %s\n", ftmp);

    /* set the initial location in the file */
    lseek(infd, 100, SEEK_SET);
    /*
     * copy the first ten out of every 100 bytes
     * to the output file
     */
    for(i = 0; i < 10; ++i) {
        read(infd, buf, 10);
        write(outfd, buf, 10);
        lseek(infd, 90, SEEK_CUR); /* jump forward 90 bytes */
    }
```

```
    close(infd);
    close(outfd);
    exit(EXIT_SUCCESS);
}
```

The input file, `devices.txt`, is included on this book's Web site in this chapter's source code directory. Instead of hard coding an output filename, the program uses the `mkstemp` call to open a uniquely named file in the current directory. After setting the file pointer 100 bytes into the file, the program then reads 10 bytes, writes them out to the output file, then seeks forward 90 more bytes. The name of the output file will vary from run to run. A test run produced the following output:

OUTPUT

```
$ ./seek
output file is tmptjcXQN
$ cat tmptjcXQN
sed: Augusnumbers an included om
ftp://fTeX versioinux Files/linux-stanly.        Alloc in the puributed wi
```

Truncating Files

Obviously, to lengthen a file, you just write more data to it or `lseek` over the end. How, then, do you truncate a file? Use the `truncate` or `ftruncate` calls, of course. Declared in `<unistd.h>`, their prototypes are as follows:

```
int truncate(const char *pathname, off_t length);
int ftruncate(int fd, off_t length);
```

Both calls shorten their file, `pathname` or `fd`, to length `length`, returning 0 on success. Recall that many of the file I/O system calls have two forms, one that takes a standard null-terminated string (`truncate`) and another, prefixed with `f`, that accepts a file descriptor instead of a pathname (`ftruncate`). If an error occurs, they return –1 and set `errno`. If you use `ftruncate`, the file must be opened for writing.

Why would you want to shorten a file using one of these calls? One typical reason is to delete unneeded data from the end of a file while preserving the rest of the file. Truncating a file to the desired length is much easier than creating a new file, reading the data you want from the old file, writing it out to the new file, and deleting the old file. The single `truncate` or `ftruncate` call replaces at least four calls, an `open`, a `read`, a `write`, and an `unlink`.

EXAMPLE

Example

The `trunc` program that follows is a handy utility for shortening files. It expects the name of the file to shorten followed by the new length to be passed on the command line.

```c
/*
 * trunc.c - Shorten named file to specified length:
 */
#include <stdio.h>
#include <stdlib.h>
#include <unistd.h>
#include <fcntl.h>

int main(int argc, char **argv)
{
    long len;

    if(argc != 3)
        exit(EXIT_FAILURE);
    len = (long)strtol(argv[2], NULL, 10);
    if(truncate(argv[1], len)) {
        perror("truncate");
        exit(EXIT_FAILURE);
    }

    exit(EXIT_SUCCESS);
}
```

Running this program on `test.txt` in the current directory yielded the following results:

OUTPUT

```
$ ls -l test.txt
-rw-r--r--   1 kwall     users          56561 Jul 24 15:56 test.txt
$ trunc test.txt 2000
$ ls -l test.txt
-rw-r--r--   1 kwall     users           2000 Jul 24 15:58 test.txt
```

After confirming that it was passed two arguments, `trunc` uses `strtol` to convert the passed-in length argument from a string to a long. It then immediately calls `truncate` using the passed-in filename and the requested length. If the `truncate` call fails, the program prints an error message and exits. If it succeeds, the program exits quietly, returning zero to the operating system.

Although functional, the `trunc` program is not nearly robust enough because it assumes that the arguments it receives are valid. A production quality program should confirm that the named file exists and that the filename passed in is a valid filename. These elements were ignored for reasons of brevity.

Getting File Information

So, now you can open, close, read, write, and truncate files. However, you can obtain lots of interesting information about a file, as the `stat(1)` command shows:

OUTPUT

```
$ stat trunc.c
  File: "trunc.c"
  Size: 420  Filetype: Regular File
  Mode: (0644/-rw-r--r--)  Uid: (500/kwall)  Gid: (100/users)
Device:  3,2   Inode: 534555   Links: 1
Access: Sat Jul 24 16:02:50 1999(00000.00:15:56)
Modify: Sat Jul 24 16:04:29 1999(00000.00:14:17)
Change: Sat Jul 24 16:04:29 1999(00000.00:14:17)
```

The `stat` command reads information from a file's information node, called an inode, and displays it for the user. Although their particulars are outside this book's scope, *inodes* are data structures that the kernel maintains for each file present in a filesystem. Among other things, they contain information such as a file's name, size, ownership, the date it was last changed, accessed, and modified, its type, and how many symbolic links there are to it. The `stat` in the example listed all this information.

There are three ways to obtain this information: `stat`, `lstat`, and `fstat`. To use them, you must include both `<sys/stat.h>` and `<unistd.h>` in your code. Their prototypes are listed here:

```
int stat(const char *filename, struct stat *buf);
int fstat(int fd, struct stat *buf);
int lstat(const char *filename, struct stat *buf);
```

All the `stat` functions fill `buf` with information taken from the file specified by `filename` or the file descriptor `fd`. On success, they return 0 and if an error occurs, they return −1 and set `errno`. The only practical difference between them is that `lstat` does not follow symbolic links, whereas `stat` and `fstat` do. The `stat` structure is defined as follows:

```
struct stat {
    dev_t st_dev;       /* device */
    ino_t st_ino;       /* inode number */
    mode_t st_mod;      /* file mode */
    nlink_t st_nlink;   /* number of hard links */
    uid_t st_uid;       /* owner's UID */
    gid_t st_gid;       /* owner's GID */
    dev_t st rdev;      /* device type */
    off_t st_size;      /* total size in bytes */
    unsigned long st_blksize; /* preferred blocksize */
    unsigned long st_blocks;  /* number of 512-byte blocks */
    time_t st_atime;    /* time last accessed */
    time_t st_mtime;    /* time last modified */
    time_t st_ctime;    /* time last changed */
};
```

The st_blksize member states the preferred block size for filesystem I/O. Using smaller chunks may result in inefficient I/O operations to the disk. Last access time, the atime, is changed by the mknod, utime, read, write, and truncate calls. The mknod, utime, and write calls also change last modification time, called the mtime. The ctime, the last change time, stores the last time that inode information was changed, including owner, group, link count, and mode information.

Using the information in the stat structure, you can implement your own stat function, as the sample program in the next section shows.

You will also want to use several macros to make sense of the file mode. The POSIX standard defines seven macros that decode a file's mode to deduce its type. They are listed in Table 7.4.

Table 7.4:   File Type Macros

Macro	Description
S_ISLNK(mode)	Returns true if the file is a symbolic link
S_ISREG(mode)	Returns true if the file is a regular file
S_ISDIR(mode)	Returns true if the file is a directory
S_ISCHR(mode)	Returns true if the file is a character device
S_ISBLK(mode)	Returns true if the file is a block device
S_ISFIFO(mode)	Returns true if the file is a FIFO
S_ISSSOCK(mode)	Returns true if the file is a socket

To use these macros, pass the st_mod member of the stat structure as the mode argument to the listed macros. The sample program that follows illustrates their usage.

Example

To run this program, pass it the name of the file that interests you.

```
/*
 * mstat.c - Naive stat(1) program
 */
#include <unistd.h>
#include <sys/stat.h>
#include <stdlib.h>
#include <stdio.h>

int main(int argc, char **argv)
{
    struct stat buf;
    mode_t mode;
    char type[80];
    if(argc != 2) {
        puts("USAGE: mstat FILENAME");
        exit(EXIT_FAILURE);
    }

    if((lstat(argv[1], &buf)) < 0) {
        perror("lstat");
        exit(EXIT_FAILURE);
    }
    mode = buf.st_mode;
    printf("    FILE: %s\n", argv[1]);
    printf("   INODE: %d\n", buf.st_ino);
    printf("  DEVICE: %d,%d\n",
            major(buf.st_dev), minor(buf.st_dev));

    printf("    MODE: %#o\n",  buf.st_mode & ~(S_IFMT));

    printf("   LINKS: %d\n", buf.st_nlink);
    printf("     UID: %d\n", buf.st_uid);
    printf("     GID: %d\n", buf.st_gid);
```

```c
        if(S_ISLNK(mode))
            strcpy(type, "Symbolic link");
        else if(S_ISREG(mode))
            strcpy(type, "Regular file");
        else if(S_ISDIR(mode))
            strcpy(type, "Directory");
        else if(S_ISCHR(mode))
            strcpy(type, "Character device");
        else if(S_ISBLK(mode))
            strcpy(type, "Block device");
        else if(S_ISFIFO(mode))
            strcpy(type, "FIFO");
        else if(S_ISSOCK(mode))
            strcpy(type, "Socket");
        else
            strcpy(type, "Unknown type");
        printf("TYPE: %s\n", type);
        printf("SIZE: %ld\n", buf.st_size);
        printf("BLK SIZE: %d\n", buf.st_blksize);
        printf("BLOCKS: %d\n", buf.st_blocks);
        printf("ACCESSED: %s", ctime(&buf.st_atime));
        printf("MODIFIED: %s", ctime(&buf.st_mtime));

        printf(" CHANGED: %s", ctime(&buf.st_ctime));

        exit(EXIT_SUCCESS);
}
```

The output from a sample run of this program is listed here:

OUTPUT

```
$ ./mstat /bin/ls
    FILE: /bin/ls
   INODE: 26740
  DEVICE: 3,1
    MODE: 0755
   LINKS: 1
     UID: 0
     GID: 0
    TYPE: 0100000
```

```
       SIZE: 50148
  BLK SIZE: 4096
    BLOCKS: 100
  ACCESSED: Sat Jul 24 16:18:15 1999
  MODIFIED: Tue Mar 23 19:34:26 1999
   CHANGED: Sun Jun 27 16:22:29 1999
```

This is, admittedly, ugly code, but it also illustrates how to use the stat
family of functions. After lstating the file, the program displays the value
of each member of the stat structure. When it comes to displaying the file
type, the code goes to considerable effort to convert a meaningless number
into a readable form, hence the if...else if structure (which should really
be cordoned off in a function). mstat used the S_IFMT constant, introduced in
Table 7.1, to mask out the file type bits of the file mode, so that the displayed file mode contains only the permission and modifier bits.

The code also uses the ctime function to turn the atime, mtime, and ctime
values into a string that users can easily comprehend. Again, this program
needs work, but it does show what is possible and is a good jumping off
point for more work. In particular, code could be added to validate that the
filename passed in is a valid filename.

Changing File Characteristics

In this section of the chapter, you meet a variety of functions that alter
inode information. Many of these routines have counterparts that are Linux
commands. These commands are usually distributed as part of the GNU
fileutils package, which is standard on almost every Linux system
around.

CHANGING ACCESS PERMISSIONS

The chmod and fchmod system calls change the permissions of a file, provided, of course, the UID and GID of the calling process indicate the sufficient rights. Only the root user and the file owner can change a file's
permissions. chmod and fchmod are prototyped in <unistd.h> as follows:

```
int chmod(const char *pathname, mode_t mode);

int fchmod(int fd, mode_t mode);
```

These routines attempt to change the permissions of the file specified by
either the null-terminated string indicated in pathname or the file descriptor
fd to mode. If the attempt succeeds, they return 0. On failure, they return
−1 and set errno to the appropriate value. To use these functions, you must
include both <sys/types.h> and <sys/stat.h>.

Example

In this program, we create an empty file with one set of permissions, and then use fchmod to change the permissions.

```c
/*
 * chgmod.c - Create a file and change its mode
 */
#include <stdlib.h>
#include <stdio.h>
#include <sys/stat.h>
#include <sys/types.h>
#include <fcntl.h>

int main(void)
{
    mode_t mode = 0755;
    int fd;

    /* create the file */
    if((fd = open("empty.file", O_CREAT, 0644)) < 0) {
        perror("open");
        exit(EXIT_FAILURE);
    }
    /* ls the file */
    system("ls -l empty.file");
    /* change its permissions */
    if((fchmod(fd, mode)) < 0) {
        perror("fchmod");
        exit(EXIT_FAILURE);
    }
    /* ls it again */
    system("ls -l empty.file");
    exit(EXIT_SUCCESS);
}
```

The output from this program should resemble the following:

```
$ ./chgmod
-rw-r--r--  1 kwall   users          0 Jul 24 20:47 empty.file
-rwxr-xr-x  1 kwall   users          0 Jul 24 20:47 empty.file
```

You can clearly see that the file has one set of permissions after its creation, and another set after the `fchmod` call. After creating the file, `chgmod` uses the `system` function to display the file's permissions, calls `fchown` to change them, and then uses another `system` call to display the change permissions.

CHANGING OWNERSHIP

Changing a file's ownership is analogous to changing its permissions. The `chown` and `fchown` calls accomplish this task. They are prototyped in `<unistd.h>` as follows:

```
int chown(const char *pathname, uid_t owner, gid_t group);
int fchown(int fd, uid_t owner, gid_t group);
```

These two calls change the owner and group of the file specified by the null-terminated string in `pathname` or the file descriptor `fd` to `owner` and `group`. As with all the functions discussed in this chapter, these two return 0 on success; upon failure, they return –1 and set `errno` to an appropriate value. The decision whether to use `chown` or `fchown` depends on several factors. If you know the file's name, you would probably want to use `chown`. If you have opened or created the file using `open` or `creat`, which return file descriptors, you would probably want to use `fchown` because you know the file descriptor. If you know both the filename and the file descriptor, which one to use is a coin toss. In this situation, I would prefer to use `fchown` because it requires less typing.

EXAMPLE

Example

This program creates a file, and then changes its ownership. Note that in order for it to work correctly, it must be run by the root user. In addition, you must replace the values assigned to `owner` and `group` with values that make sense for your system. The easiest way to accomplish this is to use the `id` command to obtain your UID and GID, and then substitute those values into the source code.

```
/*
 * chgown.c - Create a file and change its mode
 */
#include <stdlib.h>
#include <stdio.h>
#include <sys/stat.h>
#include <sys/types.h>
#include <fcntl.h>
```

```
int main(void)
{
    uid_t owner = 500;
    gid_t group = 100;
    int fd;



    /* create the file */
    if((fd = open("some.file", O_CREAT, 0644)) < 0) {
        perror("open");
        exit(EXIT_FAILURE);
    }
    /* ls the file */
    system("ls -l some.file");
    /* change its ownership */
    if((fchown(fd, owner, group)) < 0) {
        perror("fchmod");
        exit(EXIT_FAILURE);
    }
    /* ls it again */
    system("ls -l some.file");
    exit(EXIT_SUCCESS);
}
```

Here is the result of executing this program:

```
$ su
Password:
$ ./chgmod
-rw-r--r--   1 root     root            0 Jul 24 21:11 some.file
-rw-r--r--   1 kwall    users           0 Jul 24 21:11 some.file
$ exit
```

As you can see, the program first created the file. In the sample run, I first used the su command to become the superuser, so the file was created with root user and group ownership. The fchown command changes the owner and group to the specified values, 500 and 100, which correspond to kwall and users on my system. The second ls command confirms that the ownership was successfully changed.

What's Next?

In this chapter, you learned a good deal about working with Linux's basic file-handling calls. The next chapter extends this discussion by covering advanced material about topics such as the ext2 filesystem, multiplexing, non-blocking I/O, memory-mapped files, and file and record locking. This will complete the discussion of Linux's file-handling interface, which prepares you to learn about a database API and shared memory.

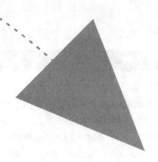

Advanced Linux File Handling

This chapter continues the discussion of Linux's file-handling interface that began in the last chapter, but covers more advanced features, such as the following:

- Manipulating file timestamps
- Features of Linux's ext2 filesystem
- I/O multiplexing
- High-speed I/O using memory mapped files
- File locking

Changing File Timestamps

Recall from Chapter 7, "Basic Linux File Handling," the kernel contains three timestamps for each file: its last access time (atime), last modification time (mtime), and last change time (ctime). The POSIX standard provides the utime routine to change the atime and the mtime. There is no user-level programmatic interface for changing the ctime, but changing the atime or mtime function causes the ctime to change, so it should not be a problem.

The utime function is prototyped in <utime.h> as

```
int utime(const char *pathname, struct utimbuf *buf);
```

You might also need to include the <sys/types.h> header file because it contains the primitive system data types defined by POSIX. Older versions of gcc and Linux did not always include <sys/types.h> in <utime.h>, so if your compiler complains about undefined values when compiling programs, add the types header file, but only if it declares the type about which the compiler complains. utime changes the access and modification times of the file specified by pathname to the actime and modtime, respectively, which are stored in buf. If buf is NULL, the actime and modtime are set to the current time. As usual, utime returns 0 on success. On error, it sets errno and returns –1. Of course, the process calling utime must have appropriate access to the file or be running with root privileges.

The utimbuf structure is defined as follows:

```
struct utimbuf {
    time_t actime;  /* access time */
    time_t modtime; /* modification time */
};
```

The time_t type is a POSIX standard type, usually a long integer, that stores the number of seconds elapsed since the Epoch. The *Epoch*, in turn, is defined by POSIX to be the date/time January 1, 1970 at 00:00:00 UTC (Universal Coordinated Time, which used to be known as Greenwich Mean Time).

NOTE

Interestingly, because many of Linux's time-related functions are based on the Epoch, the much-publicized year 2000 bug is not as big a problem for Linux as is the year 2038. Because time_t is a long integer, it will overflow in 2038. That is, time_t can hold up to 2^{31}-1 seconds, or 2,147,483,647 seconds. Disregarding leap years, there are 365×24×60×60, or 31,536,000, seconds in each year. So, time_t represents a maximum of about 68 years (2,147,483,647 / 31,536,000). Because the epoch begin in 1970, adding 68 years to this yields 2038. The exact date and time when time_t will overflow varies, depending on how many seconds exist in leap years.

Example

The program that follows creates a file and sets its `atime` and `mtime` values to September 8, 2001. For the purposes of brevity, error checking has been omitted.

```c
/*
 * chgtime.c - Using the utime routine
 */
#include <sys/types.h>
#include <sys/stat.h>
#include <utime.h>
#include <unistd.h>
#include <stdlib.h>
#include <fcntl.h>
int main(void)
{
        time_t now = 1000000000;
        struct utimbuf buf;
        int fd;

        buf.actime = now;
        buf.modtime = now;

        fd = open("foo.bar", O_CREAT, 0644);
        utime("foo.bar", &buf);
        close(fd);

        exit(EXIT_SUCCESS);
}
```

Running the program and then listing the current directory results in the following:

```
$ ls -l foo.bar
-rw-r--r--  1 kwall  users      0 Sep  8  2001 foo.bar
```

As you can see, `foo.bar` has a timestamp of September 8, 2001. After setting the `actime` and `modtime` members of the `utimbuf` structure to 1,000,000,000 (which corresponds to September 8, 2001), `chgtime` opens the file, then calls `utime` on it, passing the address of the modified structure and the filename. This causes the last access time and the last modification time (`actime` and `modtime`, respectively) to be changed to the specified (and utterly improbable) date and time.

Features of the ext2 Filesystem

The ext2 filesystem enables you to set up to four special attributes on files:

- Immutable—`EXT2_IMMUTABLE_FL`

- Append-only—`EXT2_APPEND_FL`

- No-dump—`EXT2_NODUMP_FL`

- Sync—`EXT2_SYNC_FL`

Only the root user can set or remove the immutable and append-only flags, but a file's owner may set or clear the no-dump and sync flags. What do these flags mean? The following list describes them in detail:

- *Immutable* files cannot be modified at all: You can add data to them, remove or rename them, or add links to them. Not even the superuser can do these things—the immutable flag must first be cleared.

- *Append-only* files can be written only in append mode and cannot otherwise be removed, renamed, or linked.

- The *no-dump* attribute causes the `dump` command, commonly used for creating backups, to ignore a file.

- The *sync* attribute causes the file to be written synchronously; that is, all `write`s to the file must complete before returning to the calling process (this is identical to calling `open` with the `O_SYNC` option).

Why use these attributes? Making a file immutable prevents it from being accidentally (or deliberately) deleted or modified, so it is a handy security measure for critical files. The append-only flag preserves a file's current contents while still allowing you to add data to it—again, a handy security precaution.

The no-dump flag is simply a convenience that will save you valuable space and time when you back up a system. The sync flag, finally, is especially handy for guaranteeing that critical files, such as databases, actually get written when requested. Using the sync option prevents data loss if a system goes down before cached data is physically written to disk. The downside of the sync flag, however, is that it can significantly slow down a program's performance.

To get or set these attributes, use the `ioctl` call, declared in `<sys/ioctl.h>`. Its prototype is as follows:

```
int ioctl(int fd, int request, void *arg);
```

The flags are defined in `<linux/ext2_fs.h>`. request must be set to EXT2_IOC_GETFLAGS to retrieve the attributes for the file specified by the file descriptor fd, or set to EXT2_IOC_SETFLAGS to set those attributes. In either case, arg holds the flags being manipulated.

CAUTION

The material in this section is highly specific to Linux's primary filesystem, ext2, for-mally known as the Second Extended filesystem. Other versions of UNIX may have the functions and structures we will discuss, but they surely will not behave as described here. If you use these calls in a program you intend to be portable, you must surround them with #ifdefs in order for your code to compile and run properly on non-Linux systems.

EXAMPLE

Example

The sample program that follows sets the sync and no-dump attributes on the file passed as its sole argument.

```
/*
 * setext2.c - Set ext2 special flags
 */
#include <sys/types.h>
#include <unistd.h>
#include <stdlib.h>
#include <stdio.h>
#include <fcntl.h>
#include <linux/ext2_fs.h>
#include <sys/ioctl.h>
#include <errno.h>

int main(int argc, char *argv[])
{
    int fd;
    long flags;

    /* Remind the user how to call us */
    if(argc != 2) {
        puts("USAGE: setext2 {filename}");
        exit(EXIT_FAILURE);
    }

    if((fd = open(argv[1], O_RDONLY)) < 0) {
        perror("open");
```

```
        exit(EXIT_FAILURE);
    }

    /* These are the flags we'll set on the file */
    flags = EXT2_SYNC_FL ¦ EXT2_NODUMP_FL;
    /* Set the flags, bail out gracefully if it fails */
    if(ioctl(fd, EXT2_IOC_SETFLAGS, &flags)) {
        perror("ioctl");
        close(fd);
        exit(EXIT_FAILURE);
    }

    if(flags & EXT2_SYNC_FL)
        puts(stdout, "SYNC flag set");

    if(flags & EXT2_NODUMP_FL)
        puts("NODUMP flag set");

    close(fd);
    exit(EXIT_SUCCESS);
}
```

Output from a sample run of setext2 follows:

```
$ touch foo
$ lsattr foo
-------- foo
$ ./setext2 foo
SYNC flag set
NODUMP flag set
$ lsattr foo
---S--d- foo
```

The semantics of the ioctl routine require that the file being modified be open, hence the open call. After assigning the attributes EXT2_SYNC_FL and EXT2_NODUMP_FL to the flags variable, the ioctl call attempts to set them, being sure to close the open file if the call fails. The last code block confirms that the requested attributes (sync and no-dump) were, in fact, set. The lsattr command used in the sample run further confirms this fact.

TIP

Linux has two commands, chattr and lsattr, that set and query the ext2 special attributes discussed in this section. In short, chattr enables you to set the special attributes, while lsattr displays the special ext2 attributes that are set, if any. In the sample run, the uppercase S indicates that the EXT2_SYNC_FL (sync) attribute has been set, and the lowercase d indicates that the EXT2_NODUMP_FL (no-dump) attribute has been set. See man chattr and man lsattr for more details.

Working with Directories

Although directories are simply files that contain a list of the files stored in them, they have a special programming interface for manipulating them.

Changing Directories

The call to find your current working directory is getcwd, declared in <unistd.h>. Its prototype is as follows:

```
char *getcwd(char *buf, size_t size);
```

getcwd copies the absolute pathname of the current working directory to buf, which is size bytes long. If buf is not large enough to hold the pathname, getcwd returns NULL and sets errno to ERANGE. If this occurs, increase the size of buf and try again. As an alternative, if buf is NULL and size is less than 0, getcwd will use malloc to dynamically allocate sufficient memory for buf. If you take advantage of this extension, you must remember to free the buffer to prevent memory leaks.

To change the current directory, use either the chdir or fchdir routines, prototyped in <unistd.h> as

```
int chdir(const char *path);
```

```
int fchdir(int fd);
```

chdir changes the current directory to that contained in path. fchdir works the same way, except that it must be passed an open file descriptor fd.

EXAMPLE

Examples

1. This program, cwd, uses getcwd, using both of the methods for allocating storage to hold the directory name discussed previously to return its current working directory.

```
/*
 * cwd.c - Print the current working directory
 */
#include <unistd.h>
#include <stdlib.h>
#include <stdio.h>
```

```
#include <errno.h>

#define BUFSZ 10

int main(void)
{
    char *statbuf = malloc(BUFSZ);
    char *nullbuf = NULL;
    int i = 1;
    /* Statically allocate the buffer */
    while((getcwd(statbuf, i * BUFSZ)) == NULL) {
        ++i;
        statbuf = realloc(statbuf, i * BUFSZ);
    }
    fprintf(stdout, "%d calls to realloc\n", i - 1);
    fprintf(stdout, "current dir is %s\n", statbuf);
    free(statbuf);

    /* Let getcwd allocate the memory */
    printf("current dir is %s\n", getcwd(nullbuf, -1));
    /* Have to free nullbuf to prevent a memory leak */
    free(nullbuf);

    exit(EXIT_SUCCESS);
}
```

The output from this program should resemble the following:

OUTPUT

```
$ ./cwd
3 calls to realloc
current dir is /usr/local/newprojects/lpe/08/src
current dir is /usr/local/newprojects/lpe/08/src
```

The while loop continuously increases the memory allocated to statbuf until getcwd returns non-NULL. The second code block illustrates using getcwd's alternative behavior. By using a buffer size of –1 and making the buffer itself NULL, the call still succeeds because it dynamically makes nullbuf big enough to hold the path. Because both statbuf and nullbuf are allocated off the heap, free properly releases their memory resources.

EXAMPLE

2. This program mimics the `cd` command.

```c
/*
 * chdir.c - Change to a new directory
 */
#include <unistd.h>
#include <stdlib.h>
#include <stdio.h>
#include <errno.h>

int main(int argc, char *argv[])
{

    if(chdir(argv[1]) < 0) {
        perror("chdir");
        exit(EXIT_FAILURE);
    }
    system("ls");

    exit(EXIT_SUCCESS);
}
```

OUTPUT

```
$ ./chdir $HOME
Mail/  Xwp  bin/  doc/  etc/  log/  projects/  src/  tmp/
$ pwd
/home/kwall/projects/lpe/08/src
```

The output from this program simply demonstrates that the `chdir` call succeeded. Note that when the program exits, you are still in the original directory. This is because the program executes in a subshell, and changing directories in a subshell does not affect the parent shell's current directory.

Creating and Removing Directories

Fortunately, the function names for creating and deleting directories are the same as the command counterparts: `mkdir` and `rmdir`. To use `mkdir`, include both `<fcntl.h>` and `<unistd.h>`; `rmdir` requires only `<unistd.h>`. Their prototypes are

```c
int mkdir(const char *pathname, mode_t mode);
int rmdir(const char *pathname);
```

mkdir will try to create the directory specified in pathname with the permissions in mode, as modified by the umask. rmdir deletes the directory specified in pathname, which must be empty. Both calls return 0 on success or set errno and return −1 on failure.

Examples

EXAMPLE

1. The first program creates a directory whose name is passed as the program's sole argument.

```
/*
 * newdir.c - Create a directory
 */
#include <unistd.h>
#include <fcntl.h>
#include <stdlib.h>

int main(int argc, char *argv[])
{
    if(mkdir(argv[1], 0755)) {
        perror("mkdir");
        exit(EXIT_FAILURE);
    }
    exit(EXIT_SUCCESS);
}
```

This is a simple program. It uses standard permissions, 0755, on the directory (read/write/execute for the user, read/execute for everyone else). If the call fails, the program simply bails after printing out an error message. Otherwise, error checking is absent for reasons of readability. The following output shows that the program works:

OUTPUT

```
$ ./newdir foo

$ ls -ld foo
drwxr-xr-x   2 kwall    users        1024 Jul 25 23:46 foo
```

EXAMPLE

2. The next program deletes the directory whose name is passed as the program's sole argument.

```
/*
 * deldir.c - Delete a directory
 */
#include <unistd.h>
```

```
#include <fcntl.h>
#include <stdlib.h>
#include <stdio.h>

int main(int argc, char *argv[])
{
    if(rmdir(argv[1])) {
        perror("rmdir");
        exit(EXIT_FAILURE);
    }
    exit(EXIT_SUCCESS);
}
```

This is even simpler than the first example. It attempts to delete the specified directory, exiting abruptly if it fails. The call may fail if the directory is not empty, if it does not exist, or if the user running the program lacks sufficient permissions to delete the directory.

OUTPUT

```
$ ./deldir foo
$ ls -ld foo
ls: foo: No such file or directory
```

Listing a Directory

Listing a directory simply means reading the directory's contents. The basic process is uncomplicated:

1. Open the directory using opendir.

2. Read its contents using readdir and, possibly, rewinddir, to reposition the file pointer to the beginning of the directory if you have read all the way to the end and want to start over.

3. Close the directory using closedir.

All these functions are declared in <dirent.h>. Their prototypes are

```
DIR *opendir(const char *pathname);
struct dirent *readdir(DIR *dir);
int rewinddir(DIR *dir);
int closedir(DIR *dir);
```

opendir opens the directory specified by pathname (which is just another file, after all), returning a pointer to a DIR stream. Otherwise, it returns NULL and sets errno if an error occurs. The stream pointer is positioned at the beginning of the stream. closedir, obviously, closes the stream dir, returning 0 on success or −1 on error. rewinddir moves the stream pointer back to the beginning of the stream. It also returns 0 on success or −1 on failure.

readdir does most of the work of reading a directory. It returns a pointer to a dirent structure that contains the next directory entry from dir. Each subsequent call to readdir overwrites the returned dirent structure with new data. Upon reaching the end-of-file or if an error occurs, readdir returns NULL. To obtain the filename, use the dirent.d_name[] member, which returns a pointer to the filename.

CAUTION

The dirent structure has only one member whose use is portable (that is, defined by POSIX to have predictable behavior on all POSIX-compliant systems): d_name[]. All other members are system defined and system dependent, so their names and/or the kind of data they contain might vary from system to system. Some filesystems, for example, still limit filenames to 14 characters, while others, like Linux, allow up to 256 characters.

EXAMPLE

Example

The program that follows, listdir, lists the contents of the directory whose name is passed on the command line:

```
/*
 * listdir.c - Read a directory file
 */
#include <stdio.h>
#include <stdlib.h>
#include <dirent.h>

void err_quit(char *msg);

int main(int argc, char *argv[])
{
    DIR *dir;
    struct dirent *mydirent;
    int i = 1;

    if(argc != 2) {
        puts("USAGE: listdir {pathname}");
        exit(EXIT_FAILURE);
    }
```

```
        if((dir = opendir(argv[1])) == NULL)
            err_quit("opendir");
        while((mydirent = readdir(dir)) != NULL)
            printf("%3d : %s\n", i++, mydirent->d_name);


        closedir(dir);
        exit(EXIT_SUCCESS);
    }


    void err_quit(char *msg)
    {
        perror(msg);
        exit(EXIT_FAILURE);
    }
```

The while loop is the centerpiece of this code. It repeatedly calls readdir to march through the directory stream until it returns NULL and exits the loop. On each iteration, it prints the filename (mydirent->d_name). The following output illustrates listdir's behavior:

OUTPUT

```
$ ./listdir
 1 : .
 2 : ..
 3 : listdir
 4 : Makefile
 5 : chgtime.c

 6 : 08cd.zip
 7 : cwd.c
 8 : out
 9 : setext2.c
10 : deldir.c
11 : newdir.c
12 : chdir.c
13 : listdir.c
```

I/O Multiplexing

Multiplexing is a five-dollar word that means reading from or writing to multiple file descriptors simultaneously. Examples of multiplexing include

Web browsers that open multiple network connections to download as much of a web page as they can at once and client/server applications that service dozens or hundreds of users simultaneously. Although easy to understand conceptually, multiplexing can be difficult to implement efficiently.

Fortunately, Linux has the `select` call to make multiplexing easier. `select` is a non-resource intensive means for waiting on many file descriptors to change status. Its prototype, in <unistd.h>, is as follows:

```
int select(int n, fd_set *readfds, fd_set *writefds,
➥fd_set exceptfds, struct timeval *timeout);
```

`select` monitors the following sets of file descriptors:

- The set of descriptors in `readfds` for readable characters.

- The set in `writefds` to see whether they can be written to.

- The set in `exceptfds` for exceptions.

Naturally, if you are interested only in writing to a lot of files, you might not care about the set of file descriptors that have characters ready to read. Indeed, your program might not even do any reading. If this is the case, you can pass NULL to that argument. For example, to ignore the file descriptors that are readable and the file descriptors that have some exception condition (like an error), you would call `select` as follows:

```
fd_set *writeable_fds;
select(maxfds, NULL, writefds, NULL, 10);
```

The `timeout` parameter determines how long `select` will *block*, or wait before it returns control to the calling process. If `timeout` is set to 0, `select` will return immediately. When an I/O operation returns immediately, without waiting, it is said to be a *non-blocking* I/O call. If you want to wait until an I/O operation can take place (that is, until `readfds` or `writefds` changes) or until an error occurs, pass `timeout` the value of NULL, using the same syntax as shown in the previous example.

The first parameter, n, contains the highest numbered file descriptor in any of the sets being monitored, plus 1 (the sample program shows one way to determine this value). If an error occurs, `select` returns −1 and sets `errno` to an appropriate value. In the event of an error, `select` also voids all the descriptor sets and `timeout`, so you will have to reset them to valid values before reusing them. If the `select` call succeeds, it returns either the total number of descriptors contained in the monitored (non-NULL) descriptor sets or 0. A return value of 0 means that nothing "interesting" happened, that is, that no descriptors changed status before `timeout` expired.

The select implementation also includes four routines to manipulate the descriptor sets:

```
FD_ZERO(fd_set *set);

FD_SET(int fd, fd_set *set);

FD_CLR(int fd, fd_set *set);

FD_ISSET(int fd, fd_set *set);
```

They operate as follows:

- FD_ZERO clears the set set.

- FD_SET adds descriptor fd to set.

- FD_CLR removes fd from set.

- FD_ISSET determines whether fd is in set. FD_ISSET is the routine to use after select returns in order to determine whether anything has happened that requires action. If fd is set, its status changed during the select call (it has bytes to read, can be written to, or an error occurred).

EXAMPLE

Example

The following example, mplex, watches two named pipes for data that is ready to read (the sample program uses pipes because they are the simplest way to demonstrate multiplexed I/O in a short program).

NOTE

Adapted from mpx-select.c, first published in *Linux Application Development*, Michael K. Johnson and Erik W. Troan (Addison Wesley, 1998), pp. 213-214.

✔ Named pipes are explained in detail in "Understanding FIFOs," page 330.

Perhaps the easiest way to use mplex is to build it using the makefile provided on this book's Web site, which includes rules for making the pipes. Otherwise, first build the program, and then create two named pipes (in the same directory as the mplex binary) using the following commands:

```
$ mknod pipe1 p

$ mknod pipe2 p
```

Next, start mplex. Open two other terminal windows. In the first one, type cat > pipe1, and in the second, type cat > pipe2. Anything you type after that in either window will be queued for mplex to read. The code follows:

```
/*
 * mplex.c - read input from pipe1 and pipe2 using select
 *
 * Adapted from mpx-select.c, written
 * by Michael Johnson and Erik Troan. Used with the permission of
 * the authors of _Linux Application Development_,
 * Michael Johnson and Erik Troan.
#include <fcntl.h>
#include <stdio.h>
#include <unistd.h>
#include <stdlib.h>

#define BUFSZ 80

void err_quit(char *msg);

int main(void)
{
    int fds[2];
    char buf[BUFSZ];
    int i, rc, maxfd;
    fd_set watchset;        /* Read this set of file descriptors */
    fd_set inset;           /* Copy of watchset for select to update */

    /* Open the pipes */
    if((fds[0] = open("pipe1", O_RDONLY | O_NONBLOCK)) < 0)
        err_quit("open pipe1");
    if((fds[1] = open("pipe2", O_RDONLY | O_NONBLOCK)) < 0)
        err_quit("open pipe2");

    /* Initialize watchset with our file descriptors */
    FD_ZERO(&watchset);
    FD_SET(fds[0], &watchset);
    FD_SET(fds[1], &watchset);

    /* select needs to know the maximum file descriptor */
    maxfd = fds[0] > fds[1] ? fds[0] : fds[1];
```

```
/* Loop while watching the pipes for output to read */
while(FD_ISSET(fds[0], &watchset) || FD_ISSET(fds[1], &watchset)) {
    /* Make sure select has a current set of descriptors */
    inset = watchset;
    if(select(maxfd + 1, &inset, NULL, NULL, NULL) < 0)
        err_quit("select");

    /* Which file descriptor is ready to read? */
    for(i = 0; i < 2; ++i) {
        if(FD_ISSET(fds[i], &inset)) {
            rc = read(fds[i], buf, BUFSZ - 1);
            if(rc > 0) { /* Read some data */
                buf[rc] = '\0';
                printf("read: %s", buf);
            } else if(rc == 0) { /* This pipe is closed */
                close(fds[i]);
                FD_CLR(fds[i], &watchset);
            } else
                err_quit("read"); /* Bummer */
        }
    }
}
exit(EXIT_SUCCESS);
}


void err_quit(char *msg)
{
    perror(msg);
    exit(EXIT_FAILURE);
}
```

Figure 8.1 shows how mplex looks when it's running.

This program is somewhat complex. After opening the two named pipes, it initializes a set of file descriptors using FD_ZERO, and then adds the descriptors for the two pipes. The heart of mplex is the while loop. During each iteration, it uses FD_ISSET to see if either of the pipes have data that can be read. If so, it first copies watchset to inset because watchset might have changed due to one of the pipes being closed.

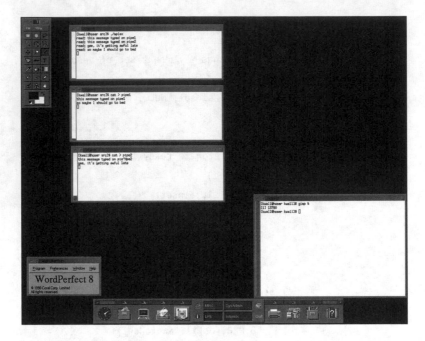

Figure 8.1: *mplex multiplexes input from two pipes.*

Next comes the select call, followed by a for loop that determines which descriptor is ready to be read (the timeout value is NULL, so select blocks until data is ready to be read). The for loop then reads the pipe and displays the data. If read returns 0, the pipe has been closed, so mplex closes that file and removes it from watchset. When the last pipe closes, mplex terminates.

Memory Mapping Files

Memory-mapped files are an identical copy in memory of a disk file. The in-core image corresponds byte for byte with the disk file. Memory-mapped files have two chief advantages. The first advantage is faster file I/O. Ordinary I/O calls, such as the read and write system calls and the fputs and fgets library calls, copy the data through kernel buffers. Although Linux uses a fast, sophisticated disk-caching algorithm, the fastest disk access will always be slower than the slowest memory access. I/O operations on a memory-mapped file bypass the kernel buffers and, as a result, are much faster. They are also simpler to use because you can access the mapped file using pointers rather than the usual file manipulation functions.

The second advantage of memory-mapped files is data sharing. If multiple processes need to access the same data, the data can be stored in a memory-mapped file. Effectively a shared memory model (see Chapter 16, "Shared Memory"), this makes the data independent of any single process and available to any process, and stores the region's contents in a disk file.

The function calls to manage memory mapping are defined in <sys/ mman.h>. They include the following calls:

- mmap—Maps a disk file into memory

- munmap—Unmaps a file, deletes the memory image

- msync—Updates the disk file with data from the memory image

- mprotect—Limits access to the memory image

- mlock—Prevents a portion of the map from being swapped to disk

- munlock—Removes a previously set lock

- mlockall—Prevents any part of the memory image from being swapped to disk

- munlockall—Removes the lock set by mlockall

These function calls are discussed in greater detail in the following sections.

Creating a Memory Map

To create a memory mapped file, call mmap. When you have finished using it, call munmap to delete the mapping from memory and return the memory to the operating system.

MAPPING A FILE

The mmap function maps a disk file into memory. It has the following prototype:

```
void *mmap(void *start, size_t length, int prot, int flags,
➥int fd, off_t offset);
```

mmap creates a memory image of the file referred to by the file descriptor fd. The memory image will start from offset bytes into the file. The argument length indicates how much of the file should be read into memory. To limit access to the memory map, you can set various protection levels using the protection argument. It can be a logical OR of one or more of the values in Table 8.1. The flags parameter sets several additional attributes for the memory map. It can a logical OR of one or more of the values listed in Table 8.2. mmap returns a pointer to the memory region or −1 on failure.

Table 8.1: *Values for* `mmap`*'s* `protection` *Parameter*

Protection	Description
PROT_NONE	No access is allowed
PROT_READ	Mapped region may be read
PROT_WRITE	Mapped region may be written
PROT_EXEC	Mapped region may be executed

NOTE

On the x86 architecture, PROT_EXEC implies PROT_READ, so PROT_EXEC is the same as specifying PROT_EXEC ¦ PROT_READ.

Table 8.2: *Values for* `mmap`*'s* `flags` *Parameter*

Flag	Description
MAP_ANONYMOUS	Creates an anonymous mapping, ignoring fd
MAP_FIXED	Fails if address is invalid or already in use
MAP_PRIVATE	Writes to region are process private
MAP_SHARED	Writes to region are copied to file
MAP_DENYWRITE	Disallows normal writes to file
MAP_GROWSDOWN	Grows the memory downward
MAP_LOCKED	Locks pages into memory

offset is usually 0, indicating that the entire file should be mapped into memory. A memory region must be marked either private, with MAP_PRIVATE, or shared, with MAP_SHARED; the other values are optional. A private mapping makes any modifications to the region process private, so these modifications are not reflected in the underlying file or available to other processes. Shared maps, on the other hand, cause any updates to the memory region to be immediately visible to other processes that have mapped the same file.

To prevent writes to the underlying disk file, specify MAP_DENYWRITE (but note that this is not a POSIX value and as such is not portable). Anonymous maps, created with MAP_ANONYMOUS, do not involve a physical file and simply allocate memory for the process's private use, such as a custom malloc implementation. MAP_FIXED causes the kernel to place the map at a specific address. If the address is already in use or otherwise unavailable, mmap fails. If MAP_FIXED is not specified and address is unavailable, the kernel will attempt to place the region elsewhere in memory. MAP_LOCKED allows processes with root privilege to lock the region into memory so it will never be swapped to disk.

NOTE

User programs cannot use MAP_LOCKED. This is a security feature that prevents unauthorized processes from locking all available memory, thus bringing the system to a standstill (also known as a *denial of service* attack).

UNMAPPING A FILE

When you have finished using a memory mapped file, call munmap to unmap the region and return the memory to the operating system. This function has the following prototype:

```
int munmap(void *start, size_t length);
```

The start argument is a pointer to the beginning of the region to unmap, and length indicates how much of the region to unmap. After a memory block has been unmapped, further attempts to access the memory to which start points will cause a segmentation fault (the signal SIGSEGV). When a process terminates, all memory maps are unmapped. The munmap function returns 0 on success. On failure, it returns −1 and sets errno.

As odd as it might seem, munmap might fail for a couple of reasons. The most common reason is that start does not point to mapped memory. Another cause for munmap to fail is that length is too long and, as a result, bleeds into memory that is not mapped.

EXAMPLE

Example

This program, mkmap, maps and unmaps a file specified on the command line.

```
/*
 * mkmap.c - Create a memory mapped file
 */
#include <sys/types.h>
#include <sys/mman.h>
#include <sys/stat.h>
#include <unistd.h>
#include <fcntl.h>

#include <stdlib.h>
#include <stdio.h>

void err_quit(char *msg);

int main(int argc, char *argv[])
{
```

```
    int fd;
    void *map;
    struct stat statbuf;

    /* Open the file to map */
    if(argc != 2) {
        puts("USAGE: mkmap {file}");
        exit(EXIT_FAILURE);
    }
    if((fd = open(argv[1], O_RDONLY)) < 0)
        err_quit("open");

    /* Get the file's length for mmap */
    fstat(fd, &statbuf);

    /* Map the input file */
    if((map = mmap(0, statbuf.st_size, PROT_READ,
                    MAP_SHARED, fd, 0)) == MAP_FAILED)
        err_quit("mmap");
    printf("map created at %p\n", &map);

    /* Close and unmap the file */
    close(fd);
    munmap(map, statbuf.st_size);
    exit(EXIT_SUCCESS);
}

void err_quit(char *msg)
{
    perror(msg);
    exit(EXIT_FAILURE);
}
```

The only output from mkmap is the mapped file's starting address. Although this program has no real functionality, it should unambiguously show how to map and unmap a file. The fstat call makes it easy to determine the file's size, which is fed to the length parameter of the mmap call.

Using a Mapped File

Of course, it is one thing to map and unmap a file, but the whole idea is to *use* and manipulate the file. The calls discussed in this section—msync, mprotect, the mlock family, and mremap—enable you to do these things.

WRITING A MAP TO DISK

The msync function writes a mapped file to disk. It has the following prototype:

```
int msync(const void *start, size_t length, int flags);
```

msync flushes length bytes of the map to disk beginning at the memory address start address. The flags argument is a bitwise OR of one or more of the following:

- MS_ASYNC—Schedules a write and returns

- MS_SYNC—Writes data before msync() returns

- MS_INVALIDATE—Invalidates other maps of the same file so they will be updated with new data

CHANGING MAP PROTECTIONS

The mprotect function modifies a memory map's protection flags. It is prototyped as follows:

```
int protect(const void *addr, size_t len, int prot);
```

mprotect sets or changes the protections for the region that begins at addr to the protection level specified in prot. prot can be a bitwise OR of one or more of the flags listed in Table 8.1. It returns 0 on success. If it fails, mprotect returns –1 and sets errno.

LOCKING MAPPED MEMORY

Memory locking means preventing a memory area from being swapped to disk. In a multitasking, multiuser system such as Linux, areas of system memory (RAM) not in active use may temporarily be written to disk (swapped out) so that memory can be put to other uses. Locking the memory sets a flag that prevents it from being swapped out. There are four functions for locking and unlocking memory: mlock, mlockall, munlock, and munlockall. Their prototypes are listed here:

```
int mlock(const void *addr, size_t len);
int munlock(void *addr, size_t len);
int mlockall(int flags);
int munlockall(void);
```

The beginning of the memory region to be locked or unlocked is specified in addr. len indicates how much of the region to lock or unlock. Values for flags may be one or both of the following:

- MCL_CURRENT requests that all pages are locked before the call returns.
- MCL_FUTURE requests that all pages added to the process's address space should be locked.

As noted in the discussion of mmap, only processes with root privilege may lock or unlock memory regions.

RESIZING A MAPPED FILE

You will occasionally need to resize a memory region. Use the mremap function to do so. It has the following prototype:

```
void *mremap(void *old_addr, size_t old_len, ]size_t new_len,
unsigned long flags);
```

An analogue of the realloc library call, mremap resizes the memory region beginning at old_addr, originally with size old_len, to new_len. flags indicates whether the region can be moved in memory if necessary. MREMAP_MAYMOVE permits the address to change; if not specified, the resize operation fails. mremap returns the address of the resized region or NULL on failure.

EXAMPLE

Example

The program that follows, mmcat, implements the cat program using memory maps. Although it is a naive implementation, it clearly shows how to perform file I/O using memory mapped files.

```
/*
 * mmcat.c - cat(1) implemented with memory maps
 */

#include <sys/types.h>
#include <sys/mman.h>
#include <sys/stat.h>
#include <unistd.h>
#include <fcntl.h>
#include <stdlib.h>
#include <stdio.h>

void err_quit(char *msg);
```

```c
int main(int argc, char *argv[])
{
    int fd;
    char *src;
    struct stat statbuf;

    /* Open the source file */
    if(argc != 2) {
        puts("USAGE: mmcat {file}");
        exit(EXIT_FAILURE);
    }
    if((fd = open(argv[1], O_RDONLY)) < 0)
        err_quit("open");

    /* Get the file length for mmap */
    fstat(fd, &statbuf);

    /* map the input file */
    if((src = mmap(0, statbuf.st_size, PROT_READ,
                    MAP_SHARED, fd, 0)) < 0)
        err_quit("mmap");

    /* write it out */

    write(STDOUT_FILENO, src, statbuf.st_size);

    /* clean up */
    close(fd);
    munmap(src, statbuf.st_size);

    exit(0);
}


void err_quit(char *msg)
{
    perror(msg);
    exit(EXIT_FAILURE);
}
```

After the file is mapped into memory, mmcat uses the character pointer, src, in the fprintf call exactly as if it had been populated by a read or fgets. We return to the memory region of the kernel by calling munmap.

TIP

From a practical point of view, using a memory mapped file in this example was overkill because it provided little in terms of performance or code length. However, in situations when performance is crucial or when you are dealing with time-sensitive operations, memory mapped files can be a definite plus. Memory mapping can also be valuable in high-security circumstances. Processes running with root privileges can lock mapped files into memory, preventing them from being swapped to disk by Linux's memory manager. As a result, sensitive data, such as password files or payroll data, would be less susceptible to scanner programs. Of course, in such a situation, the memory region would have to be set to PROT_NONE so that other processes cannot read the region.

File Locking

File locking is a method enabling multiple processes to access the same file simultaneously in a safe, rational, and predictable way. Each process that locks a file does so to prevent other processes from changing the data while it is working with the file. There is no inherent reason why two processes should not be able to read from the same file simultaneously, but imagine the confusion that would result if two processes were writing to the same file at the same time. They would likely overwrite each other's data or, in some cases, completely corrupt the file.

The general procedure if you want to access a locked file is listed here:

1. Check for a lock.

2. If the file is unlocked, establish your own lock.

3. Open the file.

4. Process the file as necessary.

5. Close the file.

6. Unlock the file.

Note how the process locks the file before beginning any I/O and completes all processing before unlocking the file. This procedure ensures that all the processing your program performs will be uninterrupted by other processes. If you open the file before establishing the lock or close the file after reading the lock, another process might be able to access the file in the fraction of a second that elapses between the lock/unlock operation and the open/close operation.

If the file is locked, you must make a decision. Many file I/O operations take, at most, only a few seconds. You can either wait a few seconds—

perhaps using the sleep call—and try again or give up and report to the user running your program that you were unable to open the file because another process is using it.

File locks come in two flavors, advisory locks and mandatory locks. *Advisory locks*, also known as cooperative locks, rely on a convention in which every process that uses a locked file checks for the existence of a lock and honors that lock. Neither the kernel nor the system as a whole enforce advisory locks; they depend on programmers honoring the convention. *Mandatory locks*, on the other hand, *are* enforced by the kernel. The kernel blocks read or write access to a file that is locked for writing until the locking process releases the lock. The price mandatory locking extracts, however, is a significant performance penalty, because every read or write operation has to check for the existence of a lock.

Just as there are two types of file locking, there are also two implementations of it, lock files and record locking.

Lock Files

Lock files are zero-length files of the form filename.lck, where .lck is appended to the end of the file, usually created in the same directory as the filename that the process wants to open. They are easy to implement. To do so, you will need a code block that resembles the following snippet of pseudo-code:

```
open with lock file using the O_EXCL flag
if the open fails and errno == EEXIST
    another process has locked the file
else
    you have locked the file
    open the file itself
    perform additional processing
    close the file
    delete (unlink) the lockfile
end if
```

Using O_EXCL when opening the lock file guarantees that the open call is *atomic*, that is, that the open call will not be interrupted by the kernel. This is important because a potential race condition exists when two processes try to open the same file. A second process could open the file while the first process's open call is interrupted by the kernel. Using O_EXCL avoids this situation. As noted earlier, by convention, lock files are named somefile.lck, where somefile is the name of the file you are locking.

✔ Race conditions are discussed in more detail in "Using fork," page 78.

EXAMPLE

Example

This program creates a lock file, and then tries to lock it a second time. The second attempt will fail. The program's purpose is to illustrate the correct logic for using lock files.

```c
/*
 * lockit.c - Using lock files
 */
#include <unistd.h>
#include <fcntl.h>
#include <errno.h> /* for EEXIST */
#include <stdlib.h>
#include <stdio.h>

int main(int argc, char *argv[])
{
    int fd, newfd;

    /* Open the lockfile */
    fd = open(argv[1], O_CREAT | O_EXCL, 0644);
    if(fd < 0 && errno == EEXIST) { /* lockfile exists */
        puts("file already locked");
        close(fd);
    } else if(fd < 0) /* some other error we don't test */
        puts("unknown error");
    else { /* file is now locked */
        puts("lock established");
            /*
             * Additional processing would take place here
             */

        /* repeat the process, this time it will fail */
        newfd = open(argv[1], O_CREAT | O_EXCL, 0644);
        if(newfd < 0 && errno == EEXIST) {
            puts("file already locked");
            close(newfd);
        } else if(newfd < 0)
```

```
            puts("unknown error");
        else
            puts("lock established");}
    close(fd);
    unlink(argv[1]);

    exit(EXIT_SUCCESS);
}
```

A sample run of `lockit` produces the following output:

```
$ ./lockit lockit.c.lck
lock established
file already locked
```

Unless something unexpected occurs, `lockit` successfully locks the file
(whose name is passed as the only command-line argument) in the first
`open` statement. Then, in the second `open` statement, `lockit` tries to lock the
file a second time by creating the same lockfile. Specifying `O_CREAT` in the
open call, along with `O_EXCL`, means that the `open` call will fail if the file
already exists. To express it another way, creating or opening a lock file
using the syntax shown is synonymous with locking a file; deleting a lock
file is synonymous with unlocking a file. Because this test fails, the program reports that the file is already locked. Back in the outer block, the
program closes the file descriptor and unlinks (deletes) the file, thus removing the lock.

Record Locking

Although lock files are easy to use, they have significant drawbacks:

- When a file is locked, it is not available to other processes that merely
  want to read it.

- The `O_EXCL` flag is reliable only on local filesystems, not on networked
  filesystems such as NFS.

- The locks are only advisory; processes can ignore them.

- If a process terminates before it removes a lock file, the lock file
  remains in place and other processes have no reliable way to determine whether it is *stale*, that is, left over from a process that died pre-
  maturely.

These shortcomings led to the development of *record locking*, which gives
programmers the ability to lock specific regions of files, called *records*.
Record locks, sometimes referred to as *POSIX locks*, allow multiple

processes to lock different portions of the same file or even read the same segments of the same file. Record locks also work across NFS and other networked filesystems. Finally, because record locks are held by the kernel, when a process terminates, its locks are automatically released.

POSIX locks come in two varieties, *read* or *shared* locks and *write* or *exclusive* locks. Read locks are called shared locks because many processes can hold read locks on the same region of a file. Exclusive locks, however, prevent access to a locked region while the write lock is in place. Furthermore, you cannot create a write lock while a read lock is in place for the same area of a file.

NOTE

Recall from Chapter 4, "Processes," that child processes do not inherit file locks after a fork, although an execed process does inherit file locks from its parent.

The fcntl call, prototyped in <fcntl.h>, manages record locks. It has the following prototype:

```
int fcntl(int fd, int cmd, struct flock *lock);
```

fd is the file descriptor to lock. cmd must be one of F_GETLK, F_SETLK, or F_SETLKW. F_GETLK checks to see if the file can be locked. If it can be locked, the l_type member of struct flock is set to F_UNLCK and if it cannot be locked, the l_pid member of struct flock is set to the PID of the process holding the lock. F_SETLK sets the lock. F_SETLKW also sets the lock, but fcntl waits to return until it successfully sets the lock.

lock is a pointer to a flock structure that describes the lock and its behavior. struct flock is defined as follows:

```
struct flock {
    short l_type;    /* Type of lock */
    short l_whence;  /* Beginning of lock */
    off_t l_start;   /* Starting offset of lock */
    off_t l_len;     /* Number of bytes to lock */
    pid_t l_pid;     /* Process holding lock */
};
```

l_type can be F_RDLCK for a read lock, F_WRLCK for a write lock, or F_UNLCK to release the lock. l_whence is one of SEEK_SET, SEEK_CUR, or SEEK_END, which have the same semantics as the lseek call. l_start indicates the starting offset of the lock, relative to l_whence, and l_len specifies how many bytes to lock. l_pid, finally, is the PID of the process holding the lock.

✔ The lseek system call is covered in "Positioning the File Pointer," page 143.

EXAMPLE

Example

The program that follows, reclck, sets a write lock on one part of a file and a read lock on another part. If you run this in two terminal windows, you can clearly see how record locks work.

```c
/*
 * reclck.c - Setting read and write locks
 */
#include <unistd.h>
#include <fcntl.h>
#include <stdlib.h>
#include <stdio.h>
#include <errno.h>

int main(void)
{
    int fd;
    struct flock lock;

    if((fd = open("test.dat", O_RDWR)) < 0) {
        perror("open");
        exit(EXIT_FAILURE);
    }

    /*
     * Set up a write lock on the last 100
     * bytes of the file
     */
    lock.l_type = F_WRLCK;
    lock.l_whence = SEEK_END;
    lock.l_start = 0;
    lock.l_len = 100;
    /* set the lock */
    if(!fcntl(fd, F_SETLK, &lock))
         puts( "write lock established");
    else {
        fcntl(fd, F_GETLK, &lock);
        printf("write locked by PID %d\n", lock.l_pid);
    }
```

```
    /* Now do a read lock */
    lock.l_type = F_RDLCK;
    lock.l_whence = SEEK_END;
    lock.l_start = 0;
    lock.l_len = 100;
    if(!fcntl(fd, F_SETLKW, &lock))
        puts("read lock established");
    else {
        fcntl(fd, F_GETLK, &lock);
        printf("read locked by PID %d\n", lock.l_pid);
    }
    getchar();
    exit(EXIT_SUCCESS);
}
```

Output from this program, running in two xterms, is shown in Figure 8.2.

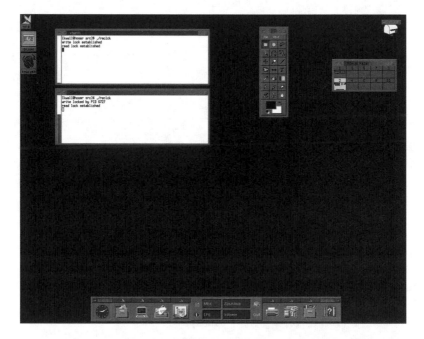

Figure 8.2: *Write locks are exclusive; read locks are shared.*

First, reclck sets a write lock on the last 100 bytes of the file. If the lock cannot be established, it calls fcntl with the F_GETLK command to retrieve the PID of the locking process. The next lock is a read lock on the first 100 bytes of the file. Read locks are shared, so multiple processes can lock the same region of the file, as Figure 8.2 illustrates.

What's Next?

This chapter extended the discussion of file I/O, focusing on advanced features such as directory manipulation, memory mapping, and file locking. The next chapter, "Daemons," looks at creating background processes, which finishes up the survey of system programming.

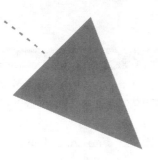

Daemons

In this chapter, you learn how to create a *daemon*, pronounced like *demon*. Daemons are background processes that run non-interactively. They usually provide some service, either for the system as a whole or for user programs. In particular, this chapter covers the following:

- The characteristics of daemons
- The rules for creating daemons
- The function calls to use when programming a daemon
- How to use the syslog facility
- How daemons should handle runtime errors

Understanding Daemons

Typically, daemons are started at boot time and, unless forcibly terminated, run until system shutdown. They also lack a controlling terminal, so any output they create must be handled specially.

Daemons also have a few characteristics that distinguish them from ordinary programs like ls and cat. To begin with, they almost always run with superuser privilege because they provide system services to user mode programs. They do not have a controlling terminal because they are non-interactive; that is, they run without user input. Daemons generally are process-group and session leaders. They often serve as the process in their process group and session. Finally, a daemon's parent is the init process, which has a PID of 1. This is because its real parent process has forked and exited before the child, hence they are orphan processes inherited by init.

✔ Controlling terminals and session leaders are discussed in "Sessions," page 76.

✔ Process groups and process leaders the subject of "Process Groups," page 76.

Creating a Daemon

To create a daemon program, you must follow a few simple rules and call several functions, all of which you have seen in previous chapters. Error handling, however, presents special difficulties for a daemon and requires the program to use the system logging facility, syslog, to send messages to the system log (often the file /var/log/messages). This topic is covered in "Handling Errors," later in this chapter.

There are a few simple steps to follow to create a daemon that both works properly and plays nice with the system.

First, fork and make the parent exit. Like most programs, daemons are started from a shell script or the command line. However, daemons are unlike application programs because they are not interactive—they run in the background and, as a result, do not have a controlling terminal. The parent forks and exits as the first step toward getting rid of the controlling terminal. If you think about it for a minute, this makes perfect sense. Daemons neither read from standard input nor write to standard output or standard error, so they do not need a terminal interface at all, except to get them started.

The second step is to create a new session using the setsid call. Calling setsid dissociates the process from any terminal. In other words, this causes the child not to have a controlling terminal. The program continues to execute, of course.

The next step is to make the root directory the process's current working directory. This is necessary because any process whose current directory is on a mounted filesystem will prevent that filesystem from being unmounted. Ordinarily, this is desirable behavior, but, if the system must go to single-user mode for some reason, a daemon process running on a mounted filesystem becomes, at best, a nuisance for the superuser (because she must find the troublesome process and kill it), or, in an emergency situation, a real threat to system integrity (because it prevents a filesystem on a disk gone bad from being unmounted). Making / a daemon's working directory is a safe way to avoid both of these possibilities.

Set the umask to 0. This step is necessary to prevent the daemon's inherited umask from interfering with the creation of files and directories. Consider the following scenario: A daemon inherits a umask of 055, which masks out read and execute permissions for group and other. If the daemon then proceeds to create a file, for example a data file, the created file will be readable, writeable, and executable by the user, but only writeable by group and other. Resetting the daemon's umask to 0 prevents such a situation. It also gives the daemon greater flexibility when creating files because, with a umask of 0, the daemon process can set precisely the permissions that are required rather than settle for system defaults.

Finally, close any file descriptors that the child inherited but does not need. This is simply a common-sense step. There is no reason for a child to keep open descriptors inherited from the parent. The list of potential file descriptors to close includes at least stdin, stdout, and stderr. Other open file descriptors, such as those that refer to configuration or data files, might also need to be closed. This step depends on the needs and requirements of the daemon in question, so it is difficult to state this rule more precisely.

Function Calls

To meet the requirements of the first item, call fork to spawn a child process and have the parent process call exit. To eliminate the controlling terminal, create a new session by calling setsid, which is declared in <unistd.h> and formatted as follows:

```
pid_t setsid(void);
```

setsid creates a new session and a new process group. The daemon will then be the session leader of the new session and the process group leader of the new process group. The setsid call also guarantees that the new session will not have a controlling terminal. If the calling process is already a process group leader, however, the setsid call will fail. setsid returns the new session ID (SID) on success. On error, it returns –1 and sets errno.

The umask call changes the daemon's umask to 0. This negates any inherited umask that could potentially interfere with file or directory creation, as explained earlier. To close unneeded file descriptors, call close.

EXAMPLE

Example

The following daemon creates a new log file, /var/log/lpedated.log, and writes a timestamp into it every minute. In order for it to work, it must be started by the root user.

```c
/*
 * lpedated.c - Simple timestamping daemon
 */
#include <sys/types.h>
#include <sys/stat.h>
#include <stdio.h>
#include <stdlib.h>
#include <fcntl.h>
#include <errno.h>
#include <unistd.h>
#include <time.h>
#include <string.h>

int main(void)
{
    pid_t pid, sid;

    int fd, len;
    time_t timebuf;

    pid = fork();
    if(pid < 0) {
        perror("fork");
        exit(EXIT_FAILURE);
    }
    if(pid > 0)
        /* In the parent, let's bail */
        exit(EXIT_SUCCESS);

    /* In the child... */
    /* First, start a new session */
```

```c
    if((sid = setsid()) < 0) {
    perror("setsid");
    exit(EXIT_FAILURE);
    }
    /* Next, make / the current directory */
    if((chdir("/")) < 0) {
        perror("chdir");
        exit(EXIT_FAILURE);
    }
    /* Reset the file mode */
    umask(0);

    /* Close stdin, etc. */
    close(STDIN_FILENO);
    close(STDOUT_FILENO);
    close(STDERR_FILENO);

    /*  Finally, do our work */
    len = strlen(ctime(&timebuf));
    while(1) {
        chaf *buf = malloc(sizeof(char) * (len + 1));

        if(buf == NULL) {
            exit(EXIT_FAILURE);
        }
        if((fd = open("/var/log/lpedated.log",
                    O_CREAT | O_WRONLY | O_APPEND, 0600)) < 0) {
            exit(EXIT_FAILURE);
        }
        time(&timebuf);
        strncpy(buf, ctime(&timebuf), len + 1);
        write(fd, buf, len + 1);
        close(fd);
        sleep(60);
    }
    exit(EXIT_SUCCESS);
}
```

lpedated uses the open and write system calls to remind you that Linux provides alternatives to the standard library's fopen and fwrite stream I/O functions. Remember, you must run this program as root because normal users do not have write access to the /var/log directory. If you try to run it as a non-root user, nothing will happen, period. The daemon will simply terminate after it fails to open its log file. After a few minutes, the log file maintained by the daemon, /var/log/lpedated.log, should resemble the following:

OUTPUT

```
$ su -c "tail -5 /var/log/lpedated.log
Wed Jul 28 01:35:41 1999
Wed Jul 28 01:36:41 1999
Wed Jul 28 01:37:41 1999
Wed Jul 28 01:38:41 1999
Wed Jul 28 01:39:41 1999
```

Note that lpedated stops writing error messages to stderr after calling setsid. The child no longer has a controlling terminal, so the output would have nowhere to go. The infinite while loop does the work of the program: Open the log file, output the timestamp, close the log file, and then sleep for 60 seconds. To kill the program, become the root user, obtain lpedated's PID, and issue kill <PID of lpedated>.

Handling Errors

After a daemon calls setsid, it no longer has a controlling terminal, so it has nowhere to send output that would normally go to stdout or stderr (such as error messages). Fortunately, the standard utility for this purpose is the BSD-derived syslog service, provided by the system logging daemon, syslogd.

The relevant interface is defined in <syslog.h>. The API is simple. openlog opens the log; syslog writes a message to it; closelog closes the log. Their prototypes are listed here:

```
void openlog(char *ident, int option, int facility);
void closelog(void);
void syslog(int priority, char *format, ...);
```

openlog initiates a connection to the system logger. ident is a string added to each message, and typically is set to the name of the program. The option argument is a logical OR of one or more of the values listed here:

- LOG_CONS—Write to the console if the system logger is unavailable.

- LOG_NDELAY—Open the connection immediately. Normally, the connection is not opened until the first message is sent.

- LOG_PERROR—Print to the stderr.

- LOG_PID—Include the process's PID with each message.

facility specifies the type of program sending the message and can be one of the values listed in Table 9.1.

Table 9.1:   *System Logger Facility Values*

Facility	Description
LOG_AUTHPRIV	Security/authorization messages
LOG_CRON	Clock daemons; cron and at
LOG_DAEMON	Other system daemons
LOG_KERN	Kernel messages
LOG_LOCAL[0-7]	Reserved for local use
LOG_LPR	Line printer subsystem
LOG_MAIL	The mail subsystem
LOG_NEWS	Usenet news subsystem
LOG_SYSLOG	Messages generated by syslogd
LOG_USER	Default
LOG_UUCP	UUCP system

priority specifies the importance of the message. Its possible values are listed in Table 9.2.

Table 9.2:   *System Logger Priority Values*

Priority	Description
LOG_EMERG	System is unusable
LOG_ALERT	Take action immediately
LOG_CRIT	Critical condition
LOG_ERR	Error condition
LOG_WARNING	Warning condition
LOG_NOTICE	Normal but significant condition
LOG_INFO	Informational message
LOG_DEBUG	Debugging message

Strictly speaking, the use of openlog and closelog is optional because syslog will open the log file automatically the first time it is called.

Example

The following program is a rewrite of lpedated, which uses the system logger:

```c
/*
 * lpedated.c - Simple timestamping daemon
 */
#include <sys/types.h>
#include <sys/stat.h>
#include <stdio.h>
#include <stdlib.h>
#include <fcntl.h>
#include <errno.h>
#include <unistd.h>
#include <time.h>
#include <string.h>
#include <syslog.h>

int main(void)
{
    pid_t pid, sid;

    int fd, len;
    time_t timebuf;

    /* Open the system log */
    openlog("lpedated", LOG_PID, LOG_DAEMON);

    pid = fork();
    if(pid < 0) {
        syslog(LOG_ERR, "%s\n", "fork");
        exit(EXIT_FAILURE);
    }
    if(pid > 0)
    /* In the parent, let's bail */
    exit(EXIT_SUCCESS);

    /* In the child... */
    /* First, start a new session */
    if((sid = setsid()) < 0) {
```

```
        syslog(LOG_ERR, "%s\n", "setsid");
        exit(EXIT_FAILURE);
    }
    /* Next, make / the current directory */
    if((chdir("/")) < 0) {
        syslog(LOG_ERR, "%s\n", "chdir");
        exit(EXIT_FAILURE);
    }
    /* Reset the file mode */
    umask(0);

    ./* Close stdin, etc. */
    close(STDIN_FILENO);
    close(STDOUT_FILENO);
    close(STDERR_FILENO);

    /*  Finally, do our work */
    len = strlen(ctime(&timebuf));
    while(1) {
        char *buf = malloc(sizeof(char) * (len = 1));

        if(buf == NULL) {
            exit(EXIT_FAILURE);
        }
        if((fd = open("/var/log/lpedated.log",
            O_CREAT | O_WRONLY | O_APPEND, 0600)) < 0) {
            syslog(LOG_ERR, "open");
            exit(EXIT_FAILURE);
        }
        time(&timebuf);
        strncpy(buf, ctime(&timebuf), len + 1);
        write(fd, buf, len + 1);
        close(fd);
        sleep(60);
    }
    closelog();
    exit(EXIT_SUCCESS);
}
```

Having added `syslog`'s logging functionality, if you try to execute the program as a normal user, `lpedated` will write an entry to the system log (usually `/var/log/messages` on Linux systems) resembling the following:

```
Sep 14 21:12:04 hoser lpedated[8192]: open
```

This log entry indicates that at the date and time specified, on the host named hoser, a program named `lpedated`, with a PID of 8192, entered the text open into the system log. Referring to `lpedated`'s source code, you would be able to see where the error occurred.

All the error messages `lpedated` generates will be logged to the system log, although the timestamps themselves will still be written to `/var/log/lpedated.log`. The output that follows, taken from the system log, was generated because a non-root user attempted to run the program. The number in brackets is `lpedated`'s PID.

```
Jul 28 11:34:06 hoser lpedated[8895]: open
```

OUTPUT

What's Next?

This chapter discussed creating *daemons*, which are background programs that are always running and usually provide some sort of service. This completes the book's coverage of system programming topics. With your knowledge of basic development tools, covered in Part I, "The Linux Programming Environment," and a solid understanding of low-level system programming (covered in Part II, "System Programming"), you are ready to learn some of Linux's most common APIs, or application programming interfaces, in Part III, "Linux APIs."

Part III

Linux APIs (Application Programming Interface)

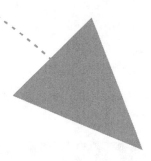

The Database API

Application programmers often must store their data in a database without requiring all the services (or wanting all the overhead) of a full-strength relational database such as Informix or Oracle. This chapter teaches you how to use the Berkeley database, an embeddable database library standard in major Linux distributions. The version discussed in this chapter is 2.7.7, but the discussion applies to any 2.x version. Note that the 2.x API incorporates all the features of the 1.x API, but also adds many elements. The following topics are covered in this chapter:

- Creating a new database
- Opening an existing database
- Adding and deleting records
- Retrieving records
- Searching for a record
- Moving around in a database
- Closing a database

> **NOTE**
>
> A complete source code distribution of version 2.7.5 of the Berkeley database is available on the Web site accompanying this book. All the examples in this book were built using a copy of the header file and library in the chapter's source code directory.

The Berkeley Database

The Berkeley database, often called *Berkeley DB* or just plain DB, uses *key/value pairs* to work with elements in the database. The *key* is the identifying element; the *value* is the data element. To find the data you want, present DB with a key and DB will return the value associated with it. The key/value pair is stored in a simple structure called a *DBT—a Data Base Thang*—that consists of a memory reference—that is, a pointer—and the length of the memory reference, measured in bytes. The key and value can be any kind of data. The length of the stored data is practically unlimited—a single key or value must fit into a system's available memory (physical RAM).

For example, if you wanted to create a database of the chapters of this book, the key/value pairs might look like the following:

Key	Value
One	Compiling Programs
Two	Controlling the Build Process: GNU make
Three	About the Project
Four	Processes
Five	Signals

DB databases support three types of storage and access methods: B+trees, hashes, and records. Record-based databases store data of fixed or variable length in sequential order; new records can be inserted between existing records or appended to the end of a series of existing records. Hash-based databases store records in a hash table for fast searching. The hash function may be supplied by the programmer, or you can use the built-in default routine. B+tree databases store data in sorted order. The sort order is determined by a programmer-supplied function or by a default function that sorts keys lexicographically. Figure 10.1 shows how the three types or storage and access methods are related.

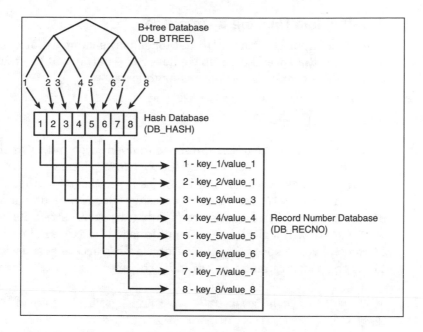

Figure 10.1: *How records are stored in Berkeley DB databases.*

The actual implementation of the storage and access methods DB supports are beyond this book's scope (indeed, many computer scientists devote their entire careers to studying sorting and searching algorithms), but the basic principles are simple. Figure 10.1 assumes a database containing eight records, denoted by the numbers one through eight. A B+tree database stores data in a tree-like structure, as shown in Figure 10.1, that makes locating a specific record extremely fast and efficient. Hash-based databases store data in a table. The location of an individual record in the table depends on an arbitrary value that is computed based on the record's key. Record number-oriented databases store records in sequential order. They are accessed and manipulated by their record number.

Creating, Opening, and Closing a Database

To use DB, include <db.h> in your source code and link against libdb.a (-ldb). Every DB function returns zero DB on success and a nonzero value on any failure. In the event of a system error, such as an illegal argument or a disk error, DB returns an errno value that can be used with the perror function. Other return codes will be documented as the functions that generate them are discussed.

Creating and Opening a Database

The function for creating a DB database is the same as for opening one, db_open. If the specified database does not exist, it will be created and then opened. The syntax for db_open is as follows:

```
int db_open(const char *file, DBTYPE type, u_int32_t flags, int mode,
➥DB_ENV *dbenv, DB_INFO *dbinfo, DB **dbpp);
```

file is the pathname of the database to open. type indicates the access method, either DB_BTREE, DB_HASH, or DB_RECNO. Use DB_UNKNOWN to open an existing database if you do not know its type. flags modifies db_open's behavior. DB_CREATE creates any necessary files if they do not already exist, DB_RDONLY opens the database read-only (any write attempts will fail), and DB_TRUNCATE will logically zero the database if it exists. The mode argument is an octal value specifying the database file's access permissions. It is similar to the mode argument required by the open system call.

✔ The open system call and its mode argument is covered in the section "The File Mode," page 134.

The dbenv and dbinfo parameters control advanced features of DB's behavior that are beyond the scope of this book and will not be covered. Pass NULL for these two arguments to obtain DB's default behavior. dbpp, finally, is a *handle* to the database opened, a pointer to a pointer to a DB (database) structure. It will be initialized to the appropriate value or NULL on failure.

The handle that db_open initializes is the key to all subsequent database operations because almost all the Berkeley DB interface takes place using function pointers contained in the handle.

Closing a Database

To close a database, use the close function. It is prototyped as follows:

```
int DB->close(DB *db, u_int32_t flags);
```

db is a handle previously returned by a db_open call. flags should be 0 or DB_NOSYNC. DB_NOSYNC tells DB not to *sync*, or flush, cached database data to disk before closing the database. If flags is 0, cached data will be written to disk.

CAUTION

DB_NOSYNC is a bad option! Berkeley DB maintains information in its own cache and writes it out independently of the kernel. Failure to synchronize the cached information will result in unreliable, inconsistent, or corrupt data.

EXAMPLE

Example

This program, opendb, opens and closes a database in the current working directory.

```c
/*
 * opendb.c - Opening a Berkeley DB database
 */
#include <stdlib.h>
#include <stdio.h>
#include <errno.h>
#include "db.h"

int main(void)
{
    DB *db;
    int ret;

    ret = db_open("test.db", DB_BTREE,
                    DB_CREATE, 0600, NULL, NULL, &db);
    if(ret) {
        perror("db_open");
        exit(EXIT_FAILURE);
    }

    db->close(db, 0);
    exit(EXIT_SUCCESS);
}
```

The db_open call attempts to open a B+tree database named test.db in the current directory. If the database does not already exist, the DB_CREATE flag tells DB to create the file. After opening (or creating, if necessary) the database, the db_close call closes the database. opendb has no output, but a quick ls in the current working directory reveals that test.db has been created. Although the test.db file will not have any records stored in it, Berkeley DB writes some administrative information into the file when it is created. You do not need to worry about this, though, because it is information that the DB API uses.

Storing Items in a Database

To add data to a database, use the put function, prototyped as follows:

```
int DB->put(DB *db, DB_TXN *txnid, DBT *key, DBT *data, u_int32_t flags);
```

db is a handle to a database previously returned by db_open; txnid is a transaction ID, an advanced feature not covered here, so set it to NULL. flags must be one of 0, which allows an existing record with the same key to be overwritten; DB_NOOVERWRITE, which disallows the put if a key/value pair with the same key is already present; or DB_APPEND, which applies only to databases of type DB_RECNO. put returns DB_KEYEXIST if the key is already present; the standard return codes also apply.

To ensure compatibility with future versions of Berkeley DB, you should always initialize the key and value arguments before using them. The easiest way to do so is to use the memset call from the standard C library. For example, suppose you need to use a key named dbkey in a program. Before using it, initialize it as the following code snippet illustrates:

```
DBT dbkey;
memset(&dbkey, 0, sizeof(DBT *));
```

In this example, memset sets the value of all memory blocks associated with DBT to zero.

EXAMPLE

Example

The next example adds a record to the database created by opendb:

```
/*
 * adddb.c - Add a record to a Berkeley DB database
 */
#include <stdlib.h>
#include <stdio.h>
#include <errno.h>
#include "db.h"

int main(void)
{
    DB *db;
    int ret, i = 0;
    DBT key, value;

    ret = db_open("test.db", DB_BTREE,
                DB_CREATE, 0600, NULL, NULL, &db);
```

```
    if(ret) {
        perror("dbopen");
        exit(EXIT_FAILURE);
    }

    /* Initialize the key/value pair first */
    memset(&key, 0, sizeof(key));
    memset(&value, 0, sizeof(value));
    /* Set the values for key, value */

    key.data = "one";
    key.size = sizeof("one");
    value.data = "Compiling Programs";
    value.size = sizeof("Compiling Programs");
    /* Store it */
    ret = db->put(db, NULL, &key, &value, DB_NOOVERWRITE);
    if(ret == DB_KEYEXIST) {
        fprintf(stderr, "key %s exists\n", (char *)key.data);
        exit(EXIT_FAILURE);
    } else {
        perror("put");
        exit(EXIT_FAILURE);
    }

    db->close(db, 0);
    exit(EXIT_SUCCESS);
}
```

Again, this example has no output. However, if you execute it twice in a row, the second run will fail because the flags value, DB_NOOVERWRITE, prohibits the put operation if the specified key already exists in the database. In this case, the output would be as follows:

```
$ ./adddb
key one exists
```

OUTPUT   It is especially important to note that, in this example, the null terminator for the strings one and Compiling Programs are stored in the database, so the size members of key and value must be the length of the strings *including the trailing null*. This explains why the code used sizeof instead of strlen when computing the length of the strings (of course, strlen+1 would also have sufficed).

TIP

Usually, programs that use Berkeley DB are not adding static data, or data compiled into the program, to a database. Instead, records are being added dynamically at run-time. The sample program used sizeof because it works well with static data (one and Compiling Programs). At runtime, however, you should use the strlen call to determine the length of the string and add 1 to its return value to store the terminating null. You are not required to store the terminating null as part of the string, but doing so enables you to use the standard library's stream output functions, such as puts and printf, which need the null terminator to work correctly (or at all).

Deleting Items in a Database

To delete data from a DB database, use the del function. It takes four of the five elements the put function takes. del is prototyped as follows:

```
int DB->del(DB *db, DB_TXN *txnid, DBT *key, u_int32_t flags);
```

The meaning of the arguments is also the same as for the put function. Because you are not interested in the data, just in its key, there is no need to specify the value you want deleted. Deleting the key will delete its associated value. At the moment, no values have been specified for flags, so it should be 0. If the specified key is not found, del returns DB_NOTFOUND; otherwise, the standard return codes apply.

EXAMPLE

Example

The following program deletes records from a database:

```
/*
 * deldb.c - Delete a record from a Berkeley DB database
 */
#include <stdlib.h>
#include <stdio.h>
#include <errno.h>
#include <string.h>
#include "db.h"

int main(void)
{

    DB *db;
    int ret;
    DBT key;
```

```
        ret = db_open("test.db", DB_BTREE,
                    DB_CREATE, 0600, NULL, NULL, &db);
    if(ret) {
        perror("db_open");
        exit(EXIT_FAILURE);
    }

    /* Initialize the key first */
    memset(&key, 0, sizeof(key));
    /* The key we want to find */
    key.data = "one";
    key.size = strlen("one") + 1;
    /* Delete it */
    ret = db->del(db, NULL, &key, 0);
    if(ret == DB_NOTFOUND) {              /* The key does not exist */
        fprintf(stderr, "key %s not found\n", (char *)key.data);
        exit(EXIT_FAILURE);
    } else if(ret) {                      /* Some other error occurred */
        perror("del");
        exit(EXIT_FAILURE);
    }

    db->close(db, 0);
    exit(EXIT_SUCCESS);
}
```

If you run this program twice, on the second run it reports that the desired key, one, was not found:

```
$ ./deldb
$ ./deldb
key one not found
```

After opening the database, deldb attempts to delete a record that has the key, one. If the key exists, the del call deletes it and its associated value. The call can fail because the key does not exist, in which case del returns DB_NOTFOUND, or because some sort of system error occurred. Note also that the program used strlen("one") + 1 to set the key's size, instead of the sizeof operator in the previous example.

Retrieving Items from a Database

The get function is the simplest way to get records from the database. It requires that you know the key for the data you want. The prototype is as follows:

```
int get(DB *db, DB_TXN, *txnid, DBT *key, DBT *data, u_int32_t flags);
```

The meaning and uses of all of get's parameters are exactly the same as for the put call, except that get will fill in the structure referenced by data. If the specified key cannot be found, get returns DB_NOTFOUND. flags may be 0 or DB_GET_BOTH, in which case, get will retrieve the key/value pair only if both the key and value match the supplied values.

EXAMPLE

Example

The next program retrieves a value from the database and displays it.

```
/*
 * getdb.c - Get a record from a Berkeley DB database
 */


#include <stdlib.h>
#include <stdio.h>
#include <errno.h>
#include <string.h>
#include "db.h"

int main(void)
{
    DB *db;
    int ret;
    DBT key, value;

    ret = db_open("test.db", DB_BTREE,
                DB_CREATE, 0600, NULL, NULL, &db);
    if(ret) {
        perror("db_open");
        exit(EXIT_FAILURE);
    }

    /* Initialize the key/value pair first*/
    memset(&key, 0, sizeof(key));
```

```
        memset(&value, 0, sizeof(value));


        /* Set the values for key, value */
        key.data = "one";
        key.size = strlen("one") + 1;
        /* Store it */
        ret = db->get(db, NULL, &key, &value, 0);
        if(ret == DB_NOTFOUND)
            fprintf(stderr, "key %s not found\n", (char *)key.data);
        else if(ret)
            perror("get");
        else
            printf("data is %s\n", (char *)value.data);



        db->close(db, 0);
        exit(EXIT_SUCCESS);
}
```

The output from this program follows:

```
$ ./getdb
data is Compiling Programs
```

OUTPUT To make sure that the get operation succeeds, the program first adds the record it will be getting. Again, if the specified key is not found or if another error occurs, the program displays an appropriate error message and exits. Otherwise, the get call fills the value structure with the data that corresponds to key, and the program displays that information.

Navigating a Database

In the previous example, you saw how to find a particular record, given the key value. Often, however, you will not know the key for which you are looking or you will want to iterate through the database and visit each record in turn. Berkeley DB maintains a logical pointer, called a *cursor*, that you can move forward and backward through a database.

Before performing cursor operations, you must create a cursor associated with the database. The call to do so is cursor, which is prototyped as follows:

```
DB->cursor(DB *db, DB_TXN *txnid, DBC **cursorp, u_int32_t flags);
```

cursor creates a cursor named cursorp that references the database db. cursorp is, like the handle returned by db_open, a database handle, except that it is used only for cursor-related operations. As usual, txnid should be NULL. flags must always be 0. cursor returns the standard DB error codes discussed at the beginning of the chapter.

Cursoring through a database, as well as obtaining the record to which the cursor is pointing, is done using the c_get call, which is prototyped as follows:

```
DBcursor->c_get(DBC *cursor, DBT *key, DBT *data, u_int32_t flags);
```

c_get retrieves a key/value pair key/data from the database using the cursor cursor, which must have been initialized by an earlier call to DB->cursor. Common flags for c_get are listed in Table 10.1.

Table 10.1: Common Flags for **c_get**

Flag	Meaning
DB_FIRST	Return the first record from the database
DB_LAST	Return the last record from the database
DB_NEXT	Return the next record from the database (or the first one, if the cursor has just been opened)
DB_NEXT_DUP	Return the next record that is a duplicate of the current one
DB_PREV	Return the previous record from the database
DB_CURRENT	Return the current record from the database
DB_SET	Return the record from the database that matches the supplied key
DB_SET_RANGE	Return the smallest record greater than or equal to the supplied key

You can also use cursors to add key/value pairs to a database via the c_put function. Its prototype is as follows:

```
DBcursor->c_put(DBC *cursor, DBT *key, DBT *data, u_int32_t flags)
```

c_put stores the key/value pair referenced by key and value, respectively, in the database at the location pointed to by cursor. The exact behavior of c_put is controlled by flags, which may be one of DB_AFTER, which adds the record immediately after the current one, DB_BEFORE, which adds the record immediately before the current one, or DB_CURRENT, which replaces the current record. flags can also be DB_KEYFIRST or DB_KEYLAST to create the first or last of a set of duplicate keys, if the database has been configured to allow duplicates. Configuring a database to permit duplicate keys is an advanced topic beyond the scope of this book.

As you might expect, the c_del call deletes the current record. Its prototype is as follows:

```
DBcursor->c_del(DBC *cursor, u_int32_t flags);
```

c_del deletes the current record from the database, returning the standard error codes or DB_KEYEMPTY if the record has already been deleted.

After you have completed all cursor operations, but before you close the database itself, use c_close to discard the cursor. It has the following prototype:

```
DBcursor->c_close(DBC *cursor);
```

After c_close has been called, you cannot use the handle again.

Syncing a Database

When a database is closed, all the data held in memory is automatically flushed to disk. While working the database, you may also want to flush in-core memory to disk. The call for this purpose is sync and it is prototyped as follows:

```
int DB->sync(DB *db, u_int32_t flags);
```

db is a database handle returned by a previous call to db_open. flags is currently unused and must be set to 0.

Why use sync? Suppose you have added and deleted a large number of records. On a heavily loaded system, you should call sync periodically to make sure that your database is written to disk to prevent data loss. Flushing the cached data to disk is also an excellent way to prevent data loss or database corruption in the unlikely event of a system crash or sudden power loss. Similarly, if your program has installed a signal handler for SIGTERM, you should call sync (and probably db_close) to flush the database to disk.

EXAMPLE

Example

This program, cursor, illustrates simple cursor operations as well as the process of using the sync call.

```
/*
 * cursor.c - Using a cursor in a Berkeley DB database
 */
#include <stdlib.h>
#include <stdio.h>
#include <errno.h>
#include <string.h>
#include "db.h"
```

```c
int main(void)
{
    DB *db;
    DBC *dbc;
    DBT key, value;
    int ret;

    ret = db_open("test.db", DB_BTREE,
                  DB_CREATE, 0600, NULL, NULL, &db);
    if(ret) {
        perror("dbopen");
        exit(EXIT_FAILURE);
    }

    /* Create a cursor */
    ret = db->cursor(db, NULL, &dbc, 0);
    if(ret) {
        perror("cursor");
        exit(EXIT_FAILURE);
    }
    memset(&key, 0, sizeof(key));
    memset(&value, 0, sizeof(value));


    /* Move sequentially through the database */
    while((ret = dbc->c_get(dbc, &key, &value,
        DB_NEXT)) != DB_NOTFOUND) {
        printf("key/value is %s/%s\n", (char *)key.data,
               (char *)value.data);

    /* Sync the database */
    db->sync(db, 0);

    /* Close the cursor */
    dbc->c_close(dbc);

    db->close(db, 0);
    exit(EXIT_SUCCESS);
}
```

The output from this program follows:

```
$ ./cursor
key/value is five/Signals
key/value is four/Processes
key/value is one/Compiling Programs
key/value is three/About the Project
key/value is two/Controlling the Build Process
```

As you can see, marching sequentially through the database, the records are, in fact, stored in sorted order based on the record key. After opening the database and creating a cursor, the program continually calls c_get to retrieve the next record from the database and then displays both the key and its associated value. When c_get returns DB_NOTFOUND, there are no more records to retrieve. The sync call is not actually necessary because no data has been changed, but it is included to illustrate its use. Note also that cursor closes the database cursor, dbc, before it closes the database. Although it is not strictly required, it is a good habit to develop to make sure that all resources allocated by the DB interface are properly returned to the operating system.

NOTE

Although not discussed, I used the program addmore.c, also on the Web site, to add records to the database. It is part of the makefile for this chapter, so you can build it to complete this example. It prompts you to enter five records at a time.

What's Next?

This chapter introduced you to the Berkeley database, the first of several Linux APIs you will learn. The next two chapters show you how to use ncurses to control the appearance of character-mode screens. You will also learn to interact with mice, create menus, and draw forms.

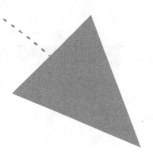

Screen Manipulation with ncurses

This chapter introduces *ncurses* (pronounced "en-curses"), the free implementation of the classic UNIX screen-handling library, *curses*. ncurses provides a simple, high-level interface for screen control and manipulation. It also contains powerful routines for handling keyboard and mouse input, creating and managing multiple windows, and using menus, forms, and panels. Topics this chapter include the following:

- ncurses' capabilities
- Terminology and concepts
- Initialization and termination routines
- Character and string output
- Character and string input

ncurses' Features

ncurses, which is short for "new curses," is a freely redistributable clone of the curses libraries distributed with the System V Release 4.0 (SVR4) of UNIX distributed by Bell Labs. The name "curses" is derived from the phrase "cursor optimization," which succinctly describes what curses does.

Terminal Independence

ncurses generalizes the interface between an application program and the screen or terminal on which it is running. Given the literally hundreds of varieties of terminals and screens, in particular the different features they possess and the commands to invoke them, UNIX programmers needed a way to abstract screen manipulation. Rather than write a lot of extra code to take into account the different terminal types, ncurses provides a uniform and generalized interface for the programmer. The ncurses API insulates the programmer from the underlying hardware.

Capabilities

ncurses gives to character-based applications many of the same features found in graphical X Window applications: multiple windows, forms, menus, and panels. ncurses' windows can be managed independently, may contain the same or different text, may or may not scroll, and can be hidden. The vi editor and the popular file manager Midnight Commander are written using ncurses.

Forms enable the programmer to create easy-to-use data entry and display windows, thus simplifying what is usually a difficult and application-specific coding task. Panels extend curses' capability to deal with overlapping and stacked windows. Menus, which give the user a simple interface to invoking application options, are easily implemented using ncurses' simple, generalized menu programming interface. The version used in this book is 4.2, although the 5.0 release is currently in beta.

Compiling with ncurses

To compile a program with ncurses, you need its function and variable definitions, so include <curses.h> in your source code:

```
#include <curses.h>
```

Many Linux systems make /usr/include/curses.h a symbolic link to /usr/include/ncurses.h, so you could conceivably include <ncurses.h>. However, for maximum portability, use <curses.h> because, believe it or not, ncurses is not available on all UNIX and UNIX-like platforms. You also need to link against the ncurses libraries, so use the -lcurses option when linking, or add `-lcurses` to the `LDFLAGS` make variable or the `$LDFLAGS` environment variable:

```
$ gcc curses_prog.c -o curses_prog -lcurses
```

By default, debug tracing is disabled in ncurses programs. To enable debugging, link against ncurses' debug library, `ncurses_g`, and either call `trace(N)` in your code or set the environment variable `$NCURSES_TRACE` to `N`, where `N` is a positive, non-zero integer. Doing so forces debugging output to a file named, appropriately, `trace`, in the current directory. The larger `N`'s value, the more detailed, and so more voluminous, the debugging output. Useful values for `N` are documented in `<ncurses.h>`. For example, the standard trace level, `TRACE_ORDINARY`, is 31.

Examples

EXAMPLE

1. This is the simplest possible ncurses program. It merely starts and stops the ncurses subsystem; no output is generated.

```
/*
 * simple.c - Simple ncurses program
 */
#include <curses.h>

int main(void)
{
    initscr();
    endwin();
    return 0;
}
```

To compile and execute it, type the following:

```
$ gcc simple.c -o simple -lcurses
```

OUTPUT

2. The next example uses the debugging library and makes a couple of extra function calls to generate output:

EXAMPLE

```
/*
 * debugit.c - ncurses program calling trace()
 */
#include <curses.h>

int main(void)
{
    initscr();
```

```
        trace(TRACE_CALLS);
        printw("set debug level to TRACE_CALLS");
        refresh();
        endwin();
        return 0;
}
```

The command line to compile this program is as follows:

```
$ gcc debugit.c -o debugit -lncurses_g
$ ./debugit
```

If you are really fast, you may see the message flash by on the screen! The trace call results in every ncurses function call being written to the file trace in the current directory. An excerpt of this file is reproduced here:

OUTPUT

```
TRACING NCURSES version 4.2 (990213)
printw("set debug level to TRACE_CALLS",...) called
called waddnstr(0x80675f8,"set debug level to TRACE_CALLS",-1)
... current {A_NORMAL}
return 0
called wrefresh(0x80675f8)
clearing and updating from scratch
ClrUpdate() called
ClearScreen() called
screen cleared
updating screen from scratch
return 0
TransformLine(0) called
TransformLine(1) called
...
TransformLine(24) called
return 0
called endwin()
return 0
```

TIP

The ncurses package comes with a script, tracemunch, that compresses and summarizes the debug information into a more readable, human-friendly format.

Terminology and Concepts

This section explains some terms and concepts that come up repeatedly when discussing ncurses.

Terms

A *screen* refers to the physical terminal screen in character or console mode. Under the X Window system, screen means a terminal emulator window. *Window* is used to refer to an independent rectangular area displayed on a screen. It may or may not be the same size as the screen.

ncurses programming relies on two pointers to data structures called WINDOWs (that is, struct WINDOW *s), stdscr and curscr. stdscr represents what you currently see on the screen. It might be one window or a set of windows, but it fills the entire screen. Think of it as a palette on which you paint using ncurses routines. curscr contains ncurses' idea of what the screen currently looks like. Like stdscr, its size is the width and height of the screen. Differences between curscr and stdscr are the changes that appear on the screen.

Refresh refers both to an ncurses function call and a logical process. The refresh function compares curscr, ncurses' notion of what the screen currently looks like, to stdscr, copies any differences between stdscr and curscr to curscr, and then displays those updates to the screen. Refresh also refers to the process of updating the screen.

Cursor, like refresh, has two similar meanings, but always refers to the location where the next character will be displayed. On a screen (the physical screen), cursor refers to the location of the physical cursor. On a window (an ncurses window), cursor refers to the logical location where the next character will be displayed. In this chapter, the second meaning generally applies. ncurses uses a (y,x) ordered pair to locate the cursor on a window.

Window Layout

ncurses defines window layout sanely and predictably. Windows are arranged such that the upper-left corner has the coordinates (0,0) and the lower-right corner has the coordinates (LINES-1, COLUMNS-1), as Figure 11.1 illustrates.

ncurses maintains two global variables, LINES and COLS, that contain ncurses' idea of the number of rows and columns, respectively, of the current window's size. Rather than using these global variables, however, use the function call getmaxyx to get the size of the window with which you are currently working.

Figure 11.1: *ncurses' window layout.*

Example

This example uses `getmaxyx` to show how many lines and columns the current window has.

```
/*
 * cols.c - How many lines and columns?
 */
#include <curses.h>

int main(void)
{
    int x, y;

    initscr();
    getmaxyx(stdscr, y, x);
    printw("maximum lines = %d\n", y);
    printw("maximim columns = %d\n", x);
    refresh();
    sleep(3);
    endwin();
    return 0;
}
```

The window this program creates is illustrated in Figure 11.2.

Figure 11.2: getmaxyx *returns a window's maximum number of lines and columns.*

Function Naming Conventions

Although many of ncurses' functions are defined to use stdscr by default, there will be many situations in which you want to operate on a window other than stdscr. ncurses uses a systematic and consistently applied naming convention for routines that can apply to any window. Functions that can operate on an arbitrary window are prefixed with the character "w" and take a (WINDOW *) variable as their first argument.

For example, the move call, which moves the cursor on stdscr, can be replaced by wmove, which moves the cursor on a specific window.

NOTE

Actually, most of the functions that apply to stdscr are pseudo-functions. They are #defined preprocessor macros that use stdscr as the default window in calls to the window-specific functions. This is an implementation detail with which you need not trouble yourself, but it may help you better understand the ncurses library. A quick grep '#define' /usr/include/ncurses.h will reveal the extent to which ncurses uses macros and will also serve as a good example of preprocessor usage.

Likewise, many ncurses input and output functions have forms that combine a move and an I/O operation in a single call. These functions prepend mv to the function name and the desired (y, x) coordinates to the argument list. So, for example, a move followed by addchstr can be combined to create mvaddchstr.

You have probably surmised by now that functions also exist that combine an I/O and a move directed to a specific window. So, wmove and waddchstr are the same as mvwaddchstr.

This sort of shorthand permeates ncurses. The convention is simple and makes for fewer lines of code.

Examples

1. The first example shows how `move`, which operates on `stdscr`, becomes `wmove`, which works on any window. The function

```
move(y, x);
```

is equivalent to

```
wmove(stdscr, y, x);
```

2. This example shows how `move` and `addchstr` become a single function. The two calls

```
move(y, x);
addchstr(str);
```

are equivalent to the single call:

```
mvaddchstr(y, x, str);
```

3. The following code snippet demonstrates the combination of `wmove` and `waddchstr`. The two calls

```
wmove(some_win, y, x);
waddchstr(some_win, str);
```

are identical to the single call

```
mvwaddchstr(some_win, y, x, str)
```

Initialization and Termination

Before you can use ncurses, you must properly initialize the ncurses subsystem, set up various ncurses data structures, and query the underlying terminal's display capabilities and characteristics.

ncurses Initialization

The `initscr` and `newterm` functions handle ncurses initialization requirements. `initscr` has two tasks, to create and initialize `stdscr` and `curscr`, and to find out the terminal's capabilities and characteristics by querying the terminfo or termcap database. If it is unable to complete one of these tasks, or if some other error occurs, `initscr` displays useful diagnostic information and terminates the application. For example, `initscr` will fail if the `$TERM` environment variable is not set to a terminal type that ncurses recognizes. In this case, `initscr` aborts with the error message "Error opening terminal: unknown."

Call `initscr` before you use any other routines that manipulate `stdscr` or `curscr`. Failure to do so will cause your application to abort with a segmentation fault. At the same time, however, call `initscr` only when you are certain you need it, such as after other routines that check for program startup errors. Functions that change a terminal's status, such as cbreak or noecho, should be called after initscr returns. The first call to refresh after initscr will clear the screen. If the call succeeds, initscr returns a pointer to stdscr, which you can save for later use; otherwise, the call returns NULL and exits the program, printing a useful error message to the display.

If your program will send output to or receive input from more than one terminal, use the newterm function call instead of initscr. For each terminal with which you expect to interact, call newterm once. newterm returns a pointer to a C data structure of type SCREEN (another ncurses-defined type), which is used when referring to that terminal. Before you can send output to or receive input from such a terminal, you must make it the current terminal. The set_term call accomplishes this. Pass as set_term's argument the pointer to the SCREEN (returned by a previous newterm call) that you want to make the current terminal.

Example

EXAMPLE

This program, initcurs, shows the standard ncurses initialization and termination idioms, using initscr and endwin. Figure 11.3 shows the window this program creates.

```c
/*
 * initcurs.c - curses initialization and termination
 */
#include <stdlib.h>
#include <curses.h>


int main(void)
{
    if((initscr()) == NULL) {
    perror("initscr");
        exit(EXIT_FAILURE);
    printw("This is an ncurses window\n");
    refresh();
    sleep(3);

    printw("Going bye-bye now\n");
    refresh();
    sleep(3);
```

```
        endwin();

        exit(0);
}
```

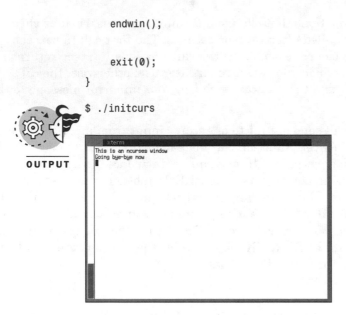

$ ./initcurs

OUTPUT

Figure 11.3: ncurses window after initialization.

The necessary function declarations and variable definitions are declared in
<curses.h>. Because there is no startup code, initialize ncurses' data struc-
tures with the call to initscr. (Ordinarily, you want to save the WINDOW
* it returns for later use.) Using the printw function (covered in more detail
in the next section), the program displays some output to the window after
calling refresh so the output will actually appear on the screen. After a
three-second pause, the endwin call, covered in the next section, "ncurses
Termination," terminates the program and frees the resources initscr
allocated.

ncurses Termination

Before exiting an ncurses-based application, you need to return the memory
resources that ncurses allocates and reset the terminal to its original, pre-
ncurses state. The initialization functions allocate memory resources and
reset the terminal state to an ncurses-friendly mode.

Accordingly, you need to free the allocated memory and reset the terminal
to its pre-ncurses mode. The termination functions endwin and delscreen do
this job. When you are through working with a SCREEN, call endwin before
making another terminal the current terminal, and then call delscreen on
that terminal to release the SCREEN resources allocated to it, because
endwin does not release memory for screens created by newterm.

If you have not called newterm, however, and have only used curscr and stdscr, all that is required is a single call to endwin before exiting. endwin moves the cursor to the lower-left corner of the screen, and resets the terminal to its non-visual, pre-ncurses state. The memory allocated to curscr and stdscr is not released because your program can temporarily suspend ncurses by calling endwin, perform other processing, and then call refresh to restore the screen.

Example

The sample program that follows, newterm, illustrates ncurses initialization and termination using newterm and delscreen.

EXAMPLE

```
/*
 * newterm.c -curses initialization and termination
 */
#include <stdlib.h>
#include <curses.h>

int main(void)
{
    SCREEN *scr;

    if((scr = newterm(NULL, stdout, stdin)) == NULL) {
        perror("newterm");
        exit(EXIT_FAILURE);
    }

    if(set_term(scr) == NULL) {
        endwin();
        delscreen(scr);
        perror("set_term");
        exit(EXIT_FAILURE);
    }

    printw("This curses window created with newterm\n");
    refresh();
    sleep(3);

    printw("Going bye-bye now\n");
    refresh();
```

```
        sleep(3);
        endwin();
        delscreen(scr);

        exit(0);
}
```

This program's output closely resembles Figure 11.3. In this program, newterm initializes the curses subsystem, pretending to be interacting with a different terminal. However, input and output will still be coming from and going to the standard locations, so stdout and stdin are the FILE pointers for outfd and infd.

Before the program can use scr, however, it has to make it the current terminal, thus the call to set_term. If the call fails, you have to make sure to call endwin and delscreen to free the memory associated with scr, hence the added code before the err_quit call. After sending some output to the "terminal," the program shuts down the curses subsystem using the required delscreen call.

Output

ncurses has many functions for sending output to screens and windows. It is important to understand that C's standard output routines *do not* work with ncurses' windows because ncurses takes over output on the terminal. Fortunately, ncurses' I/O routines behave very similarly to the standard I/O (<stdio.h>) routines, so the learning curve is tolerably flat. For the purposes of this discussion, ncurses' output routines have been divided into character, string, and miscellaneous categories. The following sections discuss each of these categories in detail.

Character Output

ncurses' core character output function is addch, prototyped in <ncurses.h> as

```
int addch(chtype ch);
```

Almost all the other output functions do their work with calls to addch. It displays the character ch in the current window (normally stdscr) at the cursor's current position and advances the cursor to the next position. If doing so would place the cursor beyond the right margin, the cursor automatically wraps to the beginning of the next line. If the cursor is positioned at the bottom of the window, it scrolls up one line. If ch is a tab, newline, or backspace, the cursor moves appropriately. Other control characters display using ^X notation, where X is the character and the caret (^) indicates that it is a control character. If you need to send the literal control character, use the function echochar(chtype ch).

NOTE

The ncurses documentation refers to characters typed in chtype format as "pseudo-characters." ncurses declares pseudo-characters as unsigned long integers, using the high bits of these characters to carry additional information, such as video attributes. This distinction between pseudo-characters and normal C characters (the char type) implies subtle differences in the behavior of functions that handle each type. These differences are noted in this chapter when and where appropriate.

As mentioned previously, mvaddch adds a character to a specified window after moving the cursor to the desired location; mvwaddch combines a move and an output operation on a specific window. waddch displays a character to a user-specified window. The echochar function, and its window-specific cousin, wechochar, combine an addch call with a refresh or wrefresh call. This combination can result in substantial performance enhancements when used with non-control characters.

A particularly useful feature of ncurses routines that use chtype characters and strings (discussed next) is that the character or string to be output can be logically ORed with a variety of video attributes before it is displayed. A partial list of these attributes includes:

- A_NORMAL—Normal display mode
- A_STANDOUT—Use the terminal's best highlighting mode
- A_UNDERLINE—Underlining
- A_REVERSE—Use reverse video
- A_BLINK—Blinking text
- A_DIM—Half-intensity display
- A_BOLD—Extra-intensity display
- A_INVIS—Character will not be visible
- A_CHARTEXT—Creates a bitmask to extract a character

Depending on the terminal emulator or hardware capabilities of the screen, not all attributes may be possible or will necessarily display correctly, however. See the curs_attr(3) manual page for more details.

In addition to control characters and characters enhanced with video attributes, the character output functions also display line graphics characters (characters from the high half of the ASCII character set, 128–255), such as box-drawing characters and various special symbols. A complete list is available in the curs_addch(3) manual page. A few of the common line graphics characters are listed here:

- ACS_ULCORNER—Upper-left corner
- ACS_LLCORNER—Lower-left corner
- ACS_URCORNER—Upper-right corner
- ACS_LRCORNER—Lower-right corner
- ACS_HLINE—Horizontal line
- ACS_VLINE—Vertical line

The functions described so far effectively "append" characters to a window without disturbing the placement of other characters already present. Another group of routines inserts characters at arbitrary locations in existing window text. These functions include insch, winsch, mvinsch, and mvwinsch.

Following the naming convention discussed earlier in this chapter, each of these functions inserts a character before (in front of) the character under the cursor, shifting the following characters to the right one position. If the right-most character is on the right margin, it will be lost. Note, however, that the cursor position does not change after an insert operation. Insertions are completely documented in the curs_insch(3) manual page. The prototypes of the functions mentioned so far are in the following list:

```
int addch(chtype ch);

int waddch(WINDOW *win, chtype ch);

int mvaddch(int y, int x, chtype ch);

int mvwaddch(WINDOW *win, int y, int x, chtype ch);

int echochar(chtype ch);

int wechochar(WINDOW *win, chtype ch);

int insch(chtype ch);

int winsch(WINDOW *win, chtype ch);

int mvinsch(int y, int x, chtype ch);

int mvwinsch(WINDOW *win, int y, int x, chtype ch);
```

Unless noted otherwise, all functions that return an integer return OK on success or ERR on failure (OK and ERR and a number of other constants are defined in <ncurses.h>). The arguments win, y, x, and ch are, respectively, the window in which the character will be displayed, the y and x coordinates at which to locate the cursor, and the character (including optional attributes) to display.

As a reminder, routines prefixed with a "w" take a pointer, win, which specifies the target window; the "mv" prefix combines a move operation to the (y, x) location with an output operation.

Example

The following program illustrates some of ncurses' character output functions. Figure 11.4 shows the ncurses character output.

The following programs illustrate how many of the routines discussed in this section might be used. To shorten the examples somewhat, initialization and termination code has been moved into a separate file, utilfcns.c. The header file containing the interface—utilfcns.h—is also included. (Both files are on the Web site that accompanies the book).

```c
/*
 * curschar.c - ncurses character output functions
 */
#include <stdlib.h>
#include <curses.h>
#include <errno.h>
#include "utilfcns.h"

int main(void)
{
    app_init();

    addch('X');
    addch('Y' | A_REVERSE);
    mvaddch(2, 1, 'Z' | A_BOLD);
    refresh();
    sleep(3);

    clear();
    waddch(stdscr, 'X');
    waddch(stdscr, 'Y' | A_REVERSE);
    mvwaddch(stdscr, 2, 1, 'Z' | A_BOLD);
    refresh();
    sleep(3);

    app_exit();
}
```

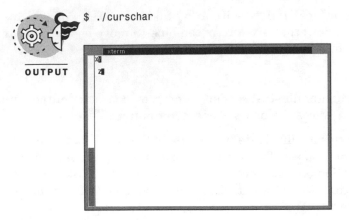

$ ./curschar

Figure 11.4: *ncurses character output.*

The addch routine outputs the desired character and advances the cursor. The two waddch calls illustrate how to combine video attributes with the character to display. The code also demonstrates a typical "mv"-prefixed function. After refreshing the screen, a short pause allows you to view the output. The second half of the program shows how to use the window-specific routines, using stdscr as the target window.

String Output

ncurses' string routines generally behave similarly to the character routines, except that they deal with strings of pseudo-characters or with normal null-terminated strings. Again, ncurses' designers created a standard notation to help programmers distinguish between the two types of functions. Function names containing chstr operate on strings of pseudo-characters, whereas function names containing only str use standard C-style (null-terminated) strings. A partial list of the functions operating on pseudo-character strings includes

```
int addchstr(const chtype *chstr);

int addchnstr(const chtype *chstr, int n);

int waddchstr(WINDOW *win, const chtype *chstr);

int waddchnstr(WINDOW *win, const chtype *chstr, int n);

int mvaddchstr(int y, int x, const chtype *chstr);

int mvaddchnstr(int y, int x, const chtype *chstr, int n);

int mvwaddchstr(WINDOW *win, int y, int x, const chtype *chstr);

int mvwaddchnstr(WINDOW *win, int y, int x, const chtype *chstr, int n);
```

All the listed functions copy chstr onto the desired window beginning at the cursor's location, but the cursor is not advanced (unlike the character output functions). If the string will not fit on the current line, it is truncated at the right margin. The four routines taking an int n argument—addchnstr, waddchnstr, mvaddchnstr, and mvwaddchnstr—copy a limit of up to n characters, stopping at the right margin. If n is –1, the entire string will be copied, but truncated at the right margin as necessary.

The next set of string output functions operates on null-terminated strings. Unlike the previous set, these functions advance the cursor. In addition, the string output will wrap at the right margin, rather than being truncated. Otherwise, the calls behave like their similarly named chtype counterparts.

```
int addstr(const char *str);

int addnstr(const char *str, int n);

int waddstr(WINDOW *win, const char *str);

int waddnstr(WINDOW *win, const char *str, int n);

int mvaddstr(int y, int x, const char *str tr);

int mvaddnstr(int y, int x, const char *str, int n);

int mvwaddstr(WINDOWS *win, int y, int x, const char *str);

int mvwaddnstr(WINDOWS *win, int y, int x, const char *str, int n);
```

Remember, str in these routines is a standard, C-style, null-terminated character array.

Example

This sample program demonstrates using the string output functions.

```
/*
 * cursstr.c - ncurses string output functions
 */
#include <stdlib.h>
#include <curses.h>
#include <errno.h>
#include "utilfcns.h"

int main(void)
{
    int xmax, ymax;
    WINDOW *tmpwin;
```

```
    app_init();
    getmaxyx(stdscr, ymax, xmax);

    addstr("Using the *str() family\n");
    hline(ACS_HLINE, xmax);
    mvaddstr(3, 0, "This string appears in full\n");
    mvaddnstr(5, 0, "This string is truncated\n", 15);
    refresh();
    sleep(3);

    if((tmpwin = newwin(0, 0, 0, 0)) == NULL)
        err_quit("newwin");

    mvwaddstr(tmpwin, 1, 1, "This message should appear in a new window");
    wborder(tmpwin, 0, 0, 0, 0, 0, 0, 0, 0);
    touchwin(tmpwin);
    wrefresh(tmpwin);
    sleep(3);

    delwin(tmpwin);
    app_exit();
}
```

The getmaxyx call on line 16 retrieves the number of columns and lines for stdscr—this routine is usually implemented as a macro, so its calling syntax does not require that ymax and xmax be pointers. The call of mvaddnstr with a value of n=15 forces the string printed to be truncated before the letter "t" in "truncated." Next, the program creates the new window, tmpwin, with the same dimensions as the current screen. Then it scribbles a message into the new window, draws a border around it, and calls refresh to display it on the screen. Before exiting, calling delwin on the window frees its resources.

The output of this program is illustrated in Figures 11.5 and 11.6.

Figure 11.5: *ncurses' *str() output functions.*

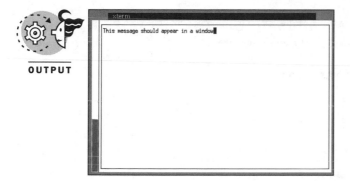

Figure 11.6: *String output in a window.*

Miscellaneous Output

The next and last group of output routines to consider are a hodgepodge of calls that draw borders and lines, clear and set the background, control output options, move the cursor, and send formatted output to an ncurses window. ncurses' "miscellaneous" output routines comprise a wide variety of calls. The most common ones are discussed in this section.

To begin with, to set a window's background property, use the set background call, bkgd, prototyped as follows:

```
int bkgd(const chtype ch);
```

ch is a logically ORed combination of the character you want to display and one or more of the video attributes previously listed. To obtain the current background setting, call

```
chtype getbkgd(WINDOW *win);
```

where `win` is the window in question. Complete descriptions of functions that set and get window backgrounds can be found in the `curs_bkgd(3)` manual page.

At least 11 ncurses functions draw boxes, borders, and lines in ncurses windows. The `box` call is the simplest; it draws a box around a specified window using one character for vertical lines and another for horizontal lines. Its prototype is listed here:

```
int box(WINDOW *win, chtype verch, chtype horch);
```

`verch` sets the pseudo-character used to draw vertical lines and `horch` sets the same for horizontal lines.

The `box` call is actually a macro, and is shorthand for the more general `wborder` function:

```
int border(WINDOW *win, chtype ls, chtype rs, chtype ts, chtype bs,
➥chtype tl, chtype tr, chtype bl, chtype br);
```

The arguments are as follows:

- `ls`—Left side
- `rs`—Right side
- `ts`—Top side
- `bs`—Bottom side
- `tl`—Top-left corner
- `tr`—Top-right corner
- `bl`—Bottom-left corner
- `br`—Bottom-right corner

Both the `box` and the `wborder` calls draw an outline on the window along its left, right, top, and bottom margins.

Use the `hline` function to draw a horizontal line of arbitrary length on the current window. `vline`, similarly, draws a vertical line of arbitrary length.

```
int hline(chtype ch, int n);
int vline(chtype ch, int n);
```

By following ncurses' function naming convention, you can also specify a window in which to draw lines using the functions listed here:

```
int whline(WINDOW *win, chtype ch, int n);
int wvline(WINDOW *win, chtype ch, int n);
```

If you want, you can move the cursor to a particular location before drawing the lines using the following functions:

```
int mvhline(int y, int x, chtype ch, int n);
int mvvline(int y, int x, chtype ch, int n);
```

You can even specify a window and request a move operation with these
two functions:

```
int mvwhline(WINDOW *win, int y, int x, chtype ch, int n);
int mvwvline(WINDOW *win, int y, int x, chtype ch, int n);
```

As usual, these routines return OK on success or ERR on failure. win indicates the target window; n specifies the maximum line length, up to the
maximum window size vertically or horizontally. The line, box, and border
drawing functions do not change the cursor position. Subsequent output
operations can overwrite the borders, so you must make sure either to
include calls to maintain border integrity or to set up your output calls such
that they do not overwrite the borders.

Functions that do not specifically set the cursor location (line, vline,
whline, and wvline) start drawing at the current cursor position. The
manual page documenting these routines is curs_border(3). The
curs_outopts(3) page also contains relevant information.

The final set of miscellaneous functions to consider clear all or part of the
screen. As usual, they are available in both plain and window-specific
varieties:

```
int erase(void);
int werase(WINDOW *win);
int clear(void);
int wclear(WINDOW *win);
int clrtobot(void);
int wclrtobot(WINDOW *win);
int clrtoeol(void);
int wclrtoeol(WINDOW *win);
```

erase writes blanks to every position in a window; clrtobot clears the
screen from the current cursor location to the bottom of the window, inclusive; clrtoeol, finally, erases the current line from the cursor to the right
margin, inclusive.

If you have used bkgd or wbkgd to set background properties on windows
that will be cleared or erased, the property set (called a "rendition" in

ncurses' documentation) is applied to each of the blanks created. The relevant manual page for these calls is `curs_clear(3)`.

EXAMPLE

Example

This program illustrates using line graphics characters and the `box` and `wborder` calls. Some ncurses output routines move the cursor after the output, others do not. Note also that the line drawing family of functions, such as `vline` and `hline`, draw top to bottom and left to right, so be aware of cursor placement when using them.

```c
/*
 * cursbox.c - ncurses box drawing functions
 */
#include <stdlib.h>
#include <curses.h>
#include <errno.h>
#include "utilfcns.h"

int main(void)
{
    int ymax, xmax;

    app_init();
    getmaxyx(stdscr, ymax, xmax);

    mvaddch(0, 0, ACS_ULCORNER);
    hline(ACS_HLINE, xmax - 2);
    mvaddch(ymax - 1, 0, ACS_LLCORNER);
    hline(ACS_HLINE, xmax - 2);
    mvaddch(0, xmax - 1, ACS_URCORNER);
    vline(ACS_VLINE, ymax - 2);
    mvvline(1, xmax - 1, ACS_VLINE, ymax - 2);
    mvaddch(ymax - 1, xmax - 1, ACS_LRCORNER);
    mvprintw(ymax / 3 - 1, (xmax - 30) / 2, "border
➥drawn the hard way");
    refresh();
    sleep(3);

    clear();
    box(stdscr, ACS_VLINE, ACS_HLINE);
```

```
mvprintw(ymax / 3 - 1, (xmax - 30) / 2, "border
►drawn the easy way");
refresh();
sleep(3);

clear();
wborder(stdscr, ACS_VLINE | A_BOLD,
►ACS_VLINE | A_BOLD, ACS_HLINE | A_BOLD,
►ACS_HLINE | A_BOLD, ACS_ULCORNER | A_BOLD,
►ACS_URCORNER | A_BOLD, ACS_LLCORNER | A_BOLD,
►ACS_LRCORNER | A_BOLD);
mvprintw(ymax / 3 - 1, (xmax - 25) / 2, "border
►drawn with wborder");
refresh();
sleep(3);

app_exit();
}
```

Figures 11.7 and 11.8 show the output from this program.

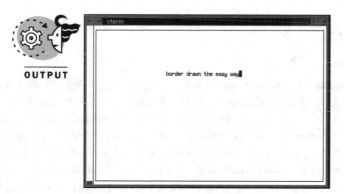

Figure 11.7: *A border drawn using lines.*

As you might expect, the mvvline call moves the cursor before drawing a vertical line. After all the gyrations to draw a simple border, the box routine is a breeze to use. The wborder function is more verbose than box, but it does allow finer control over the characters used to draw the border. The example illustrated the default character for each argument, but any character (and optional video attributes) will do, provided it is supported by the underlying emulator or video hardware.

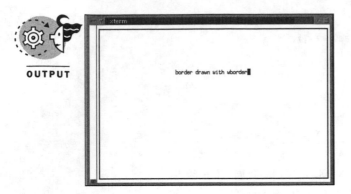

OUTPUT

Figure 11.8: *A border drawn using wborder.*

Input Routines

ncurses input routines, like its output routines, fall into several groups. This chapter focuses, however, on simple character and string input for two reasons. First and foremost, the routines discussed in this section will meet 90 percent of your needs. Second, ncurses input closely parallels ncurses output, so the material from the previous section should serve as a solid foundation.

Character Input

The core input functions can be narrowed down to three: getch, getstr, and scanw. getch's prototype is

```
int getch(void);
```

getch fetches a single character from the keyboard, returning the character or ERR on failure. It may or may not echo the fetched character back to stdscr, depending on whether echoing is enabled or disabled (thus, wgetch and variants also obtain single characters from the keyboard and may or may not echo them to a program-specified window). For characters to be echoed, first call echo; to disable echoing, call noecho. Be aware that with echoing enabled, characters are displayed on a window using waddch at the current cursor location, which is then advanced one position.

The matter is further complicated by the current input mode, which determines the amount of processing the kernel applies to the input before the program receives the character. In an ncurses program, you will generally want to process most of the keystrokes yourself. Doing so requires either crmode or raw mode. (ncurses begins in default mode, meaning that the kernel buffers text by waiting for a newline before passing keystrokes to ncurses—you will rarely want this.)

In *raw mode*, the kernel does not buffer or otherwise process any input, while in *crmode*, the kernel processes terminal control characters, such as ^S, ^Q, ^C, or ^Y, and passes all others to ncurses unmolested. On some systems, the literal "next character," ^V, may need to repeated. Depending on your application's needs, crmode should be sufficient. In one of the following sample programs, crmode is used and echoing is enabled and disabled in order to simulate shadowed password retrieval.

Example

This program uses crmode and noecho to simulate a password-checking program.

EXAMPLE

```
/*
 * cursinch.c - ncurses character input functions
 */
#include <stdlib.h>
#include <curses.h>
#include <errno.h>
#include "utilfcns.h"

int main(void)
{
    int c, i = 0;
    int xmax, ymax;
    char str[80];
    WINDOW *pwin;

    app_init();
    crmode();
    getmaxyx(stdscr, ymax, xmax);
    if((pwin = subwin(stdscr, 3, 40, ymax / 3,
    ➥(xmax - 40) / 2 )) == NULL)
        err_quit("subwin");
    box(pwin, ACS_VLINE, ACS_HLINE);
    mvwaddstr(pwin, 1, 1, "Password: ");

    noecho();
    while((c = getch()) != '\n' && i < 80) {
        str[i++] = c;
        waddch(pwin, '*');
        wrefresh(pwin);
```

```
    }
    echo();
    str[i] = '\0';
    wrefresh(pwin);

    mvwprintw(pwin, 1, 1, "You typed: %s\n", str);
    box(pwin, ACS_VLINE, ACS_HLINE);
    wrefresh(pwin);
    sleep(3);

    delwin(pwin);
    app_exit();
}
```

The screens this program creates are illustrated in Figures 11.9 and 11.10.

Figure 11.9: *Prompting for a password.*

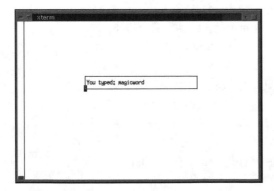

Figure 11.10: *ncurses' noecho mode.*

String Input

The `getstr` function, declared as

```
int getstr(char *str);
```

repeatedly calls `getch` until it encounters a newline or carriage return (which will not be part of the returned string). The characters input are stored in `str`. Because `getstr` performs no bounds checking, you should use `getnstr` instead, which takes an additional argument specifying the maximum number of characters to store. Regardless of whether you use `getstr` or `getnstr`, the receiving buffer `str` must be large enough to hold the string received plus a terminating null character, which must be added programmatically. `getnstr`'s prototype follows:

```
int getnstr(char *str, int n);
```

`getnstr` copies a maximum of n characters from `stdscr` to the buffer to which `str` points. Input beyond a count of n causes a beep.

`scanw` obtains formatted input from the keyboard in the manner of `scanf(3)` and family. In fact, ncurses passes the received characters as input to `sscanf(3)`, so input that does not map to available arguments in the format field goes to the bit bucket. As usual, `scanw` has variants for movement operations (the "mv" prefix) and variants that apply to specific windows (the "w" prefix). In addition, the `scanw` family of functions includes a member for dealing with variable length argument lists, `vwscanw`. The relevant prototypes are as follows:

```
int scanw(char *fmt [, arg] ...);
int vwscanw(WINDOW *win, char *fmt, va_list varglist);
```

The manual pages `curs_getch(3)`, `curs_getstr(3)`, and `curs_scanw(3)` fully document these routines and their various permutations.

EXAMPLE

Example

```
/*
 * cursgstr.c - ncurses string input functions
 */
#include <stdlib.h>
#include <curses.h>
#include <errno.h>
#include <string.h>
#include "utilfcns.h"

#define BUFSZ 20
```

```
int main(int argc, char *argv[])
{
    int c, i = 0;
    char str[20];
    char *pstr;

    app_init();
    crmode();

    printw("File to open: ");
    refresh();
    getnstr(str, BUFSZ);
    printw("You typed: %s\n", str);
    refresh();
    sleep(3);

    if((pstr = malloc(sizeof(char) * BUFSZ + 1)) == NULL)
        err_quit("malloc");

    printw("Enter your name: ");
    refresh();
    getnstr(pstr, 20);
    printw("You entered: %s\n", pstr);
    refresh();
    sleep(3);

    free(pstr);
    app_exit();
}
```

Figure 11.11 shows the program running.

Echoing remains enabled in this program because the users likely want to see what they are typing. The program uses getstr first to obtain the name of the file to open. In a "real" program, you would attempt to open the file whose name is typed. getnstr illustrates ncurses' behavior when you attempt to enter a string longer than indicated by the length limit n. In this case, ncurses stops accepting and echoing input and issues a beep after the users have typed 20 characters.

Figure 11.11: *Using ncurses' string input routines.*

What's Next?

This chapter introduced you to the ncurses API, an interface for controlling the screen in character-based programs. Although Linux is an advanced and sophisticated operating system, it still has many character based (non-GUI) applications that are very popular, so it is important to understand how to write applications that manipulate text mode screens. The next chapter continues exploring ncurses by focusing on using color, creating menus, accepting mouse input, and drawing forms and panels.

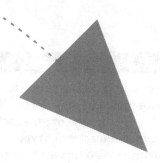

## 12

Advanced ncurses Programming

This chapter picks up where the last one left off. It explores many of ncurses' advanced features that enable to you create a more attractive and easy-to-use interface for your character mode programs. Topics covered in this chapter include the following:

- Using ncurses' color subsystem

- Creating and manipulating windows

- Interacting with the mouse

- Working with menus

- Using forms in ncurses programs

Using Color

You have already seen that ncurses supports various highlighting modes. Interestingly, it also supports color in the same fashion; that is, you can logically OR the desired color value onto the character arguments of an addch call or any other output routine that takes a pseudo-character (chtype) argument. The method is tedious, however, so ncurses also has a set of routines to set display attributes on a per-window basis.

Before you use ncurses' color capabilities, you have to make sure that the current terminal supports color. The has_colors call returns TRUE or FALSE depending on whether the current terminal has color capabilities. has_colors has the following syntax:

```
bool has_colors(void);
```

The bool return value is defined in <curses.h>.

ncurses' default colors are as follows:

- COLOR_BLACK
- COLOR_RED
- COLOR_GREEN
- COLOR_YELLOW
- COLOR_BLUE
- COLOR_MAGENTA
- COLOR_CYAN
- COLOR_WHITE

After you have determined that the terminal supports color, call the start_color function to start ncurses' color subsystem. Its prototype is

```
int start_color(void);
```

NOTE

Programs using ncurses' color routines must be run on a terminal emulator that supports color, such as a color xterm, rxvt, or nxterm.

Before you can use colors, however, you must initialize a set of color pairs. Doing so associates colors to the color pairs in the previous list. The function that does this is init_pair, prototyped as follows:

```
int init_pair(short pair, short f, short b);
```

This associates pair with a foreground color f and a background color b and returns OK on success or ERR on failure.

Rather than tediously ORing color values into chtype calls, use the attron and attroff calls. The prototypes for these two functions are as follows:

```
int attron(int attrs);
int attroff(int attrs);
```

attrs can be one or more logically ORed combinations of colors and video attributes. They both return OK on success or ERR if an error occurred.

EXAMPLE

Example

The following program draws colored lines on the screen:

```
/*
 * color.c - curses color management
 */
#include <stdlib.h>
#include <curses.h>
#include <errno.h>
#include <unistd.h>
#include "utilfcns.h"

int main(void)
{
    int n, maxx, maxy;
    char *str;

    app_init();

    if(!has_colors()) {
    printw("Terminal does not support color\n");
    refresh();
    sleep(3);
    exit(EXIT_FAILURE);
    }
    if(start_color() == ERR)
    err_quit("start_color");

    /* Set up some simple color assignments */
    init_pair(COLOR_BLACK, COLOR_BLACK, COLOR_BLACK);
    init_pair(COLOR_GREEN, COLOR_GREEN, COLOR_BLACK);
    init_pair(COLOR_RED, COLOR_RED, COLOR_BLACK);
```

```
    init_pair(COLOR_CYAN, COLOR_CYAN, COLOR_BLACK);
    init_pair(COLOR_WHITE, COLOR_WHITE, COLOR_BLACK);
    init_pair(COLOR_MAGENTA, COLOR_MAGENTA, COLOR_BLACK);
    init_pair(COLOR_BLUE, COLOR_BLUE, COLOR_BLACK);
    init_pair(COLOR_YELLOW, COLOR_YELLOW, COLOR_BLACK);

    getmaxyx(stdscr, maxy, maxx);
    if((str = malloc(sizeof(char) * maxx)) == NULL)
    err_quit("malloc");

    for(n = 1; n <= 8; n++) {
    memset(str, ACS_BLOCK, maxx);
    attron(COLOR_PAIR(n));
    printw("%s", str);
    refresh();
    }
    sleep(3);

    app_exit();
    exit(EXIT_SUCCESS);
}
```

The first conditional ensures that the terminal supports color before contin-
uing; it exits gracefully if there isn't color support. After initializing the
color system, it makes some simple color assignments using init_pair.
After the color assignments, the program draws lines filled with # across
the terminal, using memset and attron to set the current display attributes
for the current window, in this case, stdscr. attroff turns off standout
mode before moving to the next color pair.

As usual, ncurses comes with an extensive set of functions for manipulating
window display attributes. They are fully documented in the curs_attr
manual page. The curs_color manual pages discuss ncurses' color-
manipulation interface in considerable detail.

The output from this program is shown in Figure 12.1. Unfortunately, the
colors appear only as shades of gray in the figure.

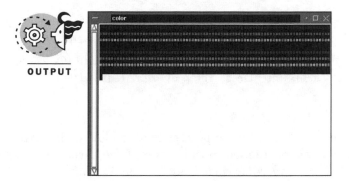

OUTPUT

Figure 12.1: ncurses uses color on a color-capable terminal.

Window Management

One of ncurses' chief advantages, in addition to complete freedom from terminal-dependent code, is the capability to create and manage multiple windows in addition to the ncurses-provided stdscr. These programmer-defined windows come in two varieties, subwindows and independent windows. All the window-manipulation routines discussed in this section are documented in the curs_window manual page.

TIP

Except where specifically noted, ncurses handles return codes very consistently: Functions that return an integer return OK on success or ERR on failure; those that return pointers return NULL on failure.

Subwindows are created using the subwin function call. They are called *subwindows* because they create a window based on an existing window. At the C language level, subwindows are pointers to pointers to a subset of an existing WINDOW data structure. The subset can include the entire window or only part of it. Subwindows, also called *child* or *derived* windows, can be managed independently of their parent windows, but changes made to the children are reflected in the parent.

Create new or independent windows with the newwin call. This function returns a pointer to a new WINDOW structure that has no connection to other windows. Changes made to an independent window do not show up onscreen unless explicitly requested. The newwin function adds powerful screen-manipulation capabilities to your programming repertoire, but, as is often the case with added power, it also entails additional complexity. You are required to keep track of the window and explicitly to display it on the screen, whereas subwindows update on the screen automatically.

Subwindows

ncurses has two functions for creating subwindows, subwin and derwin:

```
WINDOW *subwin(WINDOW *orig, int nlines, int ncols, int begin_y, int begin_x);
WINDOW *derwin(WINDOW *orig, int nlines, int ncols, int begin_y,

int begin_x);
```

subwin and derwin create and return a pointer to a window with ncols columns and nlines rows, positioned in the center of the parent window orig. The child window's upper-left corner is positioned at begin_y, begin_x relative to the screen, not the parent window. derwin behaves like subwin except that the child window is positioned at begin_y, begin_x relative to the parent window orig, not the screen.

Example

EXAMPLE

This program creates a child window, writes some text into it, and then moves it across the parent window, thus illustrating how subwindows can be managed independently of their parents.

```
/*
 * subwin.c - curses utility routines
 */
#include <stdlib.h>
#include <curses.h>
#include <errno.h>
#include <unistd.h>
#include "utilfcns.h"

int main(void)
{
    WINDOW *win;
    int ymax, xmax, n = 0;

    app_init();

    wbkgd(stdscr, 'X');
    wrefresh(stdscr);
    if((win = subwin(stdscr, 10, 10, 0, 0)) == NULL)
        err_quit("subwin");
    wbkgd(win, ' ');
    wprintw(win, "\nSUBWINDOW\n");
```

```
    wrefresh(win);
    sleep(1);

    getmaxyx(stdscr, ymax, xmax);
    while(n < xmax - 10) {
        mvwin(win, ((ymax - 10) / 2), n);
        refresh();
        sleep(1);
    n += 7;
    }

    delwin(win);
    app_exit();
    exit(EXIT_FAILURE);
}
```

First, the parent window is painted with Xs, and then a blank 10[ts]10 sub-window is created. After printing SUBWINDOW into the subwindow, the last bit of code moves it across the parent. Notice that because the contents of the subwindow never change, it is only necessary to refresh the parent window. Because of its dynamic nature, only part of the output from this program is shown in Figure 12.2.

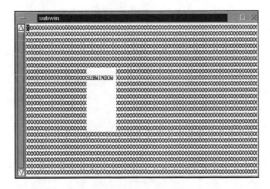

Figure 12.2: *Moving a child window across its parent window.*

New Windows

As discussed before, newwin creates a window that has no connection to other windows and must be managed independently.

```
WINDOW *newwin(int nlines, in ncols, int begin_y, int begin_x);
```

newwin creates and returns a pointer to a new window with ncols columns and nlines lines. The new window's upper-left corner is positioned at begin_y, begin_x. If you want to make a duplicate of an existing window, use dupwin, prototyped as follows:

```
WINDOW *dupwin(WINDOW *win);
```

dupwin returns a pointer to an exact duplicate of the window pointed to by win.

Example

This program behaves similarly to the last one, except that it uses newwin instead of subwin to create a window.

EXAMPLE

```
/*
 * newwin.c - curses utility routines
 */
#include <stdlib.h>
#include <curses.h>
#include <errno.h>
#include <unistd.h>
#include "utilfcns.h"

int main(void)
{
    WINDOW *win;
    int ymax, xmax;

    app_init();

    if((win = newwin(15, 30, 1, 1)) == NULL)
        err_quit("newwin");
    mvwprintw(win, 1,1, "NEW WINDOW");
    box(win, ACS_VLINE, ACS_HLINE);
    wrefresh(win);
    sleep(1);

    mvwin(win, 5, 10);
    werase(stdscr);
    refresh();
    wrefresh(win);
    sleep(2);
```

```
    getmaxyx(stdscr, ymax, xmax);
    mvwin(win, ymax - 16, xmax - 31);
    werase(stdscr);
    refresh();
    wrefresh(win);
    sleep(2);

    delwin(win);
    app_exit();
    exit(EXIT_FAILURE);
}
```

The primary difference between this program and the previous one is that it creates new windows rather than derives child windows. As a result, the code must be careful to make sure that each window, stdscr and win, refreshes and that it refreshes in order. It is a bit more code intensive but also gives you a bit more flexibility because you can prepare a window and then pop it into place with a single wrefresh call. The screen changes several times during execution, so Figure 12.3 shows it in one state during execution.

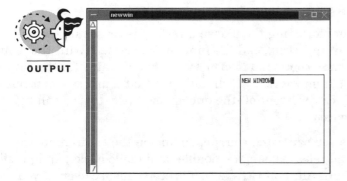

OUTPUT

Figure 12.3: Moving one window across another.

Using the Mouse

Mouse support is strictly an ncurses extension to the standard curses API. With this caveat in mind, this section shows you how to catch and use mouse events in your ncurses code.

TIP

Because the rodent interface is not supported outside ncurses, you should make sure to wrap mouse-related code in an #ifdef structure so it will not be compiled on non-ncurses system. In fact, the best design isolates mouse-related code to as few conditionally compiled modules as possible (preferably one). For example, to conditionally compile mouse code, use a construct that resembles the following:

```
#ifdef NCURSES_MOUSE_VERSION
/*
 * Mouse support is available
 * Mouse code would go here
 */
#else
/*
 * Mouse support not available
 * Come up with a work-around
 */
#endif
```

If mouse support is available, the ifdef will evaluate to 1 (true) and the section of code after #ifdef executes. If not, the code block after #else executes instead.

Overview of the Mouse Interface

The basic procedure for using the mouse interface is reasonably simple. To enable mouse event reporting, call the function mousemask. With the mouse active, your program's command loop or loops should watch for the return value of KEY_MOUSE from wgetch, which indicates that a mouse event has been queued. To pick the event off the queue, use the getmouse call before the next call to wgetch.

The mouse events you can catch can, depending on the environment, include presses and releases; single-, double- and triple-clicks; and possibly the state of the Shift, Alt, and Ctrl keys. To receive mouse events, you must be running either gpm(1), Alessandro Rubini's mouse server for the Linux console, or xterm and similar programs, such as rxvt, which report mouse events through the X server.

CAUTION

Unfortunately, most shipping versions of gpm, the console mouse driver that makes ncurses' mouse driver work, are linked against BSD curses (libcurses.[a.so]). As a result, mouse-handling code does not work properly out of the box. To get it working properly, you must download and recompile the ncurses source distribution, and then rebuild the gpm daemon and library (libgpm), thus linking it against your newly built ncurses.

DETECTING MOUSE EVENTS

Table 12.1 lists the most common mouse events you can catch. The complete list is available in the curs_mouse(3) manual page.

Table 12.1: Mouse Events Report by ncurses

Event Name	Event Description
BUTTON1_PRESSED	Mouse button 1 down
BUTTON1_RELEASED	Mouse button 1 up
BUTTON1_CLICKED	Mouse button 1 clicked
BUTTON1_DOUBLE_CLICKED	Mouse button 1 double-clicked
BUTTON1_TRIPLE_CLICKED	Mouse button 1 triple-clicked
BUTTON2_PRESSED	Mouse button 2 down
BUTTON2_RELEASED	Mouse button 2 up
BUTTON2_CLICKED	Mouse button 2 clicked
BUTTON2_DOUBLE_CLICKED	Mouse button 2 double-clicked
BUTTON2_TRIPLE_CLICKED	Mouse button 2 triple-clicked
BUTTON3_PRESSED	Mouse button 3 down
BUTTON3_RELEASED	Mouse button 3 up
BUTTON3_CLICKED	Mouse button 3 clicked
BUTTON3_DOUBLE_CLICKED	Mouse button 3 double-clicked
BUTTON3_TRIPLE_CLICKED	Mouse button 3 triple-clicked
BUTTON_SHIFT	Shift was down during button state change
BUTTON_CTRL	Control was down during button state change
BUTTON_ALT	Alt was down during button state change
ALL_MOUSE_EVENTS	Report all button state changes
REPORT_MOUSE_POSITION	Report mouse movement

Mouse button 1 is the left mouse button; mouse button 2 is the right mouse button on a two-button mouse or the middle mouse button on a three-button mouse; mouse button 3 is the right mouse button on a two- or three-button mouse.

EXAMPLE

This program illustrates the basic procedure for catching and interpreting mouse events in an ncurses program.

EXAMPLE

```
/*
 * usemouse.c - Simple mouse-aware ncurses program
```

```
        */
#include <curses.h>
#include <stdlib.h>
#include <errno.h>
#include <ctype.h>
#include "utilfcns.h"

int main(void)
{
    mmask_t mask;
    MEVENT event;
    int ch;

    app_init();
    cbreak();
    keypad(stdscr, TRUE);
    mask = mousemask(ALL_MOUSE_EVENTS, NULL);
    while((toupper(ch = getch())) != 'Q') {
        if(ch == KEY_MOUSE) {
            getmouse(&event);
            switch(event.bstate) {
            case BUTTON1_CLICKED :
                printw("button 1 clicked\n");
                break;
            case BUTTON2_CLICKED :
                printw("button 2 clicked\n");
                break;
            case BUTTON3_CLICKED :
                printw("button 3 clicked\n");
                break;
            default :
                printw("untrapped mouse event\n");
            }
        refresh();
        }
    }
    nocbreak();
    app_exit();
```

```
        exit(EXIT_FAILURE);
}
```

The program sets cbreak mode so that most key sequences will pass through the kernel terminal driver unmolested. keypad interprets the escape sequences generated by mouse clicks and other events for you, rather than you having to decode them yourself and fill up your code with lots of symbols that look like ^[[M#1).

After setting the mouse event mask to capture all mouse events, the program goes into a loop and waits for a mouse event to come through. Merely pressing one of the three buttons generates the corresponding message; otherwise, the program prints an untrapped mouse event message. Type q or Q to turn off cbreak mode and quit.

Figure 12.4 shows the output after pressing each mouse button in order, and then double-ciching the right and left buttons.

OUTPUT

Figure 12.4: *Catching mouse events with ncurses' mouse interface.*

DETECTING MOUSE LOCATION

In addition to interpreting individual mouse events such as clicks and double clicks, ncurses' mouse API also enables you to determine over which window the mouse is located and the cursor's current coordinates.

The wenclose function enables you determine which window contained the location of a mouse event. Its prototype is

```
bool wenclose(WINDOW *win, int y, int x);
```

wenclose returns TRUE if the screen-relative coordinates y and x are inside the window specified by win, and FALSE if they are not.

To determine a mouse event's coordinates, examine the x, y, and z members of the MEVENT structure. The compete structure is defined as follows:

```
typedef struct {
    short id;        /* ID distinguishing multiple mice */
    int x, y, z;     /* event coordinates */
    mmask_t bstate; /* button state bits */
} MEVENT;
```

According to the ncurses documentation (specifically, man curs_mouse) the z member is meant for use with touch screens, (which may be pressure sensitive) 3D-mice, trackballs, and power gloves. As a result, using it in programs that deal only with mice is ill-advised.

EXAMPLE

This example creates two mouse-aware windows. When you click in one of the windows, the program shows in which window the mouse event occurred and displays the event's coordinates in the appropriate window.

```
/*
/*
 * usemouse.c - Simple mouse-aware ncurses program
 */
#include <curses.h>
#include <stdlib.h>
#include <errno.h>
#include <unistd.h>
#include <ctype.h>
#include "utilfcns.h"

int main(void)
{
    mmask_t mask;
    MEVENT event;
    WINDOW *win;
    int ch;

    app_init();

    cbreak();
```

```
/* set up stdscr */
mvprintw(2, 1, "*** WINDOW 1 ***\n\n");
keypad(stdscr, TRUE);
box(stdscr, ACS_VLINE, ACS_HLINE);
refresh();

/* set up the new window */
if((win = newwin(10, 40, 10, 10)) == NULL) {
    perror("newwin");
    exit(EXIT_FAILURE);
} else {
    keypad(win, TRUE);
    mvwprintw(win, 2, 1, "*** WINDOW 2 ***\n\n");
    box(win, ACS_VLINE, ACS_HLINE);
    wrefresh(win);
}


/* set the event mask for all events */
mask = mousemask(ALL_MOUSE_EVENTS, NULL);
/* decode events until user presses [q/Q] */
while((toupper(ch = getch())) != 'Q') {
    if(ch == KEY_MOUSE) {
        getmouse(&event);
        if(wenclose(win, event.y, event.x)) {
            mvwprintw(win, 3, 1,
          "event detected in window 2\n");
            mvwprintw(win, 4, 1,
          "coords were (%d,%d)\n", event.y, event.x);
        }
        else if(wenclose(stdscr, event.y, event.x)) {
            mvprintw(3, 1,
          "event detected in window 1\n");
            mvprintw(4, 1,
          "coords were (%d,%d)\n", event.y, event.x);
        }
        box(stdscr, ACS_VLINE, ACS_HLINE);
        box(win, ACS_VLINE, ACS_HLINE);
```

```
                refresh();
                wrefresh(win);
                sleep(2);
            }
        }
        nocbreak();
        app_exit();
        exit(EXIT_FAILURE);
}
```

Figure 12.5 shows the output from a short run of this program.

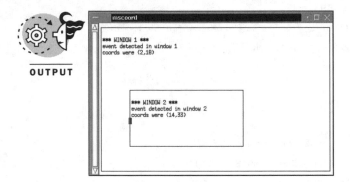

OUTPUT

Figure 12.5: *Locating the window and coordinates of the mouse.*

As you can see from the sample program, a little more setup than usual is involved to use the mouse, but the actual detection code is very simple and the payoff is a program that accepts mouse input even in a console window. The event structure is global to the program, and dereferencing the structure members to obtain the mouse event coordinates is very easy, as shown in the two calls to wenclose.

Note that the program also uses the function shorthand discussed earlier, mvprintw and mvwprintw, to reduce the number of lines of code that must be written. Note that the coordinates listed in the second window are relative to the original screen, called *window 1* in the program.

Using Menus

ncurses' menu library provides terminal-independent capabilities for creating menu systems on character mode terminals. It includes calls for creating and modifying menu items and calls that group items into menus, display menus on the screen, and handle other user interaction. Like almost all ncurses routines, you must call `initscr` before using any of the menu code. To use the menu library, you must include `<menu.h>` in your code and link against the library using the link options `-lmenu -lcurses`.

Menus are screen displays that help users choose some action or item from a set of actions or items. The ncurses menu library works by creating sets of items that are then grouped together and attached to a window, after which they are posted, or displayed on that window. You can also unpost, or detach a menu, ultimately to free its resources.

From a high level, the procedure for creating and using menus resembles the following:

1. Initialize ncurses.

2. Use `new_item` to create menu items.

3. Use `new_menu` to create the menu proper.

4. Use `post_menu` to post the menu.

5. Refresh.

6. Process user input in a command loop.

7. Use `unpost_menu` to unpost the menu.

8. Use `free_menu` to free its resources.

9. Use `free_item` to free their resources.

10. Terminate ncurses.

The key functions and macros for creating menus follow. They are explained in detail in the next few paragraphs.

```
ITEM *new_item(const char *name, const char *description);

int free_item(ITEM *item);

MENU *new_menu(ITEM **items);

int free_menu(MENU *menu);

int set_menu_format(MENU *menu, int rows, int cols);

int post_menu(MENU *menu);

int unpost_menu(MENU *menu);

int menu_driver(MENU *menu, int c);
```

`new_item` allocates a new menu entry and initializes it from the `name` and `description` passed to it. It returns a pointer to a new `ITEM` or returns `NULL` on failure. `free_item` deallocates the allocated storage, returns `E_OK` if it succeeded, E_SYSTEM_ERROR if a system error occurred (in which case, evaluate errno), E_BAD_ARGUMENT if it detected an argument that was invalid for some reason, or E_CONNECTED if item is still connected to a menu (that is, free_menu has not been called for the menu with which the item was associated).

new_menu creates a new menu that contains the menu passed in items. Note that items must be NULL terminated (see the sample program that follows). It returns a pointer to the newly created menu structure or NULL if an error occurs. free_menu, accordingly, frees the allocated resources and dissociates it from items, which can then be used in another menu. free_menu's return values are the same as free_item's, except that E_CONNECTED is replaced by E_POSTED, meaning that you are trying to free a menu that has not been unposted.

The functions post_menu and unpost_menu display and erase menu from their associated window. When posting a menu, it is necessary to call refresh or some similar function. On success, both functions return E_OK. Table 12.2 lists error conditions in addition to those already mentioned for free_item and free_menu.

Table 12.2: Errors Returned by **post_menu** *and* **unpost_menu**

Return Value	Description
E_BAD_STATE	Function called from an initialization or termination routine
E_NO_ROOM	Menu is too large for its window
E_NOT_POSTED	unpost_menu called on an unposted window
E_NOT_CONNECTED	No items are connected to the menu

set_menu_format establishes the maximum display size of menu. It will have no more than rows rows and cols columns. The default is 16 rows and 1 column. As usual, it returns E_OK on success or returns one of E_SYSTEM_ERROR, E_BAD_ARGUMENT, or E_POSTED on error.

menu_driver, the real meat of the menu library, handles all input to menu based on the value of c. It is your responsibility to channel all menu-related input to menu_driver. The c parameter receives the action or request associated with input. Menu driver requests fall into one of three categories:

- A menu navigation request
- A KEY_MOUSE special key from a mouse event
- A printable ASCII character

A navigation request corresponds to cursor motion keys, such as the up or down arrow key. KEY_MOUSE requests are the mouse events covered in the section "Using the Mouse," earlier in this chapter. Printable ASCII characters generate a progressive search up and down the menu for matching menu items, much like Microsoft Windows does. The complete list of menu driver requests are documented in the menu_driver manual page. A few examples are given in the following sample program.

EXAMPLE

Example

This program creates a simple menu with a list of beers. It shows how to navigate up and down a menu.

```c
/*
 * usemenu.c - Using ncurses menus
 */
#include <curses.h>
#include <menu.h>
#include <stdlib.h>
#include <ctype.h>
#include "utilfcns.h"

int main(void)
{
    static const char *beers[] =
    {
        "Budweiser", "Miller", "Pabst", "Schlitz", "MGD", "Coors",
        "Shiner", "Pearl", "Lone Star", "Rainer", "Carlson", NULL
    };
    const char **bp;
    int ch;
    ITEM *items[sizeof(beers)];
    ITEM **ip = items;
    MENU *mymenu;

    /* initialize ncurses */
    app_init();

    /* interpret cursor/function key input */
    keypad(stdscr, TRUE);

    /* create menu items */
    for(bp = beers; *bp; bp++)
```

```
        *ip++ = new_item(*bp, "");
    *ip = NULL;

    /* create the menu and set its format */
    mymenu = new_menu(items);
    set_menu_format(mymenu, 5, 1);

    /* post the menu and refresh */
    post_menu(mymenu);
    refresh();

    /* loop until user presses q or Q */
    while(toupper(ch = getch()) != 'Q') {
        if(ch == KEY_DOWN ¦¦ ch == KEY_NPAGE)
            menu_driver(mymenu, REQ_DOWN_ITEM);
        else if(ch == KEY_UP ¦¦ KEY_PPAGE)
            menu_driver(mymenu, REQ_UP_ITEM);
    }

    /* unpost the menu */
    unpost_menu(mymenu);

    /* free menu and menu items */
    free_menu(mymenu);
    for(ip = items; *ip; ip++)
        free_item(*ip);

    /* terminate ncurses */
    keypad(stdscr, FALSE);
    app_exit();
    exit(EXIT_FAILURE);
}
```

Output from a sample run is shown in Figure 12.6.

OUTPUT

Figure 12.6: *Using ncurses' menu library.*

The first thing this code does is create a static text array that will become the menu, as well as several other variables it will use. It uses the keypad function to interpret function and cursor keys. Next, it steps through the static text array, peeling off each string and adding it to the ITEM vector items. To create the menu, you must pass items to new_menu, which returns a pointer to mymenu that points to a properly initialized menu structure. The set_menu_format call

```
set_menu_format(mymenu, 5, 1);
```

creates a menu that is five rows long and one column wide, so that the program can demonstrate how to move up and down the menu. After the menu has been created and formatted, post_menu associates mymenu with stdscr and handles all the refreshing and updating. Finally, refreshing the screen makes the menu visible. At this point, you can scroll up and down the menu using the up and down arrow keys and the Page Up and Page Down keys.

The workhorse of the sample program is the while loop. It takes input from the keyboard and passes it to the menu_driver function, which handles all the menu manipulation. Pressing the down arrow key, for example, generates a KEY_DOWN signal that menu_driver receives as a REQ_DOWN_ITEM, thus telling menu_driver to highlight the next menu item down on the menu.

unpost_menu, free_menu, and the for loop that frees the individual menu items return allocated resources to the kernel. At last, the program terminates with the calls to app_exit and exit.

Using Forms

The form library enables you to create terminal-independent forms in character mode programs. The library's design is analogous to the menu library's: Field routines create and modify form fields. Form routines group fields into forms, display the forms to the screen, and handle user interaction. The field routines are comparable to the menu library's item routines, and the form calls map to the menu calls.

To use the form library, include the `<form.h>` header file in your source code and link against `libform`, as this gcc invocation suggests:

```
$ gcc -g formprog.c -o formprog -lform -lncurses
```

The general procedure for creating and using forms resembles the following:

1. Initialize ncurses.

2. Use `new_field` to create new fields.

3. Use `new_form` to create the form.

4. Use `post_form` to post the form.

5. Refresh.

6. Process user input in a command loop.

7. Use `unpost_form` to unpost the form.

8. Use `free_form` to free its resources.

9. Use `free_field` to free each field's resources.

10. Terminate ncurses.

Obviously, the form library's design follows the pattern set by the menu library. Unfortunately, however, the `form_driver` command loop must handle a little bit more than the menu library's input loop. The extra complication is worth the effort, though, compared to writing your own form-handling library.

The routines listed here, and explained in the following paragraphs, are sufficient to get you started creating simple, functional forms:

- `FIELD *new_field(int height, int width, int toprow, int left-col, int offscreen, int nbuffers);`

- `int free_field(FIELD *field);`

- `int set_field_buffer(FIELD *field, int buf, const char *value);`

- `int set_field_opts(FIELD *field, int opts);`

- `int set_field_userptr(FIELD *field, void *userptr);`

- `void *field_userptr(FIELD *field);`

- `FORM *new_form(FIELD **fields);`

- `int free_form(FORM *form);`

- `int post_form(FORM *form);`

- `int unpost_form(FORM *form);`

- `int form_driver(FORM *form, int c);`

The `new_field` call creates a new field with `height` rows and `width` columns. This call places the upper-left corner at (y,x) coordinates (`toprow`, `leftcol`). If any of the field's rows should be hidden, pass that number in `offscreen`. `nbuffers` is the number of additional buffers to associate with the field. `new_field` returns a pointer to the new field or `NULL` if an error occurs. `free_field` deallocates the resources associated with `field`. It returns `E_OK` on success and `E_SYSTEM_ERROR` or `E_BAD_ARGUMENT` on failure.

`new_form` creates a new form, associating the fields in `field` with it and returning a pointer to the new form (or `NULL` if an error occurs). Likewise, `free_form` frees the resources allocated to `form` and dissociates `fields` from it. If `free_form` succeeds, it returns `E_OK`. Upon error, it returns `E_SYSTEM_ERROR`, `E_BAD_ARGUMENT`, or `E_POSTED`.

`post_form` displays `form` on its window, after a forced `refresh` or similar call, and `unpost_form` erases the form from the window. `unpost_form` returns `E_OK` on success. If an error occurs, it will return one of `E_SYSTEM_ERROR`, `E_BAD_ARGUMENT`, `E_BAD_STATE`, `E_NO_ROOM`, `E_NOT_POSTED`, or `E_NOT_CONNECTED`.

`set_field_buffer` sets the buffer indicated by `buf` that is associated with `field` to the string `value`. These buffers are created by the `nbuffers` argument passed to `new_field`. Buffer 0 is the one manipulated by the menu library. All others have to be managed by the programmer. Various behavior options may be set by `set_field_opts`. All options for `field` are on by default, so `opts` contains options to disable. Table 12.3 lists the available options.

Table 12.3: Field Options

Option	Description
O_VISIBLE	The field is displayed.
O_ACTIVE	The field will be visited during processing. An invisible field cannot be visited.
O_PUBLIC	Field contents are displayed during data entry.
O_EDIT	The field can be edited.
O_WRAP	Words that do not fit on a line wrap to the next line.
O_BLANK	Field will be cleared when a character is entered at the first position.

O_AUTOSKIP	When a field fills up, skip to the next one automatically.
O_NULLOK	Allow a blank field.
O_STATIC	Field buffers are fixed to the field's original size.
O_PASSOK	Validate the field only if it is modified.

The `set_field_userptr` associates application data passed in `userptr` to `field`. Because `userptr` is a void pointer, it can point to any type of pointer. To retrieve this data, use the `field_userptr` call, which returns the pointer to `field`.

EXAMPLE

Example

Most of these calls are illustrated in the following example:

```
/*
 * useform.c - Simple form usage demo
 */
#include <curses.h>
#include <form.h>
#include <stdlib.h>
#include <ctype.h>          /* for isprint() */
#include "utilfcns.h"

int main(void)
{
    FORM *form;
    FIELD *fields[5];
    int ch, i = 0;

    /* start curses */
    app_init();
    cbreak();
    keypad(stdscr, TRUE);

    /* create the form fields */
    fields[0] = new_field(1, 12, 1, 1, 0, 0);
    set_field_buffer(fields[0], 0, "First Name: ");
    set_field_opts(fields[0], field_opts(fields[0]) & ~O_ACTIVE);

    fields[1] = new_field(1, 20, 1, 14, 0, 0);
```

```
set_field_userptr(fields[1], NULL);

fields[2] = new_field(1, 12, 2, 1, 0, 0);
set_field_buffer(fields[2], 0, "Last Name : ");
set_field_opts(fields[2], field_opts(fields[2]) & ~O_ACTIVE);

fields[3] = new_field(1, 20, 2, 14, 0, 0);
set_field_userptr(fields[3], NULL);

fields[4] = NULL;

/* create and post the form */
form = new_form(fields);
post_form(form);
refresh();

/* start the command loop */
form_driver(form, REQ_OVL_MODE);
while(toupper(ch = getch()) != KEY_F(10)) {
    if(ch == KEY_UP || ch == KEY_PPAGE)
        form_driver(form, REQ_PREV_FIELD);
    else if(ch == '\n' || ch == KEY_DOWN || ch == KEY_NPAGE)
        form_driver(form, REQ_NEXT_FIELD);
    else if(ch == KEY_BACKSPACE)
        form_driver(form, REQ_DEL_PREV);
    else if(isprint(ch))
        form_driver(form, ch);
    else
        form_driver(form, E_UNKNOWN_COMMAND);
}

unpost_form(form);
free_form(form);
for(i = 0; i < 5; i++)
    free_field(fields[i]);

keypad(stdscr, FALSE);
nocbreak();
```

```
        app_exit();
        exit(EXIT_FAILURE);
}
```

Before you learn what is going in the code, have a look at Figure 12.7, which shows this program in action. You will get a much better feeling for how it works, though, if you build the program. Use the down cursor or Page Down key to move to the next field, the up cursor or Page Up key to move the previous field, and F10 to exit. To fill in the fields, just type your entry and press Enter.

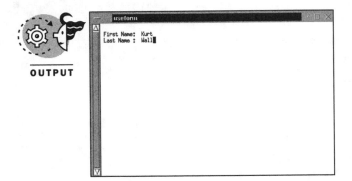

OUTPUT

Figure 12.7: *Data entry screen built with ncurses' form library.*

ncurses initialization includes setting cbreak mode so that the kernel will allow most keystrokes to pass through to the application unprocessed. The next code block creates five fields, two labels, and two text entry fields, as well as a NULL field to terminate the field vector. The fields vector is the argument to post_form, which creates the form and displays it onscreen after a refresh call.

Before entering the while loop, in which all user input is processed, the form_driver sets overlay mode for input characters. Until the user presses F10, the application processes all input. Pressing the up arrow key or Page Up key (interpreted as KEY_UP or KEY_PPAGE) maps to a request to move to the previous field (REQ_PREV_FIELD). Likewise, down arrow and Page Down map to the REQ_NEXT_FIELD event request. The program also enables the backspace key by mapping it to REQ_DEL_PREV, which deletes the previous character. Upon pressing F10, the program cleans up after itself and terminates.

What's Next?

In this chapter, you completed your introduction to some of ncurses' more advanced capabilities. The next chapter, "The Sound API: OSS/Free," continues your tour of Linux's programming interfaces.

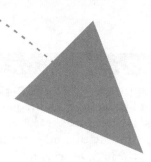

## 13

The Sound API: OSS/Free

Not too long ago, sound cards were available only as add-on devices
installed after the purchase of a PC. Now, even so-called "business PCs"
have some form of minimal sound hardware on the motherboard. This
chapter teaches you the basics of programming your sound card. It offers a
brief overview of sound card technology, and then moves on to discuss
Linux's sound API. The following topics are discussed in this chapter:

- Describing sound hardware
- General guidelines for programming sound hardware
- Manipulating mixer devices
- Programming MIDI hardware
- Writing sound playback programs
- Introducing advanced sound capabilities

Sounding Off

Sound cards are not monolithic hardware devices. Instead, they are made up of several components. Although there is considerable variety among manufacturers, and even among a single manufacturer's cards, most cards have a MIDI interface, a digital voice device, a mixer device, and a synthesizer. Linux's support for these devices is enabled through entries under the /dev filesystem: /dev/mixer, /dev/dsp, /dev/audio, /dev/sequencer, and /dev/midi.

Sound Hardware

The MIDI (*Musical Instrument Digital Interface*) interface is a port that connects external devices, particularly synthesizers, but also lighting equipment and other stage props, to a computer. The mixer is a control device that controls input and output volume levels and switches among the available input devices, such as microphones and CDs. Digital voice devices are used to record and play back digitized voice data. They are generally referred to by the *codecs*, or algorithms, used to record and encode the sample.

Synthesizer devices are used to play music and generate a wide variety of sounds and sound effects. In general, synthesizers fall into two categories. One group is based on the Yamaha OPL2 and OPL3 chips, which are common on most sound cards. The second group are wave table synthesizers—they produce sound from recorded instrument samples stored in chips on the card. Of the two types, wave table synthesizers produce far richer, more realistic sounds.

Sound Devices

Linux's /dev filesystem contains device files that correspond roughly one-to-one with the sound hardware available. All the devices end with a number N, usually 0, 1, or 2, to which the device name is symbolically linked. For example, on my system, /dev/mixer is a symbolic link to /dev/mixer0. The rest of this chapter refers to the symbolic links unless it is necessary to refer to specific device files.

/dev/mixer is the interface to the mixer hardware, whereas /dev/dsp and /dev/audio are the primary interfaces to the digital voice devices. The only differences between the two is that /dev/audio uses μ-Law (μ is the Greek letter *mu*, pronounced "mew") encoding by default, which represents 12- or 16-bit samples in 8 bits, whereas /dev/dsp uses 8-bit unsigned linear encoding. /dev/sequencer is the device used for electronic music and the sounds emitted by games. It is the interface to the synthesizer chips on the sound card and also can be used to access external MIDI devices and the wave table. /dev/midi, finally, is used for low-level MIDI output.

Guidelines for Sound Programming

The following guidelines are taken from the OSS programmer's guide, written by Hannu Savolainen, original author of the Linux sound API. The complete document can be found at http:// www.4front-tech.com/pguide/ intro.html on the World Wide Web.

First and foremost, the sound API is designed to enable applications written to it to be portable across both operating systems and sound hardware. Toward this end, the API relies on macros defined in <sys/soundcard.h>. Although the implementation has and will continue to change as the sound driver develops, the macros remain consistent. Do not, furthermore, code your applications to use the numbered devices. Instead, use the symbolic links described in the previous section, "Sound Devices." Users might have multiple sound devices or other reasons to use different device numbers, but the symbolic links will always point to the devices users want to use for a given purpose.

Avoid "feature-itis," which is the process of weighing your application down with flashy features that are secondary to its main purpose. If you are writing a CD player, for example, it does not need the capability to record sounds. On a similar note, do not assume that everyone is using the latest whiz-bang sound card. Instead, write the lowest common denominator, the Sound Blaster, and add code that detects and uses advanced or high-end features (see the section, "Advanced Audio Programming," for tips on how to do this).

Using the Sound API

To use the sound API, include <sys/soundcard.h> in your source code. No special linker commands are required, but, of course, you must have a working sound card. Before discussing the sound API in detail, you must know the ioctl call, which stands for input/output control, and is used to manipulate a character device via a file descriptor. Its prototype, declared in <ioctl.h>, is listed here:

```
int ioctl(int fd, int request, ...);
```

ioctl controls the device opened on file descriptor fd, and performs the command contained in request. A third argument, char *argp by convention, often carries a size argument. ioctl is a catch-all command for operations that do not cleanly fit into the Linux stream I/O model. A partial list of ioctl requests, typically called *ioctls*, can be found in the ioctl_list(2) manual page, but it is terribly out of date.

The mixer ioctls fall into three categories: volume control, input source, and query functions. The query capability is especially important. Some sound cards do not have a mixer, for example, or they do not have a main volume control. Generally, you should use the query macros first to establish the capabilities, or perhaps merely the presence, of a sound device before beginning to manipulate it.

Regarding the mixer, the sound API abstracts its capabilities into a set of channels, so the first thing you have to do is find out how many channels are available and what they are. Table 13.1 provides a partial list of the most common channels (a complete list is contained in <sys/soundcard.h>).

Table 13.1: Common Mixer Channels

Channel	Description
SOUND_MIXER_VOLUME	Master output level
SOUND_MIXER_BASS	Bass level of all output channels
SOUND_MIXER_TREBLE	Treble level of all output channels
SOUND_MIXER_SYNTH	Volume control of all synthesizer input such as the FM chip or the wave table
SOUND_MIXER_PCM	Output level of the audio devices /dev/audio and /dev/dsp
SOUND_MIXER_SPEAKER	Output level for the PC speaker, if it is connected directly to the sound card
SOUND_MIXER_LINE	Volume level for the line in jack
SOUND_MIXER_MIC	Volume level for microphone input
SOUND_MIXER_CD	Volume level for audio CD input
SOUND_MIXER_ALTPCM	Volume level for alternate audio device (such as the PAS16 boards Sound Blaster emulation)
SOUND_MIXER_RECLEV	Master recording volume level control

The macro SOUND_MIXER_NRDEVICES reports the maximum number of devices known to the sound driver at any given time; SOUND_MIXER_READ_DEVMASK sets a bitmask that indicates the available channels. SOUND_MIXER_READ_RECMASK sets a bitmask indicating the available recording devices. SOUND_MIXER_READ_STEREODEVS sets a bitmask indicating which channels are capable of supporting stereo output. This information gives you the ability to set the volume on each channel independently, thus providing a type of balance control. Another call, SOUND_MIXER_READ_CAPS, sets a bitmask that describes a mixer's general capabilities.

The mixer portion of the sound API also provides two macros that contain printable strings for human-readable output: SOUND_DEVICE_LABELS and SOUND_DEVICE_NAMES. The only difference between these is that the labels in SOUND_DEVICE_NAMES have no embedded blanks or uppercase letters.

To get and set the mixer volume, finally, use the
SOUND_MIXER_READ(*channel*) and SOUND_MIXER_WRITE(*channel*) macros. The
following code snippet, for example, sets the current volume of the mixer
device to 50 percent of its maximum range:

```
int vol = 50;


if((ioctl(fd, SOUND_MIXER_WRITE(SOUND_MIXER_MIC), &vol)) < 0)
    /* Call failed, so degrade gracefully */
else
    /* Call succeeded, more code here */
```

vol stores the volume level (often called *gain*) to set, and SOUND_MIXER_MIC
is the channel on which the volume is being set. The first byte contains the
volume for the left channel, while the right channel is set in the second
byte. After the call, vol contains the new value, which is slightly different
from the volume level you set due to hardware peculiarities.

Examples

EXAMPLE

1. The following program, mixer_status, queries the mixer device for its
available channels and displays their current settings:

```
/*
 * mixer_status.c - example program to display mixer settings.
 * Copyright (c) 1994-96 Jeff Tranter (jeff_tranter@mitel.com)
 * Heavily modified by Kurt Wall (kwall@xmission.com)
 */
#include <unistd.h>
#include <stdlib.h>
#include <stdio.h>
#include <sys/ioctl.h>
#include <fcntl.h>
#include <sys/soundcard.h>

/* Utility function for printing status */
void prn_stat(int condition);

int main(void)
{
    int fd;                          /* File descriptor for mixer device */
    int level;                       /* Volume setting */
    char *device = "/dev/mixer";
```

```
/* Bitmasks for device settings */
int recsrc, devmask, recmask, stereodevs, caps;
/* Names of mixer channels */
const char *labels[] = SOUND_DEVICE_LABELS;
int i;

/* Open the mixer device read only */
if((fd = open(device, O_RDONLY)) < 0) {
    perror("open");
    exit(EXIT_FAILURE);
}

/* Get mixer information */
if((ioctl(fd, SOUND_MIXER_READ_RECSRC, &recsrc)) < 0)
    perror("SOUND_MIXER_READ_RECSRC");
if((ioctl(fd, SOUND_MIXER_READ_DEVMASK, &devmask)) < 0)
    perror("SOUND_MIXER_READ_DEVMASK");
if((ioctl(fd, SOUND_MIXER_READ_RECMASK, &recmask)) < 0)
    perror("SOUND_MIXER_READ_RECMASK");

if((ioctl(fd, SOUND_MIXER_READ_STEREODEVS, &stereodevs)) < 0)
    perror("SOUND_MIXER_READ_STEREODEVS");
if((ioctl(fd, SOUND_MIXER_READ_CAPS, &caps)) < 0)
    perror("SOUND_MIXER_READ_CAPS");

/* Print mixer information */
printf("Status of %s:\n\n", device);
printf("Mixer      Recording    Active    Stereo
➥Current\n");
printf("Channel     Source      Source    Device
➥Level\n");
printf("------------------------------------
➥-------------\n");

/* Loop over all devices */
for (i = 0 ; i < SOUND_MIXER_NRDEVICES ; ++i) {
    /* Only interested in available devices */
    if((1 << i) & devmask) {
```

```c
            /* Print channel number and name */
            printf("%2d %-8s", i, labels[i]);
            /* Is it a recording source? */
            prn_stat((1 << i) & recmask);
            /* Is it active? */
            prn_stat((1 << i) & recsrc);
            /* Does it have stereo capability? */
            prn_stat((1 << i) & stereodevs);
            /* If stereo, show both levels */
            if ((1 << i) & stereodevs) {
                if((ioctl(fd, MIXER_READ(i), &level)) < 0)
                    perror("SOUND_MIXER_READ");
                printf("  %3d%% %3d%%", level & 0xff,
                    (level & 0xff00) >> 8);
            } else { /* Only one channel */
                if((ioctl(fd, MIXER_READ(i), &level)) < 0)
                    perror("SOUND_MIXER_READ");
                printf("    %3d%%", level & 0xff);
            }
        printf("\n");
        }
    }
    /* Are recording sources exclusive? */
    printf("\nNote: Choices for recording source are ");
    if (!(caps & SOUND_CAP_EXCL_INPUT))
        printf("not ");
    printf("exclusive.\n");

    /* Close mixer device */
    close(fd);
    return 0;
}


void prn_stat(int condition)
{
    condition ? printf("   YES   ") : printf("   NO    ");

}
```

The first five `ioctl` calls set bitmasks in their corresponding integer arguments (`recsrc`, `devmask`, `recmask`, `stereodevs`, and `caps`). After printing a table header, `mixer_status` loops through the available mixer channels. If the mixer has that particular channel, the conditional block executes and displays some of the available information for that channel.

Note in particular the way the bitmasks are tested:

```
(1 << channel) & bitmask;
```

The parenthesized expression left-shifts a channel number onto 1, and then bitwise ANDs the resulting value with `bitmask`. If the given channel exists, the expression evaluates to 1. If the channel is not available, it evaluates to 0. So, for example, if a channel, say, `SOUND_MIXER_VOLUME` is stereo-capable, `(1 << SOUND_MIXER_VOLUME) & stereodevs` (as set in the program) evaluates to 1.

On my system, which has a genuine Sound Blaster, `mixer_status` generated the following output:

OUTPUT

```
$ ./mixer_status
Status of /dev/mixer:
```

Mixer Channel	Recording Source	Active Source	Stereo Device	Current Level	
0 Vol	NO	NO	YES	90%	90%
1 Bass	NO	NO	YES	75%	75%
2 Trebl	NO	NO	YES	75%	75%
3 Synth	YES	NO	YES	75%	75%
4 Pcm	NO	NO	YES	100%	100%
5 Spkr	NO	NO	NO	75%	
6 Line	YES	NO	YES	75%	75%
7 Mic	YES	YES	NO	0%	
8 CD	YES	NO	YES	75%	75%
9 Mix	NO	NO	NO	0%	
12 IGain	NO	NO	YES	75%	75%
13 OGain	NO	NO	YES	75%	75%

```
Note: Choices for recording source are not exclusive.
```

As you can see, the mixer device lacks several channels, such as an alternative audio device (`SOUND_MIXER_ALTPCM`).

2. The next program, setvol, enables you to set the volume level interactively.

```c
/*
 * setvol.c - Set volume level interactively
 * mixer device
 * Copyright (c) 1994-96 Jeff Tranter (jeff_tranter@mitel.com)
 * Heavily modified by Kurt Wall (kwall@xmission.com)
 */
#include <unistd.h>

#include <stdlib.h>
#include <stdio.h>
#include <sys/ioctl.h>
#include <fcntl.h>
#include <sys/soundcard.h>

int main(int argc, char *argv[])
{
    int left, right, level;         /* Volume settings */
    int device;                      /* Which mixer device to set */
    int i;
    int fd;                          /* File descriptor for mixer */
    /* Bitmasks for mixer information *
    int devmask, stereodevs;/
    char *dev = "/dev/mixer";
    char buf[5];

    /* Open mixer for read and write */
    if((fd = open(dev, O_RDWR)) < 0) {
        perror("open");
        exit(EXIT_FAILURE);
    }

    /* Get information about the mixer */
    if((ioctl(fd, SOUND_MIXER_READ_DEVMASK,
    ➥&devmask)) < 0)
        perror("SOUND_MIXER_READ_DEVMASK");
    if((ioctl(fd, SOUND_MIXER_READ_STEREODEVS,
```

```
↪&stereodevs)) < 0)
    perror("SOUND_MIXER_READ_STEREODEVS");

/* Set the channel we want to fix */
device = SOUND_MIXER_VOLUME;

/* Get new volume level */
do {
    fprintf(stdout, "New volume level [0-100]: ");
    fgets(buf, 5, stdin);
    right = atoi(buf);
} while(right < 0 ¦¦ right > 100);
/* Set left and right channels to same level */
left = right;

/*
 * Encode both channels into one value. Left channel
 * stored in the least significant byte; right channel
 * stored in second byte, so we have to shift left 8
 * bits.
 */
level = (right << 8) + left;

/* Set the new level */
if((ioctl(fd, MIXER_WRITE(device), &level)) < 0) {
    perror("MIXER_WRITE");
    exit(EXIT_FAILURE);
}

/* Decode the level returned by sound driver */
left  = level & 0xff;
right = (level & 0xff00) >> 8;

/* Display the actual setting */
printf("%s level set to %d%% / %d%%\n",
        dev, left, right);

/* Close mixer device and exit */
```

```
        close(fd);
        return 0;
}
```

The output from this program follows:

```
$ ./setvol
New volume level [0-100]: 75
/dev/mixer level set to 75% / 75%
```

After variable declarations, setvol opens the mixer for read and write access and then uses the SOUND_MIXER_READ_DEVMASK and SOUND_MIXER_READ_STEREODEVS macros with ioctl to determine the mixer's characteristics. The next step is to get the user's preferred volume level. Note that the do-while loop continues until a valid volume level (between 0 and 100) is entered.

Setting the volume level is a bit touchy. As discussed earlier, you must use C's left-shift operator to encode the volume for the right-hand channel into the upper (or most significant) bits of level. The expression is

```
level = (right << 8) + left;
```

The parenthesized expression left-shifts the value of the right channel eight bits, moving all its bits into the upper byte, and then adds the value of left, assigning the result to level. The sound API appropriately decodes level to obtain the desired volume for the right and left channels.

Audio Programming

This section teaches you how to do simple audio programming by focusing on playback and ignoring recording, primarily due to space limitations (well, that and the trivial little detail that I have no way to record sounds on my system). The techniques for recording, however, are essentially the same. Where playback involves a write call to the audio device's file descriptor, recording requires a read call.

NOTE

At its simplest, to record sounds on half-duplex sound cards, all you must do is attach a microphone to the MIC_IN jack and start recording. Full-duplex cards, on the other hand, are more capable in this respect because you can record and play back at the same time. So, in addition to recording using a microphone, a full-duplex sound card enables you to record what it is currently playing, applying all sorts of transformations to the data.

TIP

For more information about programming multimedia, especially sound, on Linux, see Jeff Tranter's *Linux Multimedia Guide*.

UNDERSTANDING SOUND PROGRAMMING

Before jumping into programming sound players, you need some technical background to understand the concepts and terminology involved.

Computers represent sound as a sequence of samples of an audio signal taken at precisely controlled time intervals. A *sample* is the volume of the audio signal at the moment it was measured. The simplest form of digital audio is *uncompressed*, whereby each sample is stored as it is received in a sequence of one or more bytes. *Compressed* audio, on the other hand, encodes N bits of an audio signal in N-x bits to conserve space.

There are several sample formats, the most common being 8-bit, 16-bit, and µ-Law (a logarithmic format). This sample format, combined with the number of channels—that is, whether the signal is mono or stereo—determines the *sample rate*, which in turn controls how many bytes of storage are required for each sample. Typical sampling rates range from a low-grade 8 kHz to 48 kHz.

Because sound is a physical property, there are some limitations with which you must contend. Because computers are digital devices and sound is an analog property, sound cards have analog-to-digital and digital-to-analog converters (ADCs and DACs, respectively) to convert between the two forms. The conversion affects the quality of the signal. Other physical properties also affect the quality of sound.

The most basic limitation is that the highest frequency that can be recorded is half of the sampling rate, so that, for example, at a 16 kHz sampling rate, the highest frequency you can record is no more than 8 kHz. Frequencies higher than 8 kHz must be removed before the signal can be fed to a DAC or an ADC, or you will just hear loud noise. Unfortunately, to increase the quality of the sound, you must increase the sampling rate, which also increases the length of transmission time while decreasing the signal's *duration*, or how long it plays.

SETTING DEVICE PARAMETERS

To play sounds, the basic procedural flow is as follows:

1. Select the device you want to use.

2. Open the device.

3. Set the device format.

4. Set the number of channels (mono or stereo).

5. Set the sample playback speed.

6. Read a block from the file you want to play.

7. Write the block to the opened device.

8. Repeat steps 4 and 5 until EOF.

9. Close the device.

There are several constraints to keep in mind when playing back sounds. First, select the appropriate device. For all data except Sun audio (μ-Law samples), use /dev/dsp; for μ-Law, use /dev/ audio. When opening the device for playback, use O_WRONLY unless you must both read to and write from the device. Next, make sure that the device's default parameters are correct. If not, set them in the following order: sample format, the number of channels (mono or stereo), and the sampling speed. This order is less important for playback than recording, but is nevertheless worth checking.

To get and set the sample format, use the commands SNDCTL_DSP_GETFMTS and SNDCTL_DSP_SETFMT with one of the values listed in Table 13.2.

Table 13.2: Audio Format Macros

Macro	Description
AFMT_QUERY	Used when querying the current audio format (SNDCTL_DSP_GETFMTS)
AFMT_MU_LAW	Logarithmic μ-Law encoding
AFMT_A_LAW	Logarithmic A-Law encoding
AFMT_IMA_ADPCM	The standard ADPCM encoding (incompatible with the format used by Creative in the Sound Blaster 16)
AFMT_U8	Standard 8-bit unsigned encoding
AFMT_S16_LE	Signed 16-bit unsigned little endian (x86) format
AFMT_S16_BE	Signed 16-bit unsigned big endian (M68k, PPC, Sparc) format
AFMT_S8	Signed 8-bit format
AFMT_U16_LE	Unsigned 16-bit little endian format
AFMT_U16_BE	Unsigned 16-bit big endian format
AFMT_MPEG	MPEG (MPEG2) audio format

To obtain the audio formats a device currently supports, call ioctl using the command SNDCTL_DSP_GETFMTS and an argument of AFMT_QUERY. This call fills AFMT_QUERY with a bitmask that represents all the device's currently supported audio formats. The other values in Table 13.2 are the values to pass as the argument to the SNDCTL_DSP_SETFMT. For example, consider the following code snippet:

```
int format;
ioctl(fd, SNDCTL_DSP_GETFMTS, &format);
```

```
format = AFMT_U16_LE;
ioctl(fd, SNDCTL_DSP_SETFMT, &format);
if(format != AFMT_U16_LE)
    printf("AFMT_U16_LE not supported\n"):
```

The first `ioctl` call fills `format` with a bitmask of all the audio formats it currently supports. The next `ioctl` attempts to set the format to `AFMT_U16_LE`. The value that it actually sets is returned in `format`, so the conditional statement confirms whether it actually worked.

To set the number of channels, call `ioctl` with the `SNDCTL_DSP_STEREO` macro:

```
int channels = 1; /* stereo = 1, mono = 0 */
ioctl(fd, SNDCTL_DSP_STEREO, &channels;
```

Similarly, to set the sample speed, use `SNDCTL_DSP_SPEED`:

```
int speed = 11025;
ioctl(fd, SNDCTL_DSP_SPEED, &speed);
```

As always, you must check `ioctl`'s return code to make sure the system call succeeded or to handle the error.

EXAMPLE

The following program is a long, fairly comprehensive program that illustrates the material in this section dealing with audio playback:

```
/*
 * lpeplay.c - Audio playback
 */
#include <sys/ioctl.h>
#include <unistd.h>
#include <fcntl.h>
#include <sys/soundcard.h>
#include <stdlib.h>
#include <stdio.h>
#include <string.h>                    /* for strerror */
#include <errno.h>                     /* for errno */


#define BUFSZ 4096


int main(void)
{
```

```
int devfd, sampfd;                    /* File descriptors */
int len;                               /* Return value from read */
int format, speed, stereo;            /* Args for ioctls */
char *dev = "/dev/dsp";
unsigned char sampbuf[BUFSZ];          /* Buffer for sample */


/* Set some params */
speed = 8000;
stereo = 0;
format = AFMT_QUERY;


/* Open /dev/dsp */
if((devfd = open(dev, O_WRONLY)) < 0) {
    if(errno == EBUSY) {
        fprintf(stderr, "%s in use\n", dev);
    }
    fprintf(stderr, "%s: %s\n", dev, strerror(errno));
    exit(EXIT_FAILURE);
}


/* What formats are currently supported? */
if((ioctl(devfd, SNDCTL_DSP_GETFMTS, &format)) < 0) {
    perror("SNDCTL_DSP_GETFMTS");
    exit(EXIT_FAILURE);
}


/*
 * List the currently available formats.
 * Yeah, it's ugly, but it gets the job done.
 */
puts("Current formats for /dev/dsp: ");
if(format & AFMT_MU_LAW)     puts(puts("\tAFMT_MU_LAW");
if(format & AFMT_A_LAW)      puts("\tAFMT_A_LAW");
if(format & AFMT_IMA_ADPCM) puts("\tAFMT_IMA_ADPCM");
if(format & AFMT_U8)         puts("\tAFMT_U8");
if(format & AFMT_S16_LE)     puts("\tAFMT_S16_LE");
if(format & AFMT_S16_BE)     puts("\tAFMT_S16_BE");
if(format & AFMT_S8)         puts("\tAFMT_S8");
```

```
        if(format & AFMT_U16_LE)    puts("\tAFMT_U16_LE");
        if(format & AFMT_U16_BE)    puts("\tAFMT_U16_BE");
        if(format & AFMT_MPEG)      puts("\tAFMT_MPEG");

        /* Set the number of channels */
        if((ioctl(devfd, SNDCTL_DSP_STEREO, &stereo)) < 0) {
            perror("SNDCTL_DSP_STEREO");

            exit(EXIT_FAILURE);
        }
        printf("\tSet %s mode\n", stereo ? "STEREO" : "MONO");
        /* Set the sample speed */
        if((ioctl(devfd, SNDCTL_DSP_SPEED, &speed)) < 0) {
            perror("SNDCTL_DSP_SPEED");
            exit(EXIT_FAILURE);
        }
        printf("\tSPEED %d Hz\n", speed);

        /* Now read in a sample file to play */
        if((sampfd = open("8000.wav", O_RDONLY)) < 0) {
            perror("open 8000.wav");
            exit(EXIT_FAILURE);
        }

        /* Read a block, write a block */
        while((len = read(sampfd, sampbuf, BUFSZ)) > 0)
            write(devfd, sampbuf, len);

        /* Close the descriptors and get outta here */
        close(devfd);
        close(sampfd);
        exit(EXIT_SUCCESS);
}
```

Although there seems to be a lot going on here, lpeplay is quite straightforward. The BUFSZ macro simply sets a block size for reads and writes. After standard variable declarations, lpeplay opens the /dev/dsp device file and starts determining and setting its characteristics. The first ioctl sets a bitmask in format that contains the audio formats the device currently supports. This could be changed to another format, but one of the available formats, AFMT_S16_SE, will suffice. The next long block of code simply displays to stdout the formats /dev/dsp currently supports.

As written, lpeplay plays an 8-bit mono sample. Accordingly, the code sets the number of channels to 1 (although, perversely, you set it to single channel output by passing a 0—I consider it perverse because using 0 in one case and 1 in another is counter intuitive and inconsistent) and sets the output speed to 8 kHz (8000 Hz). Finally, lpeplay opens the sample file and repeatedly reads a block from the file and writes it to the output device until it reaches EOF, at which point it closes the file descriptors and terminates.

Output from a sample run on your system should resemble the following, followed by a few seconds of sound:

OUTPUT

```
$ ./lpeplay
Current settings for /dev/dsp:
    AFMT_MU_LAW
    AFMT_U8
    AFMT_S16_LE
    Set MONO mode
    SPEED 8000 Hz
```

NOTE

Several sample sounds, including 8000.wav, are available from the Web site for this book. 8000.wav must be in the same directory as the binary for lpeplay to work.

ADVANCED AUDIO PROGRAMMING

Most of the capabilities and features discussed so far are common across sound cards. This section looks at features that might or might not be present in a sound card.

One ioctl call exists that can be used to check for the availability of certain advanced sound hardware features: SNCTL_DSP_GETCAPS. It is used as follows:

```
int caps;
ioctl(fd, SNDCTL_DSP_GETCAPS, &caps);
```

caps will be set to a bitmask that describes available features. The possible bits are listed in Table 13.3.

Table 13.3: Bits Reported by **SNDCTL_DSP_GETCAPS**

Capability	Description
DSP_CAP_REVISION	Set to version number of SNDCTL_DSP_GETCAPS; reserved for future use
DSP_CAP_DUPLEX	Set if device can operate in full duplex mode; unset if in half duplex mode
DSP_CAP_REALTIME	Set if device supports high-precision reporting of the output pointer position
DSP_CAP_BATCH	Set if device has local storage for recording and playback
DSP_CAP_COPROC	Set if device has a programmable processor or DSP; reserved for future use
DSP_CAP_TRIGGER	Set if device has triggered playback or recording
DSP_CAP_MMAP	Set if direct access to the device's hardware level playback or recording buffer is possible

Full duplex simply means that a device can perform both input and output simultaneously. Most sound devices, alas, are *half duplex*. They can record and play back, but not at the same time. The DSP_CAP_REALTIME bit, if set, indicates that you can very precisely keep track of how much data has been recorded or played.

This is usually not the case for devices that use internal buffering, which the DAP_CAP_BATCH bit reports. *Triggering*, reported by the DSP_CAP_TRIGGER bit, is a feature that allows programs requiring the capability to start and stop recording or playback with tight timing. Games, in particular, need this capability.

You can also synchronize recording and playback by using /dev/sequencer in concert with /dev/dsp. For devices that have hardware-level buffers that are capable of direct access (reported by the DSP_CAP_MMAP bit), you can map those buffers into your program's address space. Unfortunately, the method to do this is dependent on the operating system and so has the regrettable side effect of making programs non-portable.

NOTE

Other than illustrating how to determine what advanced capabilities a hardware device has, this chapter does not cover these capabilities.

OUTPUT

The following output shows the rather limited capabilities of my Sound Blaster 16:

```
$ ./getcaps
/dev/dsp capabilities:
    Has triggering
    Direct hardware access possible
```

What's Next?

In this chapter, you learned the basics of programming sound cards using the kernel sound driver. Unfortunately, it is a large topic worthy of its own book, so you have only scratched the surface. The next chapter, "Creating and Using Programming Libraries," shows you how to use existing programming libraries in your programs and how to create your own libraries. Because libraries usually implement the APIs discussed throughout this part of the book, fully understanding the issues and techniques involved with creating and using libraries is essential.

Creating and Using Programming Libraries

This chapter looks at creating and using *programming libraries*, which are collections of code that can be reused across multiple software projects. Libraries are a classic example of software development's Holy Grail: code reuse. They collect frequently used programming routines and utility code into a single location.

The standard C libraries are examples of code reuse. They contain hundreds of frequently used routines, such as the output function `printf` and the input function `getchar`, that would be tedious to rewrite each time you create a new program. Beyond code reuse and programmer convenience, however, libraries provide a great deal of thoroughly debugged and well-tested utility code, such as routines for network programming, graphics handling, data manipulation, and system calls.

This chapter covers the following topics:

- Obtaining library information
- Manipulating libraries
- Creating and using static libraries
- Creating and using shared libraries
- Using dynamically loaded objects

Library Tools

Before jumping into library creation and usage, you must know about the tools at your disposal for creating, maintaining, and managing programming libraries. More detailed information can be found in the manual pages and the tex-info documents for each command and program discussed in the following sections.

The nm Command

The nm command lists all the symbols encoded in an object or binary file. It is used to see what functions a program uses or to see if a library or an object file provides a needed function. nm has the following syntax:

```
nm [options] file
```

nm lists the symbols stored in file. options controls nm's behavior. Table 14.1 lists useful options for nm.

Table 14.1: Options for the **nm** *Command*

Option	Description
-C	Converts symbol names into user-level names. This is especially useful for making C++ function names readable.
-s	When used on archive (.a) files, nm prints the index that maps symbol names to the modules or member names in which the symbol is defined in addition to the symbols the archive contains.
-u	Displays only undefined symbols (symbols that are not defined in the file being examined but that might be defined in other libraries or archives).
-l	Uses debugging information to print the line number in which each symbol is defined, or the relocation entry if the symbol is undefined.

EXAMPLE

OUTPUT

Example

The example that follows uses nm to show the symbols that the library /usr/lib/libdl.a contains:

```
$ nm /usr/lib/libdl.a ¦ head -10
dlopen.o:
00000000 T __dlopen_check
         U _dl_open
         U _dlerror_run

00000000 W dlopen
0000002c T dlopen_doit
```

```
dlclose.o:
        U _dl_close
```

The first column of output is the location (the offset in hexadecimal bytes) in the member, dlopen.o, of the various symbols, which are listed in the third column of the output. The second column is a single letter that indicates each symbol's status. U means that the listed symbol is undefined in the member, although it might be defined in another file. A T indicates that the corresponding symbol is defined in the member's text (code) area. W specifies a symbol that will either be overridden if an identically named symbol is located in another file or, if a like-named symbol is not found, it will be replaced by a 0.

The ar Command

ar creates, modifies, or extracts archives. It is most commonly used to create static libraries, which are files that contain one or more object files. *Static libraries* are object files whose code is designed to be linked into a program at compile-time rather than linked into a program dynamically at runtime. Static libraries are the conceptual opposite of Windows' dynamic link libraries (DLLs). The constituent object files are called *members.* ar also creates and maintains a table that cross-references symbol names to the members in which they are defined. An example of using the ar command is given in the section "Creating a Static Library," later in this chapter. The ar command has the following syntax:

```
ar {dmpqrtx} [options] [member] archive_file file [...]
```

ar creates the archive named archive_file from the files listed in file. At least one of the d, m, p, q, u, r or x options is required. You will normally use r. Table 14.2 describes the most commonly used ar options.

*Table 14.2: Options for the **ar** Command*

Option	Description
-c	Creates archive if it doesn't exist and suppresses the message ar would emit if archive doesn't exist. The archive will still be created whether -c is specified or not.
-s	Creates or updates the map linking symbols to the member in which they are defined.
-r	Inserts file into the archive and replaces any existing member whose name matches that being added. New members are added at the end of the archive.
-q	Appends files to the end of archive without checking for replacements.

The ldd Command

Although nm lists the symbols defined in a library, unless you know what libraries a program requires, it is not terribly helpful. This is where ldd comes in. It lists the shared libraries that a program requires in order to run. Its syntax is as follows:

```
ldd [options] file
```

ldd prints the names of the shared libraries that file requires. Two of ldd's most useful options are -d, which reports any missing functions, and -r, which reports missing functions *and* missing data objects. The other two options ldd recognizes are -v, which reports ldd's version number, and -V, which reports the version number of the dynamic linker, ld.so.

Example

EXAMPLE

OUTPUT

ldd reports that the mail client mutt (which may or may not be installed on your system) requires five shared libraries.

```
$ ldd /usr/bin/mutt
libnsl.so.1 => /lib/libnsl.so.1 (0x40019000)
libslang.so.1 => /usr/lib/libslang.so.1 (0x4002e000)
libm.so.6 => /lib/libm.so.6 (0x40072000)
libc.so.6 => /lib/libc.so.6 (0x4008f000)
/lib/ld-linux.so.2 => /lib/ld-linux.so.2 (0x40000000)
```

Note that ldd's output might be different on your system. The output indicates the libraries that the mutt binary requires to run. The first column shows the library name, which is often a symbolic link to the full pathname of the library that is listed in the second column.

The ldconfig Command

ldconfig determines the runtime links programs require to shared libraries that are located in /usr/lib and /lib, specified in libs on the command line, and stored in /etc/ld.so.conf. It works with ld.so, the dynamic linker/loader, to create and maintain links to the most current versions of shared libraries available on a system. ld.so's job is to complete the final link between programs that use functions in shared libraries and the shared libraries that define those functions. It has the following syntax:

```
ldconfig [options] [libs]
```

A bare ldconfig simply updates the cache file, /etc/ld.so.cache. options controls ldconfig's behavior. The -p option tells ldconfig to list all the shared libraries ld.so has stored in its cache, without changing anything. The -v option instructs ldconfig to update the ld.so's cache and also to list the libraries found. If you compile a program that fails to run because it cannot find a required library, execute `ldconfig -p` to list the known libraries. To actually update the library cache file, you must execute `ldconfig` as root.

NOTE

As you can see, managing shared libraries can be complex and confusing. A program that uses a function defined in shared libraries knows only the function's name, which is often called a *stub*. The program does not know how the function is defined or how, at runtime, to access the function's code. The function of `ld.so` is to connect the stub (the function name) to the actual code that implements the function (which lives in a shared library). The method `ld.so` uses to accomplish this is way beyond this book's scope. As an application programmer, all you must concern yourself with is linking your program against the appropriate libraries. You may safely take it for granted that Linux takes care of the gory details for you.

Environment Variables and Configuration Files

The dynamic linker/loader `ld.so` uses two environment variables to customize its behavior. The first is $LD_LIBRARY_PATH, a colon-separated list of directories that `ld.so` will search, in addition to the default directories /lib and /usr/lib, for shared libraries at runtime. The second variable, $LD_PRELOAD, is a whitespace-separated list of additional, user-specified shared libraries that load before all other libraries. It is used selectively to override functions that may be defined by other shared libraries.

`ld.so` also uses two configuration files whose purposes parallel the environment variables mentioned in the preceding paragraph. /etc/ld.so.conf contains a list of directories in which the linker/loader should search for the shared libraries a program requires. This is in addition to the standard directories, /usr/lib and /lib that `ld.so` always searches. /etc/ld.so.preload is a disk-based version of the $LD_PRELOAD environment variable: It contains a whitespace-separated list of shared libraries to be loaded prior to executing a program.

Static Libraries

Static libraries (and *shared libraries*, for that matter) are collections of one or more object files containing reusable precompiled code. Each constituent object file is also called a module or a *member*. Static libraries are stored in a special format along with a table or *map* that links symbol names to the members in which the symbols are defined. The map speeds up the compilation and linking processes. Static libraries are typically named with an .a (for archive) extension. Recall that code in static libraries is linked into a program at compile-time, whereas code in shared libraries is linked into a program, courtesy of `ld.so`, at runtime.

Creating a Static Library

To use library code, include the static library's header file in your source code and link against the corresponding library. To create your own library, collect your most commonly used routines into a single file, and then create a header file that declares the functions and data structures. The header file contains the interface to your library. The next example creates an error-handling library that you might find useful.

NOTE

Fans of Richard Stevens' *Advanced Programming in the UNIX Environment* will recognize this code. I have used this code for several years because it neatly meets my need for a simple, functional error-handling library. I am indebted to Stevens' generosity in allowing me to reproduce this code here.

I was also deeply saddened to hear of his death in early September 1999. Richard Stevens was a fine programmer and an outstanding expositor of the minutae of UNIX and TCP/IP programming. The clarity of expression he brought to the details of the UNIX and TCP/IP API will be sorely missed.

A few remarks about the code might be helpful. The header file includes <stdarg.h> because it uses ANSI C's variable-length argument list facility (if you are unfamiliar with variable-length argument lists, consult your favorite C reference manual). To protect against multiple inclusions of the header, it is wrapped in a preprocessor macro, LIBERR_H_. This library should not be used in daemons because it writes to stderr. Daemons usually do not have a controlling terminal, so they are not attached to stderr (see Chapter 9, "Daemons," for more information about creating daemon programs).

EXAMPLE

Example

The first listing that follows, liberr.h, is the header file for a simple error-handling library, and the second listing is the implementation of the interface defined in the header file.

```
/*
 * liberr.h
 * Declarations for simple error-handling library
 */
#ifndef LIBERR_H_
#define LIBERR_H_

#include <stdarg.h>

#define MAXLINELEN 4096
```

```c
/*
 * Print an error message to stderr and return to caller
 */
void err_ret(const char *fmt, ...);


/*
 * Print an error message to stderr and exit
 */
void err_quit(const char *fmt, ...);


/*
 * Print an error message to logfile and return to caller
 */
void log_ret(char *logfile, const char *fmt, ...);


/*
 * Print a error message to logfile and exit
 */
void log_quit(char *logfile, const char *fmt, ...);



/*
 * Print an error message and return to caller
 */
void err_prn(const char *fmt, va_list ap, char *logfile);

#undef LIBERR_H_
#endif /* LIBERR_H_ */
/*
 * liberr.c - Implement the error-handling library
 */
#include <errno.h>   /* for definition of errno */
#include <stdarg.h> /* for the vararg declarations */
#include <stdlib.h>
#include <stdio.h>
#include "liberr.h" /* our own header */


void err_ret(const char *fmt, ...)
```

```
    {
        va_list ap;

        va_start(ap, fmt);
        err_prn(fmt, ap, NULL);
        va_end(ap);
        return;
    }

    void err_quit(const char *fmt, ...)
    {
        va_list ap;

        va_start(ap, fmt);
        err_prn(fmt, ap, NULL);
        va_end(ap);
        exit(1);
    }

    void log_ret(char *logfile, const char *fmt, ...)
    {
        va_list ap;

        va_start(ap, fmt);
        err_prn(fmt, ap, logfile);
        va_end(ap);
        return;
    }

    void log_quit(char *logfile, const char *fmt, ...)
    {
        va_list ap;

        va_start(ap, fmt);
        err_prn(fmt, ap, logfile);
        va_end(ap);

        exit(1);
```

```
}

extern void err_prn(const char *fmt, va_list ap, char *logfile)
{
    int save_err;
    char buf[MAXLINELEN];
    FILE *plf;

    save_err = errno; /* value caller might want printed */
    vsprintf(buf, fmt, ap);
    sprintf(buf + strlen(buf), ": %s\n", strerror(save_err));
    fflush(stdout); /* in case stdout and stderr are the same */
    if(logfile != NULL)
        if((plf = fopen(logfile, "a")) != NULL) {
            fputs(buf, plf);
            fclose(plf);
        } else
            fputs("failed to open log file\n", stderr);
    else
        fputs(buf, stderr);
    fflush(NULL); /* flush everything */
    return;
}
```

To create a static library, you must first compile your code to object form.
Next, use the ar utility to create an archive. If all goes according to plan (if
there are no typos in your code and you do not fat finger the commands),
you will have created the static library liberr.a.

OUTPUT

```
$ gcc -c liberr.c -o liberr.o
$ ar rcs liberr.a liberr.o
$ nm liberr.a

liberr.o:
         U __errno_location
000000a4 T err_prn
00000024 T err_quit
00000000 T err_ret
         U exit
         U fclose
```

```
          U fflush
          U fopen
          U fputs
00000000 t gcc2_compiled.
00000078 T log_quit
00000054 T log_ret
          U sprintf
          U stderr
          U stdout
          U strcat
          U strerror
          U strlen
          U vsprintf
```

The second command creates liberr.a from the object file created by the compiler. The third command, nm liberr.a, lists the members of the archive followed by the functions it contains. As you can see from nm's output, the archive contains the functions defined in the liberr.o object file. They are preceded by a T in the listing.

Using a Static Library

Now that the archive has been created, you need a driver program to test it. The test program is part of the next example. Again, to use the library, include its header file in your code, use gcc's -l switch to link against it, and then use the -L option to help gcc find the library file.

EXAMPLE

Example

The following program, errtest, attempts to open a non-existent file four times, one time for each of the four error-handling functions in the library.

```
/*
 * errtest.c - Test program for error-handling library
 */
#include <stdio.h>
#include <stdlib.h>
#include "liberr.h"

#define ERR_QUIT_SKIP 1
#define LOG_QUIT_SKIP 1

int main(void)
```

```
{
    FILE *pf;

    fputs("Testing err_ret...\n", stdout);
    if((pf = fopen("foo", "r")) == NULL)
        err_ret("%s %s", "err_ret", "failed to open foo");

    fputs("Testing log_ret...\n", stdout);
    if((pf = fopen("foo", "r")) == NULL);
        log_ret("errtest.log", "%s %s", "log_ret", "failed to open foo");

#ifndef ERR_QUIT_SKIP
    fputs("Testing err_quit...\n", stdout);
    if((pf = fopen("foo", "r")) == NULL)
        err_ret("%s %s", "err_quit", "failed to open foo");
#endif /* ERR_QUIT_SKIP */

#ifndef LOG_QUIT_SKIP
    fputs("Testing log_quit...\n", stdout);
    if((pf = fopen("foo", "r")) == NULL)
        log_ret("errtest.log", "%s %s", "log_quit", "failed to open foo");
#endif /* LOG_QUIT_SKIP */

    exit(EXIT_SUCCESS);

}
```

Compiling and running errtest results in the output that follows:

OUTPUT

```
$ gcc -g errtest.c -o errtest -L. -lerr
$ ./errtest
Testing err_ret...
err_ret failed to open foo: No such file or directory
Testing log_ret...
$ cat errtest.log
log_ret failed to open foo: No such file or directory
```

The two #ifndef-#endif constructs prevent execution of the *_quit functions. To test them, comment out one of the macros and recompile, and then comment out the other and recompile. Try testing the *_quit functions as a practice exercise.

Shared Libraries

Shared libraries have several advantages over static libraries. First, they require fewer system resources. They use less disk space because shared library code is not compiled into each binary but is linked and loaded from a single location dynamically at runtime. They use less system memory because the kernel shares the memory that the library occupies among all the programs that use the library.

Another advantage of shared libraries is that they are slightly faster because they must be loaded into memory only once. Finally, shared libraries simplify code and system maintenance. As bugs are fixed or features added, users need only obtain the updated library and install it. With static libraries, each program that uses the library must be recompiled.

As already pointed out, the dynamic linker/loader, ld.so, links symbol names to the appropriate shared library in which they are defined at runtime. Shared libraries have a special name, the *soname*, that consists of the library name and the major version number. The full name of the C library on one of my systems, for example, is libc.so.5.4.46. The library name is libc.so; the major version number is 5; the minor version number is 4; and 46 is the release or patch level. So, the C library's soname is libc.so.5.

The soname of the new C library, libc6, is libc.so.6—the change in major version numbers indicates a significant library change, to the extent that the two libraries are (massively!) incompatible. Minor version numbers and patch level numbers change as bugs are fixed, but the soname remains the same, thus newer versions are usually compatible with older versions.

It's important to be aware of the soname because applications link against the soname. How does it work? The ldconfig utility creates a symbolic link from the actual library, say libc.so.5.4.46, to the soname, libc.so.5, and stores this information in /etc/ld.so.cache. At runtime, ld.so scans the cache file, finds the required soname and, because of the symbolic link, loads the actual library into memory and links application function calls to the appropriate symbols in the loaded library.

Library versions become incompatible under the following conditions:

- Exported function interfaces change
- New function interfaces are added
- Function behavior changes from the original specification
- Exported data structures change

- Exported data structures are added

To maintain library compatibility, use the following guidelines:

- Add functions to your library with new names instead of changing existing functions or changing their behavior.

- Add items only to the end of existing data structures, and either make them optional or initialize them inside the library.

- Don't expand data structures used in arrays.

Building a Shared Library

The process of building a shared library differs slightly from the one used to build a static library. The list that follows outlines the steps necessary to build a shared library:

1. When compiling the object file, use gcc's -fPIC option, which generates Position Independent Code (PIC) that can link and load at any address.

2. Don't use gcc's -fomit-frame-pointer option—doing so could possibly make debugging impossible.

3. Use gcc's -shared and -soname options.

4. Use gcc's -Wl option to pass arguments to the linker, ld.

5. Explicitly link against the C library by using gcc's -l option. This assures that your program will not compile on a program that lacks the correct version of the C library because references to new or modified functions will cause compiler errors.

EXAMPLE

Example

This example builds the error-handling library as a shared library. It first builds the object file, and then links the library. Then it creates symbolic links from the full library name to the soname, and from the full library name to the name of the shared library, which simply ends in .so.

```
$ gcc -fPIC -g -c liberr.c -o liberr.o
$ gcc -g -shared -Wl,-soname,liberr.so -o liberr.so.1.0.0 liberr.o -lc
$ ln -s liberr.so.1.0.0 liberr.so.1
$ ln -s liberr.so.1.0.0 liberr.so
```

Because you will not install this library as a system library in /usr or /usr/lib, you must create two links, one for the soname and one for the shared library. The linker will use the shared library name when linking against liberr; that is, when using -lerr.

Using a Shared Library

Now, to use the new shared library, revisit the test program introduced in the last section, errtest.c. Again, you need to tell the linker what library to use and where to find it, so use the -l and -L options. Finally, to execute the program, you need to tell ld.so, the dynamic linker/loader, where to find the shared library, so use the $LD_LIBRARY_PATH variable.

Example

EXAMPLE

This example links errtest against the shared library version of liberr and then runs errtest.

```
$ gcc -g errtest.c -o errtest -L. -lerr
$ LD_LIBRARY_PATH=$(pwd) ./errtest
```

OUTPUT

```
Testing err_ret...
err_ret failed to open foo: No such file or directory
Testing log_ret...
```

As pointed out earlier, the environment variable $LD_LIBRARY_PATH adds the path(s) it contains to the trusted library directories /lib and /usr/lib. ld.so will search the path specified in the environment variable first and will ensure that it finds your library. An alternative to using the awkward command line is to add your library's pathname to /etc/ld.so.conf and update the cache (/etc/ ld.so.cache) by running (as root) ldconfig.

Yet another alternative is to install your library as a system library. To do so, become the root user, place it in /usr/lib, and run ldconfig to update the cache file. The advantage of this last method is that you do not have to add the library search path using gcc's -L option.

Dynamically Loaded Objects

There is one more way to use shared libraries: load them dynamically at runtime, not as libraries linked and loaded automatically, but as entirely separate modules that you explicitly load using the dl (dynamic loading) interface. You might want to use the dl interface because it provides greater flexibility for both the programmer and end user, and because it is a more general solution to the issue of code reuse.

What Are They?

Dynamically loaded objects are code modules specifically loaded at runtime for the purpose of using the functionality they provide without requiring that an application be linked with modules containing the loaded code. Suppose you are writing the next killer graphics program. Within your application, you handle graphical data in a proprietary but easy-to-use way.

However, you want to be able to import from and export to any of the literally hundreds of available graphics file formats.

One way to achieve this would be to write one or more libraries to manipulate the various formats. Although it is a modular approach, each library change would require recompilation, or at least relinking, of your program, as would the addition of new formats and changes to existing ones. The effect of adding libraries is illustrated in Figure 14.1.

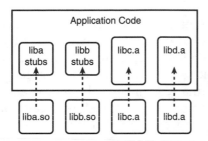

Figure 14.1: _Each library module added to a program increases its size and forces recompilation._

As you can see in Figure 14.1, each time you add another library to a program, the size (and complexity) of the program increases. This size grows especially quickly when you link with static libraries, represented by libc.a and libd.a in the figure.

The dl interface enables a different approach: you design a generic, format-neutral interface for reading, writing, and manipulating graphics files of any format. To add a new or modified graphics format to your application, you simply write a new module to deal with that format and make your application aware that it exists, perhaps by modifying a configuration file or placing the new module in a predefined directory (the plug-ins that augment the Netscape Web browser's capabilities use a variation of this approach).

To extend your application's capabilities, users simply must obtain a new module by editing a configuration file or copying the module to a preset directory. Recompiling is unnecessary. Existing code in your application loads the new modules and, voila, you can import and export a new graphic format. This approach is shown in Figure 14.2.

Each time you need code from a different library, you simply use the dl interface to load the function you require, illustrated in the figure by the arrows pointing from the application to the various libraries. The application's overall resource requirements remain low, and its disk footprint is dramatically reduced versus the linking in static or shared libraries.

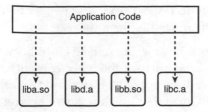

Figure 14.2: The dl *interface reduces code size and complexity.*

The dl interface (itself implemented as a library, libdl), contains functions to load, search, and unload shared objects. To use these functions, include <dlfcn.h> in your source code and link against libdl. You *don't* have to link against the library you want to use—this is the sort of necessity the dl interface is designed to eliminate. Even though you use a standard shared library, you do not use it the normal way. The linker never knows about shared objects and, in fact, the modules do not even need to exist when you build the application.

The dl Interface

The dl interface provides four functions to handle all the tasks necessary to load, use, and unload shared objects: dlopen, dlclose, dlsym, and dlerror. Use the dlopen function to load a shared object. Its prototype is as follows:

```
void *dlopen(const char *filename, int flag);
```

dlopen loads the shared object in filename using the mode specified by flag. filename can be an absolute pathname, a bare filename, or NULL. If it is NULL, dlopen opens the currently executing program—your program. If filename is an absolute pathname, dlopen opens that file. If it is a bare filename, dlopen looks in the following locations, in the order given, to find the file: $LD_ELF_LIBRARY_PATH, $LD_LIBRARY_PATH, /etc/ld.so.cache, /usr/lib, and /lib.

flag can be RTLD_LAZY, meaning that symbols from the loaded object will be resolved as they are called, or RTLD_NOW, which means that all symbols from the loaded object will be resolved before dlopen returns. Either flag, if logically ORed with RTLD_GLOBAL, will cause all symbols to be exported, just as if they had been directly linked. dlopen returns a handle to the loaded object if it finds filename, or returns NULL otherwise.

Before you can use any code in a dynamically loaded library, you must know what you are looking for and be able to access it. The dlsym function meets both needs. It is prototyped as follows:

```
void *dlsym(void *handle, char *symbol);
```

dlsym searches for the symbol or function specified by the symbol argument in the loaded object (the object loaded by dlopen) to which handle refers. handle must be a handle returned by dlopen; symbol is a standard, C-style string. dlsym returns a void pointer to the symbol or NULL on failure.

Robust code checks for and handles as many errors as possible. The dlerror function allows you to find out more about an error that occurs when using dynamically loaded objects. Its prototype is as follows:

```
const char *dlerror(void);
```

If any of the other dl interface function calls fail, dlerror returns a string describing the error. Calling dlerror also resets the error string to NULL. As a result, a second immediate call to dlerror will return NULL. dlerror returns a string describing the most recent error, or NULL otherwise.

To conserve system resources, particularly memory, be sure to unload the code in a shared object when you are finished using it. However, because of the overhead involved in loading and unloading shared objects, be certain that you will not need it before unloading it. dlclose, prototyped as follows, unloads a shared object:

```
int dlclose(void *handle);
```

dlclose unloads the object to which handle refers. The call also invalidates handle. Because the dl library maintains link counts for dynamically loaded objects, the objects are not deallocated and unloaded until dlclose has been called on an object as many times as dlopen was successfully called on it.

Using the dl Interface

To illustrate using the dl interface, return again to the trusty error-handling library used throughout this chapter. This time, however, use a new driver program, as shown in the following example.

Example

EXAMPLE

Before using this example, make sure you have built the shared library version of liberr, liberr.so, using the instructions provided in the "Creating a Shared Library" section earlier in this chapter.

```
/*
 * dltest.c - Dynamically load liberr.so and call err_ret
 */
#include <stdio.h>
#include <stdlib.h>
#include <dlfcn.h>

int main(void)
```

```
{
    void *handle;
    void (*errfcn)(); /* pointer to the loaded code to use */
    const char *errmsg;
    FILE *pf;

/* Load the object of our desire */
    handle = dlopen("liberr.so", RTLD_NOW);
    if(handle == NULL) {
        printf("failed to load liberr.so: %s\n", dlerror());
        exit(EXIT_FAILURE);
    }


/* Clear the error string, if any */
    dlerror();
    errfcn = dlsym(handle, "err_ret");
    if((errmsg = dlerror()) != NULL) {
        printf("didn't find err_ret(): %s\n", errmsg);
        exit(EXIT_FAILURE);
    }
/* Now use the loaded symbol, err_ret */
    if((pf = fopen(" foobar", "r")) == NULL)
        errfcn("couldn't open foobar");


/* Be a good citizen and unload the object */
    dlclose(handle);
    exit(EXIT_SUCCESS);
}
```

```
$ gcc -g -Wall dltest.c -o dltest -ldl
$ LD_LIBRARY_PATH=$(pwd) ./dltest
couldn't open foobar: No such file or directory
```

As you can see, you do not have to link against `liberr` or include `liberr.h` in the source code. All access to `liberr.so` comes through the `dl` interface. `dltest`'s use of the `dlerror` call illustrates the correct way to use it. Call `dlerror` once to reset the error string to NULL, call `dlsym`, and then call `dlerror` again to save its return value in another variable so you can use the string later. Call `errfcn` as you normally would call the function to which it points. Finally, unload the shared object and exit.

What's Next?

This chapter has described using and creating programming libraries. It also concludes the coverage of programming APIs. Part IV, "Interprocess Communication," looks at a variety of ways in which programs can communicate with each other. In particular, you will learn about pipes and FIFOs, shared memory and message queues, and sockets.

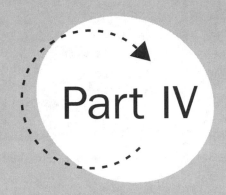

Part IV

Interprocess Communication

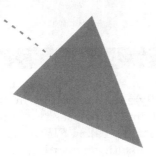

## 15

Pipes and FIFOs

This is the first of four chapters covering Linux's assortment of methods for *interprocess communication*, or IPC. IPC is a generic term referring to the methods that processes use to communicate with each other. Without IPC, processes can exchange data or other information with each other only through the filesystem or—in the case of processes having a common ancestor (such as the parent/child relationship after a fork)—through any inherited file descriptors. This chapter discusses pipes and FIFOs, the oldest forms of IPC that UNIX and UNIX-like systems have. The topics covered include the following:

- Unnamed pipes
- Opening and closing unnamed pipes
- Reading and writing unnamed pipes
- Using popen and pclose
- Understanding FIFOs
- Creating, opening, and closing FIFOs
- Reading and writing FIFOs

✔ Inheriting file descriptors is discussed in "Using fork," page 78.

Pipes

Pipes simply connect one process's output to another process's input. Like their physical analogues, a Linux pipe is (usually) unidirectional or half duplex; data flows in only one direction. This chapter discusses two kinds of pipes, unnamed and named. Named pipes are usually called *FIFOs* (First In First Out). *Unnamed pipes* are unnamed because they never have a pathname, so they never exist in the filesystem. Strictly speaking, all they are is two file descriptors associated with an in-core inode. The last process to close one of these file descriptors causes the inode, and, thus, the pipe, to vanish. *Named pipes*, on the other hand, do have a pathname and do exist in the filesystem. They are called FIFOs because data is read from them in the order it was written, so the first data into a FIFO is also the first data out of a FIFO. Figure 15.1 illustrates the differences and similarities between unnamed pipes and FIFOs.

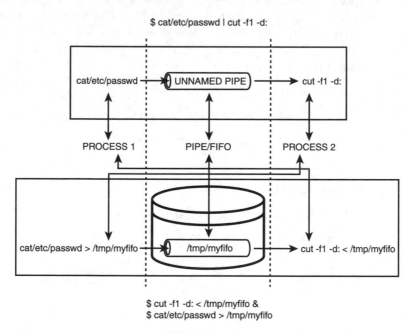

Figure 15.1: *Pipes and FIFOs function similarly but have different semantics.*

The top half of Figure 15.1 illustrates the execution of the shell pipeline cat /etc/passwd ¦ cut -f1 -d:. The bottom half of Figure 15.1 shows how the pipeline in the upper half of the figure would be executed if you used a named pipe rather than an unnamed pipe. The vertical dashed lines represent the point at which data is either being written to or read from a pipe.

The double-headed arrows show how the input and output of the two types of pipes correspond to each other. All the details will be explained in subsequent sections, so you might want to refer to this figure as you proceed through the chapter. In the top part of the figure, the output of the cat command is transmitted through an unnamed pipe created in the kernel. Its output becomes cut's input. This is a typical use of shell pipelines.

In particular, note that using named pipes requires that the order of the cat and cut commands is reversed. For reasons that will be explained later, the cut command must be executed first (and run in the background) so that you are able, in the same terminal or from the same console, to issue the cat command that provides the input to the named pipe.

The named pipe, /tmp/myfifo, and the unnamed pipe serve the same purpose, feeding their input to their output. All that really differs is the order in which commands are executed and the use of the shell redirection operators, > and <, when dealing with named pipes.

NOTE

Perhaps FIFOs are so named because they are also created using the mkfifo function!

Most Linux users are familiar with unnamed pipes, although they might not realize it. Every command such as the following uses unnamed pipes:

```
$ cat /etc/password ¦ cut -f1 -d: ¦ sort
```

In this example, the output from the cat command becomes the input to the cut command, whose output then becomes input to sort. As you know, the ¦ is the pipe symbol. What you might not realize is that your shell probably implements ¦ using the pipe function you will meet in a moment. Hopefully, it is clear that there is never an actual disk file associated with ¦.

CAUTION

A quick tip on terminology: Unless the distinction needs to be made clear, *pipe* in this chapter refers to unnamed pipes, and *FIFO* refers to named pipes. Both pipes and FIFOs, however, are *half duplex*; that is, data flows in only one direction, just as water in a drainage pipe flows in only one direction. Pipes and FIFOs are also *non-seekable*; that is, you can't use calls like lseek to position the file pointer.

Unnamed pipes have two shortcomings. First, as noted, they are half duplex, so data can travel in only one direction. Second, and more significantly, pipes can be used only between related processes, those that have a common ancestor. As you will recall from Chapter 4, "Processes," child processes created from a fork or an exec inherit their parent's file descriptors.

Figure 15.2 shows how data flows through a pipe.

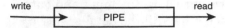

Figure 15.2: *Unnamed pipes are half duplex and are accessible only by related processes.*

As the figure shows, data is written (by the *writer*) to one end of the pipe and read (by the *reader*) at the other end.

Opening and Closing Pipes

Naturally, before you can read from or write to a pipe, it must exist. The call to create a pipe is pipe. Its prototype is declared in <unistd.h> as follows:

```
int pipe(int filedes[2]);
```

If pipe succeeds, it opens two file descriptors and stores their values in the integer array filedes. The first descriptor, filedes[0], is used for reading, so pipe opens it using read's O_RDONLY flag. The second file descriptor, filedes[1], is used for writing, so pipe opens it using open's O_WRONLY flag. pipe returns 0 on success or −1 if an error occurs, in which case it also sets the global error variable errno.

✔ The syntax of the open and close system calls is covered in "Opening and Closing Files," page 139.

Possible error conditions are EMFILE, meaning the calling process already has too many open file descriptors, EFAULT, which means that the filedes array was invalid, or ENFILE, which occurs when the kernel's file table is full (definitely *not* a good sign!). Again, it must be emphasized that the file descriptors do not correspond to a disk file, only to an inode that lives inside the kernel. Figure 15.3 illustrates this point.

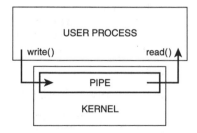

Figure 15.3: *A Linux pipe exists only in the kernel.*

To close a pipe, close its associated file descriptors using the close system call.

Example

The following example opens and closes a pipe:

```c
/*
 * pipopn.c - Open and close a pipe
 */
#include <unistd.h>
#include <stdio.h>
#include <stdlib.h>

int main(void)
{
    int fd[2];

    if((pipe(fd)) < 0) {
        perror("pipe");
        exit(EXIT_FAILURE);
    }
    printf("descriptors are %d, %d\n", fd[0], fd[1]);

    close(fd[0]);
    close(fd[1]);
    exit(EXIT_SUCCESS);
}
```

The output from this program shows that the pipe call succeeded (the descriptor values might be different on your system). The program calls the pipe function, passing it the array of file descriptors, fd. If the pipe call succeeds, the program prints the integer values of the file descriptors, closes them both, and exits.

```
$ ./pipopn
descriptors are 3, 8
```

Reading and Writing Pipes

To read from and write to pipes, simply use the read and write calls. Remember, read reads from filedes[0], and write writes to filedes[1].

✔ For a quick refresher on the read and write system calls, refer to the section, "Reading and Writing Files," page 141.

That said, there is little purpose in a process opening a pipe for its own use. Pipes are used to exchange data. Because a process already has access to the data it would share via a pipe, it doesn't make sense to share data with itself. Normally, a process calls `pipe` and then calls `fork` to spawn a child process. Because the child inherits any open file descriptors from its parent, an IPC channel has been established. The next step depends on which process is the reader and which is the writer. The general rule is that the reader process closes the write end of the pipe and the writer process closes the read end of the pipe. The following items make this process more evident:

- If the parent process is sending data to the child, the parent closes `filedes[0]` and writes to `filedes[1]` while the child closes `filedes[1]` and reads from `filedes[0]`.

- If the child is feeding data back to the parent, the child closes `filedes[0]` and writes to `filedes[1]` while the parent closes `filedes[1]` and reads from `filedes[0]`.

Figure 15.4 should help you visualize the proper procedure and remember the rule.

CAUTION

It is a serious programming error to attempt to read and write both ends of a single pipe. If two processes need the functionality of a full duplex pipe, the parent must open two pipes before `forking`.

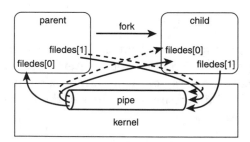

Figure 15.4: *After a* `fork`*, a process should only read or write.*

The top portion of Figure 15.4 shows the disposition of the file descriptors immediately after the `fork`: the parent and the child have both file descriptors open. Figure 15.4 assumes that the parent will be the writer and the child will be the reader. The bottom half of the figure illustrates the status of the file descriptors after the parent closes its read descriptor and the child closes its write descriptor.

CAUTION

After the write end of a pipe has been closed, reading from that pipe will return 0 to signal the end of file. However, if the read end has been closed, any attempt to write to the pipe will generate the SIGPIPE signal for the writer, and the write call itself will return –1 and set the global variable errno to EPIPE. If the writer does not catch or ignore SIGPIPE, the writing process will terminate.

✔ To review catching and ignoring signals, see "Catching Signals," page 102.

EXAMPLE

Example

The following program, piperw, shows the correct procedure for opening a pipe between related processes.

```
/*
 * piperw.c - The correct way to open a pipe and fork
 *                 a child process.
 */
#include <unistd.h>
#include <stdio.h>
#include <stdlib.h>

#include <fcntl.h>
#include <limits.h>

#define BUFSZ PIPE_BUF

void err_quit(char *msg);

int main(int argc, char *argv[])
{
    int fd[2];                  /* File descriptor array for the pipe */
    int fdin;                   /* Descriptor for input file */
    char buf[BUFSZ];
    int pid, len;

    /* Create the pipe */
    if((pipe(fd)) < 0)
        err_quit("pipe");

    /* Fork and close the appropriate descriptors */
```

```
        if((pid = fork()) < 0)
            err_quit("fork");
    if (pid == 0) {
        /* Child is reader, close the write descriptor */
        close(fd[1]);
        while((len = read(fd[0], buf, BUFSZ)) > 0)
            write(STDOUT_FILENO, buf, len);
        close(fd[0]);
    } else {
        /* Parent is writer, close the read descriptor */
        close(fd[0]);
        if((fdin = open(argv[1], O_RDONLY)) < 0) {
            perror("open");
            /* Send something since we couldn't open the input */
            write(fd[1], "123\n", 4);
        } else {
            while((len = read(fdin, buf, BUFSZ)) > 0)
                write(fd[1], buf, len);
            close(fdin);
        }
        /* Close the write descriptor */
        close(fd[1]);
    }
    /* Reap the exit status */
    waitpid(pid, NULL, 0);

    exit(EXIT_SUCCESS);
}


void err_quit(char *msg)
{
    perror(msg);
    exit(EXIT_FAILURE);
}
```

piperw expects the name of an input file or it sends 123\n to the reader. A
sample run using pipopn.c as input resulted in the following output (truncated for brevity's sake):

OUTPUT

```
$ ./piperw pipopn.c
/*
 * pipopn.c - Open and close a pipe
 */
#include <unistd.h>
#include <stdio.h>
#include <stdlib.h>
...
```

As you can see from the output, piperw behaves rather like the cat command, except that it uses a pipe rather than simply displaying input to stdout. After the fork, the child closes the write descriptor it inherits because it is only reading from the pipe. Similarly, the parent is the writer, so it closes its read descriptor.

Rather than terminate the program, if the parent is unable to open its input file (argv[1]), it sends the string 123\n through the pipe before closing. When the parent finishes piping data to its child, it closes its write descriptor. When the child reads 0 bytes from the pipe, it close the read descriptor. Finally, although it is unclear whether parent or child exits first, the parent calls waitpid to reap the child's exit status and prevent creation of a zombie or orphan.

NOTE

If multiple processes are writing to the same pipe, each process's write must be less than PIPE_BUF bytes, a macro defined in <limits.h>, to ensure *atomic writes*; that is, that data written by one process does not get intermixed with data from another process. To state the matter as a rule, to ensure atomic writes, limit the amount of data written per write call to less than PIPE_BUF bytes.

A Simpler Way

The piperw program had to do a lot of work simply to cat a file: create a pipe, fork, close unneeded descriptors in both parent and child, open an input file, write to and read from the pipe, close the open files and descriptors, and then reap the child's exit status. This sequence of actions is so common that ANSI/ISO C has encoded them in the standard library functions popen and pclose, prototyped in <stdio.h> as follows:

```
FILE *popen(const char *command, const char *mode);
int pclose(FILE *stream);
```

popen creates a pipe and then forks a child process followed by an exec, which invokes /bin/sh -c to execute the command string contained in command. The mode argument must be one of r or w, which have the same semantics as they do in standard I/O library. That is, if mode is r, the FILE stream pointer that popen returns is opened for reading, which means that the stream is attached to command's standard output; reading from the stream is the same as reading command's standard output. Likewise, if mode is w, the stream is attached to command's standard input, so that writing to that stream is like writing to command's standard input. If the popen call fails, it returns NULL. The error condition that caused the failure will be set in the error variable errno.

To close the stream, you must use pclose rather than the standard fclose call. pclose closes the I/O stream, waits for command to complete, and returns its exit status to the calling process. If the pclose call fails, it returns −1.

EXAMPLE

Example

The following program rewrites piperw to use popen and pclose:

```
/*
 * piperw.c - The correct way to open a pipe and fork
 *            a child process.
 */
#include <unistd.h>

#include <stdio.h>

#include <stdlib.h>

#include <fcntl.h>

#include <limits.h>


#define BUFSZ PIPE_BUF


void err_quit(char *msg);


int main(void)
{
    FILE *fp;                              /* FILE stream for popen */
    char *cmdstring = "cat pipopn.c";
    char buf[BUFSZ];                       /* Buffer for "input" */

    /* Create the pipe */
    if((fp = popen(cmdstring, "r")) == NULL)
        err_quit("popen");
    /* Read cmdstring's output */
    while((fgets(buf, BUFSZ, fp)) != NULL)
```

```
        printf("%s", buf);

    /* Close and reap the exit status */
    pclose(fp);
    exit(EXIT_SUCCESS);
}


void err_quit(char *msg)
{
    perror(msg);
    exit(EXIT_FAILURE);
}
```

As you can see from the listing, popen and pclose make working with pipes much less code intensive. The price is giving up a certain amount of control. For example, you are forced to use the C's stream library rather than the low-level read and write I/O calls. In addition, popen forces your program to perform an exec, which you might not necessarily want or need to do. Finally, the function call pclose uses to reap the child's exit status might not fit your program's requirements. This loss of flexibility notwithstanding, popen saves 10–15 lines of code itself, while the code to handle reading and writing is significantly simplified from the piperw code. The output, part of which follows, is unchanged. The semantics of the mode may seem odd, so just remember that r means that you read from stdout and w means you write to stdin.

OUTPUT

```
$ ./newrw
/*
 * pipopn.c - Open and close a pipe
 */
#include <unistd.h>
#include <stdio.h>
#include <stdlib.h>

...
```

FIFOs

As stated previously, FIFOs are also called named pipes because they are *persistent*, that is, they exist in the filesystem. FIFOs are especially useful because they allow unrelated processes to exchange data.

Understanding FIFOs

A simple example using shell commands can help you understand FIFOs. The mkfifo(1) command creates FIFOs:

```
mkfifo [option] name [...]
```

The command creates a FIFO named name. option is usually -m mode, where mode indicates the octal mode of the newly created FIFO, subject to modifications by the umask. After you create the FIFO, you can use it as if it were part of a regular shell pipeline.

EXAMPLE

Example

The example that follows sends the output of newrw through a FIFO imaginatively named fifo1, which in turn sends its output through the cut command.

First, create the FIFO using the following command:

```
$ mkfifo -m 600 fifo1
```

Next, execute the following two commands:

```
$ cat < fifo1 ¦ cut -c1-5 &
$ ./newrw > fifo1
```

The output of these shell commands follows:

OUTPUT

```
/*
 * pi
 */
#incl
#incl
#incl

int m

{
    int

    if((
        per
        Exit
    }
    fpri
    clos
```

```
        clos
        exit
}
```

The cat command, running in the background, reads its input from the FIFO (fifo1). cat's input is the output of the cut command, which trims off all but the first five characters of each line of input. cut's input, finally, is the output of the newrw program.

The actual output of these shell commands is the odd looking, truncated code that completes the listing. If fifo1 was a regular file, the result would be a regular file filled with newrw's output.

TIP

The output of the ls command confirms that mkfifo created the requested FIFO. It appears with a p (for pipe) in the device type field of the file mode and also, because of the -F switch, it appears with a ¦ at the end of the filename.

Creating a FIFO

The function call to create a FIFO has the same name as the shell interface, mkfifo. Its syntax is similar to that of open:

```
int mkfifo(const char *pathname, mode_t mode);
```

To use this function, include <sys/types.h> and <sys/stat.h> in your program. mkfifo creates a FIFO named pathname with the permission bits specified (in octal) by mode. As usual, the value in mode will be modified by the process's umask.

NOTE

The umask affects most calls that create files or directories with specific permissions. To determine in advance what a file or directory's mode will be after modification by the umask, simply bitwise AND the mode you are using with the one's complement of the umask's value. In code, this would look like the following:

```
        mode_t mode = 0666;
        mode & ~umask;
```

So, given a umask of 022, mode & ~umask returns 0644.

If it succeeds, mkfifo returns 0, otherwise, it sets the value of the error variable errno and returns −1 to the caller. Potential errors include EACCESS, EEXIST, ENAMETOOLONG, ENOENT, ENOSPC, ENOTDIR, and EROFS.

✔ Table 6.1, "System Call Error Codes," on page 125 lists the return codes that system calls generate.

Example

The following program creates a FIFO in the current directory:

```c
/*
 * newfifo.c - Create a FIFO
 */
#include <sys/types.h>
#include <sys/stat.h>
#include <errno.h>
#include <stdio.h>
#include <stdlib.h>

int main(int argc, char *argv[])
{
    mode_t mode = 0666;

    if(argc != 2) {
puts("USAGE: newfifo <name>");
        exit(EXIT_FAILURE);
    }
    if((mkfifo(argv[1], mode)) < 0) {
        perror("mkfifo");
        exit(EXIT_FAILURE);
    }
    exit(EXIT_SUCCESS);
}
```

A few sample runs of this program produced the following output:

```
$ ./newfifo
USAGE: newfifo <name>
$ ./newfifo fifo1
$ ./newfifo fifo1
mkfifo: File exists
```

The first time, newfifo complained because it was not called correctly; it
expects the name of the FIFO to be passed as its only argument. The second run provided a filename, and newfifo silently created it. Because the
file already existed, the mkfifo call in the third run failed and errno was
set to EEXIST. The EEXIST setting corresponds to the string that perror
printed: File exists.

Opening and Closing FIFOs

The processes of opening, closing, deleting, reading, and writing FIFOs use the same open, close, unlink, read, and write system calls, respectively, that you have already seen—one of the virtues of Linux's "everything is a file" abstraction. Because opening and closing FIFOs is identical to opening and closing pipes, you might want to review the program that opens and closes a pipe, listed in "Opening and Closing Pipes" earlier in this chapter.

You must keep a few subtleties in mind when you are reading and writing FIFOs, however. First, both ends of a FIFO must be open before it can be used. Second, and more important, is a FIFO's behavior if it has been opened using the O_NONBLOCK flag. Recall that the O_WRONLY or O_RDONLY flags can be logically ORed with O_NONBLOCK. If a FIFO is opened with O_NON-BLOCK and O_RDONLY, the call returns immediately, but if it is opened with O_NONBLOCK and O_WRONLY, open returns an error and sets errno to ENXIO if the FIFO has not also been opened for reading.

If, on the other hand, O_NONBLOCK is not specified in open's flags, O_RDONLY will cause open to block (not return) until another process opens the FIFO for writing. Likewise, O_WRONLY will block until the FIFO is opened for reading.

As with pipes, writing to a FIFO that is not opened for reading sends SIG-PIPE to the writing process and sets errno to EPIPE. After the last writer closes a FIFO, a reading process will detect an end-of-file on its next read. As mentioned in relation to pipes, to ensure atomic writes when multiple processes are writing to a single FIFO, each process's write must be less than PIPE_BUF bytes in size.

Reading and Writing FIFOs

Subject to the considerations discussed at the end of the last section, reading and writing FIFOs is similar to reading and writing pipes and regular files.

EXAMPLE

Example

This example is somewhat involved. One program, rdfifo, creates and opens a FIFO for reading, displaying the FIFO's output to stdout. The other program, wrfifo, opens the FIFO for writing. Especially interesting is the process of running several instances of the writer in different windows and watching their output in the window running the reader.

```
/*
 * rdfifo.c - Create a FIFO and read from it
 */

#include <sys/types.h>
```

```c
#include <sys/stat.h>
#include <errno.h>
#include <stdio.h>
#include <stdlib.h>
#include <fcntl.h>
#include <limits.h>

int main(void)
{
    int fd;                                 /* Descriptor for FIFO */
    int len;                                /* Bytes read from FIFO */
    char buf[PIPE_BUF];
    mode_t mode = 0666;

    if((mkfifo("fifo1", mode)) < 0) {
        perror("mkfifo");
        exit(EXIT_FAILURE);
    }
    /* Open the FIFO read-only */
    if((fd = open("fifo1", O_RDONLY)) < 0) {
        perror("open");
        exit(EXIT_FAILURE);
    }
    /* Read and display the FIFO's output until EOF */
    while((len = read(fd, buf, PIPE_BUF - 1)) > 0)
        printf("rdfifo read: %s", buf);
    close(fd);

    exit(EXIT_SUCCESS);

}

/*
 * wrfifo.c - Write to a "well-known" FIFO
 */
#include <sys/types.h>
#include <sys/stat.h>
#include <errno.h>
```

```c
#include <stdio.h>
#include <stdlib.h>
#include <fcntl.h>
#include <limits.h>
#include <time.h>

int main(void)
{
    int fd;                             /* Descriptor for FIFO */
    int len;                            /* Bytes written to FIFO */
    char buf[PIPE_BUF];                 /* Ensure atomic writes */
    mode_t mode = 0666;
    time_t tp;                          /* For time call */

    /* Identify myself */
    printf("I am %d\n", getpid());

    /* Open the FIFO write-only */
    if((fd = open("fifo1", O_WRONLY)) < 0) {
        perror("open");
        exit(EXIT_FAILURE);
    }
    /* Generate some data to write */
    while(1) {
        /* Get the current time */
        time(&tp);
        /* Create the string to write */
        len = sprintf(buf, "wrfifo %d sends %s",
                        getpid(), ctime(&tp));
        /*
         * Use (len + 1) because sprintf does not count
         * the terminating null
         */
        if((write(fd, buf, len + 1)) < 0) {
            perror("write");
            close(fd);
            exit(EXIT_FAILURE);
        }
```

```
        sleep(3);
    }
    close(fd);
    exit(EXIT_SUCCESS);
}
```

The output from these programs is shown in Figure 15.5. The reader, rdfifo, is running in the large xterm. The three smaller xterms are each running an instance of the writer, wrfifo. The PIDs of each writer are shown in their screens. Every three seconds, the writers push a message consisting of their PIDs and the current time into the FIFO, fifo1. As you can see, the reader displays the message received and prefixes it with rdfifo read to differentiate its output from the input taken from the FIFO.

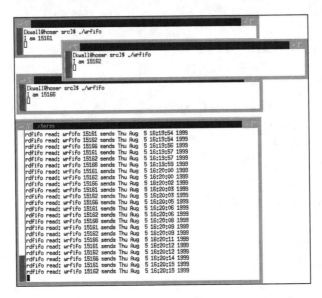

Figure 15.5: *Multiple processes writing to the same FIFO.*

It is worth noting that that these programs constitute a primitive, albeit relatively useless, *client/server* application. The server is rdfifo; it processes messages sent to it through the FIFO. The clients are each of the wrfifo processes, whose sole purpose is to send messages to the server.

A more sophisticated client/server application would perform some sort of processing on the data it receives and would send some sort of notification or data back to the client(s). In-depth coverage of client/server applications is way beyond the scope of this book, but feel satisfied that you have just written one!

What's Next?

This chapter has covered the simplest form of interprocess communication: pipes and FIFOs. The next chapter continues the discussion of IPC methods by focusing on shared memory. Although more complicated than pipes and FIFOs, shared memory IPC is more capable and flexible and is commonly used in larger, more sophisticated applications, such as relational database management systems (*RDBMS*) like Informix and Oracle.

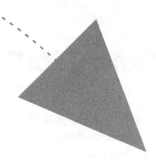

## 16

Shared Memory

Shared memory is the first of three types of *IPC*, or InterProcess Communication, you will learn. The other two styles are semaphores and message queues and are the subject of the next chapter. Taken together, the three types are usually called *System V IPC*, because they originated with System V UNIX, originally released by AT&T. BSD-derived UNIX implementations and other UNIX-like operating systems, including Linux, support them, too.

✔ Complete coverage of semaphores and message queues is provided in Chapter 17, "Semaphores and Message Queues."

The topics covered in this chapter include

- A general description of System V IPC

- Problems with System V IPC

- The use of shared memory

Introducing System V IPC

This is the first of two chapters discussing System V IPC mechanisms. System V IPC is rarely used in new applications because it has been superceded by POSIX IPC. Nevertheless, it is covered in this book because you will likely encounter it in older programs that were written before the POSIX IPC standard was proposed. All three types have the same basic interface and the same general design. This section introduces the fundamental concepts of System V IPC and looks at the features and programming idioms common to semaphores, message queues, and shared memory.

IPC structures (semaphores, message queues, and shared memory segments) exist in the kernel, like pipes, rather than in the filesystem, like FIFOs. IPC structures are sometimes referred to collectively as *IPC objects* to avoid the awkwardness of saying or writing "semaphores, messages queues, and shared memory segments." Similarly, the term *IPC object* is used to refer to one of the structure types without being specific about which type. Figure 16.1 shows how unrelated processes communicate with each other via an IPC object.

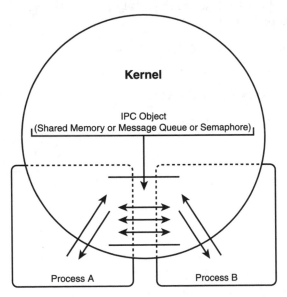

Figure 16.1: IPC objects enable unrelated processes to exchange data.

As you can see in Figure 16.1, IPC objects are maintained in the kernel (actually, in kernel memory), allowing otherwise unrelated processes (processes that do not have a common parent) to communicate with each other using one of the IPC mechanisms, shared memory, semaphores, or message queues. Data flows freely between the processes using IPC mechanisms.

Each object is referred to and accessed by its *identifier,* a positive integer uniquely identifying the object and its type. Each identifier is unique for its type, but the same identifier value may be in use for a message queue, a semaphore, and a shared memory segment. The identifier becomes the handle for all other operations on the structure.

NOTE

IPC structure identifiers are not small positive integers used and reused the way file descriptors are. In fact, as structures are created and deleted, the identifier number, formally denoted a *slot usage sequence number*, increments until it reaches a maximum value, at which point it wraps to 0 and starts over. The maximum value depends on the operating system and the underlying hardware. In Linux, identifiers are declared as integers, so the maximum value possible is 65,535.

Each IPC structure is created with a get function: semget for semaphores, msgget for message queues, and shmget for shared memory. Each time an object is created using one of the get functions, the calling process must specify a *key*, of type key_t (declared in <sys/types.h>), that the kernel uses to generate the identifier. The Linux 2.2.x kernel defines key_t as an integer.

After an IPC structure has been created, subsequent calls to a get function using the same key do not create a new structure, but merely return the identifier associated with an existing one. So two (or more) processes can call a get function with the same key in order to establish an IPC channel.

The challenge then becomes how to ensure that all processes wanting to use the same IPC structure use the same key. In one method, the process that actually creates the structure passes a key of IPC_PRIVATE to the get function, which guarantees that a new structure will be created. The creator of the IPC structure then stores the returned identifier in the filesystem where other processes can access it. When a parent forks and execs a new process, the parent passes the returned identifier to its child process as one of the arguments to the exec function that creates the child.

Another method stores a standard key in a common header file, so that all programs that include the header file have access to the same key. One problem with this approach is that no process knows if it is creating a new structure or merely accessing one that has already been created by another process. Another problem with this approach is that the key might already be in use by an unrelated program. As a result, the process using this key must have code to handle such a possibility.

A third method involves using the `ftok` function, which takes a pathname and a single `char` character, called a *project identifier*, and returns a key, which is then passed to the appropriate `get` function. It is your responsibility to ensure that the pathname and project identifier are known to all processes in advance. You can achieve this using one of the methods mentioned earlier: including the pathname and the project identifier in a common header file or storing them in a predefined configuration file. Unfortunately, `ftok` has a serious defect: It is not guaranteed to generate a unique key, which creates the same problems as the second approach discussed earlier. Due to the potential problems with using `ftok`, this chapter disregards it.

CAUTION

Bluntly stated, Linux's `ftok` implementation is broken. It generates a non-unique key in the following situations:

- When two different symbolic links link to the same file.

- When the first 16 bits of the pathname's inode number have the same value.

- When a system has two disk devices with the same minor number, which occurs in systems that have multiple disk controllers. The major device number will be different, but the minor device number can be the same.

Given the weakness of Linux's `ftok` implementation, readers are strongly encouraged to consider it anathema and ignore it.

In addition to specifying a `key`, the `get` functions also accept a `flags` argument that controls `get`'s behavior. If the specified key is not already in use for the desired type of structure and the `IPC_CREAT` bit is set in `flag`, a new structure will be created.

Each IPC structure has a *mode*, a set of permissions that behave analogously to a file's mode (as passed to `open`), except that IPC structures have no concept of execute permissions. When creating an IPC structure, you must bitwise `OR` specific permissions, using the octal notation as defined for the `open` and `creat` systems calls, into the `flags` argument or you might not be able to access the created structure. You will encounter specific examples of this later. As you might expect, System V IPC includes a call for changing access permissions and ownership of IPC structures.

✔ For a quick refresher on file modes, see "The File Mode," page 134.

Problems with System V IPC

System V IPC has several shortcomings. First, the programmatic interface is complex compared to the benefits it provides. Second, IPC structures are a more tightly limited resource than, say, the number of files a system can support or the number of active processes the system permits. Third, despite being a limited resource, IPC structures do not maintain a *reference count*, which is a counter of the number of processes using the structure. As a result, System V IPC has no automatic means of reclaiming abandoned IPC structures.

For example, if a process creates a structure, places data in it, and then terminates without properly deleting the structure and its associated data, the structure remains in place until one of the following occurs:

- The system is rebooted

- It is specifically deleted using the ipcsrm(1) command

- Another process, with appropriate access permissions, reads the data or deletes it, or both

This shortcoming constitutes a significant design defect.

Finally, IPC structures, as noted earlier, exist only in the kernel; they are unknown to the filesystem. As a result, I/O to them requires learning yet another programming interface. Lacking file descriptors, you cannot use multiplexed I/O through the select system call. If a process must wait for I/O on an IPC structure, it must use some sort of busy-wait loop. A *busy-wait loop*—a loop that continuously checks for some changed condition—is a poor programming practice almost any time because it needlessly consumes CPU cycles. The busy-wait loop is especially pernicious under Linux, which has several methods for implementing non-busy waits, such as blocking I/O, the select system call, and signals.

✔ To review multiplexed I/O and the select system call, see "I/O Multiplexing," page 169.

Understanding Shared Memory

Shared memory is a memory region (a *segment*) set aside by the kernel for the purpose of information exchange between multiple processes. Provided the segment's permissions are appropriately set, each process desiring to access the segment may map the segment into its own private address space. If one process updates the data in the segment, that update is immediately visible to other processes. A segment created by one process can be read or written (or both) by other processes. The name, *shared memory*, conveys the fact that multiple processes may share access to the segment and the information it contains.

Each process receives its own mapping of the shared memory into its address space. In fact, shared memory conceptually resembles memory mapped files. Shared memory is illustrated in Figure 16.2.

✔ The creation and use of memory mapped files is discussed in detail in "Memory Mapping Files," page 174.

Figure 16.2 oversimplifies the shared memory matter somewhat because the shared memory segment may consist of data in physical RAM as well as memory pages that have been swapped out to disk. The same caveat applies to the address space of processes attaching to the shared memory segment.

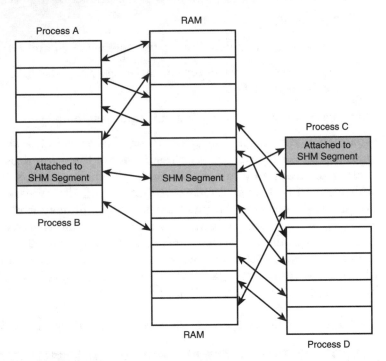

Figure 16.2: *Processes map shared memory segments into their own address space.*

Nevertheless, the figure shows a shared memory (SHM) segment created in main memory (shown as a shaded box). The shaded boxes in processes B and C illustrate that the two processes have mapped this segment into their own address spaces. The figure also shows that each of the four processes has its own address space that maps to some portion of physical RAM. However, the address space of one process is not available to another process.

Naturally, because data transfer happens strictly in memory (ignoring the possibility that one or more pages have been swapped to disk), shared memory is a fast way for two processes to communicate. It has many of the same advantages as memory mapped files.

Creating a Shared Memory Segment

The call to create a shared memory segment is shmget. To use any of the calls related to shared memory, you must include <sys/types.h>, <sys/ipc.h>, and <sys/shm.h> in your source code. shmget's prototype follows:

```
int shmget(key_t key, int size, int flags);
```

flags can be one or more of IPC_CREAT, IP_EXCL, and a set of permission bits (modes) bitwise ORed together. The permission bits are specified in octal. IPC_EXCL ensures that if the segment already exists, the call fails instead of returning the identifier to an existing segment.

TIP

The makefile for this chapter's examples (on the accompanying Web site) includes a preprocessor macro, -D _XOPEN_SOURCE. This macro is required because all the programs include <ipc.h>, which requires that _XOPEN_SOURCE is defined. Curiously, when I compiled these programs on a default Red Hat 6.0 installation, I did not need to define the macro, but I did need to define the macro when compiling on OpenLinux 2.3.

IPC_CREAT indicates that a new segment should be created if there is not already a segment associated with key. key is either IPC_PRIVATE or a key returned by the ftok function. The size argument specifies the size of the segment, but this will be rounded up to the value of PAGE_SIZE, which is the natural size of a page for a given processor (4k for current Intel processors, 8k on the Alpha). shmget returns the segment identifier on success or −1 on error.

Example

This example, mkshm, creates a shared memory segment and displays the identifier that shmget returns.

EXAMPLE

```
/*
 * mkshm.c - Create and initialize shared memory segment
 */
#include <sys/types.h>
#include <sys/ipc.h>
#include <sys/shm.h>
#include <stdio.h>
#include <stdlib.h>

#define BUFSZ 4096
```

```
int main(void)
{
    int shmid;

    if((shmid = shmget(IPC_PRIVATE, BUFSZ, 0666)) < 0) {
        perror("shmget");
        exit(EXIT_FAILURE);
    }
    printf("segment created: %d\n", shmid);
    system("ipcs -m");

    exit(EXIT_SUCCESS);
}
```

```
$ ./mkshm
segment created: 40833
```

OUTPUT

```
------ Shared Memory Segments --------
key        shmid    owner    perms   bytes    nattch   status
0x00000000 40705    kwall    666     4096     0
```

As the output shows, mkshm successfully creates a shared memory segment. The next to last column of the output from ipcs -m, nattch, shows the number of processes that have *attached* the segment (which means the processes that have mapped the segment into their own address space). Note that no processes have attached to the segment. The only thing that shmget does is create the shared memory segment; processes that want to map it into their own address space, called *attaching to the segment*, must explicitly do so, using the shmat call discussed in the next section.

Attaching a Shared Memory Segment

You cannot use a shared memory segment until you *attach* it, or map its address into your process's address space. Similarly, when you are finished working with a shared memory segment, you must detach it from your address space. Attaching is done using the shmat call, whereas detaching requires the shmdt call. These routines have the following prototypes:

```
char *shmat(int shmid, char *shmaddr, int flags);

int shmdt(char *shmadr);
```

shmid is the identifier of the segment to which you want to attach. In shmat, if shmaddr is 0, the kernel will map the segment into the calling process's address space at an address of its choosing. If shmaddr is not 0, it indicates the address at which the kernel should map the segment—obviously, doing this is a crap shoot, so always set shmaddr to 0. flags can be SHM_RDONLY, which means the segment will be attached as read-only. The default is that the segment is attached read-write. If the shmat call succeeds, it returns the address of the attached segment. Otherwise, it returns –1 and sets errno.

shmdt disconnects the segment that is attached at shmaddr from the calling process's address space; the address must have been previously returned by a call to shmget.

Examples

EXAMPLE

1. This example, atshm, attaches and detaches a shared memory segment.

```
/*
 * atshm.c - Attached to a shared memory segment
 */
#include <sys/types.h>
#include <sys/ipc.h>
#include <sys/shm.h>
#include <stdio.h>
#include <stdlib.h>

int main(int argc, char *argv[])
{
    int shmid;                  /* Segment identifier */
    char *shmbuf;               /* Address in process */

    /* Expect a segment id on the command line */
    if(argc != 2) {
        puts("USAGE: atshm <identifier>");
        exit(EXIT_FAILURE);
    }
    shmid = atoi(argv[1]);

    /* Attach the segment */
    if((shmbuf = shmat(shmid, 0, 0)) < (char *)0) {
        perror("shmat");
        exit(EXIT_FAILURE);
    }
    /* Where is it attached? */
```

```
            printf("segment attached at %p\n", shmbuf);

            /* See, we really are attached! */
            system("ipcs -m");

            /* Detach */
            if((shmdt(shmbuf)) < 0) {
                perror("shmdt");
                exit(EXIT_FAILURE);
            }
            puts("segment detached\n");
            /* Yep, we really did detach it */
            system("ipcs -m");

            exit(EXIT_SUCCESS);
        }
```

shmat returns a pointer to char, so when checking its return code, atshm casts the zero as a char * to avoid pesky compiler warnings. The example also uses the ipcs command to confirm that the calling process does in fact successfully attach and detach the memory segment. The output that follows illustrates this. Notice that the number of attached processes, nattch, increments and decrements.

```
$ ./atshm 40833
segment attached at 0x40014000
```

OUTPUT

```
------ Shared Memory Segments --------

key        shmid    owner    perms    bytes    nattch    status
0x00000000 40833    kwall    666      4096     1


segment detached

------ Shared Memory Segments --------
key        shmid    owner    perms    bytes    nattch    status
0x00000000 40833    kwall    666      4096     0
```

2. The next example attaches to a segment, writes data to it, and then writes the buffer out to the file `opshm.out`.

```c
/*
 * opshm.c - Attach to a shared memory segment
 */
#include <sys/types.h>
#include <sys/ipc.h>
#include <sys/shm.h>
#include <stdio.h>
#include <stdlib.h>
#include <fcntl.h>

#define BUFSZ 4096

int main(int argc, char *argv[])
{
    int shmid;                  /* Segment ID */
    char *shmbuf;               /* Address in process */
    int fd;                     /* File descriptor */
    int i;                      /* Counter */

    /* Expect a segment id on the command line */
    if(argc != 2) {
        puts("USAGE: opshm <identifier>");
        exit(EXIT_FAILURE);
    }
    shmid = atoi(argv[1]);

    /* Attach the segment */
    if((shmbuf = shmat(shmid, 0, 0)) < (char *)0) {
        perror("shmat");
        exit(EXIT_FAILURE);
    }

    /* Allocate storage for shmbuf */
    if((shmbuf = malloc(sizeof(char) * BUFSZ)) == NULL) {
        perror("malloc");
        exit(EXIT_FAILURE);
```

```
    }
    for(i = 0; i < BUFSZ; ++i)
  shmbuf[i] = i % 127;
    fd = open("opshm.out", O_CREAT | O_WRONLY, 0600);
    write(fd, shmbuf, BUFSZ);
    exit(EXIT_SUCCESS);
}
```

This example attaches to a previously created segment, sets values in the memory region, and then writes the entire buffer out to a disk file. The program has no visual output, but the following listing is an excerpt from the output file, opshm.out:

OUTPUT

```
$ ./opshm 40833

^@^A^B^C^D^E^F^^I

➥^K^L^M^N^O^P^Q^R^S^T^U^V^W^X^Y^ZESC^\^]^^^_

➥!"#$%&'()*+,-./0123456789:;<=>?@ABCDEFGHIJKLMNOPQRSTUVWXYZ

➥[\]^_`abcdefghijklmnopqrstuvwxyz{|}~^@^A^B^C^D^E^F^^
```

What's Next?

This chapter examined System V IPC shared memory. The next chapter, "Semaphores and Message Queues," continues your exploration of System V IPC, and then you will go on to TCP/IP and socket programming in Chapter 18.

17

Semaphores and Message Queues

This chapter continues the discussion of System V IPC that was begun in the last chapter. The coverage of message queues and semaphores here will complete the survey of System V IPC. The following material is covered in this chapter:

- Understanding a message queue
- Creating a message queue
- Attaching to an existing message queue
- Posting and retrieving messages
- Deleting a message queue
- Understanding semaphores
- Creating and removing semaphores
- Updated semaphores

✔ Using shared memory IPC objects is discussed in Chapter 16, "Shared Memory," page 339.

Linux and System V IPC

System V IPC is well-known and commonly used, but the Linux implementation of it is badly broken, as noted in this and the previous chapter. Linux's version also pre-dates POSIX IPC, but few Linux programs actually implement it even though it is available in 2.2.x kernels. POSIX IPC has a similar interface to the earlier System V incarnation discussed in this and the last chapter, but it both eliminates some of the problems that System V had and also simplifies the interface. The problem is that although System V IPC is standard, it is also perverse and poorly implemented in Linux, for reasons that are too advanced to cover here.

The outcome of this situation is that Linux, which strives (and mostly succeeds) to be POSIX compliant, implements both an early version of POSIX IPC and the System V version. The difficulty is that System V is well-established and more common, but the POSIX version is better, easier to use, and has a more uniform interface for interacting programmatically with the three types of IPC objects. The result? I chose to break my own rule and opted to cover what you are likely to encounter in both existing and new programs rather than discuss the Right Thing ©; that is, POSIX IPC.

An additional issue arises when dealing with semaphores. System V semaphores were created in the Dark Ages to address the horde of problems that arise when multiple threads of execution in a single process (and in multiple processes) need to access the same system resources approximately simultaneously. Although I consider well-written multithreaded programs an essential (indeed, an indispensable) component of any Linux system, I emphasize *well-written*. Writing multithreaded programs goes far, far beyond this book's scope; it's no place for novice programmers. Experienced programmers, even *über*-programmers, will look for other solutions before resorting to multithreading because it is difficult to implement correctly.

My point? I simplified the discussion of semaphores because the System V version was created with multithreaded processes in mind. Nonetheless, semaphores in standard, single-threaded programs are quite useful, as you will see in this chapter. The POSIX semaphore interface is simpler but not widely used, at this time, in Linux programs.

Message Queues

A *message queue* is a linked list of messages stored within the kernel and identified to user processes by a *message queue identifier*, an identifier of the sort discussed in the last chapter. For brevity and convenience, this chapter uses the terms *queue* and *queue ID* to refer to message queues and message queue identifiers. If you are adding a message to a queue, it appears to be a FIFO because new messages are added at the end of the queue. However, you do not have to retrieve messages in FIFO order. Message queues can also be considered a simple form of associative memory because, as you will see later, you can use a message's type to retrieve a message out of order. The difference between message queues and FIFOs is illustrated in Figure 17.1.

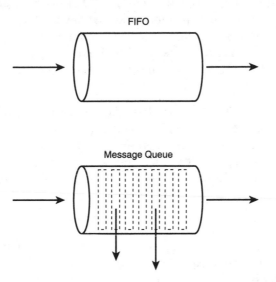

Figure 17.1: *Unlike FIFOs, messages can be read from a queue in any order.*

As you know, data is read from a FIFO in the same order as it was written. This is illustrated in the top half of Figure 17.1. However, if you know a message's message type, you can extract a given message from a queue. As shown by the arrows exiting and leaving the message queue, messages usually are read in first-in first-out order. The two dotted rectangles with outward pointing arrows on the message queue show how messages can be read in arbitrary order.

All the queue-manipulation functions are declared in <sys/msg.h>, but you must also include <sys/types.h> and <sys/ipc.h> to access the type and constant declarations they contain. To create a new queue or to open an existing one, use the msgget function. To add a new message to the bottom of a queue, use msgsnd. To grab a message off a queue, use the msgrcv call. msgctl enables you to manipulate queue features and to delete a queue, provided the calling process is the queue's creator or has superuser permissions.

Creating and Opening a Queue

The `msgget` function creates a new queue or opens an existing one. Its prototype is as follows:

```
int msgget(key_t key, int flags);
```

If the call is successful, it returns the queue ID of the new or existing queue corresponding to the value contained in key. If key is IPC_PRIVATE, a new queue is created using a key value that the underlying implementation generates; using IPC_PRIVATE is guaranteed to create a new queue if system limits on the number of queues or the total number of bytes in all queues are not exceeded.

Similarly, if key is not IPC_PRIVATE if key does not correspond to an existing queue having the same key, and if the IPC_CREAT bit is set in the flags argument, a new queue is created. Otherwise—that is, if key is not IPC_PRIVATE and if the IPC_CREAT bit is not set in flags—msgget returns the queue ID of the existing queue associated with key. If msgget fails, it returns −1 and sets the errno error variable.

EXAMPLE

Example

The sample program that follows, mkq, creates a new message queue. If you execute it a second time rather than create the specified queue, it simply opens the existing queue.

```
/*
 * mkq.c - Create a SysV IPC message queue
 */
#include <sys/types.h>
#include <sys/ipc.h>
#include <sys/msg.h>
#include <stdio.h>
#include <stdlib.h>

int main(int argc, char *argv[])
{
    int qid;        /* The queue identifier */
    key_t key;      /* The queue key */

    key = 123;

    /* Create the queue */
    if((qid == msgget(key, IPC_CREAT | 0666)) < 0) {
```

```
        perror("msgget:create");
        exit(EXIT_FAILURE);
    }
    printf("created queue id = %d\n", qid);

    /* Open the queue again */
    if((qid == msgget(key, 0)) < 0) {
        perror("msgget:open");
        exit(EXIT_FAILURE);
    }
    printf("opened queue id = %d\n", qid);

    exit(EXIT_SUCCESS);
}
```

The output from this program on my system looked as follows:

OUTPUT

```
$ ./mkq
created queue id = 384
opened queue id = 384
```

If the first msgget call succeeds, mkq displays the newly created queue ID, and then calls msgget a second time. If the second call succeeds, mkq reports this as well, but the second call merely opens the existing queue rather than creates a new one. Notice that the first call specifies read/write permissions for all users using the standard octal notation.

CAUTION

Unlike the open function's behavior, when creating a System V IPC structure, the process's umask does not modify the structure's access permissions. If you do not set access permissions, the default mode is 0, which means that not even the structure's creator has read or write access to it!

Writing a Message to a Queue

As explained earlier, to add a new message to the bottom of a queue, use the msgsnd function, which is prototyped as follows:

```
int msgsnd(int msqid, const void *ptr, size_t nbytes, int flags);
```

msgsnd returns 0 if it succeeds, but if it fails, it returns −1 and sets the global error variable errno to one of the values in the following list:

- EAGAIN
- EACCES

- EFAULT

- EIDRM

- EINTR

- EINVAL

- ENOMEM

✔ Values and explanations for errno values are listed in Table 6.1, "System Call Error Codes," page 125.

The msqid argument must be a queue ID returned by a previous call to msgget. nbytes is the number of bytes in the message posted, which should not be null-terminated. ptr is a pointer to a msgbuf structure, which consists of a message type and the data bytes that comprise the message. msgbuf is defined in <sys/ msg.h> as follows:

```
struct msgbuf {
    long mtype;
    char mtext[1];
};
```

This structure declaration is really only a template because mtext must be sized to the length of the data being stored, which corresponds to the value passed in the nbytes argument, less any terminating null. mtype can be any long integer greater than zero. The calling process must also have write access to the queue. The flags variable, finally, is either 0 or IPC_NOWAIT. IPC_NOWAIT causes behavior analogous to the O_NONBLOCK flag passed to the open system call: if the total number of individual queued messages or the queue's size, in bytes, is equal to the system-specified limit, msgsnd returns immediately and sets errno to EAGAIN. As a result, you will not be able to add any more messages to the queue until at least one message has been read.

If flags is 0 and either the maximum number of messages has been to the queue or the total number of bytes of data has been written to the queue, the msgsnd call blocks (does not return) until the condition is cleared. To clear the condition, messages must be read from queue, the queue must be removed (which sets errno to EIDRM) or a signal is caught and the handler returns (which sets errno to EINTR).

TIP

The msgbuf structure template may be expanded to meet your applications needs. For example, if you want to pass a message that consists of an integer and a 10-byte character array, just declare msgbuf as follows:

continues

continued

```
struct msgbuf {
    long mtype;
    int i;
    char c[10];
};
```

msgbuf is simply a `long` followed by the message data, which can be formatted as you see fit. The size of the structure declared in this example is `sizeof(msgbuf)` `- sizeof(long)`.

EXAMPLE

Example

This program, qsnd, adds a message to the bottom of a queue that already exists. Pass the queue ID as the program's sole command-line argument.

```c
/*
 * qsnd.c - Send a message to previously opened queue
 */
#include <sys/types.h>
#include <sys/ipc.h>
#include <sys/msg.h>
#include <stdio.h>
#include <stdlib.h>
#include <string.h>
#include <unistd.h>

#define BUFSZ 512

struct msg {                            /* Message structure */
    long msg_type;
    char msg_text[BUFSZ];
};

int main(int argc, char *argv[])
{
    int qid;                            /* The queue identifier */
    int len;                            /* Length of data sent */
    struct msg pmsg;                    /* Pointer to message structure */

    /* Expect the queue ID passed on the command-line */
```

```
        if(argc != 2) {
            puts("USAGE: qsnd <queue ID>");
            exit(EXIT_FAILURE);
        }
        qid = atoi(argv[1]);



        /* Get the message to add to the queue */
        puts("Enter message to post:");
        if((fgets((&pmsg)->msg_text, BUFSZ, stdin)) == NULL) {
            puts("no message to post");
            exit(EXIT_SUCCESS);
        }

        /* Associate the message with this process */
        pmsg.msg_type = getpid();
        /* Add the message to the queue */
        len = strlen(pmsg.msg_text);
        if((msgsnd(qid, &pmsg, len, 0)) < 0) {
            perror("msgsnd");
            exit(EXIT_FAILURE);
        }
        puts("message posted");


        exit(EXIT_SUCCESS);
}
```

A sample run of this program produced the following output. Notice that
the program uses the queue ID returned by mkq.

OUTPUT

```
$ ./mkq
created queue id = 640
opened queue id = 640
$ ./qsnd 640
Enter message to post:
this is test message number one
message posted
```

The first command, as you recall, created a new queue with a queue ID of
640. The second command, qsnd 640, prompted for a message to post and

stored the typed response (indicated in bold) directly into the msg structure declared earlier. If msgsnd completes successfully, it displays a message to that effect. Note that qsnd sets the message type to the calling process's PID. This allows you later to retrieve (using msgrcv) only those messages that this process posted.

Reading Queued Messages

To pull a message off a queue, use msgrcv, which has the syntax listed here:

```
int msgrcv(int msqid, void *ptr, size_t nbytes, long type, int flags);
```

If it succeeds, msgrcv removes the returned message from the queue. The arguments are the same as msgsnd accepts, except that msgrcv fills in the ptr structure with the message type and up to nbytes of data. The additional argument, type, corresponds to the msg_type member of the msg structure previously discussed. type's value determines which message is returned, as outlined in the following list:

- If type is 0, the first message in the queue (the topmost message) is returned.

- If type is > 0, the first message whose msg_type equals type is returned.

- If type is < 0, the first message whose msg_type is the lowest value less than or equal to type's absolute value is returned.

The value of flags also controls msgrcv's behavior. If the returned message is larger than nbytes, the message is truncated to nbytes if the MSG_NOERROR bit is set in flags (but no notification that the message has been truncated will be generated). Otherwise, msgrcv returns −1 to indicate an error and sets errno to E2BIG. The message also stays on the queue.

If the IPC_NOWAIT bit is set in flags, msgrcv returns immediately and sets errno to ENOMSG if no message of the specified type is available. Otherwise, msgrcv blocks until one of the same conditions described earlier for msgsnd occurs.

NOTE

A negative value for the type argument can be used to create a *LIFO*, or last-in, first-out type of queue, often called a stack. Passing a negative value in type enables you to retrieve messages of a given type in the reverse order in which they were placed in the queue.

EXAMPLE

Example

The following program, qrd, reads a message off a previously created and populated queue. The queue ID from which to read is passed as a command-line argument.

```c
/*
 * qrd.c - Read all message from a message queue
 */
#include <sys/types.h>
#include <sys/ipc.h>
#include <sys/msg.h>
#include <stdio.h>
#include <stdlib.h>

#define BUFSZ 512

struct msg {/* Message structure */
    long msg_type;
    char msg_text[BUFSZ];
};

int main(int argc, char *argv[])
{
    int qid;/* The queue identifier */
    int len;/* Length of message */
    struct msg pmsg;/* Pointer to a message structure */

    /* Expect the queue ID passed on the command-line */
    if(argc != 2) {
        puts("USAGE: qrd <queue ID>");
        exit(EXIT_FAILURE);
    }
    qid = atoi(argv[1]);


    /* Retrieve and display a message from the queue */
    len = msgrcv(qid, &pmsg, BUFSZ, 0, 0);
    if(len > 0) {
        printf("reading queue id: %05d\n", qid);
        printf("\tmessage type: %05d\n", (&pmsg)->msg_type);
        printf("\tmessage text: %s\n", (&pmsg)->msg_text);
    } else {
        perror("msgrcv");
```

```
        exit(EXIT_FAILURE);
    }


    exit(EXIT_SUCCESS);
}
```

The output from one run of this program follows. As before, it uses the queue ID created by mkq and also reads the message posted by the qsnd example.

OUTPUT

```
$ ./mkq
created queue id = 640
opened queue id = 640
$ ./qsnd 640
Enter message to post:
this is test message number one
message posted


$ ./qrd 640
reading queue id: 00640
    message type: 14308
    message text: this is test message number one
```

You can see from the code listing that reading from a message queue is easier than writing to one and requires less code. Of particular interest in the sample program is that it fetches the first message off the top of the queue because it passed a type of 0. In this case, because the PID of the message writing process is known or can be easily discovered (14308), qrd could have passed a type of 14308 and fetched the same message from the queue.

Removing Message Queues

The msgctl function provides a certain degree of control over message queues. Its prototype is as follows:

```
int msgctl(int msqid, int cmd, struct msqid_ds *buf);
```

As usual, msqid is the queue ID of an existing queue. cmd can be one of the following:

- IPC_RMID—Removes the queue msqid.

- IPC_STAT—Fills buf with the queue's msqid_ds structure. IPC_STAT enables you to peek into a queue's contents without removing any messages. Because it is a non-destructive read, you could consider it similar to msgrcv.

- IPC_SET—Allows you to change the queue's UID, GID, access mode, and the maximum number of bytes allowed on the queue.

EXAMPLE

Example

The program that follows uses the msgctl call to remove a queue whose ID is passed on the command line.

```
/*

 * qctl.c - Remove a message queue
 */
#include <sys/types.h>
#include <sys/ipc.h>
#include <sys/msg.h>
#include <stdio.h>
#include <stdlib.h>
#include <string.h>
#include <unistd.h>

int main(int argc, char *argv[])
{
    int qid;
    struct msqid_ds dsbuf;

    if(argc != 2) {
        puts("USAGE: qctl <qid>");
        exit(EXIT_FAILURE);
    }
    qid = atoi(argv[1]);

    if((msgctl(qid, IPC_RMID, NULL)) < 0) {
        perror("msgctl");
        exit(EXIT_FAILURE);
    }
    printf("queue %d removed\n", qid);
    exit(EXIT_SUCCESS);
}
```

OUTPUT

```
$ ./mkq
created queue id = 1280
opened queue id = 1280
$ ipcs -q
------ Message Queues --------
key         msqid      owner      perms      used-bytes  messages
0x0000007b 1280       kwall      666        0           0


$ ./qctl 1280
queue 1280 removed
$  ipcs -q

------ Message Queues --------
key         msqid      owner      perms      used-bytes  messages
```

The program output shows that the specified queue was deleted. mkq creates the queue. The ipcs call confirms that the queue was created. Using the queue ID displayed by mkq, qctl calls msgctl, specifying the IPC_RMID flag to delete the queue. Running ipcs a second time again confirms that qctl removed the queue.

The ipcs(1) command, used in several of the sample programs, shows the number and status of all System V IPC structures that exist on your system when it executes. The ipcrm(1) command will delete the IPC structure whose type and ID is specified on the command line. See the manual pages for more information. Figure 17.2 shows the output of the ipcs command.

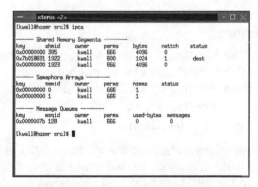

Figure 17.2: *ipcs shows all System V IPC objects that currently exist.*

Figure 17.2 shows that at least one of each type of IPC object exists. Three shared memory segments, one message queue, and two semaphores are currently in use (semaphores are discussed in the next section). Each object's key, identifier, owner/creator, and permissions are clearly listed. Statistics relative to each type of object are shown in the last one or two columns of the output, depending on the type of object.

Semaphores

Semaphores control access to shared resources. They are quite different from the other means of IPC you have seen so far, in that they do not make information available between processes, but instead synchronize access to shared resources that should not be accessed simultaneously. In this respect, semaphore operations more closely resemble file or record locking, but applied to more resources than just files. This section discusses only the simplest type of semaphore, a *binary semaphore*. A binary semaphore takes one of two values: 0 when a resource is locked and should not be accessed by other processes, and 1 when the resource is unlocked.

✔ For more information about file and record locking, see "File Locking," page 182.

Semaphores function much like traffic lights at a busy intersection. When a process needs access to a controlled resource, such as a file, it first checks the semaphore value, just as a driver checks to see if a traffic light is green. If the semaphore has a value of zero, which corresponds to a red light, the resource is in use, so the process blocks until the resource becomes available (that is, the semaphore's value becomes non-zero). In the terminology of System V IPC, this blocking is called a *wait*. If the semaphore has a positive value, which corresponds to a green light at an intersection, the associated resource is available, so the process decrements the semaphore, performs its operations on the resource, and then increments the semaphore to release the "lock."

Creating a Semaphore

Naturally, before you can increment or decrement a semaphore, it must exist. The function call for creating a new semaphore or accessing an existing one is semget, prototyped in <sys/sem.h> as follows (you also must include <sys/ipc.h> and <sys/types.h>):

```
int semget(key_t key, int nsems, int flags);
```

semget returns the semaphore identifier associated with a set of nsems semaphores. A new set of semaphores is created if key is IPC_PRIVATE or if key is not already in use and the IPC_CREAT bit is set in flags. As with shared memory segments and message queues, flags can also be bitwise ORed with permission bits (in octal) to set the access modes for the semaphore. Note, however, that semaphores have read and alter permissions rather than read and write permissions. Semaphores use the notion of *alter* rather than *write* because you never actually write data to a semaphore, you merely change (or alter) its status by incrementing or decrementing its value. semget returns –1 and sets errno if an error occurs, otherwise it returns the semaphore identifier associated with the value of key.

NOTE

System V semaphore calls actually operate on an array, or set, of semaphores, rather than just on a single semaphore. The desire here, however, is to simplify the discussion and introduce you to the material rather than cover semaphores in all their complexity. Whether working with a single semaphore or multiple semaphores, the basic approach is the same, but it is important for you to understand that System V semaphores come in sets. Personally, I think the interface is unnecessarily complex, and POSIX IPC standardizes a simpler but equally capable semaphore interface.

This chapter's discussion of semaphores also ignores their use in situations in which a process has multiple threads of execution. Multi-threaded processes and the use of semaphores in that context extends beyond this book's scope.

The semop function is the workhorse semaphore routine. It performs operations on one or more of the semaphores created or accessed by the semget call. Its prototype is as follows:

```
int semop(int semid, struct sembuf *semops, unsigned nops);
```

semid is a semaphore identifier previously returned by semget and points to the semaphore set to manipulate. nops is the number of elements in the array of sembuf structures to which semops points. sembuf, in turn, has the following structure:

```
struct sembuf {
    short sem_num; /* Semaphore number */
    short sem_op;  /* The operation to perform */
    short sem_flg; /* Flags controlling the operation */
};
```

In the sembuf structure, sem_num is a semaphore number from zero to nsems - 1, sem_op is the operation to perform, and sem_flg modifies semop's behavior. sem_op can be negative, zero, or positive. If it is positive, the resource controlled by the semaphore is released and the semaphore's value is incremented.

If sem_op is negative, the calling process is indicating that it wants to wait until the controlled resource is available, at which time the semaphore will be decremented and the resource locked by the calling process.

If sem_op is zero, finally, the calling process will block (wait) until the semaphore becomes zero; if it is already zero, the call returns immediately. sem_flg can be IPC_NOWAIT, which has behavior described earlier, or

SEM_UNDO, which means that the operation performed will be undone when the process calling semop exits.

EXAMPLE

Example

The program that follows, mksem, creates a semaphore and increments it, thus setting the imaginary resource as unlocked or available:

```c
/*
 * mksem.c - Create and decrement a semaphore
 */
#include <sys/types.h>
#include <sys/ipc.h>
#include <sys/sem.h>
#include <stdio.h>

#include <stdlib.h>

int main(void)
{
    int semid;                      /* Semaphore identifier */
    int nsems = 1;                  /* How many semaphores to create */
    int flags = 0666;               /* World read-alter mode */
    struct sembuf buf;

    /* Create the semaphore with world read-alter perms */
    semid = semget(IPC_PRIVATE, nsems, flags);
    if(semid < 0) {
        perror("semget");
        exit(EXIT_FAILURE);
    }
    printf("semaphore created: %d\n", semid);

    /* Set up the structure for semop */
    buf.sem_num = 0;                /* A single semaphore */
    buf.sem_op = 1;                 /* Increment the semaphore */
    buf.sem_flg = IPC_NOWAIT;       /* Blocking operation */

    if((semop(semid, &buf, nsems)) < 0) {
        perror("semop");
```

```
            exit(EXIT_FAILURE);
        }
        system("ipcs -s");
        exit(EXIT_SUCCESS);
    }
```

The output from one run of mksem follows. The identifier values displayed will probably be different on your system.

OUTPUT

```
semaphore created: 512

------ Semaphore Arrays --------
key        semid     owner     perms     nsems     status
0x00000000 512       kwall     666       1
```

The example uses IPC_PRIVATE to ensure that the semaphore is created as requested, and then displays semget's return value to show the semaphore identifier. The semop call initializes the semaphore appropriately: Because only one semaphore is created, sem_num is zero. Because the imaginary resource is not in use (actually, the semaphore is not programmatically associated with any particular resource), mksem initializes its value to 1, the equivalent of unlocked. Not requiring blocking behavior, the semaphore's sem_flg is set to IPC_NOWAIT, so the call returns immediately. Finally, the example uses the system call to invoke the user-level ipcs command to confirm a second time that the requested IPC structure does, in fact, exist.

Controlling and Removing Semaphores

You have already seen msgctl and shmctl, the calls that manipulate message queues and shared memory segments. As you might expect, the equivalent function for semaphores is semctl, prototyped as follows:

```
int semctl(int semid, int semnum, int cmd, union semun arg);
```

semid identifies the semaphore set that you want to manipulate, and semnum specifies the particular semaphore in which you are interested. This book ignores the situation in which there are multiple semaphores in a set, so semnum (actually an index into an array of semaphores) will always be zero.

The cmd argument can be one of the values in the following list:

- GETVAL—Returns the semaphore's current status (locked or unlocked).

- SETVAL—Sets the semaphore's current status to arg.val (the semun argument is discussed in a moment).

- GETPID—Returns the PID of the process that last called semop.

- GETNCNT—Causes semctl's return value to be the number of processes waiting for the semaphore to increment; that is, the number of processes waiting on the semaphore.

- GETZCNT—Causes semctl's return value to be the number of processes waiting for the semaphore to be zero.

- GETALL—Returns the value of all semaphores in the set associated with semid.

- SETALL—Sets the value of all semaphores in the set associated with semid to the values stored in arg.array.

- IPC_RMID—Removes the semaphore with semid.

- IPC_SET—Sets the mode (permission bits) on the semaphore.

- IPC_STAT—Each semaphore has a data structure, semid_ds, that completely describes its configuration and behavior. IPC_STAT copies this configuration information in the arg.buf member of the semun structure.

If the semctl call fails, it returns –1 and sets errno appropriately. Otherwise, it returns an integer value of GETNCNT, GETPID, GETVAL, or GET-ZCNT, depending on the value of cmd.

As you might have surmised, the semun argument plays a vital role in the semctl routine. You must define it in your code according to the following template:

```
union semun {
    int val;                    /* Value for SETVAL */
    struct semid_ds *buf;       /* IPC_STAT's buffer */
    unsigned short int *array;  /* GETALL and SETALL's buffer */
};
```

EXAMPLE

Example

By now, you should begin to understand why I complain that the System V semaphore interface is far too complex for mere mortals. This difficulty notwithstanding, the next example, sctl, uses the semctl call to remove a semaphore from the system. To do so, you will want to execute mksem to create a semaphore and then use that semaphore identifier as the argument to sctl.

```
/*
 * sctl.c - Manipulate and delete a semaphore
 */
```

```
#include <sys/types.h>
#include <sys/ipc.h>
#include <sys/sem.h>
#include <stdio.h>
#include <stdlib.h>

int main(int argc, char *argv[])
{
    int semid;/* Semaphore identifier */

    if(argc != 2) {
        puts("USAGE: sctl <semaphore id>");
        exit(EXIT_FAILURE);
    }
    semid = atoi(argv[1]);

    /* Remove the semaphore */
    if((semctl(semid, 0, IPC_RMID)) < 0) {
        perror("semctl IPC_RMID");
        exit(EXIT_FAILURE);
    } else {
        puts("semaphore removed");
        system("ipcs -s");
    }

    exit(EXIT_SUCCESS);
}
```

The following listing illustrates sctl's output operation on my system:

OUTPUT

```
$ ./mksem
semaphore created: 640

------ Semaphore Arrays --------
key        semid    owner    perms    nsems    status
0x00000000 640      kwall    666      1

$ ./sctl 640
semaphore removed
```

```
------ Semaphore Arrays --------
key       semid    owner      perms     nsems      status
```

The code for sctl simply attempts to remove a semaphore whose identifier is passed on the command line. It also uses the system call to execute ipcs -s to confirm that the semaphore was in fact removed.

What's Next?

This chapter completes your introduction to System V IPC with a look at message queues and semaphores. In the next chapter, "TCP/IP and Socket Programming," you will learn the basics of network programming. The TCP/IP and socket protocols are the best known and most widely used method for IPC between different hosts. After finishing the next chapter, you will have enough information at hand to make a well-informed decision about which of the various IPC mechanisms best suits your needs.

## 18

TCP/IP and Socket Programming

As the Internet plays an ever more central role in society and especially in the computer world, almost every non-trivial application needs to include some sort of basic network support. The subjects discussed in this chapter include

- An overview of networking concepts and terminology
- The Berkeley socket API
- Basic socket operations
- UNIX domain sockets
- TCP/IP programming fundamentals
- Network names and numbers
- TCP/IP sockets

Network Concepts and Terminology

To most people, networks seem to work like telephones. When you make a telephone call, you dial a number and reach the person you want directly. The sentences you speak are transmitted and received in the order you spoke them, and no one else can listen to your conversation or jump into the middle of it. A telephone, then, provides guaranteed delivery of your message, delivers it in order, and does not tamper with the message while it is in transit. Similarly, when you click on a link on a Web page, it takes you almost immediately to the linked page. There are no intermediate stops; the page does not get garbled or interrupted.

In reality, though, computer networks do not work so neatly and cleanly. Unlike telephone systems, which provide a direct circuit connection between two locations, computer networks work on a store and forward basis, usually called *packet switching*. A sender sends data in fixed size packages, called *packets*, to the closest intermediary, called a *router*. The router examines each incoming packet to determine whether to keep it. The router transfers packets it should keep to its own network, and forwards packets it should not keep to the next router along the line, at which point the store and forward process repeats itself. Figure 18.1 illustrates how packet switching works.

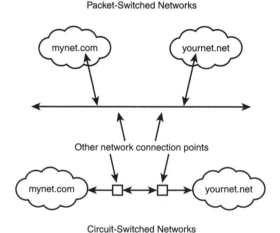

Figure 18.1: How data travels through a packet-switched network.

Figure 18.1 contrasts the way data travels across packet-switched (shown in the upper portion of the figure) and circuit-switched networks (shown in the lower portion). mynet.com and yournet.net represent two local area networks that are connected to the Internet. As you can see from the figure, on a packet-switched network, routers for mynet.com and yournet.net transfer data destined for their local networks into the network. This is represented by the vertical lines with arrows on each end connecting the flow of data across the Internet to the connected local networks. Data travelling to other networks is simply forwarded to the next router. A circuit-switched network, however, creates a connection between mynet.com and yournet.net.

Although there might be intervening network connection points, as illustrated by the small square boxes, they behave more like railroad crossings than automobile intersections. The data (the railroad train) passes through without interruption on its way to its destination. On a packet-switched network, though, like the Internet, data must negotiate several intersections (routers). The route each packet takes through the Internet is controlled by the router, much like the path an automobile takes through crowded city streets is controlled, at least in part, by the intersections it encounters.

Besides the difference in operation, packet-switched networks have other shortcomings. First, some packets will get lost. Second, long messages are broken into multiple packets that may arrive in a different order than they were sent, and anyone can intercept the packets and change their contents. These defects notwithstanding, computer networking works extremely well because the (very bright) people who designed the hardware and software devised schemes to work around or simply solve all these problems.

NOTE

Three paragraphs hardly begin to describe the complex operations of computer networks. The discussion is over-simplified considerably because the point is to provide you enough information to place programming for networks into a meaningful context without overwhelming you with details. So, please bear this in mind as you read.

Similarly, one chapter can only skim the cream off the topic of network programming. It is a complex topic that requires hundreds of pages to address completely.

Several terms arise constantly when discussing network *protocols*, the agreed-upon rules for how data is transmitted over a network. A protocol is said to be *connection-oriented* if it has two distinct endpoints, if other users cannot intrude upon the connection, and if a connection must exist between the two endpoints before communication can take place. A protocol that lacks these characteristics is considered *connectionless*.

Sequencing means that a protocol guarantees that data arrives in the same order it was sent. A protocol has *error control* if it detects corruption, discards corrupt messages, and arranges for retransmission of the data.

Networks transmit data in one of two ways: using individual bytes of data, and using packets. Byte-based transmission characterizes *streaming protocols* because they only deal with streams of bytes, much like Linux's character devices. Streaming protocols can break up long sequences of bytes but they are *sequenced*, so they arrive in the order they were sent. Streaming protocols are also known as *reliable* protocols because they take great pains to ensure that network messages are delivered intact or they otherwise notify the sender that one or more errors occurred and the message should be resent.

Packet-based protocols, on the other hand, create artificially sized packages (packets) of data with a fixed size. These protocols do not break up packets to send them, and they only deliver complete packets.

With these terms in mind, it is fairly simple to classify most network protocols, including TCP/IP, the basis of the Internet, and local IPC (formerly known as UNIX domain sockets), into one of two categories. *Datagram* protocols, such as *UDP* (the User Datagram Protocol), are packet-based, connectionless, non-sequencing, and offer no error control. *Stream* protocols, conversely, are byte-oriented and offer both sequencing and error control. TCP, the Transmission Control Protocol, is a classic example of a stream protocol.

The Berkeley Socket API

Given the huge variety of network protocols, the prospect of having to learn a new programming interface each time you want to learn or use a new protocol is surely daunting. Fortunately, the Berkeley socket API, usually called *Berkeley sockets* and so-named because it was popularized in the BSD versions of UNIX, was designed to encapsulate a variety of networking protocols and to provide a single programmatic interface for network programmers.

This generality introduces extra complexity, but the complexity is a small price to pay over not having to learn the low-level interfaces for AppleTalk, AX.25, IPX, NetRom, local IPC, and TCP/IP. This chapter uses Berkeley sockets to program both POSIX local IPC, which works only on a single machine, and TCP/IP, which enables computers across the Internet to communicate with each other.

The fundamental data structure of the socket API is the sockaddr structure, which stores a network address, the most essential feature of any network protocol. It is declared in <sys/socket.h> as follows:

```
struct sockaddr {
    unsigned short int sa_family;
    char sa_data[14];
};
```

sa_family describes the type of address stored, and sa_data contains the actual address data. sa_family is typically one of the values listed in Table 18.1.

Table 18.1: *Socket Address Families*

Address Family	Protocol Family	Description
AF_UNIX	PF_UNIX	UNIX domain sockets
AF_INET	PF_INET	TCP/IP (Version 4)
AF_AX25	PF_AX25	The AX.25 amateur radio protocol
AF_IPX	PF_IPX	The Novell IPX protocol
AF_APPLETALK	PF_APPLETALK	The AppleTalk DDS protocol

The two protocols with which this chapter concerns itself are AF_UNIX (the same as AF_LOCAL), which covers UNIX domain sockets, and AF_INET, the TCP/IP protocol.

NOTE

The complete list of supported protocol and address families is listed in <sys/socket.h>.

Socket Basics

The basic socket operations involve creating, opening, closing, reading, and writing them. Thanks to Linux's delightful habit of treating everything like a file, you can use the same I/O functions on sockets that you use on regular files.

For a brief discussion of Linux's file abstraction, see "Characteristics and Concepts," page 132.

The I/O functions (read, write, and so on) have unique semantics when applied to sockets, which this chapter covers, but the interface is identical otherwise. All socket functions require the inclusion of <sys/socket.h> and the header file appropriate to each protocol.

Creating a Socket

The only unique basic socket operation is the socket function, which creates a socket. Its prototype follows:

```
int socket(int domain, int type, int protocol);
```

The socket call creates one of at least two sockets used to establish a communications channel between two processes or systems that want to exchange data. domain specifies which network protocol to use. It will be one of the protocol families from the second column of Table 18.1. type establishes the category of the protocol, such as a streaming protocol or a datagram protocol. Not all classes of communication are available for all protocol families.

protocol indicates the default protocol to be used, based on the given domain (protocol family) and type (streaming, datagram, and so on). For the purposes of this book, this argument's value is always 0, indicating the default protocol. The list of currently supported types is given in Table 18.2, but only SOCK_STREAM is discussed in this chapter.

Table 18.2:   Berkeley Socket Types

Socket Type	Description
SOCK_STREAM	Supports connection-oriented, sequenced, error-controlled, full duplex byte streams.
SOCK_DGRAM	Supports connectionless, unsequenced, packet-oriented messages that have a fixed size.
SOCK_SEQPACKET	Supports sequenced, full duplex, connection-oriented transmissions of packets, but the receiver of the packet must read an entire packet with a single read system call.
SOCK_RAW	Is designed to provide low-level, protocol-level access. Code must be written to process data according to protocol specifications. Not for the faint-of-heart!
SOCK_RDM	Supports a connection-oriented transmission of packets, but the data is not guaranteed to be ordered.

If the socket is created successfully, socket returns a valid file descriptor to use in subsequent I/O operations. Otherwise, it returns –1 and sets errno's value to indicate the problem. Possible error values include the following:

- EACCES—The calling process lacks permissions to create the requested socket. This occurs if the process does not have sufficient directory permissions or if user-level processes (as opposed to root processes) are not permitted to create a socket of the indicated type or protocol.

- EINVAL—This error occurs because the calling process requested an unknown protocol or because the kernel does not support the protocol family specified in domain. This is often the result of a typo.

- EMFILE—Generated when the process file table is full and no more process can be created. This error indicates a heavily loaded system.

- ENFILE—The kernel lacks sufficient memory to create the necessary supporting structures to support another socket. ENFILE usually indicates a serious problem with the system.

- ENOBUFS or ENOMEM—The system (not the kernel) does not have enough memory to create the structure requested. Although not as serious as ENFILE, the system is usually in bad shape when this error occurs.

- EPROTONOSUPPORT—The protocol family specified in domain does not support either the type or the protocol (or both) requested.

Connecting to a Socket

Even though a socket has been created, it is useless without open connections to it. Moreover, the connection process is different for server processes and client processes. *Server processes* are processes that receive a request for information, data, or to grant to the requester some sort of access to a capability or facility. Accordingly, server processes generally create a socket and then wait for connection requests from clients or requesters. *Client processes*, likewise, ask the server to provide information or data via the socket, or send a request, again through the socket, for access to some service the server provides.

A server, then, has more work to do than a client. First, having created a socket, it must *bind* to it, which creates an association between the socket and an address. In the case of UNIX domain sockets, this address is simply a pathname and filename (as detailed in the next section). In the case of a normal TCP/IP socket, the address is a standard Internet address (discussed in the section, "TCP/IP Programming," later in this chapter).

After binding the address, a server must *listen* for a connection, meaning that it must wait for a client to request a connection to the socket. Upon receiving the connection request, the server ordinarily then *accepts* the request; that is, it formally opens the connection for the requesting client and starts exchanging information with it through the socket. The function calls for each of the server's tasks are intuitively named bind, listen, and accept.

The client, on the other hand, merely needs to request a connection to the socket the server has opened. Equally intuitively, the client uses the connect system call to request a connection to the socket in which it is interested. Figure 18.2 illustrates the process of creating and connecting to a socket for both a client and a server.

As you can see in Figure 18.2, the server controls the client's access to the socket through the accept call. There is no requirement that the server must accept a client's connection request.

The four calls for connecting to a socket are prototyped as follows:

```
int bind(int sockfd, struct sockaddr *addr, int addrlen);
int listen(int sockfd, int backlog);
```

```
int accept(int sockfd, struct sockaddr *addr, int *addrlen);
int connect(int sockfd, strcut sockaddr *addr, int addrlen);
```

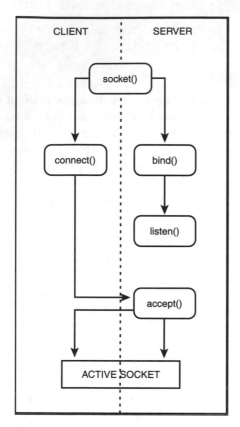

Figure 18.2: *A client and server connecting to a socket.*

For each call, `sockfd` is the file descriptor returned by a previous call to `socket`, `sockaddr` is a pointer to a socket address structure, and `addrlen` is `sockaddr`'s size (note that the `accept` call may change this value upon its return).

The `backlog` argument to `listen` defines the maximum number of pending connections that are allowed to queue on a given socket before additional connection requests are refused outright. Historically, this value has been five, but it can be changed.

`bind`, `listen`, and `connect` return zero if they succeed. As usual, if they fail, they return −1 and set `errno` to reflect the error that occurred. The `accept` call, however, returns a new file descriptor that can be used by the accepting process (usually a server) for file I/O operations using the `write` and `read` system calls. On failure, `accept` returns −1 and sets `errno`.

NOTE

Although the POSIX socket API supports some security features (namely, credentials) vis-a-vis sockets, I have not covered them here because Linux's support for POSIX sockets is in flux. Linux's implementation of POSIX-local IPC is incomplete. A lot of the material in the POSIX specification exists, but in many cases, calls supporting the new spec just seem to be wrappers around the old calls implementing the "classic," pre-POSIX spec. Even worse, the man pages are woefully out of date.

The authoritative programming reference for POSIX IPC specification is Richard Stevens' *Network Programming* series. If you attempt to use POSIX IPC, you must be aware that it might not behave as you would expect.

Examples

The sample programs that follow, mksock and sockconn, illustrate the basic socket operations. The details of UNIX domain sockets are covered in the following section, "UNIX Domain Sockets."

1. mksock

EXAMPLE

creates, binds, listens, and accepts connections on a UNIX domain socket.

```
/*
 * mksock.c - Make and bind to a socket
 */
#include <sys/socket.h>
#include <sys/un.h>
#include <stdlib.h>
#include <stdio.h>
#include "helper.h"

int main(int argc, char *argv[])
{
    int sockfd;                 /* File descriptor for socket */
    struct sockaddr_un srv;   /* Server's socket structure */
    socklen_t socklen;

    /* Expect the socket name on the command-line */
    if(argc != 2) {
        puts("USAGE: mksock <filename>");
        exit(EXIT_FAILURE);
    }

    /* Create the socket */
```

```
    if((sockfd = socket(PF_UNIX, SOCK_STREAM, 0)) < 0)
        err_quit("socket");

    /* Initialize and set up the server structure */
    memset(&srv, 0, sizeof(srv));
    srv.sun_family = AF_UNIX;
    strncpy(srv.sun_path, argv[1], sizeof(srv.sun_path));

    /* Bind the socket to an address */
    if((bind(sockfd, (struct sockaddr *)&srv, SUN_LEN(&srv))) < 0)
        err_quit("bind");

    /* Wait for incoming connections */
    if((listen(sockfd, 5)) < 0)
        err_quit("listen");
    printf("socket available: %s\n", srv.sun_path);

    /* Loop forever, accepting all connections */
    while(accept(sockfd, (struct sockaddr *)&srv, &socklen) >= 0)
        puts("new connection granted");

    exit(EXIT_SUCCESS);
}
```

mksock takes a single argument, the address of a socket to create. It first calls socket to create a stream-oriented (a protocol type of SOCK_STREAM) UNIX domain socket (a protocol family of PF_UNIX) using the default protocol. After initializing the srv structure, mksock next sets the socket family to AF_UNIX and copies the address of the socket into the sun_path member. Then, the bind call associates the file descriptor sockfd with the socket described by srv.

Notice that srv is declared as a struct sockaddr_un, the socket structure for UNIX domain sockets. To quiet compiler warnings, cast it as a struct sockaddr * to match bind's prototype. Finally, the listen call signals that the server is accepting connections on this socket, and the accept call continuously allows new connections until accept returns an error or until the program is otherwise terminated.

helper.h and its implementation, helper.c, are utility functions that all the programs in this chapter use. Their *raison d'être* is to shorten the code list-

ings. mksock and sockconn use the err_quit function, which calls perror
with the specified msg and then exits. err_quit is defined as follows:

```
void err_quit(char *msg)
{
    perror(msg);
    exit(EXIT_FAILURE);
}
```

EXAMPLE

2. sockconn connects to the socket served by mksock.

```
/*
 * sockconn.c - Connect to a socket
 */
#include <sys/socket.h>
#include <sys/un.h>
#include <stdlib.h>
#include <stdio.h>
#include "helper.h"

int main(int argc, char *argv[])
{
    int sockfd;                 /* File descriptor for socket */
    struct sockaddr_un cli;    /* Client's socket structure */
    socklen_t socklen;          /* Size of sockaddr */

    /* Expect the socket name on the command-line */
    if(argc != 2) {
        puts("USAGE: sockconn <filename>");
        exit(EXIT_FAILURE);
    }

    /* Create a socket */
    if((sockfd = socket(PF_UNIX, SOCK_STREAM, 0)) < 0)
        err_quit("socket");

    /* Set up the client */
    memset(&cli, 0, sizeof(cli));
    cli.sun_family = AF_UNIX;
    strncpy(cli.sun_path, argv[1], sizeof(cli.sun_path));
```

```
/* Connect to the socket */
socklen = SUN_LEN(&cli);
if(connect(sockfd, (struct sockaddr *)&cli, socklen))
    err_quit("connect");
printf("connected to socket %s\n", cli.sun_path);


exit(EXIT_SUCCESS);
}
```

The setup is the same for sockconn as for mksock: Create a socket and set some values in the socket. In fact, clients can also use the bind call to bind the local address, but this is optional because clients want to connect to a remote socket. Generally, clients discard the local address. The connect call binds the client's file descriptor sockfd to the socket opened by the server, which is passed as sockconn's command-line argument. The output of these two programs is illustrated in Figure 18.3.

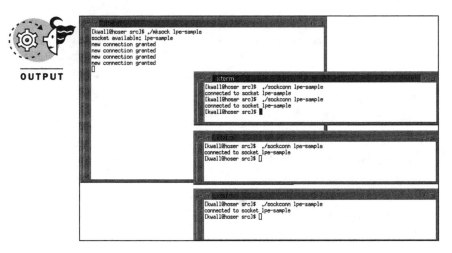

Figure 18.3: *Three clients connecting to a server socket.*

In Figure 18.3, the xterm on the left is running the server program, mksock, and is listening on a socket named lpe-sample. The client program, sock-conn, was executed in each of the three smaller xterms on the right. mksock reports each connection by displaying *new connection granted* each time it accepts a new connection. sockconn, similarly, reports successfully connecting to the server by displaying the address (name) of the socket when it successfully connects.

UNIX Domain Sockets

UNIX domain sockets work on only a single machine, so they are much more like named pipes than a network protocol. The addresses to which UNIX domain sockets bind are actual filenames in the filesystem. However, sockets cannot be opened; they must be accessed using the socket interface.

Creating a UNIX Domain Socket

Earlier, you learned that the sockaddr structure contains a network address. That was a bit of an oversimplification. Actually, that sockaddr structure is the general format. All the protocol families (domains) have their own protocol-specific versions of sockaddr. The sockaddr structure for UNIX domain sockets is defined in <sys/un.h> as follows:

```
struct sockaddr_un {
    unsigned short int sun_family; /* AF_UNIX */
    char sun_path[108];            /* Pathname */
};
```

sun_family must be set to AF_UNIX to create a UNIX domain socket. sun_path contains the name of the file to be used as the socket. The socket is bound to the file using the bind call as you would expect, but the file is created when bind is called. If the file already exists, bind fails, sets errno to EADDRINUSE, and returns –1 to the calling process. The SUN_LEN macro, also defined in <sys/un.h>, returns the size of a sockaddr_un structure.

The sockconn program illustrated the correct method for a client program to connect to a server socket, so the example will not be repeated again. Pay close attention, however, to how sockconn and mksock cast their protocol's sockaddr_un structure to a generic sockaddr structure for each call to the API's interface.

EXAMPLE

Example

This example shows what happens when you try to open a socket that is already in use. It assumes that you have already created the socket file lpe-sample by running the first two sample programs.

```
$. ls -l lpe-sample
srwxr-xr-x    1 kwall     users   0 Aug 17 18:29 lpe-sample=
$ ./mksock lpe-sample
bind: Address already in use
$ rm lpe-sample
$ ./mksock lpe-sample
socket available: lpe-sample
```

The bind call failed because the socket was already in use but, after deleting the socket file, the bind call succeeded and the server began its infinite accept loop.

Reading and Writing a UNIX Domain Socket

As stated at the beginning of the chapter, you can use standard system I/O calls to read from and write to sockets. The procedure is straightforward. The process that calls accept uses the file descriptor that accept returns for I/O. Processes that call connect, usually client processes, use the file descriptor returned by the socket call for I/O.

EXAMPLE

Example

This example shows one way to read and write UNIX domain sockets. Briefly, the writing process copies its standard input to a socket while the reading process copies data read from the socket to its standard output. wrsock is the writing, or client, process. rdsock is the reader, or server, process. To keep the code somewhat simple and easy to follow, helper.c defines a function, xfer_data, that copies data between two file descriptors. It is declared in the local header file helper.h. The listing that follows shows the definition of xfer_data:

```
void xfer_data(int srcfd, int tgtfd)
{
    char buf[1024];
    int cnt, len;

    /* Read from the input fd and write to the output fd */
    while((cnt = read(srcfd, buf, sizeof(buf))) > 0) {
        if(len < 0)
            err_quit("helper.c:xfer_data:read");
        if((len = write(tgtfd, buf, cnt)) != cnt)
            err_quit("helper.c:xfer_data:write");
    }
}
```

This function reads any input from the input file descriptor, srcfd, and then immediately writes it to the output file descriptor, tgtfd. If either the read or write encounters an error, the function exits. To use this function, add the line #include "helper.h" to your source code.

The following two code snippets show the modifications necessary to turn the server program, mksock, and the client program, sockconn, into a reader and writer, respectively. First, add the following declaration to the top of mksock:

```
int infd;
```

Then, replace lines 40–45 of `mksock.c` with the following:

```
/* Accept the first connection that comes in */
if((infd = accept(sockfd, (struct sockaddr *)&srv, &socklen)) >= 0)
    puts("new connection granted");


/* Read from the socket and write to stdout */
xfer_data(infd, fileno(stdout));
```

Rather than simply accepting every incoming connection, the new code accepts only the first connection, and then calls `xfer_data` to read incoming data from the socket's file descriptor, `infd`, and write it to `stdout`.

Finally, add the following code just above the `exit` statement of `sockconn.c`:

```
/* Copy stdin to the socket file descriptor */
xfer_data(fileno(stdin), sockfd);
```

The additional code reads input from `stdin` and writes it the file descriptor bound to the socket. The modified files are available as `rdsock.c` and `wrsock.c` from the Web site for this book.

To run these programs, run `rdsock` in one xterm or virtual console, and then start `wrsock` on another one. Each time you press Enter, lines of text entered appear in `rdsock`'s window. Sample output from these programs is illustrated in Figure 18.4.

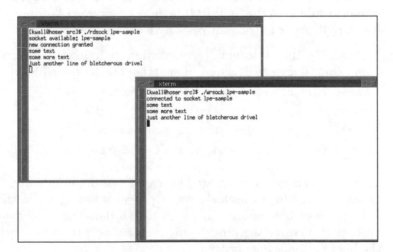

Figure 18.4: *Reading and writing UNIX domain sockets.*

In Figure 18.4, the reader/server, rdsock, is running in the xterm on the left and the writer/client, wrsock, is running in the xterm on the right. As you can see in the figure, each line of text typed into the writer appears in the reader after you press Enter.

TCP/IP Programming

TCP/IP is the protocol (actually, the protocol *family*) that runs the Internet, the largest network of interconnected machines in the world. The current version of the protocol is version 4 (IPv4), but the transition to version 6 (IPv6) has already begun. The specifications extant in current proposals for IPv6 have been integrated in the 2.2.x kernels. Because the new protocol is not in wide use, however, this section covers IPv4 instead. As remarked at the beginning of the chapter, network programming is a big topic about which whole volumes of books are written. However, you can actually write network-capable programs using fewer than 10 function calls.

Network Numbers

Before jumping into network programming *per se*, it is important to point out that the TCP/IP protocol is *big-endian*; that is, it stores the most significant bit of multibyte numbers in the lowest memory address. Many computers are similarly big-endian.

However, other computers, such as Intel's x86 processors, are *little-endian*, meaning that the least significant bit of multibyte numbers is stored in the lowest memory address (the general term for the arrangement of values in memory is *byte ordering*). The implication of this is that when feeding numeric values to the TCP/IP functions, they must be converted from the host's byte order to the network's byte order.

Fortunately, the protocol implementation includes four functions to do precisely this. They are declared in <netinet/in.h> as follows:

```
unsigned long int htonl(unsigned long int hostlong);

unsigned short int htons(unsigned short int hostshort);

unsigned long int ntohl(unsigned long int netlong);

unsigned short int ntohs(unsigned short int netshort);
```

htonl converts hostlong, a long integer, from the host system's byte order to network byte order. Similarly, htons converts hostshort, a short integer, from the host byte order to network byte order. The other two calls, ntohl and ntohs, reverse the process and thus convert from network byte order to the host system's byte order.

Network Addresses

As with UNIX domain sockets, TCP/IP network addresses are stored in a sockaddr structure, struct sockaddr_in, defined in <netinet/in.h> as follows:

```
struct sockaddr_in {
    short int sin_family;     /* AF_INET */
    uint16_t sin_port;        /* Port number */
    struct in_addr sin_addr; /* IP address */
};
```

You also must include <sys/socket.h> to get the complete socket definition. For TCP/IP (version 4, at least), sin_family must be AF_INET. sin_port is the port number to which to connect, and sin_addr is the IP address. Both sin_port and sin_addr must be in network byte order. However, sin_addr is a binary structure, so to convert it into standard dotted decimal form, use the inet_ntoa function; conversely, to convert a dotted decimal address to the binary format of sin_addr, use inet_aton. These calls are prototyped in <arpa/inet.h> as

```
char *inet_ntoa(struct in_addr addr);
```

```
char *inet_aton(const char *ddaddr, struct in_addr *ipaddr);
$I~networks;address storage, Transmission Control Protocol/Internet Protocol
(TCP/IP)>
```

inet_ntoa converts the binary IP address stored in addr and returns it as a string (the returned string is a statically allocated buffer that is overwritten by subsequent calls of inet_ntoa). inet_aton converts a dotted decimal address stored in ddaddr to the proper binary format, and then stores it in ipaddr. If the address is a valid address, inet_aton returns nonzero, otherwise it returns zero.

CAUTION

Several TCP/IP API functions return zero on failure and nonzero when they succeed. This behavior is precisely opposite the behavior of almost every library and system call you have seen so far.

TIP

You will occasionally encounter a function named inet_addr. It does the same thing as inet_aton. It has the prototype unsigned long int inet_addr(const char *ddaddr). It is an obsolete call because it does not recognize 255.255.255.255 as a valid IP address. If you encounter code that uses this function, do the world a favor and change it to use inet_aton.

TCP/IP network addresses are 32-bit numbers, usually expressed in *dotted decimal* notation such as www.xxx.yyy.zzz. Because they are 32-bit numbers, there are a potential 4,294,967,295 (counting from 0) unique network addresses. However, because each unique address might want or need to run multiple TCP/IP applications simultaneously, each address also has up to 65,535 ports to which to connect.

Ports are 16-bit numbers that represent a connection or end point on a given system (ports 0-1024 are reserved for use by processes running with root privileges). So, a unique connection point on one system is defined by the combination of the host's IP address and a port number. A complete and unique network connection between two systems is defined by two such connection points. Figure 18.5 graphically illustrates this point. $I~networks;address storage, Transmission Control Protocol/Internet Protocol (TCP/IP)>

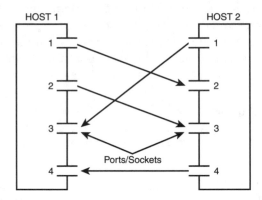

Figure 18.5: *A complete network connection is defined by two IP addresses and two port numbers.*

As you can see in the figure, HOST1 and HOST2 have four complete connections between them, HOST1:PORT1 to HOST2:PORT2, HOST1:PORT2 to HOST2:PORT3, HOST2:PORT1 to HOST1:PORT3, and HOST2:PORT4 to HOST1:PORT4.

Before looking at the sample programs, you must know about one last function, `setsockopt`. After closing a socket, its address (the IP and port number combination) is unavailable for a certain period of time. To reuse this address, you must set an option on the socket that allows it to be reused. It is declared in `<sys/socket.h>` as

```
int setsockopt(int sockfd, int level, int optname,
➥const void *optval, socklen_t optlen);
```

`setsockopt` sets the option stored in `optname` to `optval` for the socket that opened on the file descriptor `sockfd`. For sockets, `level` must be `SOL_SOCKET`.

Set optname to 0 and optval to 1. That is, the setsockopt should resemble the following:

```
int i = 1;
```

```
setsockopt(sockfd, SOL_SOCKET, 0, &i, sizeof(i));  $I-networks;address storage,
Transmission Control Protocol/Internet Protocol (TCP/IP)>
```

Examples

1. The example that follows, mknet, creates a TCP/IP socket, and then waits for and accepts all connections. It uses port number 50000, which is not likely to be used by another program.

EXAMPLE

```c
/*
 * mknet.c - Bind to and wait on a TCP/IP socket
 */
#include <sys/socket.h>
#include <netinet/in.h>

#include <arpa/inet.h>
#include <unistd.h>
#include <stdlib.h>
#include <stdio.h>
#include "helper.h"

int main(void)
{
    int sockfd;                 /* File descriptors for socket */
    struct sockaddr_in srv;  /* Server's socket structure */
    socklen_t socklen;
    int i = 1;                  /* For setsockopt */

    /* Create the socket */
    if((sockfd = socket(PF_INET, SOCK_STREAM, 0)) < 0)
        err_quit("socket");
    /* Want to reuse the local address */
    setsockopt(sockfd, SOL_SOCKET, 0, &i, sizeof(i));

    /* Initialize and set up the server structure */
    memset(&srv, 0, sizeof(srv));
    srv.sin_family = AF_INET;
    srv.sin_port = htons(50000); /* Don't forget network byte order */
```

```
                    /* Bind the socket to an address */
                    socklen = sizeof(srv);
                    if((bind(sockfd, (struct sockaddr *)&srv, socklen)) < 0)
                        err_quit("bind");

                    /* Wait for incoming connections */
                    if((listen(sockfd, 5)) < 0)
                        err_quit("listen");
                    puts("TCP/IP socket available");
                    printf("\tport %d\n", ntohs(srv.sin_port));
                    printf("\taddr %s\n", inet_ntoa(srv.sin_addr));

                    /* Loop forever, accepting all connections */
                    while((accept(sockfd, (struct sockaddr *)&srv, &socklen)) >= 0)
                        puts("new connection granted");

                    exit(EXIT_SUCCESS);
                }
```

mknet is similar to the mksock program presented earlier. The only differences are replacing the calls and data structures specific to using UNIX domain sockets with those for TCP/IP sockets. Notice that because mknet specifies an IP address of zero, the kernel assigns a default address. The output from a sample run of this program should resemble the following:

OUTPUT

```
$ ./mknet
TCP/IP socket available
        port 50000
        addr 0.0.0.0
```

EXAMPLE

2. The next program, netconn, is sockconn rewritten to use TCP/IP sockets.

```
/*
 * netconn.c - Connect to a TCP/IP socket
 */
#include <sys/socket.h>
#include <netinet/in.h>
#include <arpa/inet.h>
#include <stdlib.h>
#include <stdio.h>
#include "helper.h"
```

```
int main(int argc, char *argv[])
{
    int sockfd;                 /* File descriptor for socket */
    struct sockaddr_in cli;  /* Client's socket structure */
    socklen_t socklen;          /* Size of sockaddr */

    /* Expect the IP address on the command-line */
    if(argc != 2) {
        puts("USAGE: netconn <ip address>");
        exit(EXIT_FAILURE);
    }

    /* Create a socket */
    if((sockfd = socket(PF_INET, SOCK_STREAM, 0)) < 0)
        err_quit("socket");

    /* Set up the client */
    memset(&cli, 0, sizeof(cli));
    cli.sin_family = AF_INET;
    cli.sin_port = htons(50000); /* Don't forget network byte order */
    /* This will self-destruct if the IP address is invalid */
    if(!(inet_aton(argv[1], &cli.sin_addr)))
        herr_quit("inet_aton");

    /* Connect to the socket */
    socklen = sizeof(cli);
    if(connect(sockfd, (struct sockaddr *)&cli, socklen))
        err_quit("connect");
    puts("connected to socket");

    exit(EXIT_SUCCESS);

}
```

In addition to the code for dealing with TCP/IP sockets, netconn.c also includes a new function, herr_quit, defined in helper.c, that calls a TCP/IP-specific error-handling function, herror. It behaves exactly like the perror call. To execute netconn, pass it the IP address, in dotted decimal form, of the host to which you want to connect, as illustrated in the listing that follows (run `netconn` in one window and `mknet` in another):

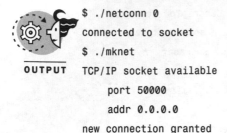

OUTPUT

```
$ ./netconn 0
connected to socket
$ ./mknet
TCP/IP socket available
    port 50000
    addr 0.0.0.0
new connection granted
```

Again, passing zero to `netconn` tells the kernel to use an address of its choosing. In place of zero, you can also pass 0.0.0.0 or your system's IP address, if it has one. Figure 18.6 shows that `mknet` is capable of communicating with any host on the Internet. From another system, I `telnet`ed to the system running `mknet` using the `telnet` syntax that enables you to specify an alternative port (`telnet`'s default port is 23).

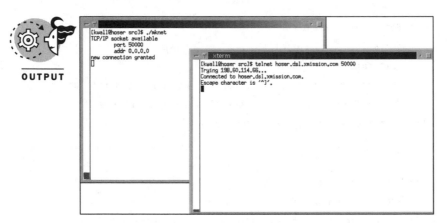

OUTPUT

Figure 18.6: *Connecting to mknet's port from another system.*

Reading and Writing TCP/IP Sockets

Reading and writing TCP/IP sockets is precisely like reading and writing UNIX domain sockets. Once again, Linux's file abstraction proves to be a real blessing. A few simple modifications to `wrsock` and `rdsock`, listed in the next example, show how simple it is.

Example

```
/*
 * rdnet.c - Make and bind to a TCP/IP socket, then read it
 */
```

EXAMPLE

```c
#include <sys/socket.h>
#include <netinet/in.h>
#include <arpa/inet.h>
#include <stdlib.h>
#include <stdio.h>
#include "helper.h"

int main(void)
{
    int sockfd, infd;       /* File descriptors for socket */
    struct sockaddr_in srv; /* Server's socket structure */
    socklen_t socklen;

    /* Create the socket */

    if((sockfd = socket(PF_INET, SOCK_STREAM, 0)) < 0)
        err_quit("socket");

    /* Initialize and set up the server structure */
    memset(&srv, 0, sizeof(srv));
    srv.sin_family = AF_INET;
    srv.sin_port = htons(50000);

    /* Bind the socket to an address */
    socklen = sizeof(srv);
    if((bind(sockfd, (struct sockaddr *)&srv, socklen)) < 0)
        err_quit("bind");

    /* Wait for incoming connections */
    if((listen(sockfd, 5)) < 0)
        err_quit("listen");
    puts("TCP/IP socket available");
    printf("\tport %d\n", ntohs(srv.sin_port));
    printf("\taddr %s\n", inet_ntoa(srv.sin_addr));

    /* Accept the first connection that comes in */
    if((infd = accept(sockfd, (struct sockaddr *)&srv, &socklen)) >= 0)
        puts("new connection granted");
```

```
        /* Read from the socket and write to stdout */
        xfer_data(infd, fileno(stdout));

        exit(EXIT_SUCCESS);
}
/*
 * wrnet.c - Write to an open TCP/IP socket
 */
#include <sys/socket.h>
#include <netinet/in.h>
#include <arpa/inet.h>
#include <stdlib.h>
#include <stdio.h>
#include "helper.h"

int main(int argc, char *argv[])
{
        int sockfd;/* File descriptor for socket */
        struct sockaddr_in cli;/* Client's socket structure */
        socklen_t socklen;/* Size of sockaddr */

        /* Expect the IP address on the command-line */
        if(argc != 2) {
            puts("USAGE: wrnet <ip address>");
            exit(EXIT_FAILURE);
        }

        /* Create a socket */
        if((sockfd = socket(PF_INET, SOCK_STREAM, 0)) < 0)
            err_quit("socket");

        /* Set up the client */
        memset(&cli, 0, sizeof(cli));
        cli.sin_family = AF_INET;
        cli.sin_port = htons(50000);
        /* This will blow up if an invalid address is passed */
        if(!(inet_aton(argv[1], &cli.sin_addr)))
            herr_quit("inet_aton");
```

```
/* Connect to the socket */
socklen = sizeof(cli);
if(connect(sockfd, (struct sockaddr *)&cli, socklen))
    err_quit("connect");
puts("connected to TCP/IP socket");
printf("\tport %d\n", ntohs(cli.sin_port));
printf("\taddr %s\n", inet_ntoa(cli.sin_addr));

/* Copy stdin to the socket file descriptor */
xfer_data(fileno(stdin), sockfd);

exit(EXIT_SUCCESS);
}
```

Very few changes have been made to these programs. In both programs, the protocol and address families were changed to PF_INET and AF_INET, respectively, and the strncpy of the socket special file was changed to a simple assignment of the port number. In wrnet.c, additional code was added that copies the IP address specified on the program's command line into the cli.sin_addr structure. The programs behave identically, sending wrnet's stdin to rdnet's stdout, as illustrated in Figure 18.7.

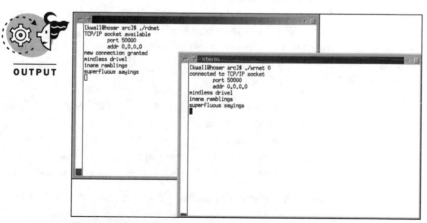

OUTPUT

Figure 18.7: *Copying wrnet's standard input to rdnet's standard output using TCP/IP sockets.*

Using Hostnames

All the discussion so far has focused on using IP addresses. This is okay because computers work as efficiently with numbers as they do with textual information. Not so mere humans, who prefer text to strings of digits.

Fortunately, the TCP/IP protocol family includes the *Domain Name System* (DNS), a distributed database that, among other things, maps names, like www.netscape.com, to IP addresses, in this case, 205.188.247.73. Although DNS encompasses many capabilities, the one covered here is how to convert a hostname to an address and vice versa. You must know about one structure, struct hostent, and two functions, gethostbyname and gethostbyaddr. They are declared in <netdb.h> as follows:

```
struct hostent {
    char *h_name;        /* Canonical machine name */

    char **h_aliases;    /* List of aliases */
    int h_addrtype;      /* AF_INET */
    int h_length;        /* sizeof(struct in_addr) */
    char **h_addr_list;  /* List of IP addresses */
};
struct hostent *gethostbyname(const char *name);
struct hostent *gethostbyaddr(const char *addr, int len, int type);
```

gethostbyname takes a hostname name, such as ftp.netscape.com, and returns a pointer to a hostent structure that contains the relevant information from the DNS. Similarly, gethostbyaddr takes an address structure, struct in_addr (which you have already seen), stored in addr, its length, stored in len, and its type, which is always AF_INET, and returns a pointer to a hostent structure. The pointer that both calls return points at a statically allocated buffer that is overwritten each time you call either function. So, if you need to save any of the information in the hostent structure pointer, save it in local variables.

Regarding the hostent structure itself, h_name is the canonical, or "official" (as in registered) machine name, h_addrtype is always AF_INET, and h_length is the size of address structure, which is sizeof(struct in_addr) at this time. h_aliases and h_addr_list, respectively, are pointers to strings containing all the names and IP addresses that a machine can have.

"Now wait a minute!" I hear you thinking. "Whaddya mean, 'all of the names and IP addresses that a machine can have?'" Simply put, the DNS is not a one-to-one mapping of hostnames to IP addresses. There are many reasons why a machine might have multiple IP addresses or multiple hostnames. In the case of multiple IP addresses, consider a *router*, a system that has multiple network cards. Each card has a different IP address to route incoming packets to the appropriate location, such as different networks or different systems.

On the other hand, a system that has multiple names (actually, it has one canonical name and one or more aliases) is typically used to allow a single physical machine to provide multiple services, such as a Web server and an FTP server. The box has one IP address but two names.

Regardless of why a system has multiple hostnames or IP addresses, `gethostbyname` and `gethostbyaddr` return the complete list of names and addresses, respectively, in the `h_aliases` and `h_addr_list` members of the `struct hostent`. If the IP address or hostname passed to these functions is invalid or if another error occurs, they return `NULL`.

EXAMPLE

Example

The sample program that follows, `hostinfo`, accepts a hostname as its command-line argument and displays the contents of its corresponding `hostent` structure.

```c
/*
 * hostinfo.c - Show the hostent structure for a hostname
 */
#include <sys/socket.h>
#include <netinet/in.h>

#include <arpa/inet.h>
#include <netdb.h>
#include <stdlib.h>
#include <stdio.h>
#include "helper.h"

int main(int argc, char *argv[])
{
    struct hostent *buf;
    struct in_addr **paddr;
    char **palias;

    /* Expect the IP addresss on the command-line */
    if(argc != 2) {
        puts("USAGE: hostinfo <host name>");
        exit(EXIT_FAILURE);
    }

    /* Do the lookup */
```

```
if((buf = gethostbyname(argv[1])) == NULL)
    herr_quit("gethostbyname");
/* Valid hostname, so ... */
printf("host info for %s\n", argv[1]);
/* The canonical hostname */
printf("name: %s\n", buf->h_name);
/* All of the aliases */
puts("aliases:");
palias = buf->h_aliases;
while(*palias) {
    printf("\t%s\n", *palias);
    palias++;
}
/* h_addrtype better be AF_INET */
if(buf->h_addrtype == AF_INET)
    puts("type: AF_INET");
else
    puts("type: unknown");
printf("length: %d\n", buf->h_length);
/* All of the IP addresses */
puts("addresses:");
paddr = (struct in_addr **)buf->h_addr_list;
while(*paddr) {
    printf("\t%s\n", inet_ntoa(**paddr));
    paddr++;
}

exit(EXIT_SUCCESS);
}
```

The following listing shows the output from this program:

OUTPUT

```
host info for ftp.redhat.com
name: ftp.redhat.com
aliases:
type: AF_INET

length: 4
addresses:
```

```
199.183.24.205
208.178.165.228
206.132.41.212
```

After performing a DNS lookup on the hostname, it displays each member of the hostent structure. The hairy-looking code that prints the IP addresses is necessary because buf>h_addr_list decays to a bare pointer, but inet_ntoa expects a struct in_addr argument.

What's Next?

This chapter gave you the nickel tour of socket and TCP/IP programming. It also completes the book's coverage of interprocess communication. The next part, "Linux Programming Utilities," introduces you to several tools and utilities that ease some of a programmer's chores. You begin with Chapter 19, "Tracking Source Code Changes," which teaches you how to use RCS, the Revision Control System. RCS is a tool that automates most of the tasks associated with tracking changes to source code files. Why keep track of source code changes? Read on and see!

Part V

Linux Programming Utilities

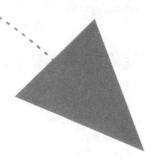

## 19

Tracking Source Code Changes: The Revision Control System

Version control is a process for keeping track of and managing changes made to source code files. Why bother? Because one day you *will* make that one fatal edit to a source file, delete its predecessor, and forget exactly which line or lines of code you "fixed." Because simultaneously keeping track of the current release, the next release, and eight bug fixes manually *will* become too tedious and confusing. Because frantically searching for the backup tape after one of your colleagues overwrote a source file for the fifth time *will* drive you over the edge. Because, one day, over your morning cappuccino, you will say to yourself, "Version control, it's the Right Thing to Do."

This chapter examines RCS, the Revision Control System, a common solution to the version control problem. RCS is a common solution because it is available on almost all UNIX systems, not just on Linux. RCS is maintained by the GNU project. Two alternatives to RCS are CVS, the Concurrent Version System, also maintained by the GNU project, and SCCS, the Source Code Control System, a proprietary product. Topics covered in this chapter include the following:

- Version control terminology
- Creating a source code repository
- Checking files in and out of the repository
- RCS keywords and the ident command
- RCS change logs
- Additional RCS commands and utilities

Why RCS?

More experienced programmers, and especially programmers familiar with other versions of UNIX or UNIX clones, might ask, "Why discuss RCS when CVS is more popular, has more features, and is better suited for use with large programming projects?" First, I consider RCS the easiest introduction to version control concepts. Few beginning programmers have ever heard of version control, much less used version control software. RCS is easy to learn, requires little setup or configuration, and has a small command set. This makes it the ideal vehicle for introducing people to version control concepts. Nevertheless, because CVS is built on and compatible with RCS, the transition to CVS will be smooth.

Moreover, although CVS definitely has a much richer feature set than RCS, these features are of little benefit to neophyte Linux programmers. Few beginning hackers will need, for example, the ability to browse their source code using a Web browser or to make anonymous read/write access to the repository available.

Finally, most beginning programmers will not be working in an environment in which multiple projects are under development or that have a single source code repository that stores the source code for multiple projects, environments for which CVS was designed.

Version Control Terminology

Before proceeding, however, Table 19.1 lists a few terms that will be used throughout the chapter. Because they are frequently used, it is important that you understand them in the context of RCS and version control.

Table 19.1:   Version Control Terms

Term	Description
RCS file	Any file located in an RCS directory, controlled by RCS and accessed using RCS commands. An RCS file contains all versions of a particular file. Normally, an RCS file has a ,v extension.
Working file	One or more files retrieved from the RCS source code repository (the RCS directory) into the current working directory and available for editing.
Lock	A working file retrieved for editing so that no one else can simultaneously edit it. A working file is locked by the first user against edits by other users.
Revision	A specific, numbered version of a source file. Revisions begin with 1.1 and increase incrementally, unless forced to use a specific revision number.

The Revision Control System manages multiple versions of files, usually but not necessarily source code files. RCS automates file version storage and retrieval, change logging, access control, release management, and revision identification and merging. As an added bonus, RCS minimizes disk space requirements because it tracks only file changes.

NOTE

The examples used in this chapter assume that you are using RCS version 5.7. To determine the version of RCS you are using, type rcs -V.

RCS can be used for more than just source code files, however. It is capable of tracking changes to any type of text file, such as reports, book chapters, or HTML code. It does not, however, handle binary files. CVS, the Concurrent Version System, does work with binary files, which is why many people use CVS rather than RCS.

Using RCS

One of RCS's attractions is its simplicity. With minimal setup and only a few commands, you can accomplish a great deal. This section discusses the ci, co, and ident commands as well as the RCS keywords.

Checking Files In and Out

You can accomplish a lot with RCS using only two commands, ci and co, and a directory named RCS. ci stands for *check in*, which means storing a working file in the RCS directory; co means *check out* and refers to retrieving an RCS file from the RCS repository.

To get started, you must create an RCS directory. By default, all RCS commands assume that a directory named RCS exists in the current working directory. So, your first step is to create this directory. Suppose you have several source files in /home/gomer/editor. Make that your current directory and create the directory, RCS, as show in the following:

```
$ cd /home/gomer/editor
$ mkdir RCS
```

All RCS commands executed in /home/gomer/editor will use this directory. The RCS directory is also called the *repository*.

TIP

RCS's default behavior is to use a repository in each working directory. This is usually sufficient for small projects. This highlights one of RCS's shortcomings: It does not make it easy to work with projects that have multiple working directories. Again, this is a reason why many people prefer CVS.

After you have created the RCS repository, the next step is to check all your existing source code files into it. The first time you check a file in, RCS asks for a description of the file, copies it to the RCS directory, and deletes the original. "Deletes the original? Ack!" Don't worry, you can retrieve it with the check-out command, co. But, first things first. The following example creates a repository, a source file to store in it, and then uses ci to check the file in.

EXAMPLE

Example

First, make an RCS directory, as shown:

```
$ mkdir RCS
```

Next, create the source file, howdy.c, in the same directory in which you created the RCS directory.

```
/*
 * $Id$
 * howdy.c - Sample to demonstrate RCS Usage
 */
#include <stdio.h>

int main(void)
{
    printf("Howdy, Linux programmer!");
    return EXIT_SUCCESS;
}
```

OUTPUT

```
$ ci howdy.c
RCS/howdy.c,v  <--  howdy.c
enter description, terminated with single '.' or end of file:
NOTE: This is NOT the log message!
>> Simple program to illustrate RCS usage

>> .
initial revision: 1.1
done
$ co -l howdy.c
RCS/howdy.c,v  -->  howdy.c
revision 1.1 (locked)
done
```

Note that if you do not use co's -1 option, the working file you just checked out is read-only; if you want to edit it, you must lock it. To do this, use the -1 option with co (co -1 howdy.c). -1 means lock (the concept of locking is defined in Table 19.1). The two lines in the output preceded by >> are lines you must type.

Making Changes to Repository Files

To see version control in action, make a change to the working file. If you haven't already done so, check out and lock the file (co -1 howdy.c). Change anything you want, but I recommend adding \n to the end of printf's string argument because Linux (and UNIX), unlike DOS and Windows, do not automatically add a newline to the end of console output.

Then, check the file back in. When you check it back in, RCS will perform the following steps:

1. Increment the revision number to 1.2

2. Ask for a description of the changes you made

3. Incorporate the changes you made into the RCS file

4. (Annoyingly) delete the original

To prevent deletion of your working files during check-in operations, use the -l or -u options with ci.

Example

This example makes the change discussed in the previous paragraph and then updates the repository file.

EXAMPLE

```
$ ci -l howdy.c
RCS/howdy.c,v  <--  howdy.c
new revision: 1.2; previous revision: 1.1
enter log message, terminated with single '.' or end of file:
>> Added newline
>> .
done
```

OUTPUT

When used with ci, both the -l and -u options cause an implied check out of the file after the check-in procedure completes. -l locks the file so you can continue to edit it, whereas -u checks out an unlocked or read-only working file.

Additional Command-Line Options

In addition to -l and -u, ci and co accept two other very useful options: -r (for revision) and -f (for force). Use -r to tell RCS which file revision you want to manipulate. RCS assumes you want to work with the most recent revision; -r overrides this default. The -f option forces RCS to overwrite the current working file. By default, RCS aborts a check-out operation if a working file of the same name already exists in your working directory. So, if you really botch up your working file, use the -f option with co to get a fresh start.

RCS's command-line options are cumulative, as you might expect, and it does a good job of disallowing incompatible options. To check out and lock a specific revision of howdy.c, you would use a command like co -l -r2.1 howdy.c. Similarly, ci -u -r3 howdy.c checks in howdy.c, assigns it the revision number 3.1, and deposits a read-only revision 3.1 working file back into your current working directory.

Examples

1. This example creates revision 2.1 of howdy.c. Make sure you have checked out and changed howdy.c somehow before executing this command.

```
$ ci -r2 howdy.c
```

EXAMPLE

```
RCS/howdy.c,v  <--  howdy.c
new revision: 2.1; previous revision: 1.2
enter log message, terminated with single '.' or end of file:
>> Added something
>> .
done
```

OUTPUT

This command is equivalent to ci -r2.1 howdy.c.

2. This command checks out revision 1.2 of howdy.c and disregards the presence of higher-numbered revisions in the working directory.

```
$ co -r1.2 howdy.c
```

EXAMPLE

```
RCS/howdy.c,v  -->  howdy.c
revision 1.2
done
```

OUTPUT

3. Here is a handy command that discards all the changes you've made and starts with a known good source file:

```
$ co -l -f howdy.c
```

EXAMPLE

```
RCS/howdy.c,v  -->  howdy.c
revision 2.1 (locked)
done
```

When used with `ci`, `-f` forces RCS to check in a file even if it has not changed.

RCS Keywords

RCS *keywords* are special, macro-like tokens used to insert and maintain identifying information in source, object, and binary files. These tokens take the form $KEYWORD$. When a file containing RCS keywords is checked out, RCS expands $KEYWORD$ to $KEYWORD: VALUE $.

Id

That peculiar string at the top of the listing for `howdy.c`, Id, is an RCS keyword. The first time you checked out `howdy.c`, RCS expanded it to something like

```
$Id: howdy.c,v 1.1 1999/07/20 04:56:08 kwall Exp kwall $
```

The format of the Id string is as follows:

```
$KEYWORD: FILENAME REV_NUM DATE TIME AUTHOR STATE LOCKER $
```

On your system, most of these fields will have different values. If you checked out the file with a lock, you will also see your login name after the `Exp` entry.

Log

RCS replaces the Log keyword with the log message you supplied during check in. Rather than replacing the previous log entry, though, RCS inserts the new log message above the last log entry.

Example

This code listing shows how the Log keyword is expanded after several check ins.

```
/*
* $Id: howdy.c,v 1.4 1999/07/20 05:00:56 kwall Exp kwall $
* howdy.c - Sample to demonstrate RCS usage
*
* **************** Revision History ****************
* $Log: howdy.c,v $
* Revision 1.4  1999/07/20 05:00:56  kwall
* Added pretty stuff around the log keyword
```

```
 *
 * Revision 1.3  1999/07/20 04:59:17  kwall
 * Changed "return" to "exit"
 *
 * Revision 1.2  1999/07/20 04:58:25  kwall
 * Added newline
 * *******************************************************
 */
#include <stdio.h>
#include <stdlib.h>

int main(void)
{
  printf("Howdy, Linux programmer!\n");
  exit(EXIT_SUCCESS);
}
```

The Log keyword makes it convenient to see the changes made to a given file while working within that file. When read from top to bottom, the change history lists the most recent changes first.

Other RCS Keywords

Table 19.2 lists other RCS keywords and how RCS expands each of them.

Table 19.2:   *RCS Keywords*

Keyword	Description
$Author$	Login name of user who checked in the revision
$Date$	Date and time revision was checked, in UTC format
$Header$	Full pathname of the RCS file, the revision number, date, time, author, state, and locker (if locked)
$Locker$	Login name of the user who locked the revision (if not locked, field is empty)
$Name$	Symbolic name, if any, used to check out the revision
$RCSfile$	Name of the RCS file without a path
$Revision$	Revision number assigned to the revision
$Source$	Full pathname to the RCS file
$State$	The state of the revision: Exp (experimental) is the default; Stab (stable); Rel (released)

The $Date$ value appears in *UTC* or Universal Coordinated Time format, formerly known as Greenwich Mean Time. The symbolic name that $Name$ represents is an alias that you can use to refer to a particular revision. To associate a symbolic name with a specific revision number, use the -n<name> switch when checking in a file. The $State$ field defaults to experimental (Exp) because RCS considers all check ins to be trial runs until they are specifically marked as stable (Stab) or released (Rel) using the -s<state> switch.

The ident Command

The ident command locates RCS keywords in files of all types and displays them to standard output. This feature lets you find out which revisions of which modules are used in a given program release. ident works by extracting strings of the form $*KEYWORD*: *VALUE* $ from source, object, and binary files. It even works on raw binary data files and core dumps. In fact, because ident looks for any instance of the $*KEYWORD*: *VALUE* $ pattern, you can also use words that are not RCS keywords.

This enables you to embed additional information into programs, for example, a company name. Embedded information can be a valuable tool for isolating problems to a specific code module. The slick part of this feature is that RCS updates the identification strings automatically—a real bonus for programmers and project managers.

Example

EXAMPLE

To illustrate using ident, create the following source file, check it in (using -u), compile and link it, ignore the warning you might get that rcsid is defined but not used, and then run the ident command on it.

```
/*
 * $Id$
 * prnenv.c - Display values of environment variables.
 */
#include <stdio.h>
#include <stdlib.h>
#include <unistd.h>

static char rcsid[] = "$Id$\n";

int main(void)
{
    extern char **environ;
    char **my_env = environ;
```

```
        while(*my_env)
            printf("%s\n", *my_env++);
        return EXIT_SUCCESS;
}
```

```
$ gcc prnenv.c -o prnenv
$ ident prnenv
prnenv:
    $id: prnenv.c,v 1.1 1999/07/20 05:57:59 kwall Exp $
```

The statement static char rcsid[] = "Id\n"; takes advantage of RCS's keyword expansion to create a static text buffer that holds the value of the Id keyword in the compiled program that ident can extract.

What happened? The Id keyword expanded as previously described and gcc compiled the expanded text into the binary. To confirm this, page through the source code file and compare the Id string in the source code to ident's output. The two strings match exactly.

Using rcsdiff

If you need to see the differences between your modified working file and its pristine counterpart in the repository, use the rcsdiff command. rcsdiff compares file revisions. In its simplest form, rcsdiff filename, rcsdiff compares the latest revision of filename in the repository with the working copy of filename. You can compare specific revisions using the -r option. The general format for comparing specific file revisions using rcsdiff is as follows:

```
rcsdiff [ -rfiles [ -rfile2 ] ] filename
```

> **TIP**
> The diff(1) command is much more powerful and generalized than rcsdiff. rcsdiff is meant only for use with RCS. If you need to compare two (or more) text files, use the diff command.

Examples

1. For basic rcsdiff use, consider the sample program prnenv.c. Check out a locked version of it and remove the static char buffer. The result should closely resemble the following:

```
/*
 * $Id: prnenv.c,v 1.1 1999/07/20 05:22:42 kwall Exp kwall $
 * prn_env.c - Display values of environment variables.
 */
```

```
#include <stdio.h>
#include <stdlib.h>
#include <unistd.h>


int main(void)
{
    extern char **environ;
    char **my_env = environ;

    while(*my_env)
        printf("%s\n", *my_env++);


    return EXIT_SUCCESS;
}
```

OUTPUT

```
$ rcsdiff prnenv.c
=======================================================================
RCS file: RCS/prnenv.c,v
retrieving revision 1.1
diff -r1.1 prnenv.c
9d8
< static char rcsid[] = "$Id: prnenv.c,v 1.1 \


1999/07/20 05:57:59 kwall Exp
kwall $\n";
```

This output means that line 9 in revision 1.1 would have appeared on line 8 of prnenv.c if it had not been deleted.

EXAMPLE

2. To compare specific revisions to each other using the -r option, check prnenv.c into the repository, check it right back out with a lock, add a sleep(5) statement immediately above return, and, finally, check this third revision back in with the -u option. You should now have three revisions of prnenv.c in the repository. First, compare revision 1.1 to the working file:

```
$ rcsdiff -r1.1 prnenv.c
2c2
<   * $Id: prnenv.c,v 1.1 1999/07/20 05:57:59 kwall Exp $
...
>   * $Id: prnenv.c,v 1.2 1999/07/20 06:00:47 kwall Exp $
```

```
9d8
< static char rcsid[] = "$Id: prnenv.c,v 1.1 1999/07/20 05:57:59 kwall
➥Exp $\n";
17a17
<
...
>       sleep(5);
```

Next, compare revision 1.2 to revision 1.3:

```
$ rcsdiff -r1.2 -r1.3 prnenv.c
===================================================================
RCS file: RCS/prnenv.c,v
retrieving revision 1.2
retrieving revision 1.3
diff -r1.2 -r1.3
2c2
<   * $Id: prnenv.c,v 1.2 1999/07/20 06:00:04 kwall Exp $
...
>   * $Id: prnenv.c,v 1.3 1999/07/20 06:00:47 kwall Exp $
16a17
>          sleep(5);
```

rcsdiff is a useful utility for viewing changes to RCS files or for preparing to merge multiple revisions into a single revision.

Other RCS Commands

Besides ci, co, ident, and rcsdiff, the RCS suite includes rlog, rcsclean, and, of course, rcs. These additional commands extend your control of your source code by allowing you to merge or delete RCS files, review log entries, and perform other administrative functions.

Using rcsclean

rcsclean does what its name suggests: It cleans up RCS working files. The basic syntax is rcsclean [options] [file ...]. A bare rcsclean command will delete all working files unchanged since they were checked out. The -u option tells rcsclean to unlock any locked files and remove unchanged working files. You can specify a revision to delete using the -rM.N format. For example, the following command removes the 2.3 revision of foobar.c:

```
$ rcsclean -r2.3 foobar.c
```

EXAMPLE

OUTPUT

Example

The following command removes an unlocked, unchanged revision of prnenv.c:

```
$ co -u -r1.1 prnenv.c
RCS/prnenv.c prnenv.c
revision 1.1 (unlocked)
done
$ rcsclean -r1.1 prnenv.c
rm -f prnenv.c
```

The first command checked out an unlocked version of prnenv.c in order to have a version to work with. The second command promptly cleaned it up (that is, deleted it).

Using rlog

rlog prints the log messages and other information about files stored in the RCS repository. The -R option tells rlog to display only filenames. To see a list of all the files in the repository, for example, rlog -R RCS/* is the proper command (of course, you could always type ls -l RCS, too). If you want to see a list of only the locked files, use the -L option. To see the log information on all files locked by the user named Gomer, use the -l option.

Example

This example displays all log information for all revisions of prnenv.c:

```
$ rlog howdy.c
RCS file: RCS/prnenv.c,v
Working file: prnenv.c
head: 1.3
branch:
locks: strict
access list:
symbolic names:
keyword substitution: kv
total revisions: 3;selected revisions: 3
description:
ew
----------------------------
revision 1.3
date: 1999/07/20 06:00:47;  author: kwall; state: Exp;  lines: +2 -1
added sleep
```

```
.............................
revision 1.2
date: 1999/07/20 06:00:04;   author: kwall; state: Exp;   lines: +1 -2
deleted buffer
.............................

revision 1.1
date: 1999/07/20 05:57:59;   author: kwall; state: Exp;
Initial revision
==============================================================================
```

Using rcs

The rcs command is primarily an administrative command. In normal usage, though, it is useful in two ways. If you checked out a file as read-only, and then made changes you can't bear to lose, rcs -l filename will check out filename with a lock without simultaneously overwriting the working file. If you need to break a lock on a file checked out by someone else, rcs -u filename is the command to use. The file is unlocked, and a message is sent to the original locker containing an explanation from you about why you broke the lock.

Recall that each time you check a file in, you can type a check-in message explaining what has changed or what you did. If you make a typographical error or some other mistake in the check-in message, or would simply like to add additional information to it, you can use the following rcs command:

```
$ rcs -mrev:msg
```

rev is the revision whose message you want to correct or modify and msg is the corrected or additional information you want to add.

EXAMPLE

OUTPUT

Example

This example uses rcs to change the check-in message for revision 1.2 of prnenv.c:

```
$ rcs -m1.2:"Deleted static buffer `rcsid[]'" prnenv.c
RCS file: RCS/prnenv.c,v
done
$ rlog -r1.2 prnenv.c
RCS file: RCS/prnenv.c,v
Working file: prnenv.c
head: 1.3
```

```
branch:
locks: strict
access list:
symbolic names:
keyword substitution: kv
total revisions: 3;    selected revisions: 1
description:
ew
- - - - - - - - - - - - - - - - - - - - - - - - - - -
revision 1.2
date: 1999/07/20 06:00:04;   author: kwall; state: Exp;   lines: +1 -2
Deleted static buffer 'rcsid[]'
========================================================================
```

The first command performed the change. The `rlog` command displayed the log information to confirm that the change took place. At the bottom of `rlog`'s output, you can see the updated log message.

For more information on RCS, see these man pages: `rcs(1)`, `ci(1)`, `co(1)`, `rcsintro(1)`, `rcsdiff(1)`, `rcsclean(1)`, `rcsmerge(1)`, `rlog(1)`, `rcsfile(1)`, and `ident(1)`.

What's Next?

In this chapter, you learned about RCS, the Revision Control System. The next chapter, "A Debugging Toolkit," continues the discussion of some essential tools you will need when programming with Linux. Bugs are an unfortunate reality, so the next chapter gets you started developing debugging skills. After you have debugged your software, applied patches and bug fixes, and recorded all these changes using RCS, you will need to distribute it, which is covered in Chapter 21, "Software Distribution."

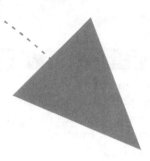

## 20

A Debugging Toolkit

As much as we all hate to admit it, software will have bugs. This chapter helps you debug your programs using gdb, the Gnu DeBugger, and some more specialized tools and techniques. You learn the following in this chapter:

- Using gdb

- Types of memory bugs

- Debugging with Electric Fence

- Using mpr and mcheck

Using gdb

To use gdb effectively, you must know only a few commands. It helps tremendously if you compile a debug version that has a special symbol table to support debugging. gdb also accepts several command-line options and arguments to customize its behavior. Time invested in learning gdb repays itself in faster, more effective debugging sessions.

But wait! What is a *debug version*? What is a *symbol table*? A symbol table is a list of functions, variables, and related information stored in a binary or object file that the C runtime environment, the linker, and the loader all use to properly load and execute your program. A debugging enhanced symbol table adds extra information, such as line numbers and more cross-references between functions and variables, that debuggers use to make debugging simpler. The section on gdb will show you how to use these features.

Compiling with Debugging Support

As you learned in Chapter 1, "Compiling Programs," you need to compile with the -g switch to create an enhanced symbol table. So, the following command:

```
$ gcc -g file1.c file2.c -o prog
```

causes prog to be created with debugging symbols in its symbol table. You can use gcc's -ggdb option to generate still more (gdb-specific) debugging information. However, to work most effectively, this option requires that you have access to the source code for every library against which you link. Although this can be very useful in certain situations, it can also be expensive in terms of disk space. In most cases, you should be able to get by with the plain -g option.

Also as noted in Chapter 1, it is possible to use both the -g and the -O (optimization) options. However, optimization transforms object code in ways that often obscure the relation between your source and what is visible in the debugger. Variables or lines of code might have disappeared or variable assignments might occur at times when you do not expect them. My recommendation is that you wait until you have debugged your code as completely as possible before starting to optimize it. In the long run, it will make your life, especially the parts of it you spend debugging, much simpler and less stressful.

CAUTION

Do not strip your binaries if you distribute programs in binary form. It is a matter of courtesy to your users and may even help you. If you get a bug report from a user who obtained a binary-only version, she will be unable to provide helpful information if you used strip to discard all symbols from the binary to make the binary smaller.

Example

This chapter uses the following program for many of its examples:

```c
/*
 * debugme.c - Poorly written program to debug
 */

#include <stdio.h>
#include <stdlib.h>

#define BIGNUM 5000

void index_to_the_moon(int ary[]);

int main(void)
{
    int intary[10];

    index_to_the_moon(intary);

    exit(EXIT_SUCCESS);
}

void index_to_the_moon(int ary[])
{
    int i;
    for(i = 0; i < BIGNUM; ++i)
        ary[i] = i;
}
```

I compiled this program and then tried to run it, as illustrated here:

```
$ gcc -g debugme.c -o debugme
$ ./debugme
Segmentation fault (core dumped)
```

The output might vary slightly on your system.

Basic Commands

Most of what you need to accomplish with gdb can be done with a surprisingly small set of commands.

STARTING gdb

To start a debugging session, simply type gdb *progname* [corefile], replacing *progname* with the name of the program you want to debug. Using a core file is optional but will enhance gdb's debugging capabilities. The first step is to start gdb, using the program name, debugme, and the core file, core, as arguments. To exit gdb, type quit at the (gdb) prompt.

```
$ gdb -q debugme core
```

The screen should resemble Figure 20.1 after gdb initializes.

OUTPUT

Figure 20.1: *The gdb start-up screen.*

The -q option suppressed annoying licensing messages. Another useful command-line option is -d *dirname*, where *dirname* is the name of a directory. This tells gdb where to find source code (it looks in the current working directory by default). As you can see in Figure 20.1, gdb displays the executable that created the core file and why the program terminated. In this case, the program caused a signal 11, which is a segmentation fault. It also helpfully displays the function it was executing and the line it believes caused the fault.

RUNNING A PROGRAM IN THE DEBUGGER

The first thing you want to do is run the program in the debugger. The command to do this is run. You can pass any arguments to the run command that your program would ordinarily accept. In addition, the program will receive a properly set up shell environment as determined by the value of the environment variable $SHELL. If you want, however, you can use gdb commands to set or unset arguments and environment variables after you have started a debugging session. To do so, type set args arg1 arg2 to set command-line arguments.

TIP

If you forget a gdb command or are not sure of its exact syntax, gdb has a rich help system. A bare `help` command typed at the gdb prompt will give a short list of available command categories, while `help [topic]` will print help information for *topic*. As always, gdb has a complete help system, TeXinfo documentation, and an excellent manual, *Debugging with GDB*, which is available online and by mail order from the FSF.

EXAMPLE

EXAMPLE

When you attempt to run this program in the debugger, it stops after receiving the SIGSEGV signal:

(gdb) run

Starting program: /usr/local/newprojects/lpe/20/src/debugme

OUTPUT

Program received signal SIGSEGV, Segmentation fault.

0x8048420 in index_to_the_moon (ary=0xbffff8c0) at debugme.c:24

24   ary[i] = i;

(gdb)

INSPECTING CODE

The question, though, is what was happening in the function index_to_the_moon? You can execute the `backtrace` command to generate the function tree that led to the segmentation fault. It is also helpful to have some idea of the context in which the offending lines of code exist. For this purpose, use the `list` command, which takes the general form, `list [m,n]`. m and n are the starting and ending line numbers you want displayed. A bare `list` command will display 10 lines of surrounding code.

EXAMPLE

EXAMPLE

The function trace looks like the following:

(gdb) backtrace

#0 0x8048420 in index_to_the_moon (ary=0xbffff8c9) at debugme.c:24

#1 0x80483df in main () at debugme.c:15

#2 0xb in ?? ()

(gdb) list

OUTPUT

19

20   void index_to_the_moon(int ary[])

21   {

22   int i;

23   for(i = 0; i < BIGNUM; ++i)

```
24          ary[i] = i;
25  }(gdb)
```

TIP

It is not necessary to type complete command names while using gdb. Any unique abbreviation will do. For example, back suffices for backtrace.

As you can see from the output, the problem was in index_to_the_moon, called from the main function. You can also see that the problem occurred at or near line 24 in the file debugme.c. With a clear picture of what is happening in the code and where it is happening, you can then determine what has gone wrong and fix it.

EXAMINING DATA

One of gdb's most useful features is its capability to display both the type and the value of almost any expression, variable, or array in a program being debugged. It will print the value of any expression legal in the language in which your program is written. The command is, predictably enough, print. print *varname* prints the value of *varname*.

You are not limited to using discrete values, either, because gdb can display the values of an arbitrary memory region. To print the first memory locations associated with an array, use the following sort of syntax:

```
(gdb) print array@number
```

where *array* is the name of the array or memory region and *number* is the number of values you want printed. Say, on the other hand, that you want to print the five values stored in an array named myarray beginning with the 71st element. The command for this is the following:

```
(gdb) print myarray[71]@5
```

The bracket notation indicates that you want to start at a specific memory location.

gdb can also tell you the types of variables using the whatis command. One of the whatis command's shortcomings is that it only gives you the type of a variable or function. If you want the structure's definition, use the ptype command.

EXAMPLE

EXAMPLE

The following example shows various print commands and their results:

EXAMPLE

```
(gdb) print i
$1 = 464
(gdb) print ary[i]
Cannot access memory at address 0xc0000000.
(gdb) print ary[i-1]
$2 = 463
(gdb) print $1-1
$3 = 463
(gdb) print ary@10
$4 = {0xbffff8c0, 0x0, 0x1, 0x2, 0x3, 0x4, 0x5, 0x6, 0x7, 0x8}
(gdb) print ary[71]@5
$5 = {71, 72, 73, 74, 75}
(gdb) print ary[0]@10
$6 = {0, 1, 2, 3, 4, 5, 6, 7, 8, 9}

(gdb) whatis i
type = int
(gdb) whatis ary
type = int *
(gdb) whatis index_to_the_moon
type = void (int *)
```

Although in this example the program crashed at i=464, where it crashes on your system depends on its memory layout. The second command, print ary[i], makes it pretty clear that the program does not have access to the memory location specified, although it does have legal access to the preceding one. The lines that begin with $1, $2, and so forth refer to entries in gdb's value history. If you want to access these values in the future, use these aliases rather than retyping the command.

Why did the first print ary command display hexadecimal values and the second one display decimal values? First, remember that arrays in C are zero-based. Remember also that the bare array name is a pointer to the base of the array. So, gdb looked at ary, saw that it was the address of the array's base, and displayed it and the following nine values as memory addresses. Memory addresses are customarily displayed in hexadecimal format. If you want to display the values stored in ary, use the indexing operator, [], as shown in the second print ary command.

TIP

gdb is usually compiled with support for the GNU `readline` library, which means that it supports the command-line editing and history features of the bash shell. For example, to recall a previous command, use the up arrow key to scroll back through the command history.

- Ctrl+A moves to the beginning of the current line.
- Ctrl+D deletes the character under the cursor.
- Ctrl+E moves to the end of the current line.
- Ctrl+K deletes everything between the cursor's current location and the end of the line.

See the `readline` manual page for more details about command-line editing.

SETTING BREAKPOINTS

As you debug problematic code, it is often useful to halt execution at some point. gdb enables you to set breakpoints on several different kinds of code constructs, including line numbers and function names. You can also set conditional breakpoints, where the code stops only when a certain condition is met.

To set a breakpoint on a line number, use the following syntax:

```
(gdb) break linenum
```

To set a breakpoint on a function name, use

```
(gdb) break funcname
```

gdb will halt execution before executing the specified line number or entering the specified function. You can then use `print` to display variable values, for example, or use `list` to review the code that is about to be executed. If you have a multi-file project and want to halt execution on a line of code or in a function that is not in the current source file, use one of the following forms:

```
(gdb) break filename:linenum
(gdb) break filename:funcname
```

Conditional breakpoints are usually more useful. They allow you to halt program execution temporarily when a particular condition is met. The correct syntax for setting conditional breakpoints is as follows:

```
(gdb) break linenum or funcname if expr
```

`expr` can be any expression that evaluates to TRUE (nonzero). To resume executing after hitting a breakpoint, type `continue`. If you have set many breakpoints and have lost track of what has been set and which ones have been triggered, you can use the `info breakpoints` command to refresh your memory. The `delete` command allows you to delete breakpoints, or you can merely disable them using the disable command and re-enable them with the enable command.

EXAMPLE

The session output that follows illustrates the use of breakpoints:

```
(gdb) break 24 if i == 15
Breakpoint 1 at 0x8048410: file debugme.c, line 24.
(gdb) run
The program being debugged has been started already.
Start it from the beginning? (y or n) y
Starting program: /usr/local/newprojects/lpe/20/src/debugme

Breakpoint 1, index_to_the_moon (ary=0xbfffffa08) at debugme.c:25
24              ary[i] = i;
(gdb) print i
$7 = 15

(gdb) info breakpoints
Num Type          Disp Enb Address    What
1   breakpoint    keep y   0x08048410 in index_to_the_moon at debugme.c:24
        Stop only if i == 15
        Breakpoint already hit 16 times
(gdb) delete 1
(gdb)
```

As you can see, gdb stopped on line 24 of the program. A quick print command confirms that it stopped at the requested value of i, 15. If the program is already running when you enter the run command, gdb will say that the program has already started and ask if you want to restart it from the beginning. Type yes and press Enter. The last two commands find out information about existing breakpoints and delete them by number.

CHANGING RUNNING CODE

If you use the print and whatis commands to display the value of an expression, and that expression modifies variables the program uses, you are changing values in a running program. This is not necessarily a bad thing, but you do need to understand that what you are doing has side effects.

If you want to change the value of a variable (keeping in mind that this change will affect the running code), the gdb command is (gdb) set variable *varname* = *value*, where *varname* is the variable you want to change and *value* is *varname*'s new value.

EXAMPLE

Delete all the breakpoints and watchpoints you might have set, and then set the breakpoint break 25 if i == 15. Then, run the program. It will temporarily halt execution when the variable i equals 15. After the break, issue the command set variable i = 10 to reset i to 10. Execute a print i command to confirm that variable's value has been reset, and then issue the step command, which executes a single statement at a time, three times, followed by another print i. You will see that i's value has incremented by one after each iteration through the for loop.

TIP

It is not necessary to type step three times. gdb remembers the last command executed, so you can simply press the Enter key to re-execute the last command, a real finger saver. This works for most gdb commands. See the documentation for more details.

VARIABLE SCOPE AND CONTEXT

At any given time, a variable is either in scope or not in scope, which affects the variables to which you have access, can examine, and can manipulate. You cannot access out of scope variables. There are a few rules that control variable scope, whether or not a variable is active or inactive:

- Local variables in any function are active if that function is running or if control has passed to a function called by the controlling function. Say the function foo calls the function bar; as long as bar is executing, all variables local to foo and bar are active. After bar has returned, only local variables in foo are active.

- Global variables are always active, regardless of whether the program is running.

- Nonglobal variables are inactive unless the program is running.

So much for variable scope. What is gdb's notion of variable context? The complication arises from the use of static variables, which are file-local; that is, you can have identically named static variables in several files, and they will not conflict because they are not visible outside the file to which they are defined. Fortunately, gdb has a way to identify to which variable you are referring. It resembles C++'s scope resolution operator. The syntax is as follows:

file_or_funcname::*varname*

where *varname* is the name of the variable to which you want to refer and *file_or_funcname* is the name of the file or the function in which it appears.

So, for example, assume two source code files, foo.c and bar.c, each containing a variable named baz that is declared static. To refer to the variable in foo.c, you might write the following:

```
(gdb) print 'foo.c'::baz
```

The single quotes around the filename are required so that gdb knows you are referring to a filename. Similarly, given two functions, blat and splat, each with an integer variable named idx, the following commands print the addresses of idx in each function:

```
(gdb) print &blat::idx
(gdb) print &splat::idx
```

Finding and Fixing Memory Problems

The subject of this chapter is bug hunting. After logic errors and typos, the most common kind of bugs are memory related. In this section, you learn what kinds of memory bugs usually occur and meet a couple of tools to help you track them down.

Types of Memory Bugs

Memory bugs fall into three broad categories: leaks, corruption, and illegal access. Memory *leaks* occur when a program allocates memory off the heap and fails to properly return it to the kernel, either by calling free or by using the termination routines that APIs define, such as the endwin call in the ncurses API. Memory *corruption* occurs when you try to use uninitialized or unallocated (or incorrectly allocated) memory, as shown in the following code snippet:

```
char *str;
char *msg;
strcpy(str, "some static text");        /* str not allocated */
printf("%s\n", msg);                     /* msg not initialized */
```

> ✔ The endwin call is discussed in "ncurses Termination," page 228.

This snippet causes a segmentation fault because, on the second line, str has not been properly malloced to hold anything, and because, on the fourth line, msg is uninitialized when used in the printf statement.

Illegal memory access errors occur when a program tries to access memory that does not belong to it. This usually occurs as some variation of an *off-by-one error*, when a program inadvertently accesses memory immediately before or after the end of an array.

Example

The following program is a problem child beset with memory bugs, including the following:

- Has a memory leak
- Overruns the end of dynamically allocated heap memory
- Underruns a memory buffer
- Frees the same buffer twice
- Accesses freed memory
- Overwrites statically allocated stack and global memory

```
/*
 * badmem.c - Demonstrate usage of memory debugging tools
 */
#include <stdlib.h>
#include <stdio.h>
#include <string.h>

char g_buf[5];                          /* global buffer */

int main(void)
{
    char *buf;
    char *leak;
    char l_buf[5];                      /* local buffer */

    /* Won't free this */
    leak = malloc(10);


    /* Overrun buf a little bit */
    buf = malloc(5);
    strcpy(buf, "abcde");
    printf("LITTLE   : %s\n", buf);
    free(buf);

    /* Overrun buf a lot */
    buf = malloc(5);
```

```
        strcpy(buf, "abcdefgh");
        printf("BIG : %s\n", buf);

        /* Underrun buf */
        *(buf - 2) = '\0';
        printf("UNDERRUN: %s\n", buf);

        /* free buf twice */
        free(buf);
        free(buf);

        /* access free()ed memory */
        strcpy(buf, "This will blow up");
        printf("FREED   : %s\n", buf);

        /* Trash the global variable */
        strcpy(g_buf, "global boom");
        printf("GLOBAL  : %s\n", g_buf);

        /* Trash the local variable */
        strcpy(l_buf, "local boom");
        printf("LOCAL   : %s\n", l_buf);

        exit(0);
}
```

badmem might or might not run on your system and it might fail at a different point. badmem's output on my system was

OUTPUT

```
$ ./badmem
LITTLE : abcde
BIG : abcdefgh
UNDERRUN: abcdefgh
Segmentation fault (core dumped)
```

Memory Debuggers

Because memory bugs are so common, programmers have developed several tools to help find them. Used in conjunction with a debugger like gdb, they have doubtless saved programmers from going bald. The two discussed here are Electric Fence and mcheck.

USING ELECTRIC FENCE

The first tool covered is Electric Fence, written by Bruce Perens. Electric Fence does not catch memory leaks, but it does an excellent job of detecting buffer overruns. You can obtain it from `ftp://metalab.unc.edu/pub/Linux/devel/lang/c`, although many Linux distributions also ship with it.

Electric Fence uses a CPU's virtual memory hardware to detect illegal memory accesses, aborting on the first instruction that commits a memory boundary violation. It accomplishes this by replacing the normal `malloc` with its own `malloc` and allocating a small section of memory after the requested allocation that the process is not permitted to access. As a result, buffer overruns cause a memory access violation, which aborts the program with a `SIGSEGV`. If your system is configured to allow core files (execute `ulimit -c` to get and set the size of core files allowed), you can then use a debugger to isolate the location of the overrun.

To use Electric Fence, you must link your program against a special library, `libefence.a`, and then simply run the program. It will dump core at the first memory violation.

EXAMPLE

This example shows how to use Electric Fence.

```
$ gcc -g badmem.c -o badmem -lefence
$ ./badmem
```

EXAMPLE

```
Electric Fence 2.0.5 Copyright (C) 1987-1995 Bruce Perens.
LITTLE : abcde
Segmentation fault (core dumped)
$ gdb -q badmem core
(gdb) run
Starting program: /usr/local/newprojects/lpe/14/src/badmem

   Electric Fence 2.0.5 Copyright (C) 1987-1998 Bruce Perens.
LITTLE  : abcde
Segmentation fault (core dumped)
$ gdb -q badmem
(gdb) run
Starting program: /usr/local/newprojects/lpe/20/src/badmem

   Electric Fence 2.0.5 Copyright (C) 1987-1998 Bruce Perens.
LITTLE  : abcde
```

OUTPUT

```
Program received signal SIGSEGV, Segmentation fault.
strcpy (dest=0x4010aff8 "abcdefgh", src=0x80495fc "abcdefgh")
    at ../sysdeps/generic/strcpy.c:38
../sysdeps/generic/strcpy.c:38: No such file or directory
(gdb) where
#0 strcpy (dest=0x4010aff8 "abcdefgh", src=0x80495fc "abcdefgh")
➥At ../sysdeps/generic/ strcpy.c:38
#1 0x8048905 in main () at badmem.c:27
#2 0x40030cb3 in __libc_start_main (main=0x8048890 <main>, argc=1,
    argv=0xbffff944, init=0x8048680 <_init>, fini=0x80495ac <_fini>,
    rtld_fini=0x4000a350 <_dl_fini>, stack_end=0xbffff93c)
    at ../sysdeps/generic/libc-start.c:78
(gdb)
```

The compile command used the `-g` option to generate extra debugging symbols. The second line from the bottom of the listing makes it crystal clear that there is a problem at line 27 in `badmem.c` in the main function. After you fix this problem, recompile and rerun the program, again linking against `libefence`, and, if it aborts again, repeat the debug/fix/recompile sequence. After you have thoroughly debugged your program, recompile without linking against Electric Fence, and you should be set.

CUSTOMIZING ELECTRIC FENCE

But wait, Electric Fence caught the big overrun on line 27, but it missed the little overrun. How could that be? This peculiar behavior results from the way the CPU aligns allocated memory. Most modern CPUs require that memory blocks be aligned on their natural word size.

Intel x86 CPUs, for example, require that memory regions begin at addresses evenly divisible by four, so `malloc` calls ordinarily return pieces of memory aligned accordingly. Electric Fence does the same. So, a request for five bytes actually results in eight bytes being allocated to meet the memory alignment requirements! As a result, the small buffer overrun slipped through the fence. Fortunately, Electric Fence enables you to control its alignment behavior using the environment variable $EF_ALIGNMENT. Its default value is `sizeof(int)`, but if you set it to zero, Electric Fence will detect smaller overruns.

Electric Fence also recognizes three other environment variables that control its behavior: EF_PROTECT_BELOW=1 for detecting buffer underruns; EF_PROTECT_FREE=1 for detecting access to freed memory; and EF_ALLOW_MAL-LOC_0=1, which allows programs to `malloc` zero bytes of memory.

EXAMPLE

After setting $EF_ALIGNMENT to 0, recompiling, and rerunning the program, Electric Fence catches the small overrun in the program.

```
$ export EF_ALIGNMENT=0
$ gcc -g badmem.c -o badmem -lefence
$ ./badmem
```

```
Electic Fence 2.0.5 Copyright (C) 1987-1998 Bruce Perens
Segmentation Fault (core dumped)
$ gdb badmem
...
(gdb) run
Starting program: /usr/local/newprojects/lpe/20/src/badmem


  Electric Fence 2.0.5 Copyright (C) 1987-1998 Bruce Perens.


Program received signal SIGSEGV, Segmentation fault.
strcpy (dest=0x4010affb "abcde", src=0x80495e8 "abcde")
    at ../sysdeps/generic/strcpy.c:38
../sysdeps/generic/strcpy.c:38: No such file or directory.
(gdb) where
#0  strcpy (dest=0x4010affb "abcde", src=0x80495e8 "abcde")
    at ../sysdeps/generic/strcpy.c:38
#1  0x80488c2 in main () at badmem.c:21
#2  0x40030cb3 in __libc_start_main (main=0x8048890 <main>, argc=1,


    argv=0xbffff934, init=0x8048680 <_init>, fini=0x80495ac <_fini>,
    rtld_fini=0x4000a350 <_dl_fini>, stack_end=0xbffff92c)
    at ../sysdeps/generic/libc-start.c:78
(gdb)
```

As you can see from the output, Electric Fence now catches the smaller overrun. I recommend always setting the EF_ALIGNMENT environment variable to 0 and using the other variables discussed to catch as many memory bugs as possible.

TIP

During the development phase, a good practice might be always to link your programs against libefence to catch memory errors that might not otherwise get caught, precisely because of the memory alignment issues discussed previously.

Using mpr and mcheck

The other memory debugging tool to consider using is Taj Khattra's mpr package, available from your favorite Metalab mirror (ftp://metalab.unc.edu/pub/Linux/devel/lang/c/mpr-1.9.tar.gz). It can be used to find memory leaks, but it does not find memory corruption errors. In addition, mpr also generates allocation statistics and patterns, but those features are not covered in this section. mpr's method uses simple brute force: It logs all allocation and free requests to an external log file that it later processes using utility programs that are part of the package.

USING mpr

To use mpr, download and compile it. The package includes several utility programs and a static library, libmpr.a, against which you link your program. Be sure to use the -g switch to generate debugging symbols because some of mpr's programs require them.

Recall from Chapter 1, "Compiling Programs," that -lmpr links badmem against libmpr.a, and -L$HOME/lib prepends $HOME/lib to the library search path. After the program is compiled and linked, set the environment variables $MPRPC to `mprpc badmem` and $MPRFI to "cat > badmem.log". mpr uses $MPRPC to traverse and display the call chain for each allocation and free request, while $MPRFI defines a pipeline command for logging and, optionally, filtering mpr's output.

With these preliminary steps out of the way, execute the program. If all goes as planned, you should wind up with a file named badmem.log in the current directory. It will look something like the following:

```
m:134522506:134516229:134514813:10:134561792
m:134522506:134516229:134514826:5:134565888
f:134522614:134520869:134514880:134565888
m:134522506:134516229:134514890:5:134565888
f:134522614:134520869:134514975:134565888
f:134522614:134520869:134514987:134565888
```

This log information is not very informative as is (the documentation explains the format, if you are interested); it merely provides the raw material for mpr's utility programs, which parse, slice, dice, and julienne the log to create meaningful information. To view leaks, use the mpr and mprlk as illustrated in the following example.

EXAMPLE

This examples compiles badmem to use mpr to locate a memory leak.

```
$ gcc -g badmem.c -o badmem -lmpr -L /usr/local/lib
$ export MPRPC=`mprpc badmem`
```

```
$ export MPRFI="cat > badmem.log"
$ ./badmem
```

```
LITTLE  : abcde
mcheck: memory clobbered past end of allocated block
Aborted (core dumped)
$ mpr -f badmem < badmem.log ¦ mprlk
m:main(badmem.c,18):10:13456992
```

The -f option reports the filename and line number where mpr detects the leak. The output indicates that line 18 of badmem.c in the main function mallocs 10 bytes of memory that it never frees (mpr and its utilities use the long decimal number to keep track of each allocation and free request). Referring to the code listing, you can see that this is correct.

USING mcheck

As mentioned a moment ago, mpr, on its own, cannot detect memory-corruption errors. Although this is true, mpr includes the mcheck function from GNU's malloc library, which enables you to detect buffer overruns, buffer underruns, and multiple frees of the same block. In fact, mpr compiles mcheck into libmpr.a by default.

So, the good news is that the buffer overruns and underruns cause it to abort unless you specifically instruct mpr not to use mcheck. The bad news is that mcheck is not terribly informative—it merely complains about a problem and leaves the programmer to determine where the problem occurs. Compiled with mcheck, the sample program aborts each time you clobber memory.

EXAMPLE

This example shows several runs of badmem compiled with mcheck, each run fixing the error encountered in the previous run:

```
$ ./badmem
```

```
LITTLE  : abcde
mcheck: memory clobbered past end of allocated block
...
$ ./badmem
LITTLE  : abcde
BIG     : abcdefgh
UNDERRUN: abcdefgh
mcheck: memory clobbered before allocated block
[...]
```

```
$ ./badmem
LITTLE  : abcde

BIG     : abcdefgh
UNDERRUN:
mcheck: block freed twice
```

Fixing the rest of the errors is left as an exercise for you.

What's Next?

You started building your debugging skills in this chapter. In the next chapter, "Software Distribution," you will learn a couple of methods for distributing your newly bug-free software. At the end of that chapter, you put all your skills together and build the programming project, a music CD database.

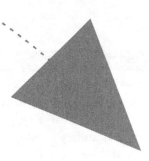

## 21

Software Distribution

The fastest, coolest code in the world will become shelfware if it is extraordinarily difficult to install or renders a user's system useless after installing it. Typically overlooked in programming texts, this chapter covers the tricky process of software distribution. You will learn the following:

- Using the `tar` command
- Using the `gzip` command
- Using the `install` command
- Using the Red Hat Package manager

Software distribution is the creation, distribution, installation, and upgrade of software in both source code and binary form. This chapter looks at the GNU project's `tar`, `gzip`, and `install` utilities and Red Hat's Red Hat Package Manager, RPM.

Using `tar` and `gzip`

`tar` and `gzip` were for many years the standard UNIX utilities for creating and distributing source code. For many people, they still are. They have limitations, however, when it comes to maintaining system integrity, particularly because they don't have a built-in facility for managing version control or checking software dependencies. This should not be seen, however, as `tar` or `gzip`'s shortcoming. The assumption behind software distribution using `tar`, `gzip`, and `install` is that the user or system administrator will take care of versioning and dependencies.

`tar` Usage

`tar`, which stands for *Tape ARchiver*, creates, manages, and extracts multi-file archives, known as *tarfiles*, or, more affectionately and idiomatically, *tarballs*. `tar` is the traditional utility used to create archives. `tar` is blessed (or plagued, depending on your perspective) with a bewildering variety of command-line options and switches.

NOTE

Long-time UNIX users will notice the absence of the `cpio` command. Why? The Linux idiom is to use `tar` (and `gzip`) to create multiple file archives for distributing software. `cpio`, when it is used at all, is used to create and manage system backups. Indeed, in the seven years I have been using Linux, I have never encountered any software that was packaged using `cpio`. That is not to say it does not happen, of course. I just have not run across it.

This chapter attempts to manage the confusion by focusing on simple, typical usage as related to the creation and management of software distribution. Table 21.1 lists some of `tar`'s command-line options, which subsequent sections discuss in more detail.

Table 21.1: **tar** *Command-Line Options*

Option	Description
c	Creates an archive
f *archive_name*	A required argument, f *archive_name* tells tar the name of the tarball with which to work
r	Appends files to the archive
u	Updates existing files in the archive
t	Lists the contents of the archive
v	Generates verbose output
z	Creates or works with a compressed archive (gzip is the default compression utility)

INVOKING tar

In its simplest form, the command to create a tarball is

```
$ tar cf archivename filelist
```

c says to create a tarball from the files indicated by *filelist*. f says to name the tarball *archivename*. You will generally want to compress the tarball to conserve disk space and minimize download time. The easiest way to do so, using GNU's tar, is to add z to the option list, which causes tar to invoke another GNU utility, gzip, on the tarball to compress it. In this case, the invocation would look like the following:

```
$ tar czf archivename filelist
```

EXAMPLES

EXAMPLE

OUTPUT

1. The following tar invocation creates a tarball named mytar.tar from all the files in the /etc directory that end in .conf:

```
$ tar cf mytar.tar /etc/*.conf
tar: Cannot add file /etc/amd.conf: Permission denied
tar: Removing leading `/' from absolute path names in the archive
tar: Cannot add file /etc/quota.conf: Permission denied
tar: Error exit delayed from previous errors
```

You might get errors because mortal users do not have access to certain files. In this case, tar will not add that file to the archive, but otherwise the archive will still be created.

EXAMPLE

OUTPUT

2. To list the contents of the archive, use the following command:

```
$ tar tf mytar.tar
etc/dosemu.conf
etc/gpm-root.conf
etc/host.conf
etc/inetd.conf
etc/isapnp.conf
etc/ld.so.conf
etc/lilo.conf
etc/logrotate.conf
etc/named.conf
etc/nscd.conf
etc/nsswitch.conf
etc/ntp.conf
etc/pwdb.conf
etc/resolv.conf
```

```
etc/smb.conf
etc/syslog.conf
```

Note that tar does not remove any of the original files, but merely creates a new tarball.

EXAMPLE

3. To create a compressed archive, simply add z to the option list. Traditionally, compressed tarballs, usually called *gzipped tarballs*, are named by adding .gz to the end. They are also often given the extension .tgz. Either one is acceptable. For purposes of consistency, this chapter will add .gz to the end of the filename.

```
$ tar czvf mytar.tar.gz /etc/*.conf
```

OUTPUT

```
etc/dosemu.conf
etc/gpm-root.conf
etc/host.conf
etc/inetd.conf
etc/isapnp.conf
etc/ld.so.conf
etc/lilo.conf
etc/logrotattar: Cannot add file /etc/quota.conf: Permission denied
tar: Error exit delayed from previous errors
smb.conf
etc/syslog.conf
```

The v option instructs tar to be verbose, that is, to list the files it is adding to the archive. Again, it is safe to ignore errors that occur due to file access violations.

TIP

Using the z option to compress a tarball slows down tar's operation somewhat, but it saves typing because you do not have to issue a second shell command, using gzip, to compress the tarball. On the other hand, calling gzip directly results in much better compression, but you have to type an additional command to prepare your package for distribution. Because programmers are lazy critters, makefiles usually include a target named dist that creates a gzipped tarball. This reduces the amount of typing you'll have to do and is convenient: simply type make dist and your package is ready to upload for the rest of the world to download.

Make sure you understand the difference between gzip, zip, and compress. gzip is the standard file compression utility on Linux systems. It is also the default compression utility used when you use tar's z option. Compressed archives created using gzip generally have a .gz extension on them. zip creates PKZIP compatible files but is a free alternative to the PKZIP utilities. Files compressed using zip have a .zip extension. compress, finally, is one of the original UNIX utilities for compressing files. A file compressed using `compress` generally has a `.Z` extension.

UPDATING `tar` FILES

So, now you have a nicely packaged and compressed tarball. But, suddenly, you realize you neglected to include the documentation. You did write documentation, didn't you? Never fear, you can easily add new files to (or update existing files in) the tarball using `tar`'s append or update options.

To append your newly written documentation to the compressed tarball we created at the end of the last series of examples, you can use the `r` option or the `u` option. The `r` instructs `tar` to append the specified files to the end of the tarball. `u`, on the other hand, simply updates a file presently in the archive with a newer version. Naturally, if it does not exist in the archive, it will be added.

EXAMPLE

This command uses `u` to update files with newer copies.

```
$ tar uvf mytar.tar /etc/*.conf
```

EXAMPLE

The output is identical to that generated when you created the tarball, so it is not repeated here. Note that the command did not use the compression option, `z`. This is because GNU `tar`, at least as of version 1.12, cannot update compressed files. As a result, it was necessary to uncompress the tarball first, using `gunzip mytar.tar`.

DELETING FILES FROM TARBALLS

To delete a file from a tarball, you have to use the long option `--delete` and specify the name of the files you want to delete. As with the update option, you cannot delete files from a compressed tarball.

EXAMPLE

This example deletes `isapnp.conf` and `host.conf` from the tarball created in earlier examples.

EXAMPLE
```
$ tar --delete -f=mytar.tar isapnp.conf host.conf
```

Note that the file deletion operation does not have a convenient single letter option; you *must* use `--delete`.

Using the `install` Command

Consider `install` a `cp` command on steroids. In addition to copying files, it sets their permissions and, if possible, their owner and group. It can also create destination directories if they do not already exist.

Invoking `install`

`install` is normally used in makefiles as part of a rule for a target named (something like) `install`. It can also be used in shell scripts. The `install` command's general syntax is

```
$ install [option[...]] source[...] dest
```

where `source` is one or more files to copy and `dest` is either the name of the target file or, if multiple files are specified in source, a directory. `option` can be one or more values listed in Table 21.2.

Table 21.2:   `install` *Command-Line Options*

Option	Argument	Description
-g	group	Sets the group ownership on files to the GID or group name specified in `group`. The default GID is that of the parent process calling `install`.
-o	owner	Sets the ownership of files to the UID or user name specified in `owner`. The default owner is `root`.
-m	mode	Sets the file mode (permissions) to the octal or symbolic value specified in `mode`. The default file mode is 755, or read/write/execute for owner and read/execute for group and other.

To specify `dest` as a directory, use the following syntax:

```
$ install -d [option [...]] dir[...]
```

The `-d` switch instructs `install` to create the directory `dir`, including any parent directories, using any of the attributes listed in Table 21.2 or the default attributes.

Examples

EXAMPLE

1. This example is taken from gdbm's makefile, the GNU database library. After expanding some of the make variables, the `install` target is

```
install: libgdbm.a gdbm.h gdbm.info
install -c -m 644 libgdbm.a $(libdir)/libgdbm.a
install -c -m 644 gdbm.h $(includedir)/gdbm.h
install -c -m 644 $(srcdir)/gdbm.info $(infodir)/gdbm.info
```

The make variables `libdir`, `includedir`, `srcdir`, and `infodir` are, respectively, `/usr/lib`, `/usr/include`, `/usr/src/build/info`, and `/usr/info`. So, `libgdbm.a` and `gdbm.h` will be read/write for the root user and read-only for everyone else. The file `libgdbm.a` gets copied to `/usr/lib`; `gdbm.h`, the header, winds up in `/usr/include`. The Texinfo file, `gdbm.info`, gets copied from `/usr/src/build/info` to `/usr/info/gdbm.info`. `install` overwrites existing files of the same name. The `-c` option is included for compatibility with older versions of install on other UNIX versions. You should include this, but, in most cases, it will be ignored.

EXAMPLE

2. This example creates a set of directories under /tmp and sets some odd file modes on the files installed. Unless you have peculiar permissions on /tmp, it should execute without any problems. The script uses some of the files from the fileutils source distribution on the Web site that accompanies this book. Feel free to delete the entire /tmp/lpe-install directory after it completes and after you have inspected its contents.

```sh
#!/bin/sh
# lpe-install.sh - Demonstrate (perverse) install usage
# ####################################################
INSTALL=$(which install)
LPE=/tmp/lpe-install
SRC=./src

for DIR in 10 20 30
do
    $INSTALL -c -d -o $USER $LPE/$DIR
    $INSTALL -c -m 111 -o $USER $SRC/*.c $LPE/$DIR
done
if [ $USER = root ]; then
    for GRP in $(cut -f1 -d: /etc/group)
    do
        $INSTALL -c -d -o $USER -g $GRP $LPE/$GRP
        $INSTALL -c -m 400 -g $GRP *.po $LPE/$GRP
    done
    echo "This part won't work if you're not root!"
fi
```

OUTPUT

```
$ ./lpe-install.sh
This part won't work if you're not root!
$ ls -l /tmp/lpe-install/10
total 388
drwxr-xr-x   2 kwall    users       1024 Jul 20 04:14 ./
drwxr-xr-x   5 kwall    users       1024 Jul 20 04:14 ../

---x--x--x   1 kwall    users      15723 Jul 20 04:14 ansi2knr.c*
---x--x--x   1 kwall    users      10045 Jul 20 04:14 chgrp.c*
---x--x--x   1 kwall    users       9522 Jul 20 04:14 chmod.c*
```

```
---x--x--x   1 kwall      users        11121 Jul 20 04:14 chown.c*
---x--x--x   1 kwall      users        24645 Jul 20 04:14 copy.c*
---x--x--x   1 kwall      users         6354 Jul 20 04:14 cp-hash.c*
---x--x--x   1 kwall      users        21121 Jul 20 04:14 cp.c*
---x--x--x   1 kwall      users        30694 Jul 20 04:14 dd.c*
---x--x--x   1 kwall      users        20320 Jul 20 04:14 df.c*
...
$ su -
Password:
# cd /home/kwall/projects/lpe/21/src
# ./lpe-install.sh
# ls -l /tmp/lpe-install
...
drwxr-xr-x   2 root       xfs           1024 Jul 20 04:21 xfs
# ls -l /tmp/lpe-install/xfs
total 1002
-r--------   1 root       xfs          67312 Jul 20 04:21 cs.po
-r--------   1 root       xfs          75552 Jul 20 04:21 de.po
-r--------   1 root       xfs          74117 Jul 20 04:21 el.po
-r--------   1 root       xfs          99148 Jul 20 04:21 es.po
-r--------   1 root       xfs          77667 Jul 20 04:21 fr.po
-r--------   1 root       xfs          65223 Jul 20 04:21 ko.po
-r--------   1 root       xfs          70329 Jul 20 04:21 nl.po
-r--------   1 root       xfs          67108 Jul 20 04:21 no.po
-r--------   1 root       xfs          67227 Jul 20 04:21 pl.po
-r--------   1 root       xfs          70748 Jul 20 04:21 pt.po
-r--------   1 root       xfs          68834 Jul 20 04:21 ru.po
-r--------   1 root       xfs          68908 Jul 20 04:21 sk.po
-r--------   1 root       xfs          65714 Jul 20 04:21 sl.po
-r--------   1 root       xfs          66882 Jul 20 04:21 sv.po
```

The interest here is in install's behavior, so do not trouble yourself trying to understand the shell syntax. Note, however, that the second code block will fail if not run by the root user. The first code block creates three directories rooted in /tmp: /tmp/lpe-install/10, /tmp/lpe-install/20, and /tmp/lpe-install/30, and copies all the C source code files from the src subdirectory of the current working directory to each of these three subdirectories. The -o option sets user ownership, which is repetitive in this case because the default owner is the user executing the script.

The second code block creates a set of directories named after each of the groups defined on your system. Each directory is owned by the default user, but the group ownership is the same as the directory name. All files ending in `*.po` are copied from `src` to the appropriate directory, again setting the group ownership to the directory name and making the files read-only for the owner/ user. No other users or groups have any privileges on these files.

This use of `install` is strange and the file modes, as the listing shows, are unusual, but the example does illustrate why `install` is a better `cp` command and how to use it.

Using RPM

The Red Hat Package Manager, although it bears Red Hat's name, is a powerful, general, and open software packaging system used by many Linux distributions, including (but not limited to) Caldera's OpenLinux, S.u.S.E., and, of course, Red Hat. It is most frequently used for Linux, but versions of it are available for many UNIX versions, including Solaris, SunOS, HP-UX, SCO, AIX, and Digital UNIX.

The discussion of RPM in this chapter focuses on creating source code packages. If you are interested in mundane issues such as installing, upgrading, and removing RPMs, read Ed Bailey's excellent book, *Maximum RPM*. Point your browser at `http://www.rpm.org/` to download the latest version of RPM, to obtain complete documentation, FAQs and HOWTOs, and even to get a downloadable version of the book.

NOTE

You are strongly encouraged to purchase *Maximum RPM* and reward both author and publisher for making it freely available. You will likely find that having hard copy is preferable to looking at a soft copy.

Minimum Requirements

To create RPMs, you need RPM itself, the source code you want to compile, an `rpmrc` file to set some RPM defaults and control its behavior, and a spec file to control the package build process. You should already have a functional development environment (compilers, tools, editors, cold pizza, Jolt cola, coffee, and such) and your source code should compile successfully.

Before proceeding, however, it is essential to convey the mindset behind RPM. RPM always begins with pristine sources. *Pristine*, in this context, means original, unpatched code as it came from the developer. RPM is designed to allow you to apply patches to the original source code. This feature enables you to use RPM to customize software to a specific system or to apply bug fixes.

The emphasis on unmodified sources allows you or your users always to begin a build from a known base and to customize it to fit particular circumstances. As a developer, this gives you considerable flexibility with respect to creating useful and reliable software and also a valuable level of control over how your software gets compiled and installed.

To boil it down to two simple rules:

1. Always start creating an RPM with unmodified sources.

2. Apply patches as necessary to fit the build environment.

Creating an RPM

Creating an RPM the first time can be somewhat daunting. Fortunately, most of the work is on the front end. The most important part of creating an RPM, generating a spec file, must be done only once. After the spec file has been created, you spend most of your time doing what you want to do, maintaining the code. Only minor modifications to the spec file are necessary.

CONFIGURING RPM

The `rpmrc` file controls almost every element of RPM's behavior. Your system administrator might have a global `rpmrc` file in `/etc`. If you would like to override one or more of the global settings, create a `~/.rpmrc` that contains your preferred settings. Before you begin, however, you may want see RPM's current configuration. `rpm --showrc` accomplishes this.

EXAMPLES

1. This is the default configuration for RPM version 3.0.2 on Red Hat 6.0:

EXAMPLE

OUTPUT

```
$rpm --showrc
ARCHITECTURE AND OS:
build arch            : i386
compatible build archs: i686 i586 i486 i386 noarch
build os              : Linux
compatible build os's : Linux
install arch          : i686
install os            : Linux
compatible archs      : i686 i586 i486 i386 noarch
compatible os's       : Linux


RPMRC VALUES:
macrofiles            : /usr/lib/rpm/macros
➥:/usr/lib/rpm/i686-linux/macros:/etc/rpm/macros
```

```
➥:/etc/ rpm/i686-linux/macros:~/.rpmmacros
optflags              : -O2
=========================
-14: GNUconfigure(MC:)
  %{__libtoolize} --copy --force
  %{__aclocal}
  %{__autoheader}
  %{__automake}
  %{__autoconf}
  %{-C:_mydir="`pwd`"; %{-M:%{__mkdir} -p %{-C*};} cd %{-C*};}
  ...
```

Your system might have slightly different settings. As you can see, the output is divided into two sections: architecture and operating system settings, which define the build and install environment; and rpmrc values, which control RPM's behavior. The global configuration file, /etc/rpmrc, should be used for settings of a systemwide sort. The local file, $HOME/.rpmrc, contains values specific to the user building an RPM. In most cases, few settings in the rpmrc file require changing.

TIP

The most common value changed in $HOME/.rpmrc is the name of the packager. However, because you can also specify this directly in the spec file, there is little reason to use this. The problem with using a personal .rpmrc file is that you might forget what it contains and propagate bad build information out to people using your RPMs. It is better to stick with the global settings in /etc/rpmrc.

THE STRUCTURE OF A SPEC FILE

The spec file, after the source code itself, is the most important element of an RPM because it defines what to build, how to build it, where to install it, and the files that it contains. Each spec file you create should be named according to the standard naming convention, *pkgname-version-release*.spec, where *pkgname* is the name of the package, *version* is the version number, typically in x.y.z format, and *release* is the release number of the current version.

For example, the name ncurses-4.2-18.spec breaks down to version 4.2, release number 18, indicating that this is the eighteenth "version" (don't get confused by the diction) of version 4.2 of ncurses. Release numbers are used by software vendors to indicated how many times they have built a specific package. Version numbers, on the other hand, are set by the maintainer of the package. Each spec file has eight sections:

- Header—The header section contains information returned by RPM queries, such as a description, version, source location, patch names and locations, and the name of an icon file.

- Prep—The prep section consists of whatever preparation must take place before the actual build process can begin. Generally this is limited to unpacking the source and applying any patches.

- Build—As you might expect, the build section lists the commands necessary to compile the software. In most cases, this is a single make command, but it can be as complex and obtuse as you desire.

- Install—Again, the name is self-explanatory. The install section lists the name of the command, such as make install, or the name of the shell script that performs the software installation after the build successfully completes.

- Install/Uninstall Scripts—These scripts, which are optional, are run on the user's system when the package is removed or installed.

- Verify Script—Usually, RPM's verification routines are sufficient, but if they fall short of your needs, this section lists any commands or shell scripts that make up for RPM's shortcomings.

- Clean—This section handles any post-build clean-up but is rarely necessary because RPM does an excellent job of cleaning up after itself.

- File List—An essential component (an RPM will not build without it), this section contains a list of files that make up your package, sets their file attributes, and identifies documentation and configuration files.

Analyzing a Spec File

The following spec file is taken from the xearth package shipped with Red Hat 6.0, /usr/src/redhat/SPECS/xearth.spec. The first part of the spec file is the header:

```
Summary: An X display of the Earth from space.
Name: xearth
Version: 1.0
Release: 12
Copyright: MIT
Group: Amusements/Graphics
Source: ftp://cag.lcs.mit.edu/pub/tuna/xearth-1.0.tar.gz
Patch: xearth-1.0-redhat.patch
BuildRoot: /var/tmp/xearth-root
```

```
%description
```

```
Xearth is an X Window System based graphic that shows a globe of the
➥Earth, including markers for major cities and Red Hat Software.  The
➥Earth is correctly shaded for the current position of the sun, and the
➥displayed image is updated every five minutes.
```

This is the end of the header section. As you can see, a ton of information is provided, which can be retrieved from RPM's database using RPM's powerful query capabilities. The name, version, and release information directly affects the build process, but the balance of the information is strictly informational.

The next section of a spec file is the prep section. It defines the steps necessary to prepare the package to be built.

```
%prep
%setup -q
%patch -p0
```

The prep section is pretty simple: It applies a patch, in this case, /usr/src/redhat/SOURCES/xearth-1.0-redhat.patch, to the pristine sources. That's it. Badda bing, badda boom.

Well, the situation is actually a bit more complex. The line %setup is an RPM macro. It accomplishes several tasks, in this case, cding into the BUILD directory, deleting the remnants of previous build attempts (if any), uncompressing and extracting the source code, a gzipped tarball, /usr/src/redhat/SOURCES/xearth-1.0.tar.gz, cding into the extracted directory, and recursively changing ownership and permission on the extracted directory and its files. This is the simplest way the %setup macro can be used. It takes a variety of arguments that modify its behavior, but in most cases, the default behavior is what you want and all you will need.

After the prep section comes the build section. It details how to build the package.

```
%build
xmkmf
make
```

The build section is fairly straightforward. In effect, the two commands are a script passed to /bin/sh to build the package. RPM checks the return codes for each step, aborting the build with a useful message if an error occurred.

After the package is built, you probably want to install it. The install section provides the information required to do so.

```
%install
rm -rf $RPM_BUILD_ROOT
mkdir -p $RPM_BUILD_ROOT/etc/X11/wmconfig

make DESTDIR=$RPM_BUILD_ROOT install install.man

cat > $RPM_BUILD_ROOT/etc/X11/wmconfig/xearth <<EOF
xearth name "xearth"
xearth description "xearth"
xearth group Amusements
xearth exec "xearth -fork"
EOF
```

Just like the prep and build sections, RPM passes each line in the install section to /bin/sh to be executed as a script. Red Hat's xearth package contains both standard make targets, install and install.man, and custom shell code to fine-tune the installation.

After a package builds and installs successfully, RPM will remove the detritus left over from the build and install process. The clean section of the spec file manages this.

```
%clean
rm -rf $RPM_BUILD_ROOT
```

Simpler still, the clean section simply makes sure that the xearth build directory is completely removed, blatantly suggesting a problem with the spec file (its commands, actually) if problems arise. You will usually not require this section if you stick with RPM's default build tree.

The next section is the files section:

```
%files
%defattr(-,root,root)
/usr/X11R6/bin/xearth
/usr/X11R6/man/man1/xearth.1x
%config /etc/X11/wmconfig/xearth
```

As noted previously, the files section consists of a list of files that make up the package. If the file does not exist in this list, it will not be included in the package. However, you must still create the file list yourself. Despite RPM's power, it cannot read your mind and create the file list. The easiest way to create the list is to use the files your makefile generates and add to that list any documentation or configuration files required.

Building the Package

With the spec file created, you are ready to build the package. If you are confident the spec file is correct, just change to the directory holding the spec file and issue the "build everything in sight" command, `rpm -ba`.

Example

The following command builds both the binary and source RPMs of `xearth`:

EXAMPLE

```
$ cd /usr/src/redhat/SPECS
$ rpm -ba xearth-1.0-12.spec
```

OUTPUT

```
+ umask 022
+ cd Patch #0:
Executing: %build
imake -DUseInstalled -I/usr/X11R6/lib/X11/config
gcc -O2 -fno-strength-reduce -I/usr/X11R6/include
➡ -Dlinux -D__i386__  -D_POSIX_C_SOURCE=199309L
➡ -D_POSIX_SOURCE -D_XOPEN_SOURCE=500L -D_BSD_SOURCE
➡ -D_SVID_SOURCE   -DFUNCPROTO=15 -DNARROWPROTO
➡ -c xearth.c -o xearth.o
...
Processing files: xearth
Finding provides...
Finding requires...
Requires: ld-linux.so.2 libICE.so.6 libSM.so.6
➡ libX11.so.6 libXext.so.6 libXt.so.6 libc.so.6
➡ libm.so.6 libc.so.6(GLIBC_2.0) libc.so.6(GLIBC_2.1)
➡ libm.so.6(GLIBC_2.1)
Wrote: /usr/src/redhat/SRPMS/xearth-1.0-12.src.rpm

Wrote: /usr/src/redhat/RPMS/i386/xearth-1.0-12.i386.rpm
Executing: %clean
```

The listing is abbreviated due to the amount of output.

If everything works correctly, you wind up with a binary package, `/usr/src/redhat/RPMS/i386/xearth-1.0-12.i386.rpm`, and a new source rpm, `/usr/src/redhat/RPMS/i386/xearth-1.0-12.src.rpm`. At this point, arrange to copy the binary package to a new machine, install it, and test it.

If it installs and runs properly, upload your source RPM to your favorite software repository, and you are finished.

If, regrettably, you run into problems, RPM's build command accepts several options that enable you to step through the build process to identify and, hopefully, fix problems. The following list contains brief descriptions of the options:

- -bp—Validate the spec file's prep section
- -bl—Validate the file list in %files
- -bc—Perform a prep and compile
- -bi—Perform a prep, compile, and install
- -bb—Perform a prep, compile, install, and build only a binary package
- --short-circuit—Add this argument to skip straight to the specified build step (p, l, c, i, b)
- --keep-temps—Preserve the temporary files and scripts created during the build process
- --test—Perform a mock build to see what would be done (also performs --keep-temps)

After you resolve the errors, rebuild using -ba, upload your masterpiece, and wait for the kudos (and patches and bug fixes) to roll in.

What's Next?

In this chapter, you looked at two different ways to distribute software, using tar, gzip, and install, and using the Red Hat Package Manager. This brings you to the end of the book. You have learned how to compile programs, covered many system programming topics, met many application programming interfaces, and briefly covered the huge subject of network programming. You were also introduced to a few essential programming utilities, such as RCS and gdb. To tie all these skills together, the next chapter walks you through building a music CD database.

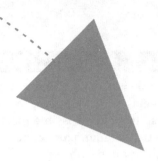

## 22

Programming Project: A Music CD Database

Chapter 3, "About the Project," gave you a whirlwind tour of the programming project you complete at the end of this book. Congratulations! You're there! Seriously, you have learned a lot about Linux programming in the previous 21 chapters, so now it is time to put that knowledge to work. This chapter walks you through a small program, a music CD database, that makes tangible (or at least as tangible as ones and zeroes can be) much of what you have learned. In particular, this chapter contains the following:

- The complete source code to the music CD database programs.

- A thorough explanation of the programs, module by module.

- Suggestions about how you can improve and extend the programs.

The Code, Module by Module

As mentioned in Chapter 3, the user-level programs, `mcdcli.c` and `mcdui.c`, rely heavily on the helper module `mcddb.c`. It seems sensible, then, to spend some time looking at the helper module, because it makes possible most of the user program's functionality. I call it the database manager because it handles almost all the interaction with the underlying database and the Berkeley database API. The header and source file follow:

```
/*
 * mcddb.h - Database module for music CD database
 */
#ifndef MCDDB_H_
#define MCDDB_H_

#include <db.h>

/*
 * Open the database named in dbpath, or, if it is NULL, assume that
 * we want PWD/mcd.db. Return 0 on success, errno or -1 on failure.
 */
int open_db(char *dbpath);

/*
 * Sync and close the currently open database. Always returns 0.
 */
int close_db(void);

/*
 * Add the record with a key of kbuf and a value of vbuf to the
 * currently opened database. Returns 0 on success, 1 if the key
 * already exists, and errno otherwise.
 */
int add_rec(char *kbuf, char *vbuf);

/*
 * Delete the record whose key matches kbuf. On success, syncs the
 * database to disk and returns 0; on failure, returns 1 if a key
 * matching kbuf was not found or errno otherwise.
```

```
 */
int del_rec(char *kbuf);


/*
 * Iterate through the database, searching for a key matching kbuf.
 * On success, returns 0 and stores the data corresponding to kbuf
 * in value. On failure, returns DB_NOUTFOUND or errno.
 */
int find_rec(char *kbuf, DBT *value);


/*
 * Retrieve the record matching key from the database. Returns 0 on
 * success and stores the corresponding value in value, 1 if the
 * indicated key is not found, and errno otherwise.
 */
int get_rec(char *kbuf, DBT *value);


/*
 * Count the number of records in the database by iterating through it
 * with a cursor. Returns the number of records if successful or 0 if
 * the database is empty or an error occurs.
 */
int count_recs(void);


/*
 * Iterate through the entire database, listing each record consecutively
 * and alphabetically by key. Returns number of records stored in kbuf and
 * vbuf on success. Returns 0 if no records available. On failure, returns
 * errno.
 */
int list_recs(char **keys, char **values);


#endif /* MCDDB_H_ */
```

The #ifndef/#endif conditional protects the header file against multiple inclusion, which would cause gcc to issue warnings or errors about variables or functions being redefined. The header file declares functions for opening and closing a database and various functions for accessing and manipulating records in the database.

One shortcoming of the interface, as it is currently defined, is that it assumes access to a Berkeley db database. The find_rec and get_rec functions expect a pointer to a DBT structure; this dependency can be resolved by making these parameters simple character string pointers.

Next up, the database manager's implementation:

```
/*
 * mcddb.c - Database manager for music CD database
 */
#include <db.h>
#include <stdlib.h>
#include <stdio.h>
#include <string.h>
#include "mcddb.h"

static DB *db;              /* Global database pointer */

int open_db(char *dbpath)
{
    int ret;
    char *defpath = "./mcd.db";

    /* If dbpath is NULL, assume the current dir name the DB mcd.db */
    if(!dbpath) {
    if((dbpath = malloc(strlen(defpath) + 1)) != NULL) {
        strcpy(dbpath, defpath);
    } else {
        return -1;
    }
    }

    ret = db_open(dbpath, DB_BTREE, DB_CREATE, 0600, NULL, NULL, &db);
    if(ret != 0) {
    return ret; /* Fatal */
    }
    return 0;
}


int close_db(void)
```

```c
{
    /* db->close should force a sync, but just in case */
    db->sync(db, 0);
    db->close(db, 0);
    return 0;
}

int add_rec(char *kbuf, char *vbuf)
{
    DBT key, value;
    int ret;

    /* Initialize the DBTs */
    memset(&key, 0, sizeof(DBT));
    memset(&value, 0, sizeof(DBT));

    /* This looks perverse, but it works */
    key.data =  kbuf;
    key.size = strlen(kbuf);
    value.data =  vbuf;
    value.size = strlen(vbuf);

    /* Store the record */
    ret = db->put(db, NULL, &key, &value, DB_NOOVERWRITE);
    if(ret == DB_KEYEXIST) /* Key already exists */
    return 1;
    else if(ret != 0) /* Some other error occurred */
    return ret;
    /* Sync the database */
    db->sync(db, 0);
    return 0; /* Success! */
}

int del_rec(char *kbuf)
{
    int ret;
    DBT key;
```

```
        memset(&key, 0, sizeof(DBT));
        key.data =  kbuf;
        key.size = strlen(kbuf);

        ret = db->del(db, NULL, &key, 0);
        if(ret != 0) {
        if(ret == DB_NOTFOUND) { /* Key not found */
            return 1;
        } else {
            return ret;
        }
        }
        /* Sync the database */
        db->sync(db, 0);
        return 0;
    }

    int find_rec(char *kbuf, DBT *value)
    {
        int ret;
        DBT key;            /* Copy kbuf here */
        DBC *dbc = NULL;        /* A database cursor */

        /* Create the cursor */
        ret = db->cursor(db, NULL, &dbc);
        if(ret != 0) {          /* Something went wrong */
        return ret;
        }

        /* Initialize DBT key; assume `value' is already init'ed */
        memset(&key, 0, sizeof(DBT));
        key.data =  kbuf;
        key.size = strlen(kbuf);

        /* Iterate through the database, looking for a match */
        while((ret = dbc->c_get(dbc, &key, value, DB_NEXT)) != DB_NOTFOUND) {
        /*
         * This is tricky. db does not store null-terminated strings,
```

```
           * so use strncmp to limit the bytes compared to the length
           * of the search string.  To make sure the match is legitimate,
           * compare the length of the search string to key.size. If they
           * are equal, assume the match is good.
           */
          if(!strncmp(key.data, kbuf, strlen(kbuf))) {
              if(key.size == strlen(kbuf)){ /* Found a match */
              break;
              }
          }
      }
      /* Did we fall through or find a match? */
      if(ret == DB_NOTFOUND) {
      return 1;
      }
      return 0;                /* Happy, happy, joy, joy */
}


int get_rec(char *kbuf, DBT *value)
{
      int ret;
      DBT key;

      /* Initialize the key DBT; assume value init'ed by caller */
      memset(&key, 0, sizeof(DBT));
      key.data = kbuf;
      key.size = strlen(kbuf);

      /* See if we can get the record */
      ret = db->get(db, NULL, &key, value, 0);
      switch(ret) {
      case 0:               /* Bliss */
      return 0;
      case DB_NOTFOUND:          /* Key not found */
      return 1;
      default:              /* Unknown error */
      return ret;
      } /* end switch */
```

```
}

int count_recs(void) {
    int ret, cnt = 0;
    DBT key, value;
    DBC *dbc = NULL;

    /* Create the cursor */
    ret = db->cursor(db, NULL, &dbc);
    if(ret != 0)
    return ret;

    /* Initialize the DBTs */
    memset(&key, 0, sizeof(DBT));
    memset(&value, 0, sizeof(DBT));

    while((dbc->c_get(dbc, &key, &value, DB_NEXT)) != DB_NOTFOUND) {
    ++cnt;
    }
    return cnt;
}

int list_recs(char **keys, char **values)
{
    int ret, cnt = 0;
    DBT key, value;
    DBC *dbc = NULL;          /* Database cursor */

    /* Create the cursor */
    ret = db->cursor(db, NULL, &dbc);
    if(ret != 0) {
    fprintf(stderr, "mcddb.c: db->cursor: %s\n", strerror(ret));
    return 0;
    }

    /* Initialize the DBTs */
    memset(&key, 0, sizeof(DBT));
    memset(&value, 0, sizeof(DBT));
```

```
    /* Move sequentially through the database */
    while((dbc->c_get(dbc, &key, &value, DB_NEXT)) != DB_NOTFOUND) {
    db->get(db, NULL, &key, &value, DB_DBT_MALLOC);
    memcpy(keys[cnt], key.data, key.size);
    memcpy(values[cnt], value.data, value.size);
        ++cnt;
    }
    return cnt;
}
```

This code defines the database interface declared in mcddb.h. In general, all the functions return zero on success, a positive integer if some sort of system error occurs, or a negative integer (usually –1) if some other (nonsystem) error occurs. Exceptions to this rule will be noted.

open_db opens the database specified in dbpath. If dbpath is NULL, a default database named mcd.db is opened in the current working directory. The DB_CREATE flag causes the database to be created if it does not already exist. The database is not set up to handle duplicate keys, either.

close_db closes the database. As the comment states, the db->close call should force the database to flush any data to disk, but to be safe close_db explicitly calls db->sync just in case. In fact, as a precautionary measure, the two functions that actually change data in the database, add_rec and del_rec, also call db->sync.

The add_rec function uses the DB_NOOVERWRITE flag to prevent overwriting an existing key/value pair. As a result, to modify an existing record in the database, you would first have to delete the record, and then add it again after making any necessary modifications. A function that updates an existing record would make an excellent addition to the database interface.

Despite their apparent similarity, find_rec and get_rec are very different. get_rec searches for a record that has a specific key. find_rec, on the other hand, is a query function. It searches the entire database to see if a given key exists. That is, where get_rec assumes that the key exists and simply retrieves the corresponding value, find_rec asks if the key exists and returns the corresponding value. find_rec must do extra work after a possible match is found.

The strcmp function works only on null-terminated strings, but the values stored in the database are not null-terminated. As a result, find_rec uses strncmp to limit the characters compared. After a possible match is found, the next step is to compare the search string's length to the length of the data in the database, which is stored in the size member of the DBT structure. If these two values are equal, find_rec concludes that the key is a valid match.

count_recs simply iterates through the database and increments a counter for each record that it encounters. It is one of the functions that returns a positive, non-zero integer when it succeeds. The Berkeley db API does not keep track of how many records exist in a B-tree database. count_recs makes it much easier to implement the list_recs function because it enables you to create a table that contains the correct number of pointers to key/value pairs. After this table's pointers are created, it is trivial to initialize each key/value pair properly.

The DB_DBT_MALLOC flag passed to db->get must be mentioned. Ordinarily, when you call db->get, the memory to which &key and &value point is valid until the next call to any Berkeley db function that uses the db handle. DB_DBT_MALLOC, however, alters this behavior. When this flag is passed to db->get and dbc->c_get (the cursor function), Berkeley db allocates memory for key and value to make the storage permanent. As a result, freeing this memory becomes the responsibility of the application.

list_recs needs this functionality because, without DB_DBT_MALLOC, the storage associated with key and value goes away after exiting the function because they are automatic variables that go out of scope at the closing brace. list_recs, like count_recs, returns a positive non-zero integer on success.

```
/*
 * mcdutil.h - Utility functions for music CD database program,
 */
#ifndef MCDUTIL_H_  /* Guard against multiple inclusion */
#define MCDUTIL_H_


/*
 * Get a string to plug into a `key' or a `value'
 */
int mcd_getstr(char buf[], int len);


#endif /* MCDUTIL_H_ */
```

This segment declares a simple function for getting a character string from the user. The definition follows in mcdutil.c:

```
/*
 * mcdutil.c - Utility functions for music CD database program
 */
```

```
#include <string.h>
#include <stdio.h>
#include <stdlib.h>
#include "mcdutil.h"

#define BUFSZ 1024

int mcd_getstr(char buf[], int len)
{
    int c, i = 0;

    while((c = getchar()) != '\n' && i < len) {
    buf[i] = c;
    ++i;
    }
    buf[i] = '\0';
    return i;
}
```

Nothing extraordinary is here. I prefer to write my own functions to read characters from the keyboard because doing so gives me much more control over how to deal with the input. For example, custom input functions such as mcd_getstr are easily modified to reject invalid input or to transform valid input into a format that your application can handle. Next, the client program, mcdcli.c.

TIP

Custom input functions are perfect candidates for inclusion into programming libraries because they can be reused in many projects.

Creating programming libraries is discussed in detail in Chapter 14, "Creating and Using Programming Libraries."

```
/*
 * mcdcli.c - Command-line driver for music CD database.  Suitable
 * for use in shell scripts.
 */
#include <stdlib.h>          /* For `exit' */
#include <unistd.h>
#include <getopt.h>          /* For `getopt' */
```

```c
#include <string.h>        /* For `memcpy' in glibc 2.1.1 */
#include "mcddb.h"         /* Database management */

#define BUFSZ 1024

void usage(void);

int main(int argc, char **argv)
{
    int ret, op, cnt, i;
    extern char *optarg;      /* From <getopt.h> */
    extern int optind;        /* From <getoph.h> */
    DBT value;
    char **keys, **values;

    if(argc < 2 || argc > 4) {
    usage();
    }

    op = getopt(argc, argv, "a:d:f:g:l");

    if(open_db(NULL) == 1) {          /* Open the database */
    puts("Error opening database");
    }

    switch(op) {
    case 'a':                 /* Add a record */
    /* But don't add an empty record or a zero-length key */
    if(argc == 4 &&
       (optarg != NULL) &&
       (strlen(optarg) >= 1) &&
       (argv[optind] != NULL)) {
      ret = add_rec(optarg, argv[optind]);
      if(ret == 1) {
      printf("Key `%s' exists\n", optarg);
      exit(EXIT_FAILURE);
      } else if (ret < 0) {
      perror("mcdcli.c: add_rec");
```

```
            exit(EXIT_FAILURE);
        }
        break;
    } else {
        usage();
    }
    case 'd':                  /* Delete a record */
    if(argc == 3) {
        if(optarg != NULL) {
        ret = del_rec(optarg);
        if(ret == 1) {
            printf("Key `%s' not found\n", optarg);
            exit(EXIT_FAILURE);
        } else if(ret < 0) {
            perror("mcdcli.c: del_rec");
            exit(EXIT_FAILURE);
        }
        break;
        }
    } else {
        usage();
    }
    case 'f':                  /* Find a record */
    if(argc == 3) {
        if(optarg != NULL) {
        memset(&value, 0, sizeof(DBT));
        ret = find_rec(optarg, &value);
        if(ret == 1) {
            printf("Key `%s' not found\n", optarg);
            exit(EXIT_FAILURE);
        } else if(ret < 0) {
            perror("mcdcli.c: find_rec");
            exit(EXIT_FAILURE);
        }
        printf("%s¦%.*s\n", optarg,
            (int)value.size, (char *)value.data);
        break;
        }
```

```
        } else {
            usage();
        }
        case 'g':            /* Get a record */
        if(argc == 3) {
            if(optarg != NULL) {
            memset(&value, 0, sizeof(DBT));
            ret = get_rec(optarg, &value);
            if(ret == 1) {
                printf("Key `%s' not found\n", optarg);
                exit(EXIT_FAILURE);
            } else if(ret < 0) {
                perror("mcdcli.c: get_rec");
                exit(EXIT_FAILURE);
            }
            printf("%.*s¦%.*s\n", (int)strlen(optarg), optarg,
                (int)value.size, (char *)value.data);
            break;
            }
        } else {
            usage();
        }
        case 'l':            /* List all records */
        if(argc == 2) {
            if((cnt = count_recs()) == 0) {
            puts("No records in database");
            exit(EXIT_FAILURE);
            }
            /* Size the pointer pointers */
            if((keys = malloc(sizeof(DBT *) * cnt)) == NULL) {
            puts("mcdcli.c: malloc keys");
            exit(EXIT_FAILURE);
            }
            if((values = malloc(sizeof(DBT *) * cnt)) == NULL) {
            puts("mcdcli.c: malloc values");
            exit(EXIT_FAILURE);
            }
            /* Size each element */
```

```
                    for(i = 0; i < cnt; ++i) {
                    if((keys[i] = malloc(BUFSZ)) == NULL) {
                        puts("mcdcli.c: malloc keys[i]");
                        exit(EXIT_FAILURE);
                    }
                    if((values[i] = malloc(BUFSZ)) == NULL) {
                        puts("mcdcli.c: malloc values[i]");
                        exit(EXIT_FAILURE);
                    }
                    }
                    ret = list_recs(keys, values);
                    if(ret == 0) {
                    perror("mcdcli.c: list_recs");
                    exit(EXIT_FAILURE);
                    }
                    for(i = 0; i < cnt; ++i) {
                    printf("%.*s¦%.*s\n",
                        (int)strlen(keys[i]), keys[i],
                        (int)strlen(values[i]), values[i]);
                    }
                    break;
                } else {
                    usage();
                }
                default:                /* Bad keystroke, show the menu */
                usage();
                break;
                } /* switch */

                close_db();        /* Close the database */
                exit(EXIT_SUCCESS);
        }


        void usage(void)
        {
            puts("USAGE: mcdcli \
            \n\t{-a <key> <value>}\
            \n\t{-d <key>}\
```

```
    \n\t{-f <key>}\
    \n\t{-g <key>}\
    \n\t{-l}");
  exit(EXIT_FAILURE);
}
```

The user program, mcdcli.c, is suitable for use in shell scripts. It expects one of five options on the command line: -a to add a record, -d to delete a record, -f to find a record, -g to get a record, or -l to list all records. The -a option requires two arguments, a key and a value to add to the database. -d, -f, and -g require one argument, a key. The -l option does not require any arguments because it simply dumps all the records in the database.

A useful enhancement would be to remove the static buffer size limit for the record listing operation. As it is written, each pointer in the table of keys and records is limited to 1024 bytes. For convenience, the code in question is reproduced here:

```
/* Size each element */
for(i = 0; i < cnt; ++i) {
if((keys[i] = malloc(BUFSZ)) == NULL) {
        puts("mcdcli.c: malloc keys[i]");
        exit(EXIT_FAILURE);
    }
    if((values[i] = malloc(BUFSZ)) == NULL) {
        puts("mcdcli.c: malloc values[i]");
        exit(EXIT_FAILURE);
    }
```

As it stands, this segment is acceptable because it is hard to imagine a musician's name or a CD title that will exceed BUFSZ bytes (which is #defined to be 1024 bytes). Nevertheless, the principle at stake is to avoid arbitrary limits such as this, no matter how reasonable they seem at the time.

To parse the command line, the program uses the POSIX getopt function, declared in <getopt.h> (you also must #include <unistd.h>), as follows:

```
int getopt(int argc, char *const argv[], const char *opstring);
```

argc and argv are the argc and argv parameters to main. getopt expects each option to be preceded by a dash (-). optstring contains a list of valid option characters. If a character in optstring is followed by a colon (:), it must be followed on the command line by an argument.

Thus, the `optstring` in `mcdcli.c`, `"a:d:f:g:l"` means that the `-a`, `-d`, `-f`, and `-g` options must be followed by an argument, but `-l` does not have an argument. `getopt` iterates through each option present in the command line and returns the corresponding character (a, d, f, g, or l) or EOF if no more options exist. If an option requires an argument, the pointer `optarg` points to that argument.

So, `mcdcli.c` first validates the number of command-line arguments it receives, and then uses `getopt` to determine the operation to perform and the corresponding arguments, if any, for that operation. When the command line is validated, it opens the database, and then goes into a long switch statement that actually performs the requested operation.

Each operation has its own code used to validate the number and value of the arguments on which it operates. If you are adding a record, for example, you need two arguments, a non-null, non-empty key, and the value to associate with that key. `del_rec`, on the other hand, needs only a key that is non-null. The same requirement also applies to `find_rec` and `get_rec`. Note that three of the cases—f, g, and l—use a variation of the following unusual `printf` statement:

```
printf("%.*s\n", (int)numeric_value, (char *)string_value);
```

Again, this is necessary because, when printing strings, `printf` ordinarily expects null-terminated strings but Berkeley db does not store null-terminated strings. Moreover, the casts are necessary because the size member of a DBT structure is actually defined as `ulen32_t`, not as an `int`, while the type of the data member of a DBT structure is `void *`.

The format specifier `%.*s` means that the next argument is to be printed as a string. `.` specifies that the string argument should be printed with a precision or field width of X characters. If X is numeric, the field width is X. In this case, however, the field width is `*`, meaning that an integral argument must be specified and that `printf` will write that many characters. For example, the line

```
printf("%.*s\n", (int)strlen(str), str);
```

prints the first `strlen(str)` characters from the string that `str` points to, while the statement

```
printf("%.5s\n", 5, str);
```

prints the first five characters of `str`.

`mcdcli.c` goes to considerable lengths to size the arrays of strings used to store and then print the entire contents of the database. After calling `count_recs`, it first allocates the correct number of character pointers in which to store the data values, and then sizes each of the strings stored in the pointer pointers. The call to `list_recs` initializes these values, and then, using the `printf` semantics discussed a moment ago, `mcdcli.c` writes each key/value pair to stdout.

As noted, `mcdcli.c` is designed to be used from a shell script, so it performs a single operation and displays its output simply. Appropriate shell code is required to format its input or output. Also be aware that input containing spaces must be surrounded by strong or weak quotes. For example, to add a key of "Joan Armatrading" and a value of "Greatest Hits," the correct invocation would be

```
$ ./mcdcli -a "Joan Armatrading" "Greatest Hits"
```

After performing the requested operation, `mcdcli.c` closes the database and exits. The usage function reminds the user how to invoke the program properly.

The support routines for the ncurses-based user interface are defined in `mcdscr.h`. It is listed here:

```
/*
 * mcdscr.h - Screen-handling for music CD database
 */
#ifndef MCDSCR_H_         /* Guard against multiple inclusion */
#define MCDSCR_H_

#include <curses.h>

/*
 * Initialize the curses subsystem. Return 0 if successful or -1
 * on error.
 */
int init_scrn(void);

/*
 * Shut down the curses sybsystem. No return value.
 */
void close_scrn(void);

/*
 * (Re)Draw the main screen. No return value.
 */
void draw_scrn(void);
```

```c
/*
 * Print a message to the status line.
 */
void status(char *msg);


/*
 * Prepare a window for input and output.
 */
void prep_win(WINDOW *win);


/*
 * Prepare a window to be redisplayed.
 */
void show_win(WINDOW *win);


/*
 * Get a key/value pair to add to the database.
 */
void add(char *kbuf, char *vbuf);


/*
 * Get the key of a record to delete.
 */
void del(char *kbuf);


/*
 * Get the key of a record to find.
 */
void find(char *kbuf);


/*
 * Display a key/value pair
 */
void show(char *kbuf, char *vbuf);


/*
 * Get a specifed key/value pair
 */
```

```
void get(char *kbuf);


/*
 * List all records real purty-like
 */
void list(char *kbuf, char *vbuf, int cnt);
#endif /* MCDSCR_H_ */
```

The interface defined in mcdscr.h is both a convenience and an effort to
maintain the system's modularity. As a convenience, it dramatically reduces
the amount of code that goes into the full-screen driver program, mcdui.c. It
improves modularity because, as already mentioned, as long as the interface defined in the header file does not change, the code that implements
the interface can be rewritten as necessary. Speaking of implementation,
you will look at it next.

```
/*
 * mcdscr.c - Screen handling for music CD database
 */
#include <curses.h>
#include <form.h>
#include "mcdscr.h"


WINDOW *mainwin;            /* Primary window */
WINDOW *menuwin;            /* Menu bar at top of mainwin */
WINDOW *statuswin;           /* Status line at bottom of mainwin */
WINDOW *workwin;            /* Input/output area of mainwin */


int init_scrn(void)
{
    int maxy, maxx;

    if((mainwin = initscr()) == NULL) {
    perror("mcdscr.c: mainwin");
    return -1;
    }
    getmaxyx(stdscr, maxy, maxx);

    /* Subwindow to write a "menu" on */
    if((menuwin = derwin(stdscr, 1, maxx, 0, 0)) == NULL) {
```

```
        perror("mcdscr.c: menuwin");
        return -1;
        }
        /* Subwindow to write status messages on */
        if((statuswin = derwin(stdscr, 1, maxx, maxy - 1, 0)) == NULL) {
        perror("mcdscr.c: statuswin");
        return -1;
        }
        /* Subwindow where input and output occurs */
        if((workwin = derwin(stdscr, maxy - 2, maxx, 1, 0)) == NULL) {
        perror("mcdscr.c: workwin");
        return - 1;
        }
        /* Set up the keyboard */
        if(cbreak() == ERR)         /* Process input ourselves */
        return -1;
        if(keypad(stdscr, TRUE) == ERR) /* Enable use of F-keys */
        return -1;
        if(noecho() == ERR)         /* Control output ourselves */
        return -1;

        return 0;
}


void close_scrn(void)
{
        nocbreak();         /* Restore cooked mode */
        delwin(menuwin);        /* Free subwindws */
        delwin(statuswin);
        delwin(workwin);
        endwin();               /* Restore terminal state */
}


void draw_scrn(void)
{
        char *menu = "F2-Add   F3-Delete   F4-Find   F5-Get   F6-List   F10-Quit";

        mvwprintw(menuwin, 0, 0, "%s", menu);
```

```
        wrefresh(menuwin);
        refresh();
}


void status(char *msg)
{
        werase(statuswin);
        mvwprintw(statuswin, 0, 0, "%s", msg);
        wrefresh(statuswin);
        refresh();
}


void prep_win(WINDOW *window)
{
        werase(window);
        echo();
}


void show_win(WINDOW *window)
{
        noecho();
        wrefresh(window);
        refresh();
}


void add(char *kbuf, char *vbuf)
{
        prep_win(workwin);
        mvwprintw(workwin, 1,0, "ARTIST : ");
        status("Enter key");
        wgetstr(workwin, kbuf);
        mvwprintw(workwin, 2, 0, "TITLE  : ");
        status("Enter value");
        wgetstr(workwin, vbuf);
        show_win(workwin);
}


void del(char *kbuf)
```

```
{
    prep_win(workwin);
    mvwprintw(workwin, 1, 0, "ARTIST : ");
    status("Enter key");
    wgetstr(workwin, kbuf);
    show_win(workwin);
}

void find(char *kbuf)
{
    prep_win(workwin);
    mvwprintw(workwin, 1, 0, "ARTIST : ");
    status("Enter key");
    wgetstr(workwin, kbuf);
    show_win(workwin);
}

void show(char *kbuf, char *vbuf)
{
    werase(workwin);
    mvwprintw(workwin, 1, 0, "ARTIST : %s", kbuf);
    mvwprintw(workwin, 2, 0, "TITLE  : %s", vbuf);
    show_win(workwin);
}

void list(char *kbuf, char *vbuf, int cnt)
{
    int maxx, maxy, nexty;

    getmaxyx(workwin, maxy, maxx);
    if(cnt == 0) {
    werase(workwin);
    mvwhline(workwin, cnt, 0, ACS_HLINE, maxx);
    mvwprintw(workwin, cnt + 1, 0, "ARTIST");
    mvwprintw(workwin, cnt + 1, maxx / 2, "TITLE");
    mvwhline(workwin, cnt + 2, 0, ACS_HLINE, maxx);
    }
    nexty = cnt + 3;
```

```
        mvwprintw(workwin, nexty, 0, "%s", kbuf);
        mvwprintw(workwin, nexty, maxx / 2, "%s", vbuf);
        show_win(workwin);
}

void get(char *kbuf)
{
    prep_win(workwin);
    mvwprintw(workwin, 1, 0, "ARTIST : ");
    status("Enter key");
    wgetstr(workwin, kbuf);
    show_win(workwin);
}
```

A lot is going in this code, but not as much as it might seem as first glance. init_scrn initializes the ncurses subsystem, creates three subwindows used throughout the program, and sets up an ncurses-friendly keyboard state. As mentioned in Chapters 11 and 12, most ncurses programs must interpret keyboard input directly, hence the call to cbreak. The keypad call enables easily interpreted cursor and function key calls. noecho prevents any keystrokes from being echoed to the screen, unless specifically enabled. The three subwindows that are created simplify management of the screen. As you will see in the screen driver program in a moment, handling input and output via separate windows makes redrawing the screen much simpler.

close_scrn restores keyboard input to standard cooked mode and deallocates the memory resources given to three subwindows. Finally, it calls endwin to allow ncurses to perform its cleanup. These steps restore the terminal's state to its pre-ncurses status. draw_scrn simply displays the initial screen users will see when they first start the program.

The status routine updates a status line maintained at the bottom of the screen. The status line is used to give the user additional information and to display error messages. status and other routines use two utility routines, prep_win and show_win, to simplify window management. prep_win erases a window and turns on echo mode, making data entry screens easy to read. show_win updates the window you have been working on and also stdscr, so that any changes that have been made get displayed on the user's screen.

The add, del, find, show, and get functions in mcdscr.c implement the functionality for adding, deleting, finding, showing, and getting individual records, respectively. They transfer data retrieved from the database to the ncurses screen. The list function deserves special comment. It is designed to display all the records in the database (comparable to the -1 option of mcdcli.c). It tries to arrange the output in an attractive fashion on the screen. The cnt argument is key. When cnt is 0, no records have yet been displayed, so list first creates a header before displaying a record. Thereafter, list updates the working window, workwin, with the next record. A useful improvement in this function would be to enable scrolling in the working window if the total number of records to show exceeds the number of rows that workwin has.

The real meat of the interactive interface lives in mcdui.c, presented next.

```c
/*
 * mcdui.c - Ncurses-based driver for music CD database.
 */
#include <stdlib.h>          /* For `exit' */
#include <unistd.h>
#include <getopt.h>          /* For `getopt' */
#include <string.h>          /* For `memcpy' in glibc 2.1.1 */
#include "mcddb.h"           /* Database management */
#include "mcdscr.h"          /* Screen handling */

#define BUFSZ 1024

void usage(void);

int main(int argc, char **argv)
{
    int ret, opt, fkey, cnt, i;
    extern char *optarg;      /* From <getopt.h> */
    char kbuf[BUFSZ], vbuf[BUFSZ];
    char **keys, **values;
    DBT value;

    /* Parse the command line */
    switch(argc) {
    case 3:                   /* Use the specified database */
    opt = getopt(argc, argv, "f:");
    if(opt == 'f') {
        if(optarg == NULL) {
        usage();
        } else {
```

```
                if(open_db(optarg)) {
                    fprintf(stderr, "Error opening database %s\n", optarg);
                    exit(EXIT_FAILURE);
            }
        }
    }
    break;
    case 1:              /* Use the default database */
    if(open_db(NULL)) {
        puts("Error opening database");
        exit(EXIT_FAILURE);
    }
    break;
    default:             /* Malformed command-line */
    usage();
    break;
    } /* end switch */



    /* Start ncurses */
    if(init_scrn() < 0) {    /* Bummer, ncurses didn't start */
    puts("Error initializing ncurses");
    close_db();
    exit(EXIT_FAILURE);
    }
    /* Draw the initial screen */
    draw_scrn();

    /* The primary command loop */
    while((fkey = getch()) != KEY_F(10)) {
    switch(fkey) {
    case KEY_F(2) :          /* F2 -Add a record */
        add(kbuf, vbuf);
        ret = add_rec(kbuf, vbuf);
        if(ret > 0)
        status("Key already exists");
        else if(ret < 0)
        status("Unknown error occurred");
```

```
        else
        status("Record added");
        break;
    case KEY_F(3) :          /* F3 - Delete a record */
        del(kbuf);
        ret = del_rec(kbuf);
        if(ret > 0)
        status("Key not found");
        else if(ret < 0)
        status("Unknown error occurred");
        else
        status("Record deleted");
        break;
    case KEY_F(4) :          /* F4 - Find a record */
        find(kbuf);
        memset(&value, 0, sizeof(DBT));
        ret = find_rec(kbuf, &value);
        if(ret > 0)
        status("Key not found");
        else if(ret < 0)
        status("Unknown error occurred");
        else {
        status("Record located");
        sprintf(vbuf, "%.*s",
            (int)value.size, (char *)value.data);
        show(kbuf, vbuf);
        }
        break;
    case KEY_F(5) :          /* F5 - Get a record */
        get(kbuf);
        memset(&value, 0, sizeof(DBT));
        ret = get_rec(kbuf, &value);
        if(ret > 0)
        status("Key not found");
        else if(ret < 0)
        status("Unknown error occurred");
        else
        status("Record located");
```

```
            sprintf(vbuf, "%.*s",
                (int)value.size, (char *)value.data);
            show(kbuf, vbuf);
            break;
        case KEY_F(6):          /* F6 - List all records */
            if((cnt = count_recs()) == 0) {
            status("No records in database");
            break;
            }
            /* Size a table of pointers */
            if((keys = malloc(sizeof(DBT *) * cnt)) == NULL)
            status("Memory error");
            if((values = malloc(sizeof(DBT *) * cnt)) == NULL)
            status("Memory error");
            /* Size each pointer in the table */
            for(i = 0; i < cnt; ++i) {
            if((keys[i] = malloc(BUFSZ)) == NULL) {
                status("Memory error");
                break;
            }
            if((values[i] = malloc(BUFSZ)) == NULL) {
                status("Memory error");
                break;
            }
            }
            /* Get all of the records */
            ret = list_recs(keys, values);
            if(ret == 0) {
            status("Problem with database manager");
            break;
            }
            /* Show 'em on the screen */
            for(i = 0; i < cnt; ++i) {
            sprintf(kbuf, "%.*s", (int)strlen(keys[i]), keys[i]);
            sprintf(vbuf, "%.*s", (int)strlen(values[i]), values[i]);
            list(kbuf, vbuf, i);
            }
            status("Last record displayed");
```

```
        break;
    default:          /* Bad keystroke, nag user */
        status("Key not defined");
        break;
    } /* End switch(fkey) */
    }


    close_db();                 /* Close the database */
    close_scrn();            /* Close curses subsystem */
    exit(EXIT_SUCCESS);
}


/*
 * Simple usage nag
 */
void usage(void)
{
    puts("USAGE: mcdui [-f database]");
    exit(EXIT_FAILURE);
}
```

mcdui.c should look familiar. Its overall flow, and a lot of its code, closely resembles the code in mcdcli.c. This is deliberate. The design of the database interface is such that the only real difference between the command-line client and the interactive is that data retrieved by the database must be formatted in an ncurses-friendly way.

Of course, there are some differences. mcdui.c has a much simpler invocation. It accepts one command-line option, -f, that enables you to use a database other than the default, mcd.db. Invalid arguments or options result in a usage message, an example of which is show here:

```
$ mcdui -f some database
USAGE: mcdui [-f database]
```

EXAMPLE

The next few blocks of code open the database, start the ncurses subsystem, and draw the initial screen. The initial screen that init_scrn and draw_scrn create are shown in Figure 22.1.

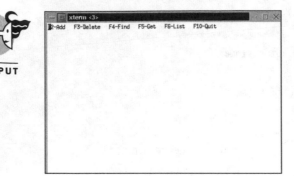

OUTPUT

Figure 22.1: *The main* mcdui *screen.*

All the action takes place in the while loop. The switch statement processes keyboard input, calling the appropriate routine. Valid input consists of one of the following:

- F2—Add a record
- F3—Delete a record
- F4—Find a record
- F5—Get a record
- F6—List all records
- F10—Quit the program

Any other keystroke, when looking at this screen, causes the message Key not defined to be displayed in the status area. The success or failure of each operation is displayed on the status line using the status function. You can easily extend the program to accept other keystrokes as aliases for the currently defined commands. For example, typing a or A would allow the user to add a record, and typing l or L would list all records currently in the database.

When you press F2, you are first asked to enter the musician's name and then the CD title. The appearance of the screen after completing an add operation is shown in Figure 22.2.

If the key already exists in the database, an error message to that effect is displayed in the database.

To delete a record from the database, press F3. The screen that results from deleting a record in shown in Figure 22.3.

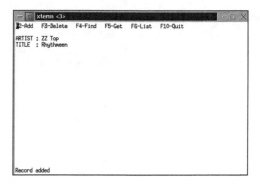

Figure 22.2: *mcdui after adding a new CD to the database.*

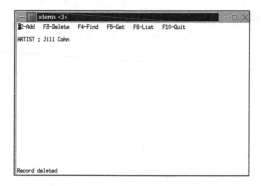

Figure 22.3: *mcdui after deleting a CD from the database.*

The find operation, invoked when you press F4, searches the entire database for a key that matches the key the user inputs. As with `mcdcli.c`, it knows ahead of time if the key exists. Figure 22.4 shows the screen after entering the key for which to search, and Figure 22.5 shows the screen after a successful search. `mcdui` uses the `show` function to display the record it found. Figure 22.6 illustrates the screen when a search fails.

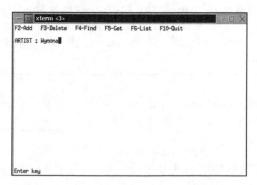

Figure 22.4: *mcdui after entering a key for which to search.*

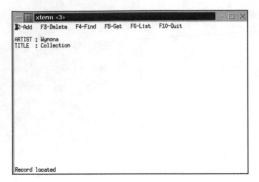

Figure 22.5: *mcdui displaying a successful search.*

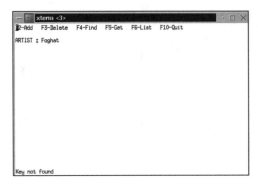

Figure 22.6: *mcdui's appearance after an unsuccessful search.*

As noted with respect to mcdcli, the get operation looks for a specific key instead of searching the entire database for a match. From the user's point of view, the resulting screen display is identical.

The code to list all the records in the database is the most interesting code in mcdui.c. Again, its functionality in the interactive application is almost identical to its cousin in the command-line client. It begins by obtaining a count of records in the database. If the count is zero, the program writes a message on the status line to this effect. Otherwise, mcdui.c begins by sizing tables of pointers to keys and values and then sizes each pointer in the two tables.

TIP

Again, a valuable improvement would be to size each table element dynamically rather than size them statically.

The list_recs call fills the keys and values tables. The next code block uses the list helper routine to display all the CDs in the database to the screen. Figure 22.7 shows the screen's appearance after `list` has updated the status line to indicate that the last record has been displayed.

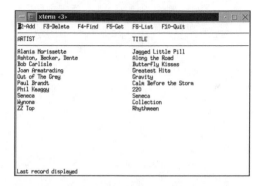

Figure 22.7: *Listing all the records in the CD database.*

`mcdui.c`'s `list` operation does a passable job of listing all the CDs in the database. If you want to enhance its functionality, modify it so that you can scroll back and forth in the list.

What's Next?

What's next? Why, closing the book and becoming a famous Linux programmer, of course! Seriously, you have covered a great deal of material in this book and have a solid foundation for further programming. What remains is simply to write lots of programs that use what you have learned. There is really no other way to become a proficient Linux hacker except by practice. Although a book can show you the basic principles and idioms, experience is the best teacher. Go forth and code!

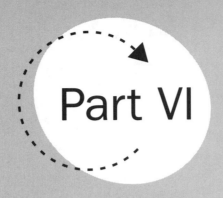

Part VI

Appendixes

A Additional Resources

B Additional Programming Tools

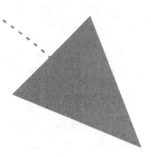

Additional Resources

Annotated Bibliography

Advanced Programming in the UNIX Environment, W. Richard Stevens (Addison-Wesley, 1993), ISBN 0-201-56317. The classic work on programming for UNIX. Although not Linux specific (it never even mentions Linux, in fact), it completely covers all of the issues regarding POSIX compliance. Since Linux is a UNIX clone, most of the techniques mentioned also apply to Linux. Stevens is currently revising APUE, as it is conventionally known.

The Art of Computer Programming, Volume 1: Fundamental Algorithms, 3rd Edition, Donald Knuth (Addison-Wesley, 1997), ISBN 0-201-89683-4.

The Art of Computer Programming, Volume 2: Seminumerical Algorithms, 3rd Edition, Donald Knuth (Addison-Wesley, 1998), ISBN 0-201-89684-2.

The Art of Computer Programming, Volume 3: Sorting and Searching, 3rd Edition, Donald Knuth (Addison-Wesley, 1998), ISBN 0-201-89685-0. These three volumes are the classic works on software development. They are tool- and language-neutral, but the distilled knowledge of 30 years of programming, as well as thousands of algorithms, are well worth the investment (the three-volume set costs over $125.00).

Beginning Linux Programming, Neil Matthews and Rick Stones (Wrox Press, 1996). This book, although dated at this point, covers basic Linux/UNIX programming techniques. It is mis-titled, however, as it covers UNIX programming too.

The C Answer Book: Solutions to Exercises in the C Programming Language, 2nd Edition, Clovis L. Tondo, Scott E. Gimpel (Prentice Hall, 1989), ISBN 0-13-109653-2. This book contains solutions for each exercise Kernighan and Ritchie put in their book, *The C Programming Language*. Unfortunately, the solutions assume knowledge of language features not yet introduced.

C Programming: A Modern Approach, K. N. King (W. W. Norton and Company, 1996). King's book is generally recommended as *the* tutorial introduction to C for those who find *The C Programming Language* too terse.

The C Programming Language, 2nd Edition, Brian W. Kernighan, Dennis M. Ritchie (Prentice Hall, 1988), ISBN 0-393-96945-2. A concise but complete manual of the C programming language, as standardized by ANSI and ISO, written by the two men who created C.

Developing Linux Applications with GTK+ and GDK, Eric Harlow (New Riders, 1999), ISBN 0-7357-0021-4. GTK+ and GDK provide the toolkits and libraries underneath GNOME, the Enlightenment window manager, and the popular GIMP image manipulation program, an Adobe PhotoShop clone.

GNU Make: A Program for Directing Recompilation, Richard M. Stallman and Roland McGrath (Free Software Foundation, 1998), ISBN 1-882114-80-9. Written by the creator's of GNU make, this book covers make front to back and top to bottom. If it is not covered in this book, you'll have to look at the source code.

Introduction to Computer Graphics, James D. Foley, Andries van Dam, Steven K. Feiner, John F. Hughes, Richard L. Phillips (Addison-Wesley, 1993), ISBN 0-201-60921-5. The classic work on computer graphics. This version is actually an abridged version of *Computer Graphics: Principles and Practice*. If you want to understand computer graphics, this book, or its larger cousin, is the one to own.

Learning the bash Shell, 2nd Edition, Cameron Newham, Bill Rosenblatt (O'Reilly, 1998), ISBN 1-56592-347-2. A tutorial introduction to the bash shell, it contains several chapters devoted to bash shell script programming.

Learning the Korn Shell, Bill Rosenblatt (O'Reilly, 1993), ISBN 1-56592-054-6. A tutorial introduction the Korn shell, it contains several chapters to Korn shell script programming. Everything in it should apply to pdksh, the public domain incarnation of the Korn shell.

Learning Perl, 2nd Edition, Randal L. Schwartz & Tom Christiansen (O'Reilly, 1997), ISBN 1-56592-284-0. If you want to learn Perl, this is the book to read.

Linux Application Development, Michael K. Johnson, Erik W. Troan (Addison-Wesley, 1998), 0-201-30821-5. Written by two of Red Hat Software's top application programmers, this book does an excellent job of explaining the subtleties of writing Linux applications. It does not cover kernel hacking, however.

Linux Device Drivers, Allesandro Rubini (O'Reilly, 1998), ISBN 56592-292-1. This is *the* book on how to write device drivers for Linux; it contains several complete, useful examples.

The Linux Kernel Book, Remy Card, Eric Dumas, Franck Mével (John Wiley and Sons, 1998), ISBN 0-471-98141-0. Translated from French, Card and his co-authors explain almost every single line of code in the 2.0.x kernel. It is out of date now, of course, due to the release of the 2.2 kernel, but it is still an excellent introduction. The translation is rough and uneven. This book can't see the forest for the trees.

Linux Kernel Internals, 2nd Edition, Michael Beck, Harald Böhme, Mirko Dziadzka, Ulrich Kunitz, Robert Magnus, Dirk Verworner (Addison-Wesley, 1998), ISBN 0-201-33143-8. One-third the size of *The Linux Kernel Book*, Beck and company give the reader a much better introduction to the Linux kernel.

Linux Programming, Patrick Volkerding, Eric Foster-Johnson, Kevin Reichard (MIS Press, 1997), ISBN 1-55828-507-5. Volkerding, creator of the popular Slackware distribution, surveys the broad landscape of Linux programming, covering a lot of ground in a short period of time.

Linux Programming Unleashed, Kurt Wall, Mark Watson, Mark Whitis (Macmillan Computer Publishing, 1999), ISBN 0-672-31607-2. This is an intermediate-to-advanced level book covering many aspects of Linux programming.

Practical Programming in Tcl and Tk, Second Edition, Brent B. Welch (Prentice Hall, 1997), ISBN 0-13-616830-2. Tcl/Tk is the most fully-featured of UNIX/Linux scripting languages. Tcl is the character mode part and Tk adds an X Window interface. This book is the recommended text for learning Tcl/Tk.

Programming Perl, 2nd Edition, Larry Wall, Tom Christiansen, Randal L. Schwartz (O'Reilly, 1996), ISBN 1-56592-149-6. Written by three Perl luminaries, including the creator of the language, Larry Wall, it covers the entire breadth of programming with Perl, version 5.

Programming with GNU Software, Mike Loukides, Andy Oram (O'Reilly, 1997), ISBN 1-56592-112-7. Written by members of Cygnus Solutions, vendors of support and commercial version of GNU tools, this is an excellent book on using GNU development tools such as gcc, Emacs, make, and gdb, the GNU debugger.

Programming with Qt, Atthias Kalle Dalheimer (O'Reilly, 1999), ISBN 1-56592-588-2. At the moment, this is the only published book-length treatment of programming with Qt. If you intend to do serious programming using the Qt toolkit, this book is a must have.

Sams Teach Yourself Linux Programming in 24 Hours, Warren W. Gay (Macmillan Computer Publishing, 1999), ISBN 0-672-31582-3. Good introduction to Linux programming.

Internet Resources

The Internet is overflowing with information about Linux. This appendix hardly scratches the surface of what is available.

Web Sites

GENERAL

The Association of Computing Machinery

http://www.acm.org/

The Free Software Foundation

http://www.fsf.org/

The GNU Project

http://www.gnu.org/

Institute of Electrical and Electronics Engineers

http://www.ieee.org/

Linux.com

http://www.linux.com/

The Linux Documentation Project

http://metalab.unc.edu/LDP

The Linux Gazette

http://www.ssc.com/lg/

The Linux Journal

http://www.linuxjournal.com/

The Linux Kernel

http://www.kernel.org/

http://www.linuxhq.com/guides/TLK/index.html

The Linux Kernel Hacker's Guide

http://www.redhat.com:8080/HyperNews/get/khg.html

Linux Online

http://www.linux.org/

The Linux Programmer's Bounce Point

http://www.ee.mu.oz.au/linux/programming/

The Linux Programmer's Guide

http://linuxwww.db.erau.edu/LPG/

Linux Magazine

http://www.linux-mag.com/

LinuxToday

http://www.linuxtoday.com/

Linux Weekly News

http://www.lwn.net/

LinuxWorld

http://www.linuxworld.com/

Linux WWW Mailing List Archives

http://linuxwww.db.erau.edu/mail_archives

Mailing List Archives

http://www.mail-archive.com/

The UNIX Programming FAQ

http://www.landfield.com/faqs/unix-faq/programmer/faq/

Usenet FAQs

http://www.landfield.com/faqs/

http://www.faq.org/

Usenix - The Advanced Computing Systems Association

http://www.usenix.org/

Linux Center: Development

http://www.linux-center.org/en/development/

GAMES

The Linux Game Developers Web Ring

http://www.kc.net/~mack-10/LGDRing.htm

Linux GSDK

http://sunsite.auc.dk/penguinplay/index.html

GRAPHICS

Graphic File Formats

http://www.cis.ohio-state.edu/hypertext/faq/usenet/graphics/
➥fileformats-faq/top.html

Mesa

http://www.ssec.wisc.edu/~brianp/Mesa.html

NETWORK PROGRAMMING

Beej's Guide to Network Programming

http://www.ecst.csuchico.edu/~beej/guide/net/

Spencer's Socket Site

http://www.lowtek.com/sockets/

The UNIX Socket FAQs

http://www.landfield.com/faqs/unix-faq/socket/

OPERATING SYSTEM DEVELOPMENT

The OS Development Web Page

http://www.effect.net.au/os-dev/osdev/index.html

Writing Linux Device Drivers

http://www.redhat.com/~johnsonm/devices.html

SECURITY

Designing Secure Software

http://www.sun.com/sunworldonline/swol-04-1998/swol-04-security.html?040198i

The Secure UNIX Programming FAQ

http://www.whitefang.com/sup/

SOFTWARE DISTRIBUTION

Building RPM Packages

http://www.rpm.org/

MULTIMEDIA

Linux CD-ROM Drive Programming

http://www.ee.mu.oz.au/linux/cdrom/

Open Sound System Programmer's Guide

http://www.4front-tech.com/pguide/

GUI TOOLKITS

GTK

http://www.gtk.org/

GTK Tutorial

http://levien.com/~slow/gtk/

KDE Developer's Centre

http://www.ph.unimelb.edu.au/~ssk/kde/devel/

LessTif

http://www.lesstif.org/

Troll Tech's QT

http://www.troll.no/

Xforms Home Page

http://bragg.phys.uwm.edu/xform/

UNIX PROGRAMMING

Sun Developer's Connection

http://www.sun.com/developers/developers.html

X WINDOW PROGRAMMING

The Open Group (formerly X Consortium)

http://www.opengroup.org/

Technical X Window System Sites

http://www.rahul.net/kenton/xsites.html

X Image Extension info

http://www.users.cts.com/crash/s/slogan/

XPM format and library

http://www.inria.fr/koala/lehors/xpm.html

DISTRIBUTION VENDORS

Caldera Systems

http://www.calderasystems.com/

Debian

http://www.debian.org/

Red Hat Software

http://www.redhat.com/

Slackware

http://www.slackware.com

http://www.cdrom.com

Stampede

http://www.stampede.org/

S.u.S.E

http://www.suse.com/

Usenet

`comp.admin.policy`—Site administration policies.

`comp.lang.c`—Covers programming with ANSI/ISO C.

`comp.os.linux.development.apps`—Covers the details of application programming under Linux.

`comp.os.linux.development.system`—Covers everything you always wanted to know about Linux system programming, but were afraid to ask.

`comp.os.linux.setup`—Setting up and administering a Linux system.

`comp.shell.programmer`—Covers shell programming.

`comp.unix.admin`—Administering a UNIX system.

`comp.unix.programmer`—Discusses programming in the UNIX environment.

Mailing Lists

The following lists are supported by Majordomo. To subscribe to a list, send a message to `majordomo@vger.rutgers.edu` with `subscribe` followed by the mailing list name in the body of the message. Commands in the "subject" line are not processed.

`linux-apps`—Software applications

`linux-c-programming`—Programming and development with C

`linux-config`—System configuration

`linux-doc`—Documentation projects

`linux-fsf`—The Free Software Foundation

`linux-gcc`—Issues of importance to those developing under Linux

`linux-kernel`—General kernel discussion

`linux-kernel-announce`—Kernel announcements

`linux-kernel-digest`—Digest of linux-kernel

`linux-kernel-patch`—Kernel patches

`linux-linuxss`—Linux Mach single sever development

`linux-oi`—Using the Object Interface toolkit

`linux-opengl`—Programming with OpenGL on Linux

`linux-pkg`—Making package installation easier

`linux-raid`—Software and hardware RAID development and usage

`linux-scsi`—SCSI drive development and usage

`linux-smp`—Linux on symmetrical multi-processing machines

`linux-sound`—Using sound cards and utilities under Linux

`linux-svgalib`—SVGA library discussion

`linux-tape`—Using Tape storage devices under Linux

`linux-term`—Using the term suite of programs

`linux-x11`—Using the X Window system under Linux

Linux Software Development List for Linux software developers—To subscribe, send a message to `lsd-list-request@cannonexpress.com` with nothing in the body of the message except `SUBSCRIBE`.

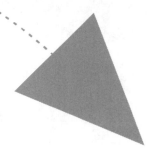

Additional Programming Tools

Certification

- Caldera Systems Linux Training

  http://www.calderasystems.com/education/

- Linux Professional Institute

  http://www.lpi.org/

- Red Hat Software Developer Training

  http://www.redhat.com/about/1999/press_dev_training.html

- Red Hat Software Linux Certification

  http://www.redhat.com/products/training.html

Compilers and Languages

- Allegro CL, a LISP/Common LISP Rapid Application Development System

  http://www.franz.com/dload/dload.html

- CINT, a C/C++ Interpreter

  http://root.cern.ch/root/Cint.html

- EGCS

  http://egcs.cygnus.com/

- FORTRAN90

  http://www.tools.fujitsu.com/download/index.html

- FreeBuilder, a Java-based IDE

  http://members.xoom.com/_XOOM/ivelin/FreeBuilder/index.html

- JDK, the Java Development Kit 1.2

  http://www.blackdown.org/java-linux/mirrors.html

- PGCC, the Pentium GCC

  http://www.gcc.ml.org/

- PGCC Workstation

  http://www.pgroup.com/

- Tcl/TK

  http://www.scriptics.com/products/tcltk/index.html

Database Software

- DISAM96, ISAM (Indexed Sequential Access Method) databases

  http://www.bytedesigns.com/disam/register.htm

- Informix

  http://www.informix.com/linux/

- MySQL, a popular SQL database for Linux

  http://www.mysql.com/

- Oracle

  http://platforms.oracle.com/linux/

- PostgreSQL

  http://www.postgresql.org/

Editors

- Cforge, an integrated C/C++ development environment

  http://www.codeforge.com/cgi-bin/Custom/NevinKaplan/
  ↪Register.cgi?Register=Free

- C Meister, a platform/compiler independent IDE

  http://www.cmeister.com/

- Code Crusader

  http://www.coo.caltech.edu/~jafl/jcc/

- GNUPro, a commercial version of the GNU development tools

  http://www.cygnus.com/gnupro

- Jessie, a cross-platform IDE developed by Silicon Graphics

  http://oss.sgi.com/projects/jessie/

Graphics

- General Graphics Interface, a cross-platform graphics system
  http://www.ggi-project.org/
- MESA, a clone of SGI's OpenGL Toolkit
  http://www.mesa3d.org/

Libraries

- Epeios, a C++ encapsulation of most of the UNIX API
  http://www.epeios.org/
- LibWWW, a general Web library for client and servers
  http://www.w3.org/pub/WWW/Distribution.html
- Sfio, a robust implementation of the Standard I/O Library
  http://www.research.att.com/sw/tools/sfio/

Application Frameworks

- JX application framework
  http://www.coo.caltech.edu/~jafl/jx/
- Lesstif, a Motif clone
  http://www.lesstif.org
- Xforms, a high-level X Window toolkit
  http://bragg.phys.uwm.edu/xforms/
- Crystal Space, a 3D engine written in C++
  http://crystal.linuxgames.com/

Miscellaneous

- Insure++, a static code validation tool (like LCLint)
  http://www.parasoft.com/products/insure/index.htm
- PowerRPC, a rapid development tool for remote procedure calls
  http://www.netbula.com/products/powerrpc/download/v11port.html
- Xaudio SDK, a toolkit for building MP3 software
  http://www.xaudio.com/downloads/#linux
- Wotsit's Format, a resource for hundreds of file formats
  http://www.wotsit.org/

- Willows API, for porting Windows applications to Linux

  `http://www.willows.com/`

- Code Medic, an X-based interface to the GBU debugged (gdb)

  `http://www.its.caltech.edu/~glenn/medic.html`

- Online C Library Reference

  `http://www.dinkumware.com/htm_cl/index.html`

Scientific and Mathematical Software

- DISLIN Data Plotting

  `(LIBC5/GLIBC1)`

  `http://www.linmpi.mpg.de/dislin/libc5.html`

  `(LIBC6/GLIBC2)`

  `http://www.linmpi.mpg.de/dislin/libc6.html`

- PV-WAVE/JWAVE, visual data analysis tools

  `http://www/vni.com/products/wave/wave621register.html`

- VARKON, engineering and CAD libraries

  `http://www.microform.se/sources.htm`

Software Distribution

- Red Hat Package Manager Home Page

  `http://www.rpm.org/`

Tools

- LCLint, a static code-verification tool

  `http://www.sds.lcs.mit.edu/lclint`

- Checker, for locating runtime memory errors

  `http://www.gnu.org/software/checker/checker.html`

- CCMalloc, another memory profiler

  `http://iseran.ira.uka.de/~armin/ccmalloc/`

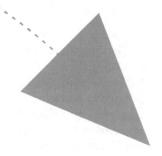

Index

The IT site
you asked for...

It's
Here!

InformIT is a complete online library delivering
information, technology, reference, training, news
and opinion to IT professionals, students
and corporate users.

Find IT Solutions Here!

www.informit.com

Other Related Titles

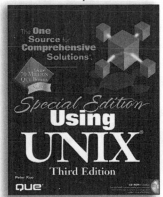